AF600391

The Atlantic and Africa

FERNAND BRAUDEL CENTER

STUDIES IN HISTORICAL SOCIAL SCIENCE

Series Editor: Richard E. Lee

The Fernand Braudel Center Studies in Historical Social Science will publish works that address theoretical and empirical questions produced by scholars in or through the Fernand Braudel Center or who share its approach and concerns. It specifically seeks to promote works that contribute to the development of the world-systems perspective, engaging a holistic and relational vision of the world—the modern world-system—implicit in historical social science, which at once takes into consideration structures (long-term regularities) and change (history). As the intellectual boundaries within the sciences/social sciences/humanities structure collapse in the work scholars actually do, this series will offer a venue for a wide range of research that confronts the dilemmas of producing relevant accounts of historical processes in the context of the rapidly changing structures of both the social and the academic world. The series will include monographs, colloquiums, and collections of essays organized around specific themes.

VOLUMES IN THIS SERIES:

Questioning Nineteenth-Century Assumptions about Knowledge: Determinism
Richard E. Lee, editor

Questioning Nineteenth-Century Assumptions about Knowledge: Reductionism
Richard E. Lee, editor

Questioning Nineteenth-Century Assumptions about Knowledge: Dualism
Richard E. Lee, editor

The *Longue Durée* and World-Systems Analysis
Richard E. Lee, editor

New Frontiers of Slavery
Dale Tomich, editor

Slavery in the Circuit of Sugar: Martinique and the World-Economy, 1848–1860
Dale Tomich

The Politics of the Second Slavery
Dale Tomich, editor

The Trade in the Living
Luiz Felipe de Alencastro

Race and Rurality in the Global Economy
Michaeline A. Crichlow, Patricia Northover, and Juan Guisti-Cordero, editors

Power, Political Economy, and Historical Landscapes of the Modern World: Interdisciplinary Perspectives
Christopher R. DeCorse, editor

Atlantic Transformations: Empire, Politics, and Slavery during the Nineteenth Century
Dale Tomich, editor

Premises and Problems
Luiza Franco Moreira, editor

The Atlantic and Africa: The Second Slavery and Beyond
Dale W. Tomich and Paul E. Lovejoy, editors

The Atlantic and Africa

The Second Slavery and Beyond

Edited by

Dale W. Tomich and Paul E. Lovejoy

FERNAND BRAUDEL CENTER
STUDIES IN HISTORICAL SOCIAL SCIENCE

Cover image "Caravan Arriving at Timbuctoo, 1853," *Slavery Images: A Visual Record of the African Slave Trade and Slave Life in the Early African Diaspora,* accessed March 25, 2021, http://www.slaveryimages.org/s/slaveryimages/item/1795.

Published by State University of New York Press, Albany

© 2021 State University of New York

All rights reserved

Printed in the United States of America

No part of this book may be used or reproduced in any manner whatsoever without written permission. No part of this book may be stored in a retrieval system or transmitted in any form or by any means including electronic, electrostatic, magnetic tape, mechanical, photocopying, recording, or otherwise without the prior permission in writing of the publisher.

For information, contact State University of New York Press, Albany, NY
www.sunypress.edu

Library of Congress Cataloging-in-Publication Data

Names: Tomich, Dale W., 1946– editor. | Lovejoy, Paul E., editor.
Title: The Atlantic and Africa : the second slavery and beyond / edited by Dale W. Tomich and Paul E. Lovejoy.
Description: Albany : State University of New York Press, [2021] | Series: Fernand Braudel Center studies in historical social science | Includes bibliographical references and index.
Identifiers: LCCN 2021016736 (print) | LCCN 2021016737 (ebook) | ISBN 9781438484433 (hardcover : alk. paper) | ISBN 9781438484440 (pbk. : alk. paper) | 9781438484457 (ebook)
Subjects: LCSH: Slavery—America—History. | Slavery—Africa—History. | Slavery—Economic aspects. | Slave trade—History. | Economic history—1750–1918.
Classification: LCC HT1048 .A877 2021 (print) | LCC HT1048 (ebook) | DDC 306.3/6209—dc23
LC record available at https://lccn.loc.gov/2021016736
LC ebook record available at https://lccn.loc.gov/2021016737

10 9 8 7 6 5 4 3 2 1

In honor of Catherine Coquery-Vidrovitch

CONTENTS

ILLUSTRATIONS

Figures

Tables

Introduction

Atlantic/Africa

Dale W. Tomich and Paul E. Lovejoy

This book explores the connections between two bodies of scholarship that have developed separately from one another. On the one hand, the "second slavery" perspective has reinterpreted the relation of Atlantic slavery and capitalism by emphasizing the extraordinary expansion of new frontiers of slave commodity production—cotton in the US South, sugar in Cuba, and coffee in Brazil during the nineteenth century—and their role in the economic, social, and political transformations of the nineteenth-century world-economy. On the other hand, Africanist scholarship has demonstrated the expansion, redirection, and restructuring of slavery in Africa and its role in the formation of new, and in some instances, revolutionary states associated with the end of the Atlantic slave trade.

Despite their independent development, these two historiographical approaches raise a number of problems that are deeply interconnected. In order to facilitate and structure the integration of these two literatures, this introduction sketches out a conceptual framework that engages the problems posed by the interrelation of their historical interpretations. The approach presented here is not a simple comparison between two independent slave systems. Rather, it examines the changing position of each slave complex within the capitalist world-economy and their interrelations in the economic and political transformations of the nineteenth century. By examining these two bodies of scholarship from the perspective of the capitalist world-system, we are able to trace the inner connections between the second slavery,

slavery in Africa, and what Karl Polanyi has termed the "Great Transformation" of the European economy. Through this procedure it is possible to situate these particular regional histories in world-economic processes. We may then spatially and temporally specify local slave systems in Africa and in the Americas as parts of the historical transformation of the nineteenth-century world-economy while at the same time delineating the constellation of structures and processes historically forming the world-economy itself.

Over the course of the nineteenth century, the widening and deepening of industrial production; urbanization and population growth; new patterns of consumption by middle-class and working-class consumers; the development of competitive mass markets for industrial goods, raw materials, and food products; the introduction of railroads, steamships, and canals; decolonization and the consolidation of national states on both sides of the Atlantic as well as colonial expansion in Africa and Asia; and the rise of abolitionism and liberalism reconfigured the capitalist world-system. The Congress of Vienna of 1815 and the Berlin Conference of 1884–1885 frame the economic and political conjuncture of this "Great Transformation." Vienna established the European state system under British hegemony. It provided the political-legal framework not only for relations among states but also for the development of the world market and industrialization. The Berlin Conference provided a global division of territorial control and influence that consolidated that world order.

Both the African and Atlantic slave complexes underwent transformation as part of the profound geographical, economic, and political expansion and restructuring of the capitalist world-economy in the course of the nineteenth century. They had been deeply implicated in one another through the Atlantic slave trade for several centuries. Nonetheless, they remained distinct systems. Atlantic slavery had been an integral part of the European world-economy since its inception, while Africa was not incorporated into the European world-economy except as a source of unfree labor. Even though Africa had provided enslaved manpower for European colonization of the Atlantic since the sixteenth century, factors of production in Africa were not configured in ways that subordinated the continent to the control of European capital and state power as a space of commodity production, exchange, and consumption. African economic and political structures retained their regional integrity and autonomy in the face of the Atlantic slave trade, and the internal African slave trade and slavery operated to a large extent independently from it. Africanist scholarship has nonetheless established the importance of slavery and slave trading in Africa to the political, economic, and social organization of African societies during the nineteenth century. In Africa slaves were deployed in a variety of economic, social, and political roles. They were key to the acquisition of power, wealth, and prestige for African polities and they played a central role in long-distance trade, both as a means of transport and as merchandise. Slavery within Africa coexisted with the Atlantic slave trade. However, the internal slave trade and slavery enabled African economic and political structures to maintain their integrity and autonomy in the face of the Atlantic slave trade.

In the Americas industrialization, free markets, and decolonization created the conditions for the second slavery and the strengthening of the transatlantic slave trade to Cuba and Brazil. The old zones of colonial slavery declined relative to the expansion of the world-economy, and slavery was abolished in them sometimes progressively and other times through abrupt violent change. They were superseded by new, extended geographical zones of slavery that presupposed and further developed the emergent industrial division of labor. Slave relations in the US cotton frontier, the Cuban sugar frontier, and the Brazilian coffee frontier were restructured as masses of slaves were transported to these new zones and incorporated into new labor processes. Between 1815 and 1850 the transatlantic slave trade approached the highest level in its history, but enslaved Africans were transported overwhelmingly to the new commodity frontiers in Brazil and Cuba, while US expansion was fed largely through domestic migration. The scale of production in each zone increased continuously. New industrial production and transportation technologies were adopted. They kept pace with ever-increasing demand and drove down the price of these key industrial raw materials and foodstuffs. Atlantic trade was restructured. Raw cotton from the United States was exported to Britain and to a lesser extent retained within the domestic economy, while the US became the leading importer of Cuban sugar and Brazilian coffee. The volume of production and trade and the restructuring of markets and states integrated the new slave zones more closely than ever into the new industrial division of labor. Beyond the Atlantic, commodity production was reorganized in the Dutch East Indies in ways that were analogous to the second slavery in the Americas and were part of the same movement of world-economic expansion.

However, abolition of the slave trade was also integral to the transformation of the nineteenth century. As part of the Congress of Vienna, Britain insisted that ending the international slave trade was a key provision of the new order. The destruction of the colonial system and the formation of independent states in the Americas meant the nationalization of the slavery issue. Consequently, the abolition of slavery became a problem of national, not colonial politics. Cuba, of course, remained a colony, but with considerable autonomy with respect to Spain, and after 1815 the slavery issue in colonial Cuba became analogous to a national question. Britain's strategy of abolishing the slave trade put pressure on the internal slave regimes of Cuba and Brazil. At the same time, securing abolition of the trade by the consent of the slaveholding states was a means of establishing stable market relations and a political-legal order between sovereign states under British hegemony. After mid-century, the suppression of the Atlantic slave trade severed the direct ties between the Americas and Africa and produced opposite effects on each slave complex on the two sides of the Atlantic.

In the Americas, the ending of the transatlantic slave trade to Cuba and Brazil in combination with the violent destruction of slavery in the US Civil War and the depression of the 1870s marked the crisis and decline of the second slavery. Cuba and Brazil were cut off from renewed supplies of manpower from the African trade, while political, economic, and social pressures made the reproduction of the slave system in each country more difficult and contested. The rate of expansion of sugar and coffee production slowed. In the US reconstruction of cotton production after the Civil War was oriented toward the expansion of a national market rather than the export market. Slave emancipation first in Cuba in 1886 and then in Brazil in 1888, the last country in the western hemisphere to end chattel slavery, brought the conjuncture of the second slavery to an end. With the end of slavery in the Americas, the countries of the second slavery were firmly integrated into the world division of labor through the state system and the world market, which provided the framework for the further growth of commodity production. Each was able to develop new internal commodity frontiers and restructure the labor force—migrant labor in Brazil, tenancy and sharecropping in US cotton cultivation in the South, and a racialized rural proletariat in Cuba. Each continued to be a major producer of its particular crop well into the twentieth century.

In Africa the progressive suppression of the Atlantic slave trade had stimulated the growth of slavery and the reorientation of the internal slave trade and other commercial activity toward North Africa, East Africa, and the Indian Ocean, and most importantly toward internal domestic employment as African elites attempted to compensate for the loss of the Atlantic trade. In West Africa this expansion and restructuring of the slave trade supported the rise of the Sokoto Caliphate and other Muslim states formed in jihad, each of which attempted to restrict the slave trade to non-Muslims. Other polities in both West Africa and East Africa diverted their participation in the slave trade as well as slave production into new commodity markets. African political elites, particularly in West Africa, promoted peasantization in order to take advantage of new commercial opportunities presented by the "legitimate trade" that followed the abolition of the Atlantic slave trade. The growth of independent African states and an African slave system was, however, an obstacle to the further expansion of the European world-economy. The incorporation of Africa into the capitalist world-economy entailed dismantling the independent initiatives taken in Africa after the abolition of the external slave trade. It was achieved through the imposition of formal colonial control and the subordination of African societies to the economic and political interests of the colonizing powers of Europe. The need to suppress slavery in Africa was then used as a justification of European colonialism. Abolitionist ideology was mobilized against slavery in Africa and became a part of Europe's "civilizing mission." The agreement that nominally partitioned Africa among the European powers took place at the Berlin Conference in 1884–1885, which immediately preceded the abolition of slavery in Brazil.

The second slavery consolidated the processes of decolonization and the integration of the Americas into the new world division of labor, state system, and world market. In Africa the growth of the internal slave trade and of independent states was the justification for European colonial expansion and the forced integration of Africa into the European world-economy. These two distinct but interlinked processes provided the platform for the New Imperialism and the Second Industrial Revolution of the 1870s and 1880s. The approach presented here at once situates particular histories in global processes and reconstructs the temporal rhythms and spatial configurations forming the world-economy itself. Taken together, these two movements enable us to delineate the processes forming the capitalist world-economy, establish its specific geographical and historical structure, and reintegrate Africa into the transformations in the world-economy. The chapters in this volume explore this paradigm at diverse levels ranging from state formation and the reorganization of world markets to the creation of new social roles and identities.

This volume grows out of a conference held at Binghamton University's Fernand Braudel Center to honor Catherine Coquery-Vidrovitch, a pioneering historian of Africa whose commitment, passion, and generosity have made her an inspiration, example, and mentor to others, including many of those who have contributed to this volume. We wish to thank Sven Beckert and Michael Zeuske for their help in conceptualizing the conference. We would also like to remember our late friend and colleague Joseph Miller. When one of the participants was unable to attend the conference at the last minute, Joe, with characteristic grace and generosity, volunteered from the audience to make an extemporaneous presentation. Richard Lee, Amy Keough, and Kelly Pueschel of the Fernand Braudel Center did a superb job organizing the conference and assisting in the production of this book.

Chapter 1

African Slavery in the Nineteenth Century

Inseparable Partner of the Atlantic Slave Trade

Catherine Coquery-Vidrovitch

This chapter seeks to explain the extent to which the emergence of industrial capitalism in the West during the nineteenth century was closely connected to African slavery, both in the Americas and in Africa. The expansion and then the destruction of the second slavery in the Americas was intimately linked to the expansion of slavery in Africa. To return to an earlier but nonetheless useful terminology, it will be shown here how the Western "capitalist mode of production" was fed by the African "slave mode of production" over the course of the nineteenth century, and, conversely, how the destruction of Atlantic slavery stimulated the growth of slavery in Africa. This connection varied according to time and place, first because of the growth of the Atlantic slave trade between 1780 and 1830, then because of the progressive disappearance of this trade after the 1850s. After explaining what we mean by the "slave mode of production" in Africa, we analyze the forms taken by the interdependence of this mode and Western capitalism in different parts of Africa. West Africa suffered the full force of the interdiction of the Atlantic slave trade, which compelled it to reenter the capitalist world through the growth of an internal slavery of "production." East Africa, in contrast, intensified its involvement in the slave trade thanks to Western industrialization, which nourished it through

Translated by Dale Tomich.

the massive introduction of armaments whose sale was forbidden in the Atlantic. In the two cases, the result was an intensification of the African "slave mode of production" that was inseparable from Western capitalism.

The Affirmation of the "Slave Mode of Production" in Africa during the Nineteenth Century

During the nineteenth century, the economic transformations were as fundamental in Africa as they were in America. From the last third of the eighteenth century the production of slaves in Africa assumed literally industrial proportions because, with the Industrial Revolution, what Dale Tomich has termed "the second slavery" emerged (2017). Plantation slavery producing, above all, sugar and secondarily tobacco had dominated the preindustrial mercantilist epoch. Through the first third of the nineteenth century American plantations, with cotton in the lead, were integrated into the emergent Western capitalist system. The production of cotton, the premier raw material of the British textile industry, as well as sugar and coffee would depend on slave plantations in the United States (until 1863), Cuba (until 1880), and Brazil (until 1888). Britain accorded these plantation zones the privilege of prolonging the slave trade south of the equator (that is, with Angola and Mozambique) until the middle of the century.

Since the eighteenth century the tracks of both the internal and the external slave trade crisscrossed the African continent. The internal trade was accentuated as the legal Atlantic slave trade was progressively closed. At the same time, Europeans demanded growing quantities of raw materials from Africa for their infant industries. The economy of tropical Africa was transformed by the new demands of the Western Industrial Revolution. In West Africa palm oil (from 1802) and peanut oil (from the 1830s–1840s), tropical oil-producing plants that were lacking in temperate countries, were indispensable for lubricating machines, providing illumination before electricity, and providing the raw material for the new soap industry. In Zanzibar it was cloves, which employed one hundred thousand slaves in 1830. In the rain forest it was red and yellow dyewoods, which were required by the British textile industry because the chemical industry was not yet able to produce synthetic dyes. The demand for ivory increased exponentially (piano keys, etc.), while at the end of the century natural rubber was required for the fabrication of automobile tires before the rubber plantations of the twentieth century.

The use of a servile African labor force was generalized in order to export all these products. To put it another way, the development of the capitalist economy in the West did not reject slave labor at all. On the contrary, in America as well as in Africa, the industrial economy profited from it.

African societies had known slavery for a very long time, and, contrary to what some anthropologists dreamed only a short while ago, slavery in Africa was not necessarily more "mild" or more "domestic" than elsewhere. But what is certain is that the demand from buyers from outside the continent brought about the formation and rapid expansion of intensive internal networks. Beginning in the eighteenth century, there were numerous chiefs on the coast and in the interior who became great slave traders, and more and more organized supply networks reached into the heart of the continent. The internal use of slaves was amplified at the same time, especially when the progressive closing of the Atlantic market increased the number of captives available. African sovereigns looked more and more to utilize in place the servile labor force that had become unsalable across the seas. The situation in Africa fit international conditions well. The Industrial Revolution centered in Britain changed conditions at the same time. Claude Meillassoux has thus demonstrated that a "slave mode of production" was veritably in place in Africa during the nineteenth century (1991; Lovejoy 1983). The first evaluations of the early French colonizers at the end of the nineteenth century estimated that perhaps one-half of the population had servile status, a much higher percentage than what it had been a century earlier (Klein 1998). At the same time, the utilization of slave soldiers increased. The conquering powers of the West African jihads (Ousman dan Fodio, El Hadj Omar, Samori, etc.) largely used these slaves to reinforce their production and their armies. And here is the extreme paradox: at the end of the nineteenth century, Western colonizers justified the conquest by the need to struggle against the internal African slavery that they themselves had stimulated.

The Expansion of Internal Slavery in West Africa: The Different Spaces

Despite British efforts, nearly 1.3 million slaves embarked from West Africa destined for the Americas in the first part of the nineteenth century. Three-fourths of them originated in the Bights of Benin and Biafra, and they still came from the Senegambian coast and the Volta River. The slave trade and slavery continued to be very closely tied together. Nevertheless, the growing difficulties of the Atlantic trade led local sovereigns to promote the export of "legitimate" products such as gum, palm oil, peanuts, and so on, to intensify other activities such as gold mining, or to create networks that went in new directions such as the redistribution of kola nuts by the Asante in the Sudanese zone where massive conversions to Islam increased demand. Alongside long-standing demand for slaves (as soldiers, personal retainers of chiefs, or wives), this reorientation of production and porterage made the demand for slaves explode, and in turn, the growing number of slaves encouraged the reorganization of economy and society.

In Senegambia or among the Fulbe in Fuuta Jalon servile labor already existed, but more than ever it became the major mode of exploitation. Even where British antislavery pressure was strongest, as in Sierra Leone where thousands of "liberated" Africans flowed over the course of the century, internal local slavery was forbidden only in 1928. The commerce stimulated by European presence multiplied the exchanges of salt, rice, and imported manufactured goods for vegetable oils and food products from the backcountry. By the end of the century, it is estimated that half of the Mende population were in servile status (Lovejoy 1983). Internal slavery developed even more when there was no longer an overseas market. The beneficiaries were the coastal states and the urban Muslim aristocracies of the Sahel. For example, the great Hausa city of Kano in the interior established a cottage industry producing cotton cloth whose main labor force was exclusively servile (Frishman 1977). The Kano manufacturers, along with secondary textile centers, supplied the whole of the West African market before British colonization substituted cotton goods imported from England in the twentieth century.

The regions producing agricultural products for export were also quick to adopt a "slave mode of production," especially when the political structure and the organization of landed property lent themselves to production on a grand scale. This was the case regarding the Kingdom of Dahomey, with Abomey as its capital, and the city-states of the Nigerian coast, which produced palm oil, and the Empire of Asante, which produced gold and kola nuts (Wilks 1975). The adjustment was not always easy. Initially, following British abolition of the slave trade, the price of slaves in the trade fell drastically and momentarily affected the lifestyle of the elite merchants on the coast. But prices soon returned to normal (because of the risks of the contraband trade) and the level of the trade recovered in the Bight of Biafra. The regions also adapted readily to the substitution of "legitimate" products (above all vegetable oils). King Ghezo of Dahomey was able to take advantage of the new situation by simultaneously playing off the interests of Régis, a Marseilles merchant who wanted to trade in both slaves and oil (Coquery-Vidrovitch 1971). As for the Asante Kingdom, it found new resources after a brief conjunctural crisis thanks to its position between the coast and the Sokoto Caliphate, the great consumer of its kola nuts (Lovejoy 1980; Terray 1994).

Obviously, the coastal forts such as Cape Coast, Elmina, and Accra on the Gold Coast experienced a period of crisis at the beginning of the century, and the coastal Fante were its first victims. Yet the change did not affect everyone. Until the 1840s the Danes continued to trade slaves as usual in the southwest of the Gold Coast in order to support their slave plantations, which produced more food for local consumption than export products (Kea and Law 1995). Moreover, the Fante, like the Asante, did not lack resources that could be substituted for slaves, in particular gold as well as kola nuts. The Asante of the interior gradually converted the annual raids by means of which they obtained slaves to exchange for guns and powder. At first, large numbers of captives were taken to the capital of Kumasi and its environs, and, with no one knowing what to do with them, many were executed. As in the Kingdom of Dahomey, human ritual sacrifices were celebrated each year and on an even grander scale on the occasion of royal funerals (Terray 1994). But soon the king and the provincial chiefs employed the slaves in harvesting nuts or mining gold. In the 1870s it is estimated that half of the Asante population lived in servile status. The kings of Abomey and Porto Novo did the same by encouraging the exploitation of natural palm groves that formed the wealth of their kingdoms. The Afro-Brazilians of the coast, former slaves returned from Brazil and slave traders themselves, imitated them as did the principal local dignitaries. Around 1860 Quenum, son of a great merchant from Abomey, had thousands of slaves, as did the "Brazilian" Domingo Martinez. On the vast plantations clusters of slaves guaranteed palm nut production and porterage for "legitimate" commerce. In the capitals (Porto Novo, Kumasi, and Abomey where in 1851 a third of the thirty thousand inhabitants were slaves) or the great centers of kola trade such as Salaga, Bondoukou, or Bouna, slaves performed all of the necessary labor: supplying wood and water and food supplies for the merchants and caravans leaving from the great plantations surrounding the towns, each of which had several hundred slaves who were often grouped in villages of farmers or artisans.

Even in those scattered societies where there was no power beyond that of the village chief, such as those societies inhabiting the lagoons in Ivory Coast (Memel-Fote 2007), slavery existed and became more and more extensive. There were hardly any free peasants who did not possess at least one or two slaves, not to mention the frequent phenomenon of young people held in pawn for payment of a debt or the atonement of an offense (Lovejoy and Falola 1994). Local slavery seems to have been least common in the regions that were the most subject to slave raiding, such as the Mossi countries or Gourounsi (present-day Burkina-Faso). These regions served as the reservoirs for the trade of others.

In Igbo country, where palm oil was produced on village scale, a class of notables established their wealth through control of lineage lands, the importance of their commercial affairs, and the number of their clients and slaves. The firms that traded on the river employed hundreds of slaves who were organized in a paramilitary manner. A slave master who possessed two hundred slaves for the production of oil and yams was recorded there in 1841 (cited by Ohadike 1994, 186). The process of enslavement only grew. Merchant cities like Onitsha or the ports of the Niger Delta such as Bonny or Opobo ended up holding thousands of slaves as porters or boatmen. In about 1880 a merchant from Calabar possessed about three thousand, the majority divided among his three plantations.

The same phenomenon occurred in the great Yoruba city-states (Ibadan, Ijebu, Abeokuta, Lagos) as a result of the incessant wars of the nineteenth century (Hopkins 1968). Freemen did not constitute more than a minority of the population. Whether animist, Muslim, or Christian, both war chiefs and large merchants, the latter including a few women, amassed hundreds if not thousands of slaves who served them as workers or soldiers. Thus, in 1859 Chief Kurumi of Ijaye had three hundred women and an army of a thousand slaves, not counting all those who worked on his plantations. Because of insecurity, it was necessary for the armies, largely constituted by slaves, to be fed by other hordes of slaves. Besides Lagos before English occupation (1851), Ibadan was the most deeply implicated in slavery. Several thousand slaves passed through each year. The majority of them were Muslims, most of whom spoke Hausa. Those suitable for local employment were sold. Women were placed in harems; the more fit served as soldiers. Others were used as artisans or as porters. The great majority of these slaves were sent to the fields where they worked under the supervision of overseers who were slaves themselves. There they risked being captured again at the least disturbance. Between 1860 and 1870 some one hundred families alone possessed more than fifty thousand slaves. Madame Efustan had two thousand on her lands without counting those she kept in town (Lovejoy 1983, 173–75). But in contrast to Asante where the matrilineal system meant that the children of a slave woman remained slaves, the patrilineal system of Dahomey or Yoruba country made the assimilation of the second generation much easier because the child of a slave wife enjoyed the status of its father.

The Transfer of the Atlantic Slave Trade toward the Indian Ocean

The rise of the Atlantic slave trade and then its decline beginning in the 1840s, at the time of the first Industrial Revolution, had an analogous effect for opposite reasons in Africa—that of increasing the internal slave trade. With the rise of the Atlantic trade the demand for slaves in intertropical Africa increased exponentially, while with its decline slaves already accumulated who could no longer find purchasers elsewhere were deployed in place as instruments of production and as soldiers.

This turning point is apparent in East Africa. The trade toward the Indian Ocean was active, but for a long time it was less intense than that of the west because Arab-Muslim demand was not based on plantation agriculture. A reason for that is undoubtedly the memorable and massive slave revolt that lasted for thirty years in Mesopotamia during the ninth century and provoked the massacre of five hundred thousand to a million primarily Zanj (black) slaves (Popović 2011). The lesson of the dangers of such concentrations of an enslaved labor force demonstrated by that revolt lasted for a long time.

All that changed with the Industrial Revolution, which reintegrated the Sultanate of Zanzibar into the world-economy. Clove trees were introduced as contraband to Zanzibar in 1820. The plants began to yield fruit in 1828 when the sultan of Oman, the ruler of Zanzibar, passed through the island. While there, the sultan met an American businessman from Boston who convinced him that it was in his interest to break the Dutch monopoly on this rare and expensive spice. The American returned in 1833 with a contract that the sultan signed. He became the American commercial consul and clove fever seized the island. Along with the neighboring island of Pemba, it quickly became the world's leading exporter of cloves. The majority of plantations were of medium size with fifty to a hundred slaves. The Americans offered in exchange pearls, copper and iron coins, and coarse cotton cloth that caused a sensation and spread rapidly in the backward country. Called *merikani* because of its origin and often dyed black because it showed less dirt, it is still very much in demand though it is no longer produced in the

United States. The paradox was that the consul, representing an antislavery state (Massachusetts) and pleading for the end of the slave trade before the sultan, encouraged cotton production by the slaves in the Southern United States, whose labor supplied the textile mills of Massachusetts (Cheriff 1987).

In 1840 the wealth of Zanzibar, which rested on both the slave trade and the plantations, led the sultan of Oman to transfer his capital there. At the same time, Arab and Swahili notables created plantations producing cloves, sugar, coconut palms for copra oil, as well as food crops to feed a growing population and provision the caravans that streamed in from the interior (Cooper 1977; Glassman 1995). In contrast to the densely populated and cultivated regions to the south of present-day Tanzania around Lakes Nyasa and Malawi and the Usumbara Hills behind Tanga, the immediate semiarid hinterland was depopulated and it became necessary to go further and further into the interior to search for slaves. Raids for Manama slaves were also conducted in the eastern Upper Congo and around Lake Nyasa in the territories of the Nyasa and Yao in Mozambique. Cherif (1987) estimates that in the 1860s 20,000 slaves arrived in Zanzibar, of whom 12,000 supplied the plantations of the country. The hunt for slaves and ivory combined with a plantation economy that penetrated the interior. The case of the great Arab-Swahili merchant Tippu Tip, whose real name was Muhammad el Murjebi, is well-known. The son of a merchant, Tippu Tip organized a commercial and slave empire in the Upper Congo on the Lualaba River, west of Lake Tanganyika. There, and then later in Zanzibar, he established some twenty plantations where slaves obeyed the sound of the gong that regulated their work. Tippu Tip recognized the authority of the sultan, but he also had his own political relations with the Europeans. He met the explorers Stanley and Livingstone. The king of the Belgians tried to use him by naming him governor of the Upper Congo. Finally, Tippu Tip retired to Zanzibar where he again bought a series of plantations in 1895, where, according to the missionaries of the time, he had 10,000 slaves. His fortune rose to about £50,000 sterling. When he died in 1905, his obituary appeared in *The Times of London.*

The trade undoubtedly reached its peak in the last third of the nineteenth century. By then the number of slaves in Zanzibar had risen from 6,000 to 20,000 (Cherif 1987). A report from London probably exaggerated when it estimated the number of slave departures for the Indian Ocean at 50,000. The report caused the British government to demand in 1873 that the sultan forbid the international slave trade. But that demand only made the internal slave trade increase. Departures to the Kenyan and Somalian coasts and to the Lamu Islands remained numerous and the plantations prospered. The hurricane that struck the same year devastated Zanzibar and led to the intense utilization of slaves to open plantations on the island of Pemba.

One of the reasons for the rise of the slave trade in the interior of the continent is that the traffic had almost entirely disappeared on the Atlantic coast. The "trade guns" produced by Western industry then flowed into the Mediterranean where they were bought by Eastern merchants. The high level of firearm production was at once the result of the end of the Napoleonic Wars and of the Industrial Revolution. The peace of 1815 demobilized hundreds of thousands of European soldiers whose equipment became useless. What to do with it? This was the origin of the industrial transformation that now made military weapons in response to the demands of African chiefs. Birmingham in England and, above all, Liège in Belgium became the principal centers for the production of weapons that were destined to be sold in the Mediterranean to Muslim merchants. As the arms industry in Europe periodically advanced, stimulating the modernization of armies, the stocks of obsolete weapons continued to accumulate throughout the course of the century. The opening of the Suez Canal in 1869 facilitated their massive exportation through the Red Sea to the Indian Ocean (Coquery-Vidrovitch 2009). These guns allowed a series of Arab, Swahili, and African war chiefs to arm themselves and to utilize the geographical and cartographical knowledge furnished by Western explorers who crossed the backcountry caravan routes beginning in the 1840s. The end of the century witnessed the construction of formidable African slave empires like that of Rabih in the Chad Basin and of Mirambo in Tanzania. Internal slavery was solidly established in the interior of the continent. It is estimated that on the eve of its conquest, 40 percent of the population of the Kingdom of Buganda were slaves, the majority of whom were women (Wright 1993), and for the societies of West Africa the figure rose to some 60 percent. These slaveholding potentates (Rabih, Mirambo in Tanzania, or Msiri in Katenga, not to speak of the Sultanate of Zanzibar or of Tippu Tip) were not backward chiefs. They were *modern* rulers well attuned to the Western market whose resources they knew how to exploit. Rabih secured his ammunition from the Red Sea and his eyeglasses from Tripoli. He refused to ally with the British who wanted to use his forces against the French. Tippu Tip retired to his beautiful mansion in Zanzibar where he died in 1905; his death notice appeared in *The Times of London*. All of this demonstrates that Western capitalist globalization developed in and around Africa in proportion to its development in the West. African sovereigns and their states were not marginal auxiliaries of the process; they were, like others, indispensable partners.

References

Akintoye, Stephen Adebanji. 1980. "The Economic Foundation of Ibadan in the 19th Century." In *Topics on Nigerian Economic and Social History,* edited by I. A. Akinjogbin and Segun Osoba, 55–65. Ile-Ife, Nigeria: University of Ife Press.

Barry, Boubacar. 1998. *Senegambia and the Atlantic Slave Trade.* Cambridge, UK: Cambridge University Press.

Cheriff, Abdul. 1987. *Slaves, Spices, and Ivory in Zanzibar: Integration of an East African Commercial Empire into the World Economy, 1770–1873.* Athens: Ohio University Press.

Cooper, Frederick. 1977. *Plantation Slavery on the East Coast of Africa.* New Haven, CT: Yale University Press.

Coquery-Vidrovitch, Catherine. 1971. "De la traite des esclaves à l'exportation de l'huile de palme au Dahomey." In *The Development of Indigenous Trade and Markets in West Africa,* edited by Claude Meillassoux. London: Oxford University Press for the International African Institute.

———. 2009. *Africa and the Africans in the Nineteenth Century: A Turbulent History.* Translated by M. E. Sharpe (revised translation of *L'Afrique et les Africains au XIXe siècle: Mutations, révolutions, crise* [Paris: Colin, 1999]). Armonk, NY: M. E. Sharpe.

———. 2018. *Les routes de l'esclavage africaines du VIe au XXe siècle.* Paris: Albin-Michel.

Coquery-Vidrovitch, Catherine, and Henri Moniot. 1974. *L'Afrique noire, de 1800 à nos jours.* 5th rev. ed. Paris: PUF, Nouvelle Clio.

Frishman, Alan. 1977. "The Population Growth of Kano, Nigeria." *African Historical Demography.* Proceedings of a seminar at the Centre of African Studies, University of Edinburgh, April 29–30, 1977, vol. 1, 212–50.

Glassman, Jonathan. 1995. *Feasts and Riots: Revelry, Rebellion, and Popular Consciousness on the Swahili Coast, 1856–1888.* Portsmouth, NH: Heinemann.

Hopkins, Anthony. 1968. "Economic Imperialism in West Africa: Lagos, 1880–1892." *Economic History Review* 21, no. 3: 580–606.

Kea, Rey, and Robin Law, eds. 1995. *From Slave Trade to "Legitimate" Commerce: The Commercial Transition in Nineteenth-Century West Africa.* Cambridge, UK: Cambridge University Press.

Klein, Martin. 1998. *Slavery and Colonial Rule in French West Africa.* Cambridge, UK: Cambridge University Press.

Lovejoy, Paul. 1980. *Caravans of Kola: The Hausa Kola Trade 1700–1900.* Zaria, Nigeria: Ahmadu Bello University Press.

———. 1983. *Transformations of Slavery: A History of Slavery in Africa.* Cambridge, UK: Cambridge University Press.

Lovejoy, Paul, and Toyin Falola, eds. 1994. *Pawnship in Africa: Debt Bondage in Historical Perspective.* Boulder, CO: Westview.

Médard, Henri, and Shane Doyle, eds. 2007. *Slavery in the Great Lakes Region of East Africa.* Oxford, UK: James Currey.

Meillassoux, Claude. 1991. *The Anthropology of Slavery: The Womb of Iron and Gold.* Chicago: University of Chicago Press; London: Athlone.

Memel-Fote, Harris. 2007. *L'esclavage dans les sociétés lignagères de la forêt ivoirienne (XVIIe-XXe siècle).* Paris: Éditions du CERAP—IRD.

Ohadike, Don C. 1994. *Anioma: A Social History of the Western Igbo People.* Athens: Ohio University Press.

Popović, Alexandre. 2011. *The Revolt of African Slaves in Iraq in the 3rd/9th Century.* Princeton, NJ: Princeton University Press.

Terray, Emmanuel. 1994. "Le pouvoir, le sang, la mort dans le royaume ashanti au XIXe siècle." *Cahiers d'Études africaines* 34, no. 136: 549–62.

Tomich, Dale, ed. 2017. *Slavery and Historical Capitalism in the Nineteenth Century.* Lanham, MD: Lexington Books.

Wilks, Ivor. 1975. *Asante in the Nineteenth Century: The Structure and Evolution of a Political Order.* New York: Cambridge University Press.

Wright, Marcia. 1993. *Strategies of Slaves and Women: Life-Stories from East/Central Africa.* New York: L. Barber; London: J. Currey.

Chapter 2

The Great Transformation

World Capitalism and the Crisis of Slavery in the Americas

Tâmis Parron

In February 1861, the Constitutional Convention of the Confederate States of America (CSA) in Montgomery, Alabama, discussed a clause forbidding the slaveholding nation from reopening the transatlantic slave trade. As soon as he got wind of the news, Leonidas Spratt, a publicist and former newspaper editor from South Carolina, protested with a pamphlet entitled *The Philosophy of Secession* (1861). Spratt had been advocating the revival of the Middle Passage to the United States for nearly eight years. Now he said the new founding fathers were about to make a fatal blunder. If the leading CSA politicians thought they could perpetuate black slavery by doing nothing more than simply sealing off the South from the political antislavery of the North, they were wrong. Reopening the transatlantic slave trade was a life-or-death issue for the CSA.

Spratt argued that many slaveholders, and to his great surprise the founding fathers of the CSA too, tended to regard "the slave as property," a static thing with constitutionally protectable fixed attributes. In their opinion, the South was a "geographical section" (1861, 1) soon to be invested with powers to determine

---

This research was supported by a Fapesp grant and the Prêmio Capes de Tese.

its own future irrespective of any kind of changes in the surrounding world. Such reasoning made no sense because it was too formalist, and Spratt offered a wholly different vision of slavery to reframe the question. Southerners should not regard "the slave as a property" but instead "slavery as a relation" (1861, 5). While the phrasing "slave as a property" evoked a constant interpersonal bond between two people or a kind of object that one might calmly put in the constitutional safe, Spratt contended that human bondage was a multiscalar relational system that realized itself through distinct social instances, such as regional markets, national politics, and global economy. In other words, it was dynamic, complex, and context-bound (1861, 5–6). In Spratt's eyes the CSA needed to entertain the reopening of the transatlantic slave trade as a permanent political possibility so that the new nation could better adjust to the changing global scenario of which it was part. Containerizing slavery would never do.

The geopolitical implications of Spratt's argument were far-reaching. If slavery was a relational phenomenon within a multilayered shifting context, then its content, form, and strength rested on the interplay of local resources and global processes within the worldwide self-expansion of capital. Not only in *Philosophy of Secession* but also in many writings published in the 1850s, southern pro-slave-trade writers had been pressing the point over and over again that world commodity markets, breakthrough technologies, and the rise of an international market of uncoerced labor required prompt adaptive responses from the South. For some years past, they argued, cotton mills had been mushrooming across the North Atlantic and cotton consumption was reaching unprecedented levels in the East, as vast areas of the Indo-Pacific complex (broadly speaking, India, Indochina, China, and Australia) became gradually subordinated to the capitalist world-economy as spaces of commodity production and exchange. "While the demand for slave products is an increasing quantity," wrote editor James De Bow to an Alabama politician, "represented by the growing civilization of the unnumbered millions of Europe and of Asia, the capacity of supply is a constant and almost fixed quantity, represented by the increase of a few millions of Africans upon our shores" (1859, 234). An uneasy question, then, arose for those who inquired into the matter: "Does increased capacity for production, under the natural increase of slave labor, keep pace with this increased demand?" (*Charleston Mercury*, August 3, 1858, 2). "Future security," South Carolinians said, "depends upon an increased production proportionate to the increased demand" (*Report* 1857, 18). Preserving chattel slavery in the Americas meant holding the economic weight of slavery constant within a variable world. Hence, human bondage should expand at increasingly higher rates in order to stabilize the relational proportion between slavery and self-globalizing capitalism. For the so-called reopeners, the transatlantic slave trade seemed to best solve the problem of global-local proportionality.

By mid-century the connection between ongoing world industrialization and commodity production was also leading to a new concept of international mobility of labor on a world scale. According to Spratt, the fact that Europeans had been flooding the North was making the Southern states "less populous than the Northern" and putting the South in a position of relative "inferiority in some departments of material progress." He added, "Though less efficient than the slave, [the Europeans] still have been compelled to work; they have dug canals, constructed railroads." If migration made the transportation revolution, Spratt further pointed out, the transportation revolution also made migration. "It is in virtue of this [infrastructure building] that the North has an excess of near 5,000,000 population" and was beginning to have a decided edge over the thriving and otherwise unbeatable slaveholding economy of the South (1855, 14). A Northern editorialist captured the essentials of this argument: "Vast number of free laborers who are constantly migrating to the unoccupied parts of our country and . . . , by the new facilities of transportation, in a few days and at a trifling expense are set down in the wilderness of our vast interior. . . . The most obvious way of counteracting the effects of this emigration is the revival of the slave trade" (*Evening Post*, June 21, 1854, 2). In this sense, the Middle Passage would not only address a potential unbalance between global consumption and Southern production that imperialism was creating in the realm of world commodity markets, but also remedy a real unbalance in the realm of world labor markets created by the conjunction of epochal technology and the rise of international uncoerced labor mobility.

Apparently blind to these great transformations involving massive mechanization, a transportation revolution, imperialism, and the rise of international labor markets, the founding fathers of the CSA were happy to think that slavery was a static reality and that their Confederacy was a constitutional warrantor of slaves, understood as a stable collection of commodities. Against this formalist worldview, Spratt argued that perpetuating human bondage required continuous articulation of multiple spatiotemporal instances within the global social system—operative mechanisms of national politics creating elastic sources of labor recruitment in line with evolving global markets. In analytical terms, Spratt came close to the idea that capitalism was developing unforeseen patterns of commodity production and exchange. He then claimed that the North was benefiting most from the evolving scenario; and that New World slavery could keep pace with the North or the world-economy as a whole only if it revamped itself by enslaving Africans as an alternative to European mass migration. Had his plans worked out well, a human nightmare would have taken the form of some monstrosity like "the Third Slavery"—a continental system of bondage fed by a superindustrialized transatlantic slave trade, comparable in volume only to the first uncoerced intercontinental migration in Atlantic history, that would resolve the emerging worldwide accumulation contradictions of industrial capitalism. What happened instead was the expansion of enslaving practices in other social forms within Africa (cf. Huzzey 2012; P. Lovejoy 2016) under the banner of antislavery-inspired imperialism and away from the New World slaveholding states, which were just entering the stage of collapse (1860s–1888).

Long dismissed as radical and highly politicized, the writings of Spratt and other reopeners are not so off the mark as they are deemed to be. For all their biased values, pro–slave trade diehards did flesh out events engendered by world-historical processes that scholars tend to overlook all too easily when dealing with the crisis of New World slavery: the worldwide transformation of commodity production and exchange caused by breakthrough transportation technologies, international mobility of labor, and imperialism-based market expansion, that is, processes through which what we may call the first nineteenth century (1780–1840/1860) morphed into the second nineteenth century (1840/1860–1918/1945). In the following pages I suggest that the world-systemic processes touched upon by fire-eaters structured the geopolitical crisis and eventual abolition of New World black slavery. My aim is to emphasize the world-historical origins of the American Civil War, which led to the ultimate extinction of slavery in the Americas as part of the reorganization of nineteenth-century capitalism. Once internalized by the United States in the 1840s and 1850s, the global process magnified the organizational power, popular range, and ideological scope of political abolitionism both in the American republic and beyond.

My argument is threefold. I first maintain that Great Britain faced a dialectical combination of over- and underproduction crises arising out of contradictions between the unprecedented increasing composition of industrial fixed capital and other social forms of value within a worldwide historically specific context, the post-Napoleonic world order (1815–1840s). Hard-pressed, British entrepreneurs and politicians alike increased surplus-value extraction by assuring the final realization of value through mass consumption in colonial markets (imperialism), stimulating investments in railways (railroadization), and widening the sources of food commodity chains that regulated the value of wage labor (free-trade food regime). British responses to deeply felt contradictions unleashed historical-geographical processes that gave impetus to new patterns of commodity, capital, and labor markets worldwide. I then argue that the United States internalized the restructuring of the world-economy in the 1840s and, thereby, also assimilated the contradictions between an increasing composition of fixed capital and other social forms of value. Instead of exporting these contradictions (sort of the "British way"), the United States embraced and even intensified them by designing a new means to expand fixed capital, here called *the agrofinancial-migratory strategy of accumulation*. Finally, I suggest that this strategy—a by-product of globalizing value relations unleashed by the British Empire and internalized by the American Republic—placed regional differentiation within the United States on a new level of magnitude, boosting the rise of the Republican Party, and pushed the South into secession.

The Big Breakthrough of Great Britain, 1815–1840s

Sometimes regarded as little more than a bump in the *longue durée* of capitalism, the Industrial Revolution took the contradiction between fixed capital and other social forms of value to unprecedented levels in human history (Harvey 1982). Machine-based production, designed to increase accumulation through relative surplus value, required extraordinary amounts of input in ways that would make raw materials prohibitively expensive if their supply chains were not properly reorganized (Burkett 1999; Foster 2000; Moore 2010; Tilzey 2018). The input-form of value became key to ongoing industrialization. On the other hand, mass production implied accelerated expansion of consumer markets both in industrializing arenas and elsewhere. The challenge here was not so much the input-form but the wage-form of value. "Workers are important for the market as buyers of commodities," Marx wrote. Therefore, it would be in the interest of entrepreneurs to increase their wages. "But as sellers of their commodity—labor-power—capitalist society has the tendency to restrict them to their minimum price" (1992, 2: 391), a behavior that tended to cut short the local effective demand and make the process of industrialization highly reliant on the growth of foreign markets. After 1815 these so-called immanent limits to the self-expansion of industrial capital were dramatically aggravated by a series of political decisions that established pervasive protectionism and restrictive monetary policies as the hallmarks of the post-Napoleonic world order (Parron 2018).

Producing a long-term impact on the dynamics of nineteenth-century capitalism, both post-1815 fiscal and monetary policies emerged from the Atlantic Revolutions. Tariffs are a case in point. Several factors tilted state policies toward protectionism after 1815. European colonial powers such as France and Spain had lost their main possessions during the liberal revolutions. They then had to address their balance of trade and needed high tariffs to scale down the volume of imports in accordance with their new trading realities. Moreover, virtually all European countries, as well as the United States, incurred crippling war debts and raised tariffs to pay them off. Finally, most important, governments manipulated tariffs on competing imports to protect marginal producers favored during the revolutionary wars. For a fabulous twenty-four-year period (1791–1815), wars, revolutions, and embargoes sent some relative prices sky-high across the world economy, allowing farmers and planters in both Europe and the Americas to save capital, allocate labor, and advance cash crops on marginal lands where they cultivated wheat, sugarcane, or coffee according to local socioecological conditions of production (cf. Tomich 2018; Marquese and Tomich 2020; Hunter 2005). Thanks to the upswing, manufacturing entrepreneurs also set up otherwise uncompetitive cotton mills in the United States and Continental Europe (Beckert 2014). With the end of the conflicts high tariffs became a peacetime means to preserve long-standing wartime prices (O'Rourke 2006; Cardoso 2013), and protectionism became an appealing policy strategically designed to increase state power, unify national economies, and prevent social unrest in a shaky postrevolutionary setting. The British Corn Laws and the French Échelle Mobile (grain protectionist tariff), the reestablishment of the Navigation Acts and the rise of sugar duties in France, and the postwar tariffs on textiles both in the United States and Continental Europe were at once outcomes and causes of the rising world conjuncture.

Widespread Atlantic protectionism coincided with two unrelated events that disrupted the global supply of capital in its money-form in the 1820s. Silver output in Mexico, the leading silver-mining region at the end of the eighteenth-century world-economy, fell "in the face of war and insurgency" after Mexico plunged into its own revolutionary turmoil in the 1810s (Tutino 2016, 7; 1998). Silver had integrated global trade networks in previous centuries, and its breakdown simply meant that money capital would become more expensive—or that commodity prices would plummet. Simultaneously, the British Parliament passed an act in 1819 for the resumption of the gold standard (the Bank of England had abandoned it during the Atlantic Revolutions in order to finance war expenses). Because London had taken over Amsterdam's position as the world's leading capital market, where most exchange bills within the world-economy were redeemed, the convertibility policy of postwar London implied a systemwide restriction on world money (Vilar 1984, 309–40; O'Brien 2000). Coupled with widespread protectionism, both the fall of silver output and the resumption of the gold standard helped throw the capitalist world-economy into a typical Kondratieff downturn, or the B-phase of a wave, during which world prices slumped and the Atlantic GDP growth rates seem to have been lower than those of the subsequent phase (Grinin, Korotayev, and Tausch 2016, 23–54; Wallerstein 2011).

The new conditions of trade and production of the world-economy intensified an accumulation crisis within the powerhouse of nineteenth-century capitalism, Great Britain. This accumulation crisis was not a simple problem of overproduction, nor a mere problem of underproduction, but a combination of both (Marx 1992, 3; Moore 2010). Great Britain started facing an overproduction crisis in the first half of the nineteenth century partly because post-Napoleonic protectionism restricted the potential growth of foreign cotton markets when British mill owners were fully capitalizing production through the widespread use of power looms (Giles 1993; Holden 2017). Coupled with the issues of effective demand, collapse of "silver capitalism," and resumption of the gold standard, restrictions of foreign markets for cotton proved to be devastating. Cotton goods had been the leading articles in British exports since 1805 (Davis 1979, 15, 25). The stagnating value of their exports to Atlantic powers, shown in figure 2.1, sheds light on the outstanding economic challenges to industrial Britain.

Pressed by the contradictions between rising fixed capital, world tariffs, and international monetary policies, Britain explored several "solutions" to its challenges. One of them was to force open the home markets of peripheral powers. While Brazil and Argentina became textbook examples of Western countries diplomatically or militarily bullied into opening their economies, it was in the East that the British made more promising inroads. Gradually they managed to build international credit chains linking India, Indochina, China, and the Australian colonies (the Indo-Pacific complex), subordinating them to the world-economy as a unified space of commodity production and exchange. This imperial decentering from the Atlantic Basin to the Indo-Pacific, the so-called "swing to the East"

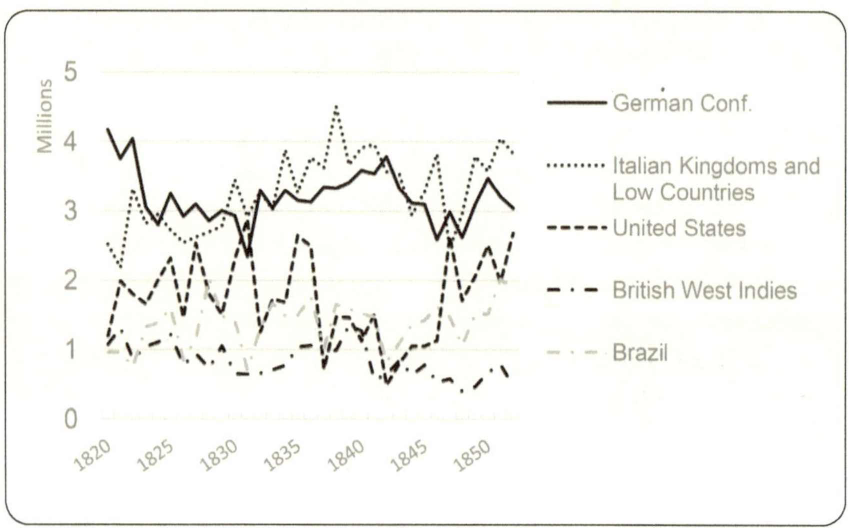

Figure 2.1. British cotton goods exported to Atlantic countries, 1820–1854 (pounds sterling). Sources: *Tables of the Revenue* 1833: 65–70; 1835: 194–97; 1835: 96–97; 1836: 96–97; 1837: 102–3; 1838: 124–25; 1839: 116–17; 1840: 112–13; 1841: 116–17; 1843: 113; 1844: 110; 1845: 112; 1846: 115–416; 1847: 119; 1848: 119; 1849: 125; 1850: 129; 1851: 147; 1852: 149.

(Harlow 1964), was self-evidently violent. In India imperialism implied reshaping environment, labor relations, social customs, and patterns of land tenure to make the colony export opium, cotton, indigo, and rice in order to have capital to buy British textiles (Bosma 2013; Ludden 1990; Harnetty 1972). In China it implied war to unlock massive local markets to both Indian opium and British textiles (Greenberg 1969). And it implied high human costs for settlement in the Australian colonies (Wolfe 2001). The chart below, which shows data from the previous figure plus a line representing British cotton exports to parts of the Indo-Pacific, suggests a dramatic correlation: protectionism-based social peace in the postrevolutionary North Atlantic boosted a disruptive high-geared British colonialism in the East.

The second factor that could smooth out contradictions between the increasing composition of fixed capital and market restrictions involved speeding up and cheapening commodity circulation within Britain itself through massive investment in railroads. "The age of crisis for textile industrialism," Hobsbawm wrote, "was the age of breakthrough for coal and iron" (1999, 87). Indeed, for fifteen years (1835–1850) Britain led the rate of railroad expansion among European nations,

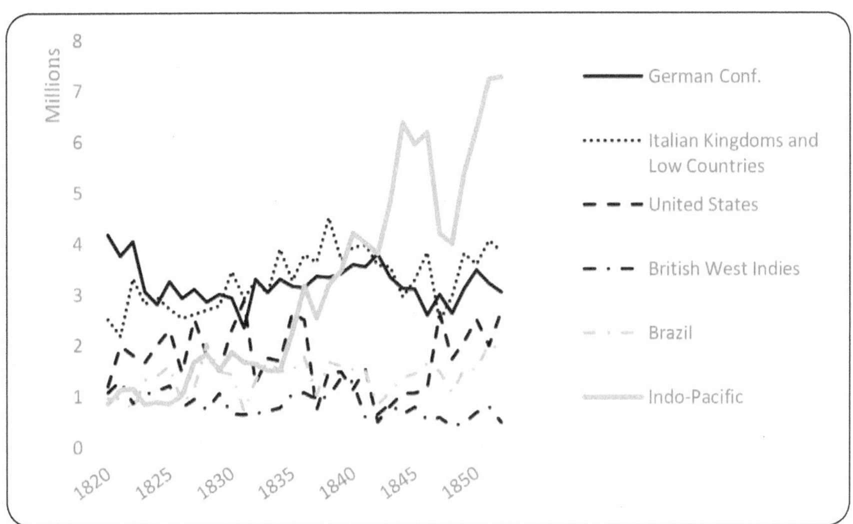

Figure 2.2. Re-Orient: British cotton goods exported, 1820–1852 (pounds sterling). Sources: *Tables of the Revenue* 1833: 65–70; 1835: 194–97; 1835: 96–97; 1836: 96–97; 1837: 102–3; 1838: 124–25; 1839: 116–17; 1840: 112–13; 1841: 116–17; 1843: 113; 1844: 110; 1845: 112; 1846: 115–16; 1847: 119; 1848: 119; 1849: 125; 1850: 129; 1851: 147; 1852: 149. ("Indo-Pacific" includes only East India Company territories and China.)

even though it already had Europe's most unified national economy thanks to its widespread system of roads, turnpikes, and canals (Braudel 1996, 291–356). Such a massive railroad expansion resulted in the growth of secondary and tertiary sectors immediately around railroad stations and the growth of agriculture employment over larger distances. Thereby it deepened the regional division of labor between town and country within Britain and, thus, increased the domestic demand for manufactured goods both in towns and countryside (Bogart et al. 2018). By 1850 Britain's total railroad trackage was equal to the total mileage of lines in Continental Europe, as seen in figure 2.3.

Imperialism in the East and railroadization at home were demand-side "solutions" for the overproduction crisis of British capitalism in the post-Napoleonic world order. Their very success, however, allowed for further proletarianization and urbanization, pushing Britain toward an underproduction crisis. Full proletarianization, or the conversion of part-time peasant workers into full-time wage laborers, implied that wages became the only source of revenue for laboring masses and that markets became the only means for them to obtain consumption goods. In other words,

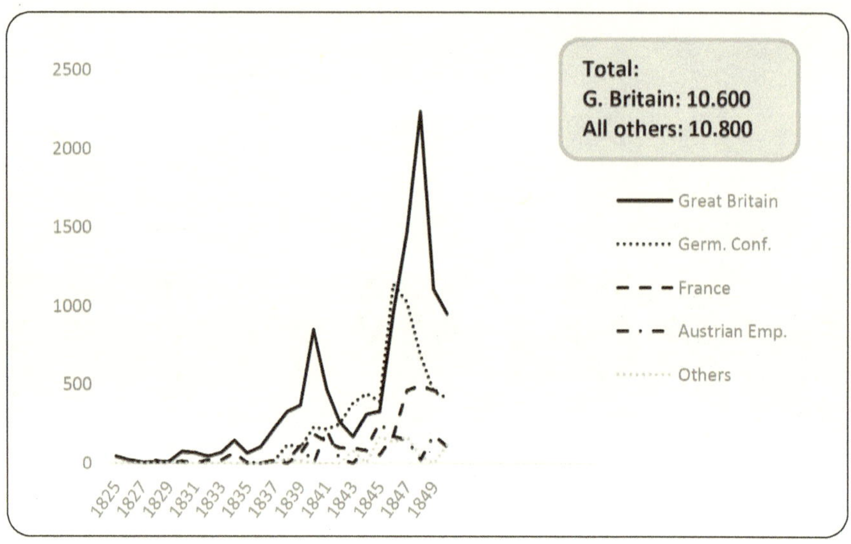

Figure 2.3. Railroad tracks annually opened, Europe (km). Source: Mitchell (1992, 655–56).

more and more people started having "two-side contacts" with markets, both as sellers (of labor) and buyers (of their needs). Coevolving with urbanization, this massive wage and market dependence, a decisive aspect of nineteenth-century industrial capitalism, put the British imperial agroecology under strain. In the metropolis, low yields of marginal lands—taken up in the Atlantic Revolutions because of high prices and kept in cultivation thereafter because of high tariffs—and the famous four-field rotation system of grain production turned out to be wholly inadequate to sustain proletarianization. Ecological exhaustion followed, and food prices rose (Foster 2016; Overton 1996). Meanwhile, rising costs of colonial labor due to the "mighty experiment" with black-slave abolition (Drescher 2002) pushed sugar prices up. As metropolitan workers fought back against the run-up in living costs and fed Chartism in the late 1830s, the British state pondered two alternatives to escape the revolutionary subversion of the social order: either raise wages or lower food prices (Schonhardt-Bailey 2006). From 1842 onward the British Parliament took the second option, slashing tariffs on sugar, meat, flour, and a good many petty consumer articles. The flagships of this reformism, the Repeal of the Corn Laws and the Sugar Act, both passed in 1846, crowned the so-called British free-trade food regime (Tilzey 2018; McMichael 2013; Friedmann and McMichael 1989).

Instead of fulfilling a sort of manifest destiny, the unilateral adoption of free trade by Britain made sense only in the historically specific context of British industrialism and the post-Napoleonic world order. By the thirties, the massive rise of market-dependent and wage-dependent producers in Britain tended to make a worker's wage equal to the exchange value of her or his basic needs (food, clothing, housing), food alone probably being responsible for 65 percent of total household expenditures (Araghi 2003; Levi 1885, 34–35). For the industrial class, then, two mutually reinforcing sources of surplus value achieved a wholly new order of magnitude. Not only was productivity of labor within the unit of production important, which lowered the value of the commodity, but equally decisive was the cheapening of food outside the unit of production, which lowered the value of labor (Marx 1976, 1, ch. 12; Tomich 1980, 2004). Failing to open the domestic markets of central powers and, thus, relieve its internal contradictions, Britain globalized food provisioning as the main regulatory mechanism of its social reproduction. It was in this specific setting that the free-trade food regime arose as a pattern of capital accumulation designed to organize the financing, production, marketing, and consumption of agrofood on a world scale so as to regulate the value of wage labor and control class struggle (McMichael 1991, 1999, 2013). Over the years, distinct social organizations of labor across the world entered the repertoire of global sources of industrial wage-value. The more the double dependence (wage- and market-dependence) moved center stage, the more commodity-producing labor within the capitalist world-system became value-regulating commodity production.

High-geared imperialism in the Indo-Pacific, railroadization at home, and the British free-trade food regime were distinct moments of the globalization of value relations necessary to neutralize the contradictions of capital accumulation of industrial capitalism in Britain in the post-Napoleonic world order. Before the 1840s the world order was ruled by what might be called *periphery-intensive commodity market integration.* This was a conjuncture in which global conditions of commodity exchange and production favored mobility of enslaved laborers, as well as world trade in articles mostly produced by New World slave labor. The political and technological foundations of this conjuncture boosted slave-made rather than free articles as the former (cotton, sugar, coffee) were not nearly as taxed as the latter (textiles and grains) at custom houses; and they fed slave rather than free intercontinental labor mobility because protected wheat markets in postrevolutionary Europe, coupled with prerailroad transportation technology, helped keep the numbers of European out-migration below those of the transatlantic slave trade to the Americas up to the 1840s. Against this background, Britain globalized the value-generating and value-realizing commodity chains of wage labor through imperialism, railroadization, and free-trade food regime. Because of its disproportional weight in the whole of the capitalist world-economy, Britain's pursuit of self-preservation gave rise to a new world conjuncture, an international pattern of trade that also favored a *core-intensive commodity market integration* (that is, in non-slave-made articles) and fostered mobility of the uncoerced labor force.

The emerging worldwide sociospatial composition of value relations—designed by free trade, railroads, and imperialism—expressed itself through several specifically localized clusters of interstate and intrastate interactions. Some of these were as far-flung as (1) the suspension of the transatlantic slave trade to Cuba in 1845, (2) the suppression of the transatlantic slave trade to Brazil in 1850, (3) the US conquest of California during the Mexican War (1846–1848), (4) the US Compromise of 1850, and (5) the increasing regional differentiation within the United States in the 1840s and 1850s. Each of those events deserves an in-depth, encompassing world-historical analysis from a global value relations perspective. In the following pages, I focus on the last one.

The Big American Incorporation, 1840s–1850s

The conjuncture of core-intensive commodity market integration triggered the rise of an unintendedly revolutionary strategy of capital accumulation in the United States. This strategy, pivoting on British imperial reconfiguring, rested on the territorialization of finances, massive labor mobility on both regional and international levels, and a new regional division of labor between town and country. At the end of the day, it helped reshape the ecological and labor surpluses of the United States in ways that shifted the political and material power from the South to the North in the two decades leading to the outbreak of the American Civil War (1861). Although noticeable in several socioeconomic sectors, this transformation is most clearly visible in the railroadization of the United States.

The globalizing value relations of the British Empire boosted railroad investments in the United States in more than one sense. To begin with, by globalizing family-based agriculture, the British free-trade food regime built up expectations for the sustained growth of grain markets throughout the Atlantic (Martin 1935; Fairlie 1959; Araghi 2003). Thereby it induced capital market actors in Boston, Philadelphia, and New York to invest in "merchant railroads" toward the West, where the best lands for grains were located—that is, railroads boomed in order to attend to the commercialization of petty-commodity production, not for big industrial needs (Fishlow 1971, 237–61). Likewise, Britain also played a role on the supply side. The railroad mania in Britain came to a halt in 1847 after massive free-trade speculation on corn and sugar and the bursting of railway financial bubbles squeezed corporate profits. Because of this reversal of fortunes, enormous quantities of iron lay idle and were shipped to the United States and Germany, which needed them badly if they were "to capture the commercial gains likely to result from repeal of the Corn Laws" (Lake and James 1989, 23). Finally, congressional politics kicked in. American railroad demand and British iron supply induced federal representatives of New England, Pennsylvania, and New York to vote for articles of the Walker Tariff (1846) that slashed duties on imported iron. So, as British iron prices dropped 50 percent between 1847 and 1850 (Fishlow 1971, 247), US import duties plummeted 60 percent for pig iron and 80 percent for shaped iron (*H. R. 384*, 1846, 11). During the 1850s the railroad network expansion within the world-economy moved from Britain to the United States. By 1860 American railroads occupied the position in the North Atlantic (figure 2.4) that the British lines had occupied in Europe a decade earlier.

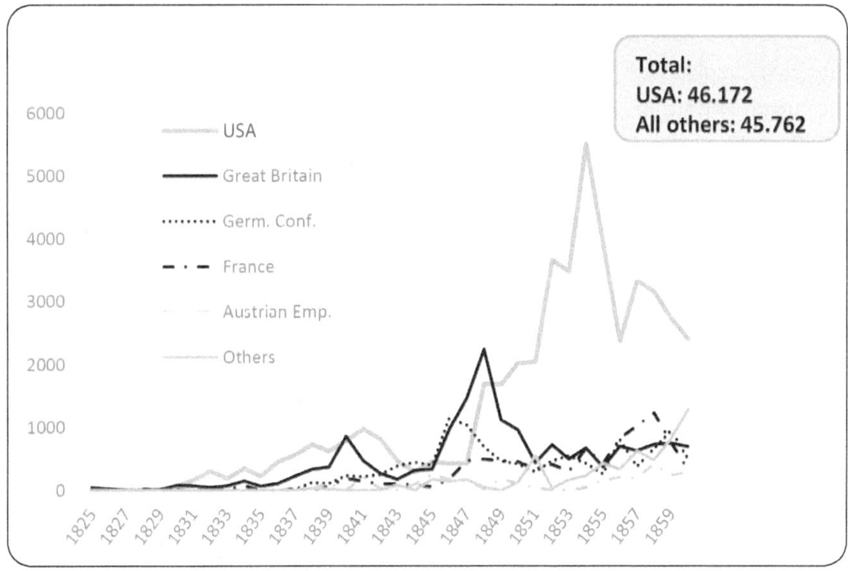

Figure 2.4. Railroad tracks annually opened, North Atlantic (km). Source: Mitchell 1992, 655–56; Shuman 1883, 308.

The unequaled American railroad boom was both formed by and formative of an emerging strategy of capital accumulation based on large-scale financial capitalization through massive labor mobility and state-sponsored land commodification. That strategy closely followed the basics of nineteenth-century railroad microeconomics. As many scholars have suggested, railroads were a costly industry (Chandler 1965; White 2012; Nelson 2012). It was so expensive to build them that laying a single line on a flat area where no grading work or curves were necessary, as with the Illinois Central for example, could absorb more capital than the total value of slave-grown coffee annually exported from Brazil to its main consumer market at the time, the United States. The unprecedented magnitude of investment within a single corporation represented real challenges for extant mechanisms of credit, which had to find new ways to patch up the rift between the huge amount of fixed capital with slow turnover time and the relatively small amount of incoming circulating capital resulting from the railroad operations. Finally, not only were their costs high, constant, and relatively traffic-inelastic (Ripley 1912, 55; Mercer 1982, 18–31) but also their maintenance required large constant reinvestments, since the material they were made of in the antebellum period, wood and wrought iron, had a short lifespan of three to seven years (Fishlow 1971). In analytical terms, antebellum railroads had a good deal of large-scale past dead labor, that is, fixed capital that would undergo quick devaluation and, therefore, had to be realized through maximal use (Harvey 1982). Facing gigantic outlays (inputs, wages, interests) coupled with rapid devaluation, railroad entrepreneurs sought to cut short the turnover time of incoming capital as much as possible. The means to do so rested on the only resource they could possibly foster: traffic, traffic, and traffic.

Intensity of traffic was a shorthand for extremely violent commodification processes. American business experience in the 1840s gradually convinced investors that track networks needed densely populated rural markets, for local traffic proved to generate a larger slice of earnings than through traffic (*Railway Times*, September 1, 1860, 341). Investors also learned that densely populated rural markets would be better fed by massive migration, as they realized that passenger fares were as crucial as freight for most of railroad budgets (Poor 1860, 93, 228, 381, 423; Majewski 2000). To their happiness, investors finally learned that the United States could count on such a mobility of people. Between the Repeal of the Corn Laws and the American Civil War, nearly four million foreigners, mainly from Ireland, Germany, and England, made their way to the republic, a number almost as large as the entire enslaved population that the South had been able to accumulate after three hundred years of slaveholding (*Historical Statistics* 1960, 57). In a five-year period (1851–1855), the United States took in as many immigrants as it had absorbed since the fall of Napoleon in 1815 (Bromwell 1856, 174–75). Compared to its population in 1845, the republic would never again receive such a deluge of foreigners as it did between 1846 and 1855.

While historians cite push and pull factors to explain the mid-century mass migration to the United States (Wilkinson 1970; Thomas 1973; Cohn 2009, 70–80), virtually all of its key elements were formed through the globalizing value relations that Britain was promoting within the world-system. The most important migration factor was the series of potato-harvest failures that caused the tragic Irish Famine (1845–1848). Beginning with the pathogen *Phytophthora infestans*, the blight turned into a man-made catastrophe when British politicians decided to address the problem relying on the recently passed Repeal of the Corn Laws. They expected the efficiency of the free market in food to secure grain supplies, a strategy that condemned starving millions to either death or out-migration across the Atlantic (Kenealy 1998, 2002). Moreover, English and German migrants were moving out due partly to lifetime-income expectations raised by the international free-trade regime in grains (Van Vugt 1988; Fairlie 1969) and partly to the railroad-made regional division of labor between countryside and towns not only in England but also in Germany, which, like the United States, benefited from British iron surpluses in the wake of the 1847 railroad bust (Fremdling 1977). In this setting, American railroadization and migration evolved in a circular causality. Allowing cheap fares to cheap distant lands to produce cheap food, railroads boosted the very migratory chains they were produced by. Tracks became the conveyor belt between depeasantization in Europe and repeasantization in the United States, unifying both as a world-systemic process constitutive of the first uncoerced international market of the workforce in the Atlantic.

To further stimulate mass migration and create densely populated rural markets, American federal congressmen designed a policy of land grants in 1850 that eventuated in large-scale territorialized financing. The workings of this policy are well-known. Congress enclosed federal land in a checkerboard pattern and transferred the property rights to corresponding states; state legislatures gave corporations half of the land within the granted area in the form of alternate plots; those corporations used those plots as collateral of bonds they issued in capital markets; at the same time, they mortgaged the same plots to farmers, who provided the companies with future cash payment, passenger traffic, and freight (Nelson 2012, 126–58).

In the end, capital and land markets (stock exchange and mortgage), intertwined with a new agrofood world market, helped construct the emerging international market of the uncoerced workforce.

The asymmetrical development of those world-historical markets in capital, commodities, and labor morphed into a revolutionary form to valorize capital in the United States, or what I will call the *agrofinancial-migratory strategy of accumulation.* Globally conditioned, nationally regulated, and locally materialized, this strategy promoted greater regional differentiation within the United States in the 1840s and 1850s in ways that structured the geopolitical crisis leading to Southern secession. To put it differently, when the United States internalized, and reinvented, the world-historical forces emanating from British imperial reconfiguring as the agrofinancial-migratory strategy of accumulation, it also internalized, and exacerbated, the contradictions between the increasing composition of fixed capital and other social forms of value. To understand why the "big American incorporation" brought sharp regional differentiation to a new level, it is necessary to see how the increasing composition of fixed capital in the United States interacted with the distinct locational geographies of labor in the slaveholding South and the free North.

The locational geographies of slavery and free labor were two modes of organizing spatial relations for capital accumulation in the republic. As noted by Wright (2007), the operations of the locational geography of slavery were as simple as they were violent. Once the chattel slave was defined as property, the enslaved person was at once input (allocable resource) and collateral (pledged property for debts). Not only could an enslaved man, woman, or child morph into the money-form through the slave trade as any regular commodity (C → M), but he or she could also make money into more money as assets for securities (M → M'). Thanks to this fictional duality of the enslaved, slave markets thrived and slave-owners could buy captives to set up correspondingly larger operating production units than farmers in regions where no ready supply of labor was available. By the same token, using the whip of law and the right to whip, slaveholders moved their human factors of production around, violently allocating labor in strategically located land plots where agroecological conditions (waterways included) allowed large-scale cotton production. This built-in violence of the locational geography of slavery enabled land speculation in specific areas without present or prospective dense settlement.

In contrast, the size of rural properties and patterns of land speculation in the North were closely related to labor markets and demography. Here no coerced mobility of workers applied and demographic density dictated nearly everything.

Relative inelasticity of the labor supply, as well as the slow-paced rhythm of population growth, meant that families had to have recourse to self-exploitation to make ends meet and that the size of operative rural units tended to be relatively small, as it was proportional to the availability of family labor. While the locational geography of slavery produced "blotches of high-value lands" scattered in the South, the locational geography of uncoerced labor fashioned a rather uniform "progression of land values from east to west" pushed by demographic density (Wright 2006, 64; Weiman 1990). Partly because of its pattern of land tenure, the North presented a significantly higher proportion of improved to unimproved land than the South: 58 percent against 32 percent by 1860 (*Agriculture* 1864, table 1, California and Texas excluded for their recent occupation by the republic).

The locational geography of slavery gave the South competitive advantages over the North *before the arrival of railroads*—just think of a social institution so productive that it makes population surplus relatively superfluous to frontier speculation—but it turned into a relative handicap when the United States caught the "railroadization fever." Dispersal was the pest for the new, fixed-capital-dependent strategy of accumulation. Railroads required a gigantic measure of money capital, circulating goods, and circulating people to pay off the massive fixed capital embodied in their astronomically expensive, quickly devaluating facilities. As a consequence, railroads found in the locational geography of family grain farming, not of cotton plantations, the socioecology for dense concentrations of human beings within the emerging core-intensive commodity market integration.

Perhaps the most straightforward way to assess the relation between railroads and the locational geography of labor regimes is through data extracted from the American railroad share lists published in the 1850s for investors interested in railroad securities. Produced for most of the operating lines and periodically inserted in newspapers like *American Railroad Journal* and the *American Railway Times*, share lists contain figures such as the sum of existing companies in each state, the amount of dividend-paying companies, and the average net income per mile for each company. In any of these entries, Northern railroads performed much better than Southern railroads.

As shown in figure 2.5, investors could easily realize that future earnings were potentially bigger in the petty-commodity production areas fed by large-scale immigration than in areas where social-property relations of slavery prevailed. As a result, railroad companies in free states disproportionately outnumbered those in slaveholding states (figure 2.6).

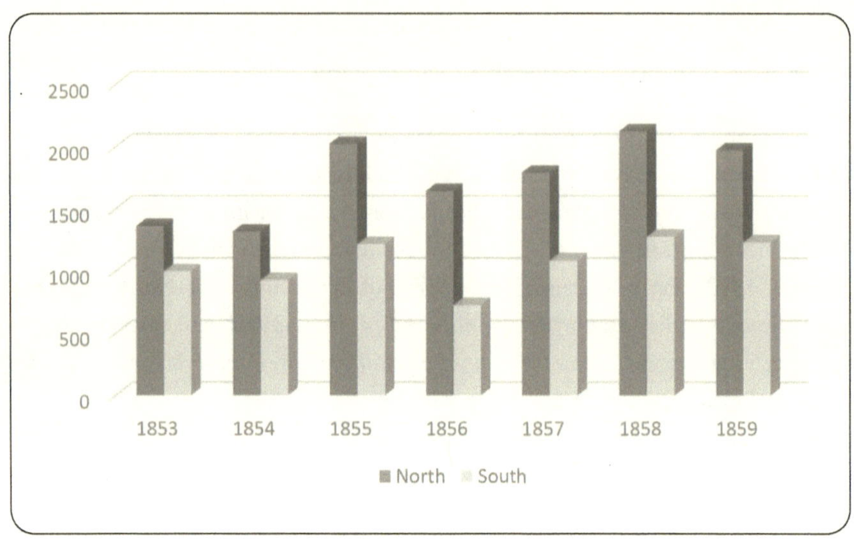

Figure 2.5. Average net income per mile (US$). Sources: *American Railroad Journal*, June 11, 1853, 376; October 7, 1854, 632; December 29, 1855, 822; *American Railway Times*, July 3, 1856, 3; March, 19, 1857, 3; March 27, 1858, 3; February 19, 1859, 3.

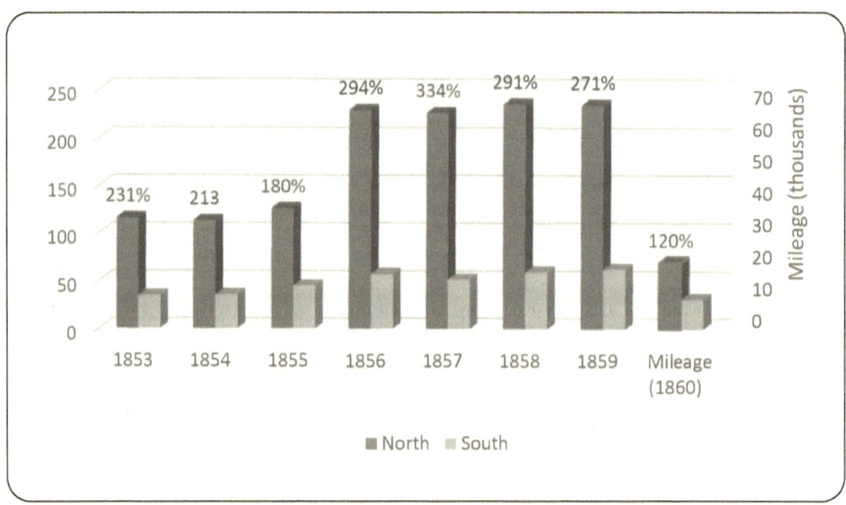

Figure 2.6. Number of railroad companies per section: a highly speculative business. Sources: *American Railroad Journal*, June 11, 1853, 376; October 7, 1854, 632; December 29, 1855, 822; *American Railway Times*, July 3, 1856, 3; March 19, 1857, 3; March 27, 1858, 3; February 19, 1859, 3.

Dividends are not equally reliable data. They do not cover the full financial operations of railroad companies, as shareholders could receive "interest payments during the construction period" and get new equity "at a discount" by accepting "payment in stock" (Fishlow 1971, 187). Likewise, companies could pay dividends by getting subsidized money from the state—a practice called "stock watering"—so that shareholders could gain even when the company lost. Nonetheless, the number of dividend-paying companies (figure 2.7) still reflects similar disparities between Southern and Northern railroadization within the world-historical context of mass migration.

None of the foregoing assertions suggests any incompatibility between the slaveholding South and modernity. As scholars have long observed, slaveholding states showed high productivity rates in several sectors and were able to mechanize land transportation in the 1840s and 1850s. What I am arguing is that slavery had a spatial pattern of land occupation that shaped the form and content of railroadization within the context of the first emerging uncoerced mass migration of the capitalist world-system. Not only did Northern lines pay better but their multiplier effects were far larger. While the locational geography of slavery gave the wealthiest greater control over land markets and cotton prices—slaveholders were

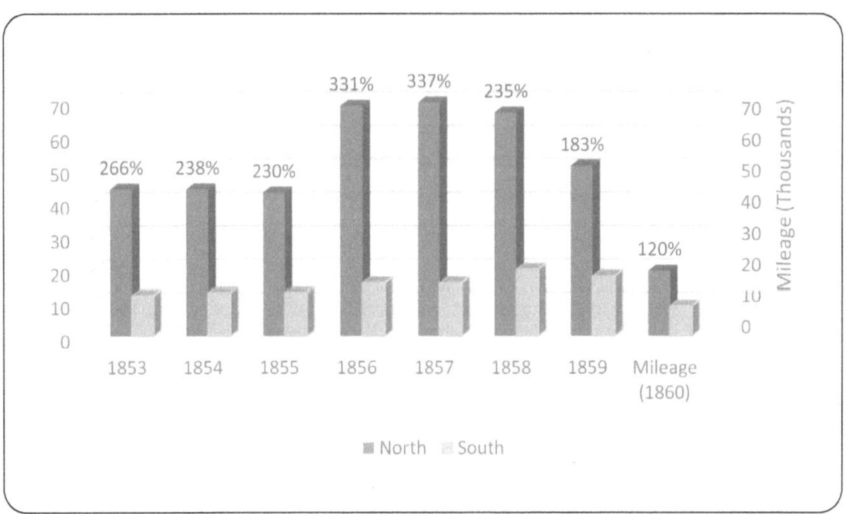

Figure 2.7. Dividend-paying companies. Sources: *American Railroad Journal*, June 11, 1853, 376; October 7, 1854, 632; December 29, 1855, 822; *American Railway Times*, July 3, 1856, 3; March 19, 1857, 3; March 27, 1858, 3; February 19, 1859, 3.

"settlers with means"—wheat prices and land markets in the North were shaped by more affordable, family-sized operative units run by "men with small means," as the press then put it. Along with climate and agrarian cultures, the economic spatiality of labor was one of the reasons why incoming Europeans made their way mostly to the North (Lewis 1978). Even when making good money, railroads in slaveholding states did not repeat the virtuous cycle based on territorialized financing and massive labor mobility that was revolutionizing the Northern economy. An apparently abstract universal category, or a comparable factor of production, technology is better understood as historically formed through specific clusters of social relations (Tomich 2018). As seen in the opening section of this chapter, pro-slave-trade writers were quick to recognize these differences.

But they were not the only ones. When the Republican Party arose as the most powerful American political organization in the 1850s, it had a firm ideological commitment to antislavery. Its leaders read the Federal Constitution as a document that unequivocally denied property rights in human beings and, accordingly, were determined to disentangle the federal government from the proslavery structure that the South had built over the previous decades: the national flag would not fly on slave-trading ships; Washington, DC, would be rid of slavery; slavery would be blocked from the territories (Oakes 2013; Sewell 1976). The party seems to have been the machine responsible for turning the 1850 Compromise, the Kansas-Nebraska Act of 1854, the Bloody Kansas confrontations, and the Dred Scott decision into a linear, cumulative chain of events culminating in the Civil War. Without a doubt, the Republicans performed such a role. Still, it was one thing to have a political antislavery agenda, a position that harked back to the late 1830s; it was another to become popular pursuing that agenda. What was, after all, the social engine propelling and popularizing political antislavery so extraordinarily in the 1850s? When Republicans speak, they are quite explicit on this matter: the expansion of slavery was not only morally wrong, it was prejudicial to Western farmers, incoming settlers, immigrating Europeans, financial investors, land speculators, industrial interests, and railroad shareholders. The windfall of the Northern economy rested on the agrofinancial-migratory strategy of accumulation. Expanding slavery over the territories was bad economics.

"The North is rapidly filling up," a Republican editorialist wrote. "The changes that have been wrought in the last ten years we can now appreciate." As for the future, "we are to have substantial men from Germany, England, and Ireland, in numbers that we have heretofore not dreamed of. Where are all these to find land?" (*National Era*, October 4, 1855, 158). The problem of losing the West to slavery went beyond political balance and morality. Without the West, said John Jay, "the vast emigration from abroad that is now poured into our midst and overflows westward" would "be stopped suddenly by a line of slave States" (1856, 11). William Seward, an equally well-known vocal opponent of slavery, also touched on the world-historical processes that made political antislavery popular politics in the United States: "When I became acquainted with the shore of Lake Ontario, some thirty years ago, it had little more than historical importance. . . . There were no colleges, no ships, no manufactures, no railroads, no canals. The new and scattered settlements in this part of the state were ruled from Albany. . . . How majestic the change which has come over Western New York within that short period. . . . The whole region is traversed with canals and railroads, which leave no farm distant ten miles from some avenue which conducts to the great markets of the world." Migration, he said, was "the real spring of the prosperity and expansion of Oswego, of Western New York, of the State of New York, and of the United States of America." If the South faced "a relative decline of commercial and political wealth and influence," it was because slavery inhibited migration (1857, 3–5).

As the United States internalized the world-systemic contradictions between the increasing composition of fixed capital and the labor-form of value, the agrofinancial-migratory nexus became the sinew and muscle of the Republican body politic. Republicans pointed out that financial investments in massive fixed capital enterprises made more sense in densely populated areas fed by constant foreign labor, and they argued that the necessary labor mobility, both international and national, depended on the interplay of world commodity markets, world labor markets, and the distinct locational geographies of labor within the United States. For the first time ever in US history, conservative abolitionism merged with rational exploitation of large-scale economic opportunities. Or, to put it another way, the cultural level of general norms framing human behavior as right or wrong interacted, in the context of the great transformation, with a cultural perception of how resources of material life should be allocated, building a cycle of mutual reinforcement. This synergy was established through a broader, large-scale social change within which sectional grievances eventually flared into the American Civil War, paving the way—as we know—for the end of slavery in the Americas.

Final Remarks

Spratt lost his bet. The Montgomery Convention ignored his plea and kept the constitutional clause prohibiting the resumption of the Middle Passage by the CSA. But the Founding Fathers also lost theirs: slavery was crushed from without by invading Northern troops and from within through large-scale slave flights. This national stage for abolition, however, should not obscure the world-systemic origins of the American Civil War. The social process that ushered the United States into its bloodiest conflict ever was not a simple cumulative result of national phenomena—say, different rates of growth between two regions possessing fixed social attributes (Genovese 1976; Foner 1995; Ashworth 2007; Freehling 2007), or simmering feuds between politically opposite sections (Holt 1978; Potter 2011). The social dynamic leading to the American Civil War was rather the working out of systemwide accumulation processes embodied in the rise of massive fixed capital and industrial wage labor. The rising global value relations of industrial wage labor, transformed through distinct locational geographies of labor regimes within the United States, redefined the place that black slavery occupied both in the Republic and within the world-system. In this sense the American regional differentiation—or the rise of the Midwest—should not be interpreted as the direct result of an internally driven, self-propelling move to the West (Egnal 2009). Nor, perhaps, should it show up as an exclusive effect of "social-property relations" of "petty-commodity production," or family-based cash crop agriculture, in the North (Post 2011). It is not that regionally distinct social relations of production did not matter. On the contrary, it seems that the emerging agrofinancial migratory chain—which crowned the United States as the most thriving world land market in nineteenth-century capitalism—colonized, scaled up, and recast preexisting social-property relations of petty-commodity production within an evolving global set of value relations.

In other words, *The American Road to Capitalism* may not have been *The Road to Civil War*—to mention two thoughtful books on the origins of the Civil War. The great transformation that took place in the United States in the 1840s and 1850s seems to have been part of a compositional, deeper, infinitely more massive structural reconfiguring of the capitalist world-system under the hegemony of British capital in the post-Napoleonic world order. When the United States internalized and redefined this multiscalar, systemwide transformation of industrial capitalism, domestic conservative abolitionism resonated with rational exploitation of large-scale economic opportunities for the first time in American history, a setting that the Republican Party quickly enshrined in its agenda. Reinforced by the outcome of the Civil War, the same synergy would play a decisive role some years later in Cuba and Brazil, paving *The Global Road* to the abolition of black slavery in the Americas. While, however, the Americas escaped the human tragedy of a "third slavery," the increasing composition of fixed capital in the world arena and the rising global value relations of industrial wage labor stimulated, cunningly, massive enslaving networks in Africa and beyond.

References

Agriculture of the United States in 1860. 1864. Washington, DC: Government Printing Office.

Araghi, Farshad. 2003. "Food Regimes and the Production of Value: Some Methodological Issues." *Journal of Peasant Studies* 30, no. 2: 337–68.

Ashworth, John. 2007. *Slavery, Capitalism, and Politics in the Antebellum Republic.* Vol. 2. *The Coming of the Civil War, 1850–1861.* Cambridge, UK: Cambridge University Press.

Beckert, Sven. 2014. *Empire of Cotton: A Global History.* New York: Knopf.

Bogart, Dan, Leigh Shaw-Taylor, and Xuesheng You. 2018. "Railways and Structural Change: Evidence from Industrializing Britain." In *The Online Historical Atlas of Transport, Urbanization and Economic Development in England and Wales c. 1680–1911*, edited by L. Shaw-Taylor, D. Bogart, and M. Satchell, ch. 3, http://www.campop.geog.cam.ac.uk/research/projects/transport/onlineatlas/.

Bosma, Ulrich. 2013. *The Sugar Plantation in India and Indonesia: Industrial Production, 1770–2010.* Cambridge, UK: Cambridge University Press.

Boswell, Terry, and Mike Sweat. 1991. "Hegemony, Long Waves, and Major Wars: A Time Series Analysis of Systemic Dynamics, 1496–1967." *International Studies Quarterly* 35, no. 2: 123–49.

Braudel, Fernand.1996. *Civilização material, economia e capitalismo, século XV–XVIII.* Vol. 3. *O tempo do mundo.* São Paulo: Martins Fontes.

Bromwell, William. 1856. *History of the Immigration to the United States.* New York: Redfield.

Burkett, Paul. 1999. *Marx and Nature: A Red and Green Perspective.* New York: Palgrave.

Chandler, Alfred. 1965. *The Railroads: The Nation's First Big Business.* New York: Harcourt, Brace & World.

Cardoso, José Luís. 2013. "Lifting the Continental Blockade: Britain, Portugal and Brazilian Trade in the Global Context of the Napoleonic Wars." In *A Global History of Trade and Conflict since 1500*, edited by Lucia Coppolaro and Francine McKenzie, 87–104. New York: Palgrave Macmillan.

Cohn, Raymond L. 2009. *Mass Migration under Sail: European Immigration to the Antebellum United States.* Cambridge: Cambridge University Press.

Davis, Ralph. 1979. *The Industrial Revolution and British Overseas Trade.* Atlantic Highlands, NJ: Humanities Press.

De Bow, J. D. B. 1859. "African Labor Supply Association." *De Bow's Review*, no. 27: 231–35.

Drescher, Seymour. 2002. *The Mighty Experiment: Free Labor versus Slavery in British Emancipation.* Oxford, UK: Oxford University Press.

Egnal, Marc. 2009. *Clash of Extremes: The Economic Origins of the Civil War.* New York: Hill & Wang.

Fairlie, Susan. 1959. "The Anglo-Russian Grain Trade" (PhD diss., London School of Economics).

———. 1969. "The Corn Laws and British Wheat Production, 1829–76." *Economic History Review* 22, no. 1: 88–116.

Fishlow, Albert. 1971. *American Railroads and the Transformation of the Ante-bellum Economy.* Cambridge, MA: Harvard University Press.

Fogel, Robert, and Stanley Engerman. 1974. *Time on the Cross: The Economics of American Negro Slavery.* Boston: Little, Brown.

Foner, Eric. 1995. *Free Soil, Free Labor, Free Men: The Ideology of the Republican Party before the Civil War.* Oxford, UK: Oxford University Press.

Foster, John Bellamy. 2000. *Marx's Ecology: Materialism and Nature.* New York: Monthly Review.

———. 2016. "Marx as a Food Theorist." *Monthly Review* 68, no. 7.

Freehling, William. 2007. *The Road to Disunion.* Vol. 2. *Secessionists Triumphant, 1854–1861.* Oxford, UK: Oxford University Press.

Fremdling, Rainer. 1977. "Railroads and German Economic Growth: A Leading Sector Analysis with a Comparison to the United States and Great Britain." *Journal of Economic History* 37, no. 3: 583–604.

Friedmann, Harriet, and Philip McMichael. 1989. "Agriculture and the State System: The Rise and Decline of National Agricultures, 1870 to the Present." *Sociologia Ruralis* 29, no. 2: 93–117.

Genovese, Eugene. 1976. *A economia política da escravidão.* Rio de Janeiro: Passas.

Giles, Colum. 1993. "Housing the Loom, 1790–1850: A Study of Industrial Building and Mechanisation in a Transitional Period." *Industrial Archaeology Review* 16, no. 1: 27–37.

Greenberg, M. 1969. *British Trade and the Opening of China, 1800–42.* Cambridge, UK: Cambridge University Press.

Grinin, Leonid, Andrey Korotayev, and Arno Tausch. 2016. "Kondratieff Waves in the World System Perspective." In Grinin, Korotayev, and Tausch, *Economic Cycles, Crises, and the Global Periphery.* New York: Springer.

Harlow, Vincent T. 1964. *The Founding of the Second British Empire, 1763–1793: New Continents and Changing Values*. Vol. 2. London: Longmans.

Harnetty, Peter. 1972. *Imperialism and Free Trade: Lancashire and India in the Mid-Nineteenth Century*. Vancouver: University of British Columbia Press.

Harvey, David. 1982. *The Limits to Capital*. Chicago: University of Chicago Press.

Hobsbawm, Eric. 1999. *Industry and Empire: From 1750 to the Present Day*. New York: Penguin Books.

Holden, Roger. 2017. *Manufacturing the Cloth of the World: Weaving Mills in Lancashire*. Stockport, Cheshire, UK: Roger Holden.

Holt, Michael. 1978. *The Political Crisis of the 1850s*. New York: Wiley.

H. R. [House of Representatives] *384*. 1846. *An Act Reducing the Duty on Imports, and for other purposes*.

Hunter, Brooke. 2005. "Wheat, War, and the American Economy during the Age of Revolution." *William and Mary Quarterly* 62, no. 3: 505–26.

Huzzey, Richard. 2012. *Freedom Burning: Anti-Slavery and Empire in Victorian Britain*. Ithaca, NY: Cornell University Press.

Jay, John. 1856. *America Free—or America Slave: An Address on the State of the Country*. New York: NY Tribune.

Johnson, Walter. 2013. *River of Dark Dreams: Slavery and Empire in the Cotton Kingdom*. Cambridge, MA: Belknap.

Kenealy, Christine. 1998. "Peel, Rotten Potatoes and Providence." In *Free Trade and Its Reception, 1815–1960*, vol. 1, edited by Andrew Marrison, 50–62. London: Routledge.

———. 2002. *The Great Irish Famine: Impact, Ideology and Rebellion*. New York: Palgrave.

Lake, D. A., and S. C. James. 1989. "The Second Face of Hegemony: Britain's Repeal of the Corn Laws and the American Walker Tariff of 1846." *International Organization* 43, no. 1: 1–29.

Levi, Leone. 1885. *Wages and Earnings of the Working Classes*. London: John Murray.

Lewis, Arthur. 1978. *The Evolution of the International Economic Order*. Princeton, NJ: Princeton University Press.

Lovejoy, Paul. 2016. "Jihad and the Era of the Second Slavery." *Journal of Global Slavery*, no. 1: 28–43.

Ludden, David. 1990. "World Economy and Village India 1600–1900: Exploring the Agrarian History of Capitalism." In *South Asia and World Capitalism*, edited by Sugata Bose, 159–77. New York: Oxford University Press.

Majewski, John. 2000. *A House Dividing: Economic Development in Pennsylvania and Virginia before the Civil War*. Cambridge, UK: Cambridge University Press.

Marquese, Rafael, and Dale Tomich. 2020. "Slavery in the Paraíba Valley and the Formation of the World Coffee Market in the Nineteenth Century." In *Atlantic Transformations:*

Empire, Politics, and Slavery during the Nineteenth Century, edited by Dale Tomich, 193–223. Albany: State University of New York Press.

Martin, Thomas P. 1935. "Cotton and Wheat in Anglo-American Trade and Politics, 1846–1852." *Journal of Southern History*, v. 1, no. 3: 293–319.

Marx, Karl. 1976. *Capital: A Critique of Political Economy*. Vol. 1. Middlesex, UK: Penguin Books.

———. 1992. *Capital: A Critique of Political Economy*. Vols. 2–3. London: Penguin Books.

McMichael, Philip. 1991. "Slavery in the Regime of Wage Labor: Beyond Paternalism in the U.S. Cotton Culture." *Social Concept* 6, no. 1: 10–28.

———. 1999. "The Global Crisis of Wage-Labor." *Studies in Political Economy*, no. 58: 11–40.

———. 2013. *Food Regimes and Agrarian Questions*. Halifax/Winnipeg: Fernwood.

Mercer, Lloyd J. 1982. *Railroads and Land Grant Policy: A Study in Government Intervention*. New York: Academic.

Mitchell, B. R. 1992. *International Historical Statistics: Europe, 1750–1988*. London: Macmillan.

Moore, Jason. 2010. "The End of the Road? Agricultural Revolutions in the Capitalist World-Ecology, 1450–2010." *Journal of Agrarian Change* 10, 3: 389–413.

Nelson, Scott Reynolds. 2012. *A Nation of Deadbeats: An Uncommon History of America's Financial Disasters*. New York: Vintage Books.

Nitzan, Jonathan, and Shimshon Bichler. 2009. *Capital as Power: A Study of Order and Creorder*. London: Routledge.

Oakes, James. 2013. *Freedom National: The Destruction of Slavery in the United States, 1861–1865*. New York: Norton.

O'Brien, Patrick. 2000. "Merchants and Bankers as Patriots or Speculators? Foreign Commerce and Monetary Policy in Wartime, 1793–1815." In *The Early Modern Atlantic Economy*, edited by John McCusker and Kenneth Morgan, 250–77. Cambridge, UK: Cambridge University Press.

O'Rourke, Kevin. 2006. "The Worldwide Economic Impact of the French Revolutionary and Napoleonic Wars, 1793–1815." *Journal of Global History* 1, no. 1: 123–49.

Overton, Mark. 1996. *Agricultural Revolution in England: The Transformation of the Agrarian Economy, 1500–1850*. Cambridge, UK: Cambridge University Press.

Parron, Tâmis. 2018. "The British Empire and the Suppression of the Slave Trade to Brazil: A Global History Analysis." *Journal of World History* 29, no. 1: 1–36.

Poor, Henry. 1860. *History of the Railroads and Canals of the United States*. New York: Schultz.

Potter, David. 2011. *The Impending Crisis: America before the Civil War, 1848–1861*. Edited by Don E. Fehrenbacher. New York: Harper Perennial.

Post, Charles. 2011. *The American Road to Capitalism: Studies in Class-Structure, Economic Development and Political Conflict, 1620–1877*. Leiden: Brill.

Report of the House of Representatives of South Carolina. 1857. Columbia: Carolina Times.

Ripley, William Z. 1912. *Railroads: Rates and Regulations.* New York: Longmans, Green.

Schoen, Brian. *The Fragile Fabric of Union: Cotton, Federal Politics, and the Global Origins of the Civil War.* Baltimore: Johns Hopkins University Press, 2009.

Schonhardt-Bailey, Cheryl. 2006. *From the Corn Laws to Free Trade: Interests, Ideas, and Institutions in Historical Perspective.* Cambridge, MA: MIT Press.

Seward, William. 1857. *Immigrant White Labor, or Imported Black African Slave Labor.* Washington, DC: Republican Association of Washington.

Sewell, Richard H. 1976. *Ballots for Freedom: Antislavery Politics in the United States, 1837–1860.* New York: Norton.

Shuman, Armin. 1883. *Statistical Report of the Railroads in the United States.* Washington, DC: Government Printing Office.

Silver, Beverly. 1995. "World Scale Patterns of Labor-Capital Conflict: Labor Unrest, Long Waves and Cycles of Hegemony." *Review: A Journal of the Fernand Braudel Center* 18, no. 1: 155–92.

Spratt, Leonidas. 1855. *A Series of Articles on the Value of the Union to the South.* Charleston, SC: James, Williams, Gitsenger.

———. [1861]. *The Philosophy of Secession. A Southern View, Presented in a Letter Addressed to the Hon. Mr. Perkins of Louisiana, in Criticism on the Provisional Constitution Adopted by the Southern Congress at Montgomery, Alabama.* [Charleston, SC: n.p.].

Tables of the Revenue, Population, Commerce etc. of the United Kingdom and Its Dependencies. 1833–1852. London: William Clowes.

Thomas, Brinley. 1973. *Migration and Economic Growth: A Study of Great Britain and the Atlantic Economy.* London: Cambridge University Press.

Thomas, William G. 2011. *The Iron Way: Railroads, the Civil War, and the Making of Modern America.* New Haven, CT: Yale University Press.

Tilzey, Mark. 2018. *Political Ecology, Food Regimes, and Food Sovereignty Crisis, Resistance, and Resilience.* London: Palgrave.

Tomich, Dale. 1980. "Rapporti sociali di produzione e mercato mondiale nel dibattito recente sulla transizione dal feudalesimo al capitalismo." *Studi Storici* 21, no. 3: 539–64.

———. 2004. *Through the Prism of Slavery: Labor, Capital, and the World-Economy.* New York: Rowman & Littlefield.

———. 2018. "The Second Slavery and World Capitalism: A Perspective for Historical Inquiry." *International Review of Social History* 63, no. 3: 477–501.

Tutino, John. 1998. "The Revolution in Mexican Independence: Insurgency and the Renegotiation of Property, Production, and Patriarchy in the Bajío, 1800–1855." *Hispanic American Historical Review* 78, no. 3: 367–418.

———. 2016. "Introduction: Revolutions, Nations, and a New Industrial World." In *New Countries: Capitalism, Revolutions, and Nations in the Americas, 1750–1870,* edited by John Tutino, 1–24. London: Duke University Press.

Van Vugt, W. E. 1988. "Running from Ruin? The Emigration of British Farmers to the U.S.A. in the Wake of the Repeal of the Corn Laws." *Economic History Review* 41, no. 3: 411–28.

Vilar, Pierre. 1984. *A History of Gold and Money, 1450–1920.* London: Verso.

Wallerstein, Immanuel. 2011. *The Modern World-System IV: Centrist Liberalism Triumphant,* 1789–1914. Berkeley: University of California Press.

Weiman, David. 1990. "The First Land Boom in the Antebellum United States: Was the South Different?" In *Structures and Dynamics of Exploitations: Studies in Social and Economic History,* vol. 5, edited by Erik Aerts et al., 27–39. Louvain, Belgium: Leuven University Press.

White, Richard. 2012. *Railroaded: The Transcontinental and the Making of Modern America.* New York: Norton.

Wilkinson, Maurice. 1970. "European Migration to the United States: An Econometric Analysis of Aggregate Labor Supply and Demand." *Review of Economics and Statistics* 52, no. 3: 272–79.

Wolfe, Patrick. 2001. "Land, Labor, and Difference: Elementary Structures of Race." *American Historical Review* 106, no. 3: 866–905.

Wright, Gavin. 2006. *Slavery and American Economic Development.* Baton Rouge: Louisiana State University Press.

Chapter 3

The Jihad Movement and the Development of "Second Slavery" in West Africa in the Nineteenth Century

Paul E. Lovejoy

The dramatic expansion of slavery in the Americas during the first half of the nineteenth century revitalized the transatlantic slave trade, which attained levels that matched those at the height of traffic in the last decades of the eighteenth century. Despite the emergence of Haiti as an independent country in 1804 on the ruins of the highly successful French colony of Saint-Domingue, the abolition of the transatlantic slave trade by Britain and the United States in 1807, and the constraining impact of the Napoleonic Wars before 1815, Brazil, Cuba, and the southern United States led the way in fashioning a period that has been termed a "second slavery" that distinguishes the nineteenth century from the earlier slavery that was concentrated in the French and British colonies of the Caribbean and the Portuguese colony of Brazil. As developed by Dale Tomich (2004), "second slavery" not only distinguishes developments in the nineteenth century from the earlier period but also was closely intertwined with the consolidation of a capitalist world order. The question that remains, however, relates to the origins of the enslaved population that enabled the period of second slavery. For the United States, an internal enslaved migration accounts for the labor supply, but for Brazil, Cuba, and elsewhere the continued enforced migration out of Africa was the basis for economic expansion, and US involvement in that migration through ship construction and capital investment was an underlying factor in sustaining the trade. But from where in Africa did the slave population for Cuba, Brazil, and elsewhere, including the Mascarene Islands in the Indian Ocean, come? In what ways was the nineteenth-century traffic different from the period before ca. 1804–1807?

While it is generally accepted that an increasing proportion of the enslaved came from West Central Africa and Southeast Africa, it is argued here that a major factor in sustaining this trend was the jihad movement in West Africa. From the 1780s through the ending of the transatlantic slave trade in the 1860s, a steadily decreasing proportion of the enslaved population that left Africa for the centers of the second slavery originated in West Africa, falling from almost half to less than 20 percent after 1830. Moreover, the reasons for this decline had less to do with British anti-slave-trade suppression than the policies of the states that were established through jihad. Hitherto, internal African factors in shaping developments have generally been overlooked as if continental Africa was not part of the Atlantic World. This study examines the shift in the origins of the enslaved population of the nineteenth century and considers the consequences of the shift in terms of the impact on West Africa. In doing so, it is argued that the concept "second slavery" has to be modified to explain the resurgence of slavery in West Africa, which might be called a similar period of "second slavery" but one that was not tied to the capitalist world system.

A jihad movement overthrew most established governments in West Africa between 1780 and 1850 and installed new regimes based on strict adherence to Islamic law (sharia) (P. E. Lovejoy 2016a, 2016b). Beginning in Senegambia, that is, the basins of the Senegal and Gambia Rivers in the western Sudan, the emergence of Fuuta Jalon and Fuuta Toro in the 1770s began the transformation of the political map of West Africa. Jihad spread across the interior of West Africa thereafter, with the establishment of the Sokoto Caliphate in 1804–1808, Hamdullahi in 1817, and the 'Umarian state after 1837. This political movement was based in part on opposition to the transatlantic slave trade and effectively advocated a process of self-imposed isolation from the Atlantic World that ended only with the European conquest of the region, which was effectively completed in 1903 despite sporadic resistance thereafter. Based on a profound intellectual outpouring of literature in Arabic and the radical teaching of Muslim clerics, jihad fulfilled several aims that consolidated a new political order, despite frontier pockets of opposition and the inability of the jihad leadership to adhere always to its principles and stated intentions (P. E. Lovejoy 2016b). Despite these qualifications, jihad ushered in a period of major adjustments in the contours of the Atlantic World (figure 3.1). On the one hand, jihad resulted in massive enslavement and economic development that not only paralleled the rise of the "second slavery" in the Americas but also entailed a comparable period of slavery in West Africa. On the other hand, jihad accelerated a shift in the sources of the enslaved population that was destined for the Americas away from West Africa that was already well underway. Through its politically and religiously sanctioned policies, Islamic West Africa had a dramatic impact in shaping second slavery in the Americas and introducing a comparable period of slavery regeneration in West Africa.

The interlocking argument presented here rests on three propositions. First, the jihad movement that revolutionized most of West Africa from the 1770s through the middle of the nineteenth century was based in part on opposition to the transatlantic slave trade, which thereby discouraged Muslim participation in Atlantic commerce in slaves. Second, as a result, there was a major shift in the regional origins of transatlantic slavery away from West Africa, so that the peak period of

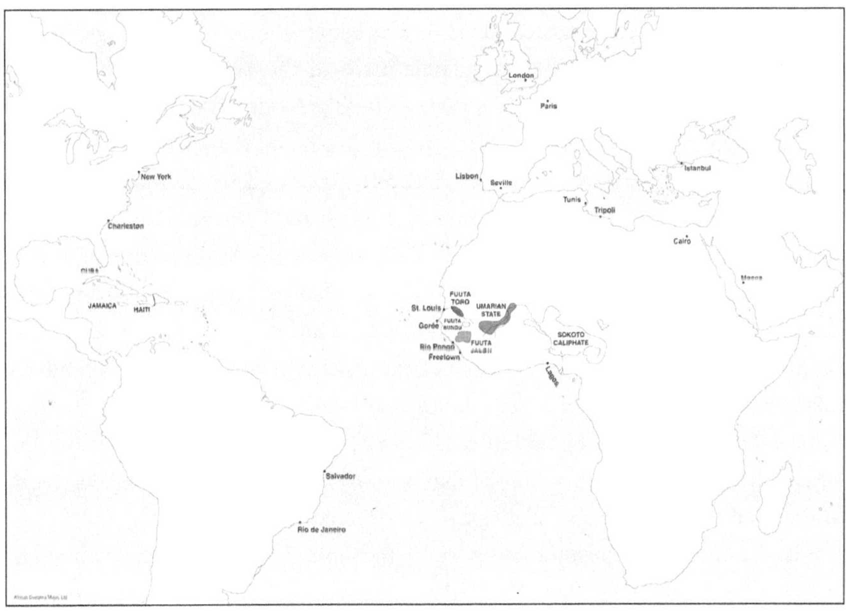

Figure 3.1. Jihad states in the Atlantic World. Source: Courtesy of Henry B. Lovejoy, *African Diaspora Maps Ltd.*

the transatlantic slave trade to the Americas that fueled the second slavery came to rely almost entirely on areas that were not affected by jihad. Third, jihad states nonetheless continued a campaign of massive enslavement but rather than feed the second slavery of the Americas redeployed the newly enslaved population within West Africa. The result was that second slavery in the Americas drew relatively less on West Africa than might otherwise have been the case but instead led to a corresponding second slavery in the jihad states, which mirrored the Americas. Demographically, West Africa could have supplied many more times the enslaved population than it did, and indeed potentially might even have supplied all of the enslaved population for the Americas after 1807, but did not do so. Instead West Africa, and the areas of the jihad states in particular, accounted for a steadily decreasing proportion of the enslaved population sent to the Americas.

The jihad movement that revolutionized most of West Africa from the 1770s through the middle of the nineteenth century was based in part on opposition to the transatlantic slave trade, as demonstrated in the literature in Arabic that was generated in the course of the jihad (Muhammad Bello 1812). While there are two important qualifications to this generalization, the long-term trend in West Africa nonetheless limited Muslim interaction with Atlantic merchants, especially with regard to the slave trade. Muslim merchants dominated all long-distance trade in West Africa from the Senegambia basin in the west through the Niger-Benue and Lake Chad basin in the east, including the interior trade of all areas from the upper Guinea coast, the Sierra Leone River, and the kola-nut forests that stretched from the headwaters of the Niger River eastward to the Akan states and the Volta River basin, and further east still through the Bight of Benin hinterland to the lower Niger River (Lofkrantz and P. E. Lovejoy 2015). Even the important slave-supplying states of Asante, Dahomey, and Oyo depended on Muslim commercial networks for their links inland, including sources of slaves other than those assembled through their own military campaigns, legal mechanisms, and tribute collections. This Muslim commercial domination was propagated, moreover, through two overlapping systems, one based on Hausa as the commercial language and the other using the Juula dialect of Malinke, as well as Arabic as the religious, legal, commercial, and diplomatic language of communication.

The two important qualifications relate to the limitations on Muslim involvement in the transatlantic slave trade. First, friction between the jihad states in Senegambia sometimes spilled over into the Atlantic trade because of war with those states resisting the jihad. Second, frontier areas of confrontation generated captives who required disposal, and sometimes those who were captured bypassed the centers of the jihad states and were taken to the coast. The state policies of Fuuta Jalon allowed officially sponsored sale of captives to the coast who were allegedly screened to exclude the possible sale of freeborn Muslims, but the other jihad states do not appear to have sanctioned such expeditions. Individually, Muslim merchants could not be prevented from circumventing Islamic prohibitions and religiously based reluctance to sell slaves to non-Muslims, but they did so on an individual basis. Prohibitions on the sale of enslaved captives to non-Muslims otherwise discouraged the organization of a sustained, large-scale trade in slaves to the coast. As the statistics for departing ships make clear, a sustained export trade was effectively prevented. In many contexts, freeborn Muslims who had been captured in war or seized along trade routes were protected through ransoming procedures that were more profitable than trade, since the cost of ransoming was traditionally twice as high as sale prices (Lofkrantz 2012). As the surviving biographies of enslaved Muslims demonstrate, however, ransoming was not always achieved. Those whose freeborn status could not be verified but who may have been nominally Muslim or came from areas where Muslims were influential also made it onto slave ships, and hence jihad-inspired policies may have restricted the trade but did not prevent it.

The first jihad states emerged in the Senegambia region of West Africa. The antecedents stretched back to the 1680s and 1690s, and a more intensive eruption occurred in the 1720s, but the real impetus took hold in the 1770s when Fuuta Toro consolidated its hold on the Senegal River valley and a resurgent movement in Fuuta Jalon consolidated the highlands behind the upper Guinea coast (figure 3.2). Subsequently, the interior Niger delta region fell under the domination of the Caliphate of Hamdullahi after 1817 and then was further unified through the wars of al-Haj 'Umar after 1837.

The establishment of the Sokoto Caliphate, initially through jihad in the separate Hausa states between 1804 and 1808 but then extending to Borno and Nupe by 1810, was the most significant development in the jihad movement. A comparison of the political map of the interior of the Bight of Benin in approximately 1800, before the jihad erupted, with the map several decades later clearly establishes the transformation (figures 3.3 and 3.4). The two dominant states in 1800, Borno and Oyo, were affected most dramatically. Borno's tributary influence over several of the Hausa states was completely undermined and indeed Borno lost about half its territory in the jihad wars and survived only by overthrowing its ancient aristocracy and substituting a new regime that was similar in aims and principles

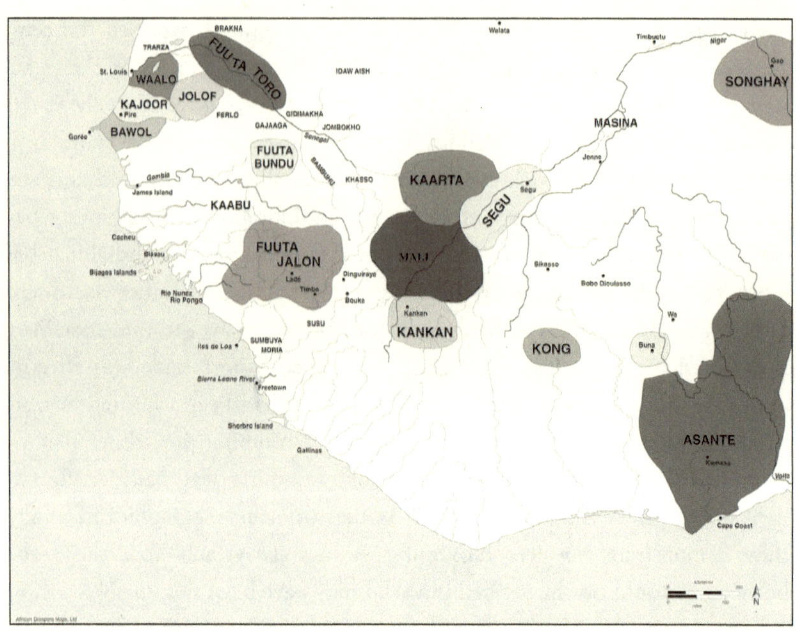

Figure 3.2. Fuuta Jalon and Fuuta Toro, ca. 1975. Source: Courtesy of Henry B. Lovejoy, *African Diaspora Maps Ltd.*

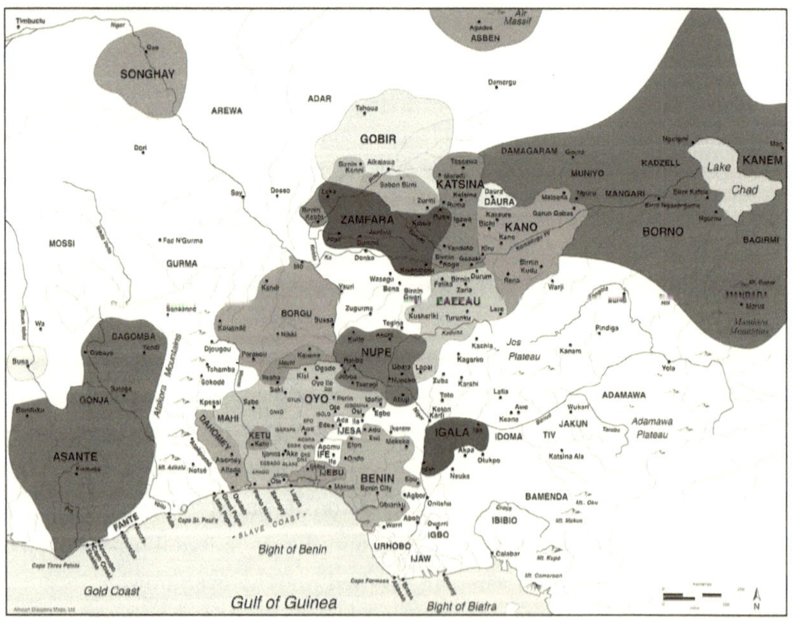

Figure 3.3. Bight of Benin interior, ca. 1800. Source: Courtesy of Henry B. Lovejoy, *African Diaspora Maps Ltd.*

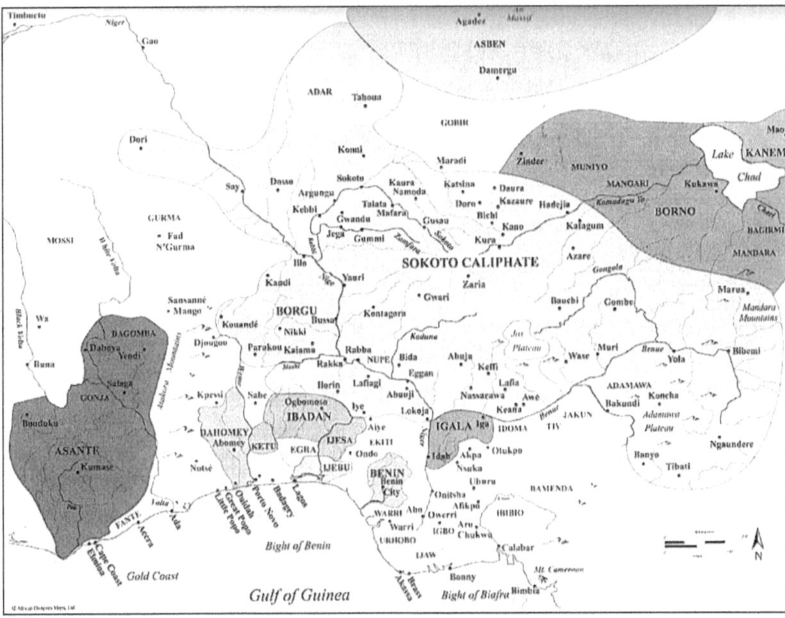

Figure 3.4. Sokoto Caliphate, ca. 1850. Source: Courtesy of Henry B. Lovejoy, *African Diaspora Maps Ltd.*

to the jihad states themselves. Oyo, which had dominated the trade of the Bight of Benin throughout most of the eighteenth century, lost control over Dahomey and ultimately collapsed in the face of the jihad, with much of its heartland incorporated into the Sokoto Caliphate.

Most important for the transatlantic slave trade, the collapse of Oyo in jihad after the military uprising at Ilorin in 1817, the incorporation of Ilorin as an emirate in the Sokoto Caliphate in 1823, and the subsequent campaigns that led to the final destruction of the Oyo capital and the abandonment of its metropolitan district in 1835–1836 prompted the massive enslavement and deportation of enslaved that accounts for the Yoruba diaspora in Brazil, particularly Bahia, and in Cuba and Sierra Leone (P. E. Lovejoy 2016b). This enslavement not only ended the involvement of Oyo as the major slave supplier in the Bight of Benin interior but resulted in the enslavement of a considerable portion of its population. The impact of the jihad on the destruction of Oyo can be visualized graphically on the animated maps developed by Henry Lovejoy (2016), which show the profound changes in the Yoruba region beginning with the military uprising in Ilorin in 1817, the Owu wars, the declaration of Ilorin as an emirate within the Sokoto

Caliphate in 1823, the intervention of Dahomey in Oyo politics in the late 1820s, and the final destruction of the Oyo capital in the dry season of 1835–1836. The jihad movement that prompted the Yoruba migration of the second-slavery era was a direct cause of enslavement and displacement, qualifying my assertion that jihad opposed the transatlantic slave trade because in the Yoruba case there was a direct link. The jihad leadership, as first revealed in the pronouncements of Muhammad Bello in *Infāq al-Maysūr fī taʾrīkh bilād al-Takrūr* (1812), accused Oyo of complicity in the enslavement of freeborn Muslims and their sale to Christians. Thereafter the jihad targeted Oyo, and while the intention may not have been to supply the transatlantic slave trade, military destruction ironically thrust Oyo's own citizenship onto slave ships and launched the continuing enslavement in the Bight of Benin interior that lasted for several decades after 1836 (Barcia 2014).

Although an enslaved exodus continued from the upper Guinea coast and Senegambia and the Bight of Benin after British and US abolition of the transatlantic slave trade in 1807, the trend in population displacement shifted dramatically away from West Africa toward the Bight of Biafra, West Central Africa, and Southeast Africa, accelerating a shift that was already underway. This pattern can be seen through the division of the transatlantic migration into four periods, namely, the period before 1775, the period from 1776 to 1807, the period from 1807 to 1830, and the period after 1830 when British suppression spread south of the equator and into the Indian Ocean, which is highlighted in the following tables.

The parts of West Africa that became the focus of the jihad movement included Senegambia, the upper Guinea coast before the nineteenth century and continuing thereafter, and the interior of the Bight of Benin in the nineteenth century. The interior of the Gold Coast can also be included, but the slave departures from west of the Volta River virtually ended after 1800. As a benchmark, West Africa to the west of the Niger River delta accounted for slightly over three million slave departures (45.6 percent of total departures) before 1775, while the Bight of Biafra and the southern third of Africa accounted for 3.6 million departures or 54.4 percent of the total.

For the period from 1776 until the end of the transatlantic migration, by contrast, approximately 1.7 million enslaved (28.3 percent) came from West Africa to the west of the Niger delta, while 4.2 million (71.7 percent) came from areas not affected by the jihad movement. These latter estimates can be broken down into three periods, namely, 1776–1807, when British and US abolition took effect; 1808–1830, when British suppression was confined north of the equator and effectively excluded West Central and Southeast Africa; and 1831–1865,

Table 3.1. Regional Origins of Enslaved, 1501–1775

	Jihād Regions					*Non Jihād* Regions			
	Senegambia	**Upper Guinea**	**Forests of West Africa**	**Gold Coast**	**Bight of Benin**	**Bight of Biafra**	**West Central**	**South East**	**Total**
1501–1775	562,000	116,000	219,000	838,000	1,293,000	*763,000*	*2,796,000*	*52,000*	**6,639,000**
	8.5%	1.7%	3.3%	12.6%	19.5%	*11.5%*	*42.1%*	*0.8%*	
Total		**3,028,000**			**45.6%**		***3,611,000***	***54.4%***	

Table 3.2. Departures by Region, 1776–1865

	Senegambia	Upper Guinea	Forests of West Africa	Gold Coast	Bight of Benin	Bight of Biafra	West Central	South East	Total
1776–	128,000	133,000	98,000	357,000	326,000	453,000	1,091,000	92,000	2,677,000
1807	4.8%	5.0%	3.7%	13.3%	12.2%	16.9%	40.8%	3.4%	
1808–	53,000	71,000	16,000	11,000	164,000	253,000	921,000	207,000	1,697,000
1830	3.1%	4.2%	0.9%	0.6%	9.7%	14.9%	54.3%	12.2%	
1831–	13,000	70,000	3,000	3,000	216,000	125,000	887,000	191,000	1,508,000
1866	0.9%	4.6%	0.2%	0.2%	14.3%	8.3%	58.8%	12.7%	
1808–	**66,000**	**141,000**	**19,000**	**14,000**	**380,000**	**378,000**	**1,808,000**	**398,000**	**3,205,000**
1865	**2.1%**	**4.4%**	**0.6%**	**0.4%**	**11.9%**	**11.8%**	**56.4%**	**12.4%**	
TOTAL	**194,000**	**274,000**	**117,000**	**371,000**	**706,000**	**831,000**	**2,899,000**	**490,000**	**5,882,000**
	3.3%	**4.7%**	**2.0%**	**6.3%**	**12.0%**	**14.1%**	**49.3%**	**8.3%**	

when suppression was extended south of the equator and into the Indian Ocean. Abolition in 1807 effectively ended the first period of slavery in the Americas and marked the era of second slavery. From 1776 to 1807, 1,169,000 of the enslaved (43.7 percent) came from west of the Niger delta, with 1,636,000 originating in the interior of the Bight of Biafra, West Central Africa, and southeast Africa. The dramatic shift in the origins of the enslaved is clear thereafter, with 620,000 captives coming from west of the Niger delta and 2,584,000 departures leaving from the other regions after 1807. The proportion coming from West Africa dropped from 43.7 percent to 19.3 percent, while the proportion from the Bight of Biafra and regions to the south increased from 56.3 percent to 80.6 percent.

For purposes of the present analysis, the coastal designations introduced by Philip Curtin and used in the Voyages database (www.slavevoyages.org) are continued here, although revision of these regions is warranted. First, Guinea-Bissau is more accurately associated with the upper Guinea coast and not with Senegambia; second, Sierra Leone is not a region but a river and the region more accurately should be labeled "upper Guinea coast"; third, the eastern portion of what has been referred to as the Windward Coast should be identified with the Gold Coast, while the region behind the European-designated Windward Coast more appropriately can be identified with the forested region of West Africa. Once these adjustments are introduced, the figure for Senegambia would be lower and the figure for upper Guinea would increase correspondingly. Similarly, the Gold Coast estimates would be somewhat higher and the forested region reduced accordingly. Nonetheless, these adjustments do not affect the present analysis significantly.

During the era of the jihads in West Africa after the mid-1770s, there was a corresponding shift in the destinations of the enslaved population sent to the Americas. As can be seen in table 3.3, more captives were sent to the British Caribbean and North America (972,000) than to Brazil (926,000), while the numbers sent to Spanish colonies (158,000), including Cuba, were far behind the French Caribbean (474,000) and more in line with the number that were sent to Dutch and Danish colonies (142,000). After 1807 there was a dramatic shift, with the emergence of the Cuban market, the expansion of slavery in Brazil, and the virtual disappearance of almost all other markets except a modest resurgence in the French Caribbean. After 1830 the Cuban market became even more important, increasing to almost one-third of the traffic. British suppression certainly impeded the traffic in some areas but nonetheless only accounted for about 7 percent of the trade. These estimates clearly delineate Cuba and Brazil in the consolidation of the era of second slavery.

Table 3.3. Destinations of Enslaved Population, 1776–1865

	North America	British Caribbean	French Caribbean	Spanish America	Brazil	Dutch Danish	Sierra Leone	Total
1776–1807	121,000	851,000	474,000	158,000	926,000	142,000	6,000	**2,677,000**
	4.5%	31.9%	17.7%	5.9%	34.6%	5.3%	0.2%	
1808–1830	8,000	17,000	81,000	301,000	1,209,000	15,000	66,000	**1,696,000**
	0.5%	1.0%	4.8%	17.7%	71.3%	0.9%	3.9%	
1831–1865		11,000	1,000	481,000	912,000		101,000	**1,508,000**
		0.7%	0.1%	31.9%	60.5%		6.7%	
1776–1865	**130,000**	**880,000**	**555,000**	**940,000**	**3,047,000**	**157,000**	**173,000**	**5,881,000**
	2.2%	15.0%	9.4%	16.0%	51.8%	2.7%	2.9%	

Despite the qualifications stated above with respect to the ways in which the enslaved entered the transatlantic migration in West Africa during the era of the jihads, it is clear that there was an overwhelming transformation in West Africa during the nineteenth century. That transformation involved the greatly reduced participation of the region in the transatlantic trade. Accordingly, jihad shaped the demographic profile of second slavery in Cuba, Brazil, and other affected regions outside of Africa. Second slavery rested on the expanded traffic in slaves from regions that were not affected by jihad. Specifically, the enslaved population of Cuba and Brazil in the nineteenth century did not come from the region of the jihad states of West Africa but rather overwhelmingly from West Central Africa and Southeast Africa; over 80 percent of the 770,000 who went to Cuba and the 1,995,000 sent to Brazil came from regions not affected by the jihad movement. The exceptions are instructive: the Yoruba population in Brazil, Cuba, and Sierra Leone largely originated in jihad, and in many ways their influence in diaspora was out of proportion to their numbers for reasons that are not entirely clear but may well reflect this history. Rebellions in Brazil, Cuba, and Sierra Leone are attributed to their presence, sometimes in association with allegiance as Muslims, often newly converted. Similarly, Muslims from Senegambia and the upper Guinea coast were sometimes involved in jihad or the resistance to jihad, and as recent analysis has demonstrated, they may have been more numerous in Cuba than previously thought. The jihad state of Fuuta Jalon at least occasionally sold slaves to the coast at Rio Pongo, Rio Nunez, and Iles de Los who were a product of its jihad policies, although it is claimed that those being sold to Europeans were not Muslims, which has not been confirmed. Nonetheless, the enslaved from Senegambia and the upper Guinea coast only constituted 6.3 percent of the deported population to Cuba and Brazil.

The startling feature of the demography of migration from West Africa after 1807 was not the continued involvement of the region in the transatlantic slave trade but rather the massive redeployment of population within West Africa itself, especially in the areas that were consolidated into the states founded in jihad. While Senegambia, the upper Guinea coast, and the Bight of Benin continued to be sources of slaves as described above, the relocation of the enslaved population within West Africa was far more significant in terms of scale and with consequences that concentrated the enslaved population in a fashion that mirrored the second slavery of the Americas. While it cannot be measured with precision, it can be estimated that approximately 620,000 enslaved left West Africa for the Americas after 1807 and perhaps 200,000–300,000 were sent across the Sahara in the period ca. 1810–1865, almost entirely from the jihad states (P. E. Lovejoy 1984, 2012). The numbers that were retained within West Africa had to have been far larger, if the estimates of the scale of slavery in West Africa are reasonably accurate. My own projections suggest that the scale of slavery in the jihad states was on the order of several million by the mid-nineteenth century. Hence we can refer to a period of second slavery in the jihad states of West Africa that helped determine the profile of the second slavery of the Americas.

The best that can be done in terms of estimating the scale of slavery in the jihad states is to derive estimates from early colonial calculations at the end of the nineteenth century and the first years of the twentieth century. French colonial officials were more systematic in attempting to determine the size of the slave population, but the level of accuracy varied widely depending on local circumstances and the competence of the officials themselves. Often officials just made up figures that they thought would be acceptable to their superiors, who equally often were not that interested in the degree of accuracy. British officials and observers were even more sketchy in their projections, although both French and British observers were virtually unanimous in stating that a very large percentage of the population was enslaved. The colonial regimes wanted to know the size of the population for tax purposes but did not conduct censuses that might have helped clarify the extent of slavery and indeed other matters that were important for tax assessment. Neither regime undertook even a superficial attempt to determine the tax base, let alone the size of the population. In realistic terms, such a venture was simply beyond the administrative capabilities of the early colonial state. Hence the estimates summarized in table 3.4 are nothing more than a best guess on scale, with no claim

Table 3.4 Slave Populations of the Western and Central Sudan, ca. 1900

Region	**Enslaved Population**	**Percent of Total Population**
Haut-Sénégal-Niger	822,000	21
Guinée	687,000	51
Sénégal	330,000	31
Sokoto Caliphate	1,250,000–2,500,000	25–50
TOTAL	3,089,000–4,399,000	25–50

to any accuracy.[1] The conquered population could easily have been twice as large as either the French or British thought, which would implicitly suggest that the number of enslaved was greater.

The significance for West Africa of a period comparable to the second slavery of the Americas and elsewhere relates to two factors. First, the intensity of enslavement and slavery did not diminish during this period but if anything intensified. Rather than promoting a flow of enslaved migration to the Americas, however, most of this enslavement was consumed within West Africa and to a lesser extent favored Saharan and trans-Saharan markets thereby supplying the Muslim world and not the Americas. Correspondingly, therefore, transatlantic demand had to be fulfilled elsewhere in Africa. The subsequent expansion of slavery in West Africa can be estimated to have been on the same order as the enslaved population of the Americas. Second, the economic impact of slavery in the jihad states mirrored the Americas, especially in the production of cotton and the expansion of the internal West African textile industry. Unlike the Americas, however, this expansion was confined to regional markets and had little influence on capitalist developments that characterized second slavery elsewhere. Moreover, economic development in West Africa was ultimately undermined by French and British colonial conquest. Nonetheless, slavery was pervasive in all walks of life, and the importance of slavery in agricultural production is to be noticed in particular.

The implications for applying the concept of "second slavery" to the changes of the nineteenth century and the development of capitalist relationships of production are profound. The concept distinguishes periods of slavery in innovative ways that allow a consideration of the interface between slavery and capitalism. Nonetheless, it must be asked what factors influenced the origins of the enslaved population in Africa. The jihad states cannot be ignored in a discussion of the intensification of slavery, which suggests that slavery might be linked to the capitalism of the global order but that slavery was also associated with efforts to remain beyond the pull of capitalist forces. Although in the end European conquest and colonial occupation of Africa undermined the Islamic assertions of autonomy, slavery was just as important to the alternate thrust to economic development as it was to capitalism itself. While it is impossible to conceive of the nineteenth century without a consideration of "capitalism's slavery," it is important to understand how the jihad movement shaped the Atlantic World through its own preoccupation with retaining a large, enslaved population within West Africa for its own ends.

Note

1. For the size of the slave population in the area that became Afrique Occidentale Française, see Klein (1998, 252–56), who bases his estimates largely on the reports of colonial officials, especially the K series in Dakar, which are summarized in the reports of E. Poulet and E. Deherme (Kanya-Forstner and P. E. Lovejoy 1994). The relative scale of slave populations in Islamic West Africa is also discussed in P. E. Lovejoy (2012, 186–96).

References

Barcia, Manuel. 2014. *West African Warfare in Bahia and Cuba: Soldier Slaves in the Atlantic World, 1807–1844*. Oxford, UK: Oxford University Press.

Eltis, David et al. *Voyages: The Trans-Atlantic Slave Trade Database*, http://www.slavevoyages.org.

Kanya-Forstner, A. S., and Paul E. Lovejoy, eds. 1994. *Slavery and Its Abolition in French West Africa: The Official Reports of G. Poulet, E. Roume, and G. Deherme*. Madison: African Studies Program, University of Wisconsin.

Klein, Martin A. 1998. *Slavery and Colonial Rule in French West Africa*. Cambridge: Cambridge University Press.

Kriger, Colleen E. 2006. *Cloth in West African History*. Lanham, MD: AltaMira.

Lofkrantz, Jennifer. 2012. "Intellectual Discourse in the Early Sokoto Caliphate: The Triumvirate's Opinions on the Issue of Ransoming, c. 1810." *International Journal of African Historical Studies* 45, no. 3: 385–401.

Lofkrantz, Jennifer, and Paul E. Lovejoy. 2015. "Maintaining Network Boundaries: Islamic Law and Commerce from Sahara to Guinea Shores." *Slavery & Abolition* 36, no. 2: 211–32.

Lovejoy, Henry B. "West African Historical GIS and the Liberated African Project." College Park: Maryland Institute for Technology in the Humanities, University of Maryland, March 8, 2016, https://vimeo.com/159831363.

Lovejoy, Paul E. 1984. "Commercial Sectors in the Economy of the Nineteenth-Century Central Sudan: The Trans-Saharan Trade and the Desert-Side Salt Trade." *African Economic History*, no. 13: 85–116.

———. 2012. *Transformations in Slavery: A History of Slavery in Africa*. 3rd ed. Cambridge: Cambridge University Press.

———. 2016a. "*Jihād* and the Era of the Second Slavery." *Journal of Global Slavery* 1, no. 1: 28–42.

———. 2016b. *Jihād in West Africa during the Age of Revolutions, 1780–1850*. Athens: Ohio University Press.

Lovejoy, Paul E., and Jan Hogendorn. 1993. *Slow Death for Slavery: The Course of Abolition in Northern Nigeria, 1897–1936.* Cambridge: Cambridge University Press.

Muhammad Bello. 1812. *Infāq al- Maysūr fi ta'rīkh bilād al- Takrūr.* Edited by Bahija al- Shadhili. Rabat: Institute of African Studies, 1996.

Shea, Philip. 2006. "Big Is Sometimes Best: The Sokoto Caliphate and Economic Advantages of Size in the Textile Industry" *African Economic History*, no. 34: 5–21.

Tomich, Dale. 2004. "Atlantic History and World Economy: Concepts and Constructions." *Proto Sociology*, no. 20: 102–21.

Zeuske, Michael. 2014. "The Second Slavery: Modernity, Mobility, and Identity of Captives in Nineteenth-Century Cuba and the Atlantic World." In *The Second Slavery: Mass Slaveries and Modernity in the Americas and in the Atlantic Basin*, edited by Javier Lavina and Michael Zeuske, 113–42. Berlin: Lit Verlag.

Chapter 4

The Atlantic and Atlantic Slavery, Second Slavery, the *Hidden Atlantic*, and Capitalism

Michael Zeuske

Setting the Stage: Africa, the Slavery Atlantic, and Atlantic Slavery

The Atlantic as a spatial concept (Tomich 2004a, 221–40) and as a historical-geographic category is mostly associated with "discoveries," European expansion, European trade to the Americas, and the silver transports of Spain between Peru, New Spain, and Europe, as well as with colonial empires, world trade, piracy, and maritime wars of the European maritime powers. However, the Atlantic as *mares oçéanas* (ocean seas) arose and developed, in reality, with the search for luxury goods in Africa, slaving raids, transportation of enslaved persons (often for African elites), slave trade, and slavery—all initially mostly at the level of captains and ship crews as well as deserters from ships, interlopers, or raiding teams (called in Portuguese and Spanish *lançados/huestes*). It has an Arabic and North African

Research for this chapter is based on the research project: Michael Zeuske, "Der Mediziner und Sklavenhändler Dr. Daniel Botefeur. Der Übergang zum illegalen Sklavenhandel auf dem Atlantik sowie in den Amerikas und der Menschenhandel in Westafrika. Mikrogeschichten des Wissens" (DFG [German Research Foundation]—ZE 302/22-1).

prehistory, related to Islamicate culture (Obenaus 2013). From its beginnings in European-Iberian shores and port towns, *mares oçéanas* was a very important dimension of capitalism in modern history (ca. 1415 onward in the Atlantic): first on the south-north Atlantic axis (Iberians/Portuguese on the west coast and on islands of West Africa to Portugal/Andalusia), then on the southwest-northeast Atlantic axis (Columbus, Iberians/Castilians/Spaniards in the Antilles and in the Caribbean to Andalusia/Seville), and finally, until the end of the Slavery Atlantic (around 1900), especially the south-south Atlantic orientation from west and east (Africa) across the Atlantic to the west (America) and back. It was, to repeat, from ca. 1520 essentially a south-south relationship. In its most developed form, around 1800–1900, when second slaveries, the Hidden Atlantic, and Slavery Capitalism[1] were at their heights, it formed a transcontinental, a transatlantic, and most of all, a transcultural infrastructure of violence between the interiors of Africa, the Atlantic, and the second slaveries of the Americas (Tomich 2017, 2018, 477–501; Zeuske 2015d, 296–364).

The beginnings were tiny. The origins of the Slavery Atlantic[2] and Atlantic slavery (as slavery on land *and* maritime slave trade, Zeuske 2015e, 280–301) lay in the indigenous slaveries of Africa, in raid slaveries, and in "new" island slaveries of the Iberian "empire of islands" including Arguim, Cabo Verde, São Tomé, and Príncipe, and the Canaries, Madeira, and the Azores on the eastern side of the Atlantic, and, since 1493, Hispaniola (later Saint-Domingue/Haiti and Santo Domingo) (Duncan 1972; Lobo Cabrera 1985; Vieira 1995, 2004; Hawthorne 2003; Mann 2005; Hernández González 2006; Viña Brito 2006; Phillips 2011; Green 2011, 2012b; Caldeira 2013b; Horta and Freire 2013, 37–53), East Cuba, and Puerto Rico on the western side of the Atlantic (Caribbean/West Indies). (The English/British also controlled an "empire of islands" on the American side of the Atlantic more than a hundred years later, first of all Barbados and Jamaica, as did the French—Saint Domingue, Guadeloupe, Martinique—and others as well.) On the African side of this "empire of islands," the Iberians had to learn from African elites the use of human bodies as capital, just as they had to "aprender os trópicos" (learn to know the tropics) (Caldeira 2013a, 25–54). Later, all the other European colonial and slavery powers learned from the Iberians (Zeuske 2021, forthcoming). The birth of Atlantic plantation slavery with its massive slave trade took place in a microregion—on the northern plain of São Tomé (1500–1530) (Alencastro 2000, 63–67; Fábregas García 2000, 59–85; Seibert 2013, 54–78; Zeuske 2018a, 79–119). This Atlantic slavery of captives jumped over the Cabo Verde and Canary

Islands relatively quickly (around 1510–1520) to Hispaniola and the Caribbean. There the Iberians, first of all Castilians and some Genoese, intended to develop a slavery of the "yndios" (a new governmental category, invented by the Castilian *letrados* [lawyers of the crown] about 1494–1495), another Atlantic slavery (Mira Caballos 2000, 46–48, 141–43; Zeuske 2019b, 11–36) that was called "the other slavery" by Andrés Reséndez (2016). The Castilian crown, as well as the crown of imperial Spain later, banned it legally at all levels but were able to enforce this ban only with difficulty in its Atlantic dimension. They also used the category "yndio" for their other dominions, such as the Philippines, with the same problems but without massive slavery of Africans (Sánchez 2015, 95–172).

Since about 1550, the "first" Slavery Atlantic developed, based on the slave trade of *negros* from Africa, usually referred to as the *Iberian Atlantic* (Fuente et al. 2008). In reality, the Slavery Atlantic was always an *African-Iberian Atlantic* (whether called that or not) (Boubacar 1998; Thornton 1998, 2012; Klein 2001, 49–65, 2002, 37–49; Hawthorne 2003, 2010; Shumway 2011; Green 2012b, 2016, 91–122; Araujo 2012, 1–19; Wimmler 2012; Ferreira 2012b, 242–48; Graden 2014; Santana Pérez 2014, 11–25; Zeuske 2015d, 296–364; Schneider 2015, 3–29; Wheat 2016; Soule 2018, 16–39; Zeuske 2021, forthcoming). This was so, above all, because of the supply and customer function of African and Arab elites in the trade in enslaved persons as well as the mediating function of Iberian-African elites between Atlantic factors and captains as well as Afro-creole deliverers from the *slaving zones* (Fynn-Paul and Pargas 2018) in Africa; second, because the mass of the deportees and victims of the enslavement and the slave trade came from Africa; and third, because many enslaved, quasi-enslaved, and former enslaved as *Atlantic Creoles* formed the main personnel of the Atlantic slave trade (local brokers and traders [including also women], sailors, boys, translators, cooks, guards, oarsmen, healers/priests, dispensers, captains' slaves [*grumetes*], but also "free African traders") (Brooks 1976b, 19–44; 1976a, 295–319; 1993; Lopes 1993; Heintze 2002, 155–74; Rodrigues 2005; Rediker 2007; Heywood and Thornton 2007; Candido 2010, 395–409; Reis et al. 2010; Ipsen 2015; Zeuske 2015c, 172–205). African slave traders, who traversed the Slavery Atlantic between African regions and the Americas, first of all Brazil and the Caribbean, established the "early rise of intercontinental mobility [that] involved free African traders as well as the agency of enslaved Africans" (Green 2016, 91–122, at 100).

Beginning around 1600 (for England with Hawkins and Drake), a Northwestern European superposition or overlay of the African-Iberian Slavery Atlantic developed involving England/Great Britain, the Netherlands, Atlantic France, and Baltic countries such as Denmark, Sweden, and Brandenburg-Prussia. This restructuring is traditionally known as the *English Atlantic* (there are many more conceptualizations of "Atlantics" and the so-called "triangular trade" for the period 1660–1808) (Degn 1974/2000, 2006; J. C. Miller 1997, 9–36; Marzagalli 1999, 70–83; Pritchard 2004; Vries 2005; Coclanis 2005; Cañizares Esguerra 2006; Cañizares Esguerra and Seemann 2017; C. L. Miller 2008; Lloyd and O'Neill 2009; Turgeon 2009, 33–56; Dubois and Scott 2010; Pérez Tostado and García-Hernán 2012; Ferreira 2012b, 242–48; Cañizares Esguerra, Childs, and Sidbury 2013; Cañizares Esguerra and Breen 2013, 597–609; De Almeida Mendes 2013, 137–57; Obenaus 2013; Schnakenbourg 2013, 229–42; Bethencourt 2013, 15–36; Bassi 2014; Zeuske 2015d, 296–394; 2015b, 280–301; Oostindie and Roitman 2014, 2–10; Weaver 2014; Klooster 2016; Wimmler 2017).[3] While this English Atlantic is at the center of traditional slave-trade research, in this chapter the African-Iberian Atlantic from 1450 to 1890 is central (first of all because of the simple evidence of numbers: about two million for the English/British slave trade over the Atlantic vs. six to seven million for the Iberian slave trade over the Atlantic) (see Zeuske 2013a, 51–63; Borucki, Eltis, and Wheat 2015, 433–61). With the revolution of Saint-Domingue/Haiti (1791–1803) and the waves of abolition by the European and American slave-trade powers (Great Britain, Denmark, France, Netherlands, Spain, Portugal, United States, and Brazil as well as the Latin American republics), the slave trade (years of formal abolitions of Atlantic slave trade, 1803–1808, 1820, 1840–1850) as well as slavery itself (years of formal abolitions of slavery, 1794, 1838, 1848, 1863–1865, 1886, 1888) formally ended. But a "third" Atlantic originated between 1800 and 1890, again essentially on African and Iberian foundations, which I call here the *Hidden Atlantic* (Zeuske 2015a, 49–54; 2018a, 212–44; 2018b, 103–35).[4] This was because despite the prohibitions, the assault of the British Royal Navy on the Atlantic slave trade (Grindal 2016), and the formal governmental abolition, once again two to three million people were brought out of Africa (Zeuske 2018b, 103–35; Harris 2016, 409–29) and since the mid-nineteenth century millions of people from the eastern hemisphere were deported and transported as "new slaves" (coolies) to the Americas and other parts of the world (Allen 2013, 183–99; Zeuske 2016d, 35–57).

Slave traders, most of them Iberians or African-Iberians, and their personnel as well as, during the crossings, the enslaved were extremely mobile across large spaces and often polyglot. They were Atlantic cosmopolites "from below." The direct use of the concept of "cosmopolitanism" for actors and victims (who were also actors) of the Atlantic slave trade is new. So far, the cultural-ideological concept of cosmopolitanism has been reserved for actors of "honorable" trade (especially large merchants), ideologues of globalism and world capitalism (mostly "white" Europeans or North Americans), travelers, "discoverers," intellectuals, and scientists. But the real cosmopolitans of the Slavery Atlantic were "secret" (*hidden*) cosmopolitans—slavers (especially merchants, captains, and factors) and their staffs (especially all kinds of Atlantic Creoles, translators, and healers). During their time in the slave trade, they developed all the attributes of cosmopolitanism (knowledge of several cultures and languages, many long-distance travels, mobility across large areas and oceans and between cultural spaces, forms of trade, knowledge of food, corporeal performance, diseases, sexuality, medicine, customs and habits, networks) (see, e.g., Rodrigo y Alharilla 2013, 93–119; Zeuske 2016a, 129–55). In the case of slave merchants, bankers, and captains, for their contemporaries in their native environment this was a hidden cosmopolitanism à la *The Count of Monte Cristo*. *Negrero*, the common Spanish term for a slave trader (Zeuske 2015a),[5] was never used in face-to-face situations for large merchants in the nineteenth century (they were called *capitalistas* in contemporary Spanish language); those directly referred to as *negreros*—though or just because it was an insult—became captains, the factors of sales barracoons as well as *factorías* (slave factories) in West Africa, and lower employees of the contraband trade (Moreno Fraginals 1978, 1:269–74; Ortega 2006, 225–52; Nerín 2015, 38–47).

Atlantic slavery in its main dimension, as well as the African-Iberian Atlantic, Hidden Atlantic, and global dimensions of the second slavery (see the next section) at the times of their real existence, remain in the margins (see also Eltis and Richardson 2008, 2010; on the perceptual paradox of British Atlantic vs. African-Iberian Atlantic, see Sweet 2009, 1–45; Zeuske 2013b, 51–63; Borucki, Eltis, and Wheat 2015, 433–61). They were recorded in hidden text genres (diaries, logbooks) or in novels and memoirs (and also, of course, in port import and export documents that were not accessible to the general public). The most famous memoirs of a slave trader and captain of the Hidden Atlantic are those of Théodore Conneau (Zeuske 2015b, 55–100; Mayer [Conneau] 1845; Schwarz 2008).[6] The most important contemporary information and memoiristic material for the literate society in relation to *negreros* and Atlantic smuggling of human beings were to be found in the belles lettres literature such as *The Count of Monte Cristo* (Alexandre Dumas, 1844–1846), and in Spain especially the works of Pío Baroja (such as *Los pilotos de altura*), but long after the fact in the twentieth century (Surwillo 2014).

Indigenous Slaveries, an "Other Slavery" of *Yndios*, "First Slaveries," and the Second Slavery

What has all this to do with second slavery and world capitalism or capitalism as slavery (Slavery Capitalism, Conermann and Zeuske 2021, forthcoming)? First, in a very basic form and in the very big picture of global history, the control of human bodies by violence (which is central to the definition of any slavery, Zeuske 2018) in its historical form as value in exchange and currency (beginning with indigenous slaveries) always included strong dimensions of capital accumulation—the capital of human bodies, involving mostly status capital (captives as dominated bodies, slave warriors, elite slaves, women for the reproduction of human bodies) and productive capital in the case of enslaved men, mostly productive and reproductive capital in the case of enslaved women.

Second, and related to the "Atlantics," the spatial dimension is of central importance. Until the beginning of the nineteenth century, the Iberian Atlantic until the 1820s to 1845 (during which there were formal abolitions of the Atlantic slave trade by Spain, Portugal, and Brazil) and the Northwest European Atlantic until the 1790s to 1808 (a period that saw the abolition of the Atlantic slave trade in French possessions of the Caribbean and in the US and the UK) were spatially networked systems, financed by African corporeal capital, commodities produced by and for enslaved people, European debts, insurance profits, credits, and other profits from the slave trade and colonial slaveries themselves. These networks were formed by caravans of enslaved people from the interior of Africa (*slaving zones*, Fynn-Paul and Pargas 2018, controlled by African and Arab-African elites). The contact points to the networks of "Atlantic" slave-ship voyages (until 1808–1820 mostly European, from 1800–1820 to 1890 mostly American, from all of the Americas) were African loading points, developing cities (Coquery-Vidrovitch 2005; Eltis, Lovejoy, and Richardson 1999, 12–34; Cañizares Esguerra, Childs, and Sidbury 2013; D. Silva 2017), and the famous *factorías*, which were not industrial factories but slave factories, with systems of barracoons and other types of camp constructions and barracks for merchandise and defensive structures (Nerín 2015), controlled or partly controlled by "Atlantic" slave traders (from an African perspective), but the delivery of enslaved *cativos* was under the control of African elites and with smaller networks of petty Atlantic Creole slave traders (as middlemen between African elites and "Atlantic" traders, Law 1989, 45–68; Austen and Derrick 1999; Perbi 2002, 33–41; Zeuske 2021, forthcoming). In the *factorías* the Atlantic (sea-)trajectory of the AAA networks (AAA=Africa-Atlantic-Americas, and back) began, with all the traumas of sea transport for enslaved people (Zeuske 2015b, 55–100). On the Western Atlantic side of these slave-trade voyages was the coastal corollary of American East Coast harbor cities as slave ports—from Providence/ Rhode Island, New York, New Orleans, and Charleston through the ports of the Caribbean, Cartagena, Caracas, Cumaná, the Guyanas, the Brazilian ports (first of all Bahia and Rio), and Montevideo as well as Buenos Aires among others (Zeuske 2021, forthcoming). These cities were also the first "places of slavery" in the Americas (house slaveries, slavery of institutions including the Catholic Church, the Jesuits, and other orders, state slavery, military slavery, slavery infrastructures/port slavery). But from these port cities, enslaved were moved by violence (American slave caravans) to towns of the interior and rural "places of slavery" (mines, plantations, and big estates with cattle, horses, mules, etc.—in Spanish, *hatos*) (Sluyter 2010 98–120, 2012; O'Malley 2014; O'Malley and Borucki 2017, 314–38). In the epoch that in the general development of capitalism is traditionally called *mercantilism* (I call it "crown capitalism/ colonialism")—in the Netherlands until 1660, in England and later Britain until more or less 1690, in the Iberian countries until more or less 1760–1790—this Atlantic infrastructure of slavery was based on very tiny points including river estuaries and zones near the Atlantic coasts on both the African and American sides. It practically did not exist "beyond the Atlantic." Beyond the Atlantic in Africa indigenous slaveries existed and beyond the Atlantic in the Americas there were also indigenous slaveries, "other slaveries," (including slaves from Asia/ Philippines (Seijas 2014)) and later "first slaveries" (Reséndez 2016; Lovejoy 2018, 220–47; Santos-Granero 2018, 191–219), as well as ubiquitous urban slave trades (Adelman 2006). This spatial big picture changed dramatically in the first forty years of the nineteenth century. In Europe the policy of abolitions and the "work of forgetting" the slave trade and slavery began (Hall, Draper, and McClelland 2016, 1–32), as well as the "liberation" of the European consumers. I call the latter "*biedermeier* capitalism" (romantic capitalism) (Zeuske 2016b, 96–144).[7] Beginning with courts, aristocratic groups and bourgeois middle classes, European and later also North American consumers wanted to have hot water with sugar and coffee, tea, or cocoa, in a formerly unknown meal called breakfast; they also wanted other tropical luxuries, and to smoke and wear cotton clothes (and also underwear, handkerchiefs, socks, etc., Blackburn 2016, 48–54). All these "commodities," with the exception of cheap tobacco (especially in Europe) and later beet sugar, were produced beyond the "North" by enslaved people or people in tropical bond-relations, as well in mixed free/bond-relations. Under discourses of "freedom" and "abolition," the slavery spaces with their capitalism of human bodies in the Atlantic World expanded dramatically, moving from tiny *factorías* and port places/port cities, and cities beyond the Atlantic, deeply into continental spaces and big islands (like Cuba, Madagascar, and Java), contributing to the industrial development of world capitalism (with *Welthandel*—the German term for the nineteenth-century concept of world capitalism) with its giant spaces known as hemispheres or *the global* as a term referring to all the world (continents, large islands, oceans, seas, and hemispheres—for example, in Africa, the Indian Ocean domain, the Pacific, all far *beyond the Atlantic*). These were the spaces of second slaveries and of the Hidden Atlantic (the contraband trade of human bodies despite abolitions, or better, under the discourses of "freedom," [Western] "civilization," and abolition)—the nineteenth-century epoch of capitalist globalization. In the writings of contemporary economists, social scientists, and historians, the term *world* (or *universal*) was usually used; since 1990, almost always the term *global.*

Third, related first to the Caribbean as a region of concentrated world/global history, the temporal dimension (indigenous slaveries; "other slavery," first with an Atlantic dimension; "first slaveries"; and second slavery), world capitalism, and the conflicts between workers and capitalists of the nineteenth and twentieth centuries did not develop "after" or "without" slavery; they developed as the base and as part of the history of modern capitalism (Zeuske 2016b, 96–144; Tomich 2018, 477–501). Global and local forms of slavery existed before, during, and after what we call "Atlantic slavery." When European, initially Iberian-Mediterranean, expansion started around 1400, there were everywhere indigenous slaveries, including the house and port slaveries, as well as raid slaveries (piracy) of Mediterranean, Southern, and Southwestern Europe. In combination with African slaveries from more or less 1460 onward, Iberians learned new forms of mass slavery of African *cativos* (war captives—first of all men), which they called slavery, legalizing it by reinventing "Roman" law. They began to concentrate these *cativos*,[8] as well as enslaved African women and Atlantic Creoles, under their control, as discussed above, in the tiny tropical islands of their "empire of islands."

The first lesson from local forms of African slavery for the Iberians concerned the extremely important function of human bodies as capital under the climatic and social conditions of the tropics and a type of base currency in operations of value exchange with African elites (Caldeira 2013a, 25–56). The second lesson was that *slaving* (the operations of enslavement, transport, and interchange in the capital of human bodies, as well as the accumulation of the profits from commercial operations with enslaved people or the status-related, productive, and reproductive use of them) was one of the fastest channels to getting rich and improving status (C. L. Miller 2008, 70–102; J. C. Miller 2012). The first to learn all that on the African coasts were captains and nonmonopolistic traders, middlemen, and other personnel involved in the exchange (*lançados*, Jews, *tangomãos*, as well as African women; *lançados* is the Portuguese word for monopoly violators/interlopers—in other regions of Africa also *pombeiros*; *tangomãos* or *tungumás* is the word referring to their sons with African women). The second large group of the first-slavery learners—to repeat, learning from African forms of slavery and capital mobilization—were speculators and big merchants in the Iberian and Italian (and some German) metropolises or commercial centers (Lisbon, Seville, Florence, Genoa, Augsburg, etc.) and their factors in Africa (Alencastro 2000; Fernández Cháves and Pérez García 2010, 5–34; 2016, 385–414; Wheat 2016; Zeuske 2021, forthcoming). One of the first to take these lessons from Africa to the western shores of the Atlantic Basin (from an American perspective, the East Coast) was Columbus himself—as a representative of the group of captains of the Iberian Atlantic. Columbus was a slave trader (Keegan 1996, 95–121; Zeuske 2019, 11–36). He and his family and their personnel, as well as their enemies under the Castilians, founded the abovementioned "other slavery" in "the Indies" (Reséndez 2016)—that of "yndios," using local indigenous slaveries among the *tainos* (the peoples of Hispaniola) and other indigenous populations, as well as Iberian and African traditions, the African experiences of the Iberians (in *Guiné*—the Portuguese term for Sub-Saharan Africa), and the legal concepts and customs of Roman law as well as indigenous slaveries (Zeuske 2021, forthcoming). Columbus and others tried to develop, through slaving, an Atlantic dimension of this "other slavery" (together with local forms of indigenous slavery, like *naboría*). The Castilian and the Aragonese crown, as well as later the Spanish crown, intervened in and interdicted this Atlantic dimension, that is, the transport of enslaved *indígenas* from the Greater Antilles (first of all Hispaniola) to the Iberian Peninsula and the selling of them there as slaves under the conditions of "Roman" law. But the "other slavery," mostly "outside of the Atlantic" but within the Caribbean and what we may call the inter-American dimensions, remained in the Americas until 1900 as informal slaveries, raid slaveries, and other forms of private slaveries, as well as forms of collective slaveries (Reséndez 2016[9] Zeuske 2018a).

The Iberian crowns of Spain (under Charles I as king of Spain and Charles V as emperor of the German Empire) and Portugal, fearing that the African elites and their *tangomão*/Atlantic Creole relatives could gain control over the tiny islands of the African west coast, opened the way to the "first slaveries" under Iberian/European control in the Americas. They allowed or, to put it better, made official the direct slave trade from the tiny African islands to the Greater Antilles and later to the American mainland (Green 2012b, 2016, 91–122; Wheat 2016; Eagle and Wheat 2020, 47–72), that is, first of all, the developing cities and villas, as well as ports, under Spanish control. This "first slavery" entailed a mixture of high-priced Africans (also as a type of surrogate settlers) (Wheat 2016)) and low-priced Indians, as well as some *chinos* (from Macau and from the Philippines from the 1570s onward, Seijas 2008, 19–38; 2014). We could call this "first slavery" or, in the words of Jeremy Adelman, the "hinterland-slaveries" of Spanish America, especially in their mixture with the "other slavery" (Adelman 2006, 56–100; Reséndez 2016). This "first slavery" worked well, for the slavers and slave-owners, the state and big institutions like the church, in urban spaces and in some mining regions. In most of the rural zones of Spanish America it worked less well because of Indian resistance, *cimarronaje* (Maroons, sometimes in combination with piracy), and the fierce resistance of the enslaved (Laviña and Ruiz-Peinado 2006). Thus only some regions had profitable "first slaveries" (the coastal valleys and river estuaries of today's Venezuela, the Guyanas, some parts of Brazil, and regions of the East Coast of North America); "first slaveries" failed, for example, in early Louisiana, early Florida, or on the coast of today's Colombia and the interior, as well as on some coasts of Panama (then part of New Granada).

Then a "second slavery" began (Tomich 2018, 477–501). The first island of this "modern" slavery was Barbados, the nucleus of the inner Caribbean development of this second slavery, on the American/Caribbean side of the Atlantic. Whether there are also examples of "second slaveries" on the African Atlantic side or in East Africa is a matter of controversy. For the Indian Ocean domain there are the examples of Mauritius, Réunion, and so on (Allen 1999, 9–31; 2013, 183–99; 2014). Barbados demonstrates the pattern. Dominated by a small group of big white Protestant landowners and slaveholders with great capital of human bodies, this island was fully commodified rapidly after English occupation—land, properties, human bodies, products (food, commodities), infrastructures, housing, and so on (Appleby 1996, 86–104). In other words, the first "modern" capitalist society of the world was Barbados. It also represented the roots of second slavery; nearly everything on this island was commodified and therefore also capitalized. The English took over the Iberian institution of the large tropical land system (*engenhos*, *ingenios*, *haciendas*; the Portuguese and Spanish terms for specialized sugar estates), calling it the *plantation* (as in Ireland, their first colony) or estate. But what was very new was the extreme dynamic of the organization of slave work in this property institution, which followed the model of penal work gangs. Gangs of enslaved from different (African) "nations" (*coromantee*, *mina*, etc.) were assigned tasks of rural labor, and they worked in competition with other gangs (mostly of other "nations"). Another consequence of this organization was that a strong hierarchy of the enslaved of one estate—through the concurrence of the different groups ("nations")—helped in effect to maintain the power of the slave-owners and their personnel (drivers, administrators, etc.) (Newman 2013). By contrast, because Barbados was so tiny and wood so expensive, the entrepreneurs began to develop sugar technology (windmills and ovens) and improve the living conditions of the enslaved (providing "modern" barracoons with slave gardens, as well as healers and surgeons on slave ships and larger plantations). All this was accompanied by pressures against the free Black and colored population (involving racism, the legal system, and local racial hierarchies). As on other Caribbean islands, the indigenous Indian population had been liquidated by the so-called demographic catastrophe. The "second slavery" was a slavery of African people in the Americas, starting from very tiny islands, like Barbados or Martinique (Tomich 2004a), or regions of Antillean islands or coasts (like the coastal regions of Venezuela and the Guyanas; Zeuske 2016a, 2017). These very beginnings of the "second slavery" jumped to other islands (like Jamaica) and, in the eighteenth century, also to the competing French colonies of "L'Amérique" (Martinique, Saint-Domingue, etc. (Burnard and Garrigus 2016), failing, as noted, in Louisiana and on the Colombian coasts. Because there was still no "modern" transportation system, the plantations were very near to coasts, or on small coastal plains or river estuaries, as mentioned above. And they needed masses of enslaved, not only for production but also for infrastructure, houses and transportation. So, the most important feature of this "modern" slavery was that masses of enslaved were brought by a chaotic Atlantic slavery (slave trade) to the British and French colonies between 1763 and 1808 (the French delinked from the Atlantic slave trade already in 1791). The Haitian Revolution in this sense was also a breakdown of an uncontrollable slavery demography, made by *slaving*. The most important accumulation of capital for these extremely dynamic economies of "modern" mass production occurred along the AAA (Africa-Atlantic-Americas) axis if we take the perspective of the enslaved and the capital of human bodies, or along the E/A (Europe/Americas)–AAA (Africa-Atlantic-Americas) axis if we take the perspective of credit, banking, discourses, and history of "modern" capitalist property and its legal development, production of goods and artifacts (weapons, machetes, tools, textiles) for the slave trade, ship construction and sales, and the investment of profits.

The hour of the second slavery arrived with the Haitian Revolution (and the Louisiana Purchase as one of the most important consequences for the young United States), the Anglo-American Abolition of 1808 (with the consumer revolution and *biedermeier* capitalism in the longer-lasting background), the Congress of Vienna (1815), the global discourses of abolition, (Western) "civilization," bonded labor by contract, and the new global expansion of Europe after 1840, followed by the United States from the 1850s onward.[10] The most important second slaveries, each with a real landscape as spatial base, developed with the new technologies of mobility, transportation, and communication (first of all ships, railways, newspapers, and new forms of communication and visualization) for fifty to seventy years in the American South, the South of Brazil, and the *Cuba grande* (Cantero 1857; García Mora; Santamaría García 2005; Zeuske 2004; Tomich 2018, 477–501). This *Cuba grande* developed around Havana, Matanzas until Cienfuegos, Cárdenas, and Sagua la Grande with the most productive landscape of sugar in the world—the plain of famous red earth known as *llanura de Colón* (Marrero Cruz 2006, 2007, 21–33; Funes 2017). It was connected by sea with two giant valleys, namely, the Mississippi Valley (Johnson 2013) to the north and the Paraíba Valley to the south (Marquese 2008, 1:195–216; 2009, 215–51). With these new frontiers, slavery got its very own capitalism (Tomich 2015, 2016; Conermann and Zeuske 2021, forthcoming), its own modernity (Kaye 2014, 174–202) alongside medicine, science, literature, art, communications, and architecture, its own modern slavery society based on Slavery Capitalism, and its own industrial and technological revolutions. And all this was with worldwide dimensions (Beckert 2004) and occurred despite, or should I say because of the formal abolitions in the West Atlantic, together with the functional "war capitalism" of nineteenth-century globalization (Beckert 2014, 7–18).[11] This Slavery Capitalism was based on formal (until 1865–1888) and mixed with informal "slave labor" of the Americas, as well as with the surviving "other slaveries," indigenous slaveries, bond-slaveries, and local slaveries all over the world (which bore their own names and were far from the legalistic forms of "Roman" law), as well as "new slaveries" of contractual bond-labor (Allen 2013, 183–99; Zeuske 2016d,

35–57). In sum, these global second slaveries, though based on older capitalism of human bodies, were new and modern, and they brought industrial organization by violence to rural resource areas, in combination, to repeat, with worldwide but local slavery regimes, "new" collective slaveries based on mass migration of people called coolies, as well as on the rapid development of some indigenous slaveries (such as slavery in Zanzibar, Egypt, Madagascar, Sokoto, and other North African caliphates, South Asia and Southeast Asia, China, or in Arab regions, Campbell 2004; Sheriff 1987; Dal Lago 2012; Zeuske 2019a; Rossum 2021, forthcoming).

Second Slavery and Its *Hidden Atlantic*—and World Capitalism

The core of the second slavery as Slavery Capitalism lay in the Americas. Since about 1815, if one tries to find an essential geography, it lay from the catchment area of the river of dark dreams (Johnson 2013) with its hinterland across the Gulf of Mexico to the northern coast of Cuba, and from there by rail to the plain of Colón and some port points in the south of the island, such as Batabanó and Cienfuegos. From there these modern slaveries firmly communicated accumulation spaces of the capital of human bodies—despite or because of the abolition discourses (Zeuske 2018a)—along the AAA (Africa-Atlantic-Americas/Americas-Atlantic-Africa) axis, reaching East Africa in the nineteenth century. Since 2008 I called this space of informal but extremely profitable contraband trade of human bodies the *Hidden Atlantic* (Zeuske 2018c, 212–44). Since more or less 1800, the Hidden Atlantic expanded into the eastern hemisphere (the Indian Ocean domain, China, India, Dutch India, southeast India, etc.). In the Atlantic hemisphere there was something like a return to the spaces of the "first" or African-Iberian Atlantic from the La Plata region over the coasts of Brazil and the Guiana to the Caribbean, especially Cuba and Puerto Rico. Europeans from Europe were more or less out, but many European Spaniards or Portuguese who were slaving from colonies (like Cuba or Puerto Rico) or ex-colonies (like Brazil) participated in the formation of the Hidden Atlantic. First of all, Cuba (1820–1880), and in Cuba first of all Spanish *negreros*, smuggled between 700,000 and 1,000,000 enslaved to the island (and perhaps a high number to the United States) and withdrew the larger parts of their capital from the Hidden Atlantic contraband trade (Zeuske 2015a), not only for investments in second slavery and its continuous modernization in Cuba (for example, from *ingenios* to *centrales*, as specifically industrialized plantations and huge sugar factories with sugarcane cultivation, or the elite architecture of Havana, Matanzas, or Cienfuegos) but also for reinvestment in Spain, especially in Barcelona, Catalonia, or Cádiz, as well as for financing the Spanish Empire (Morgado García 2013; Rodrigo y Alharilla and Chaviano 2017). The second-richest man in the Atlantic World in 1870 was the former slave smuggler Tomás Terry (Rodrigo y Alharilla 2013, 93–119). Spanish-Cuban *negreros* and Portuguese-Brazilian *negreiros* abducted between two and three million enslaved from West Africa, Congo/Angola, and Mozambique to the south of Brazil from 1810 until the 1850s (Zeuske 2014b, 156–64). Brazilian second slavery did not undergo technological transformation as did Cuban second slavery or some dimensions of the slavery of the American South, first of all because the Brazilian slavers had access to such masses of enslaved that they could maintain their second slavery based until the 1860s on the preindustrial features of the older stages of this slavery mentioned above (as in Saint-Domingue—for example, in transportation). Hidden Atlantic slave smuggling was accompanied by strong inner networks of slave trading in Brazil (from the northeast to the south) (Johnson 2004; L. Marques 2017, 340–59). The American South with its second slavery was formally delinked from the Hidden Atlantic but participated in it outside of US shores relatively directly with many ships, captains, factors (also in Africa), personnel, surgeons, cargoes, and so on. Their space of operation was also the Hidden Atlantic, but they often departed for it from Havana or other Cuban port towns: "Cuando yo salí de la Habana, válgame díos" (the first words of the song "La Paloma," written in 1863 in Havana and Mexico by Sebastián de Yradier). The main source of bodies for human capital, commodities, and workforce for the American South was the formal inner slave trade (Johnson 2004). We still do not know the numbers of the contraband slave trade from Cuba to the North American South (Zeuske 2018c, 212–44). Thus, Slavery Capitalism in the Americas was based on and financed by the illegal slave trade of human bodies. But it was more than simply "financing"; the system and its financial institutions relied on land as capital and on the capital of human bodies (not only for production but also for reproduction).

Slavery elites throughout all of the Americas changed only after failed reforms and bloody wars (the US Civil War and the Cuban anticolonial wars of 1868–1898, as well as imperial breakdown in Brazil). The now "normal" mode of formally "free" capitalist societies in the West prevailed. The European societies of this "free" capitalism maintained collective slaveries/forced labor and slaveries that were not named as such until the second half of the twentieth century (Miers 2003).

The concept of "second slavery" should be localized in individual research history from the perspective of the question of who were the main actors of the second slavery. Under the influence of joint fieldwork with Rebecca J. Scott between 1993 and 2003, I changed the orientation of my research from the global history of "bourgeois revolutions" and their elites (Zeuske 2015f, 99–145) to, on the one hand, a more culturally oriented microhistory, focusing on life histories and slave names and the classical postcolonial theme of "voices of the enslaved," and, on the other, a larger project of a history of Cuba as an African and an Atlantic history of the enslaved who were brought (through Atlantic slavery) to Cuba, as well as their role in the formation of the Cuban nation. That also meant I was interested in the African part of the life histories of "my" enslaved in Cuba. For me by that time, the problem of slave names concerned how we could know, in written texts after slavery, who once was a slave and what was the prehistory of these enslaved in the AA (Africa-Atlantic) and in the AAA (Africa-Atlantic-Americas), and in slavery itself (Zeuske 2002a, 235–66; 2002b, 125–40; 2014a). These questions brought me to the provincial archives and local archives of notaries, as well as to my main source: the notarial records of commercialization and capitalization of human bodies "without their African names" and with Christian slave names. All notarial records of sold or purchased enslaved people contain a short description of the individual human body to be sold: man, woman, or child, age (more or less, but very important for the productive or reproductive value), the characterization "from Africa" or *bozal*, then often with markers of a larger African cultural region: *lucumí* (*yoruba*), *mandinga*, *gangá*, *mina*, *arará*, *carabalí*, *congo*, *loango*, *angola*, *macuá*, or *mozambique* or *criollo* (born in Cuba),[12] wounds, (sometimes) tattoos, scarification, teeth deformations (la Rosa Corzo 2011)[13] and sicknesses of the concrete body, as well as whether the enslaved were drinkers, rebels, or Maroons (Zeuske 2014c). This is what we can know about real bodies of enslaved people—*in slavery*, not in the so-called slave narratives (or better, "freedom narratives") after slavery (Zeuske 2016c, 65–114; Sanz and Zeuske 2017, 9–21). My point here—regarding the history of slavery as capitalism—is that these bodies were not only goods or commodities to be sold; they were always capital, that is, capital of human bodies or corporeal capital. They were the most important capital for Slavery Capitalism and, at the same time, the most important "hands" for production, services, and reproduction (involving the entire body—above all for women).

Thus the treatment of human bodies avant la lettre (for all types of capitalization and commodification, debt, mortgage, borrowing, credit, all types of monetary and bank actions, and regarding human bodies as "money," that is, the most important exchange values, as Europeans and Americans had to learn in West Africa as discussed above), and in written form as notarial records, constituted the first step to one of the central elements of a global history of slavery—human bodies as capital, property, and general currency.

In 2005 or so, I noted that I had read and analyzed some 200,000–300,000 notarial records of buying and selling (and manumitting) enslaved people in Cuba (from the estimated two million in total), and that I was using more and more of a micro approach and getting farther from the world history I had learned at Leipzig with Manfred Kossok and as part of comparative world history in the time of the German Democratic Republic (1949–1990) (Zeuske 2015f, 99–145). So in 2006, as I began a new period of historical research (Zeuske 2006, 9–44), I stopped focusing on the original "voice of the enslaved" (*in* slavery, not after!), meaning that my involvement with postcolonial cultural history was (relatively) over. The change to new forms of larger histories of slavery, global history, and world capitalism helped me in 2002–2003 (Zeuske 2002b, 125–40). I met Dale Tomich personally in Cologne in 2003 (at a colloquium on "Five Hundred Years of Slavery in the Americas"), and in the same year the journal *Comparative Studies in Society and History* sent me an article about the "Adam Smith" of American plantation economy, Francisco de Arango y Parreño (1765–1837) (Arango 1952, 2005), written by Dale Tomich (Tomich 2003, 4–28), for evaluation. Since 2002 I had been struck by the explanatory power of his concept of "second slavery" (Tomich 1988, 103–17; 2018, 477–501). But I still had no idea about slavery as corporeal capitalism, not only in Atlantic slavery but above all in global history. Slavery and capitalism were for me still relatively clearly separate. They were in communication because slavery was a kind of cheap resource production for the capitalism of Western colonial powers in modern times, initially in the late eighteenth and nineteenth centuries, but they were conceptually separate. But having found in the famous *ANC* of Havana (the *Archivo Nacional de Cuba* in Calle Compostela) the papers of Ramón Ferrer, the captain of the slave ship *Amistad* (Zeuske 2014a, 2014b, 156–64), I decided to move forward in two directions: first, from Cuba—though this meant moving me spatially "back" (in the perspective of the enslaved African people, from their homes in Africa to the spaces of slavery in America/ Cuba) along the AAA (Americas(Cuba)-Atlantic-Africa) axis, which involved an Atlantic history of slave trade in the era of abolition (1808/1820–1888), including slave-trader sources on Africa, which I later called the era of the Hidden Atlantic (Zeuske 2018b, 103–35). The intention was first to find Ferrer's second ship *Bella Antonia* (which had sailed in the 1830s from Cuba to Africa, Zeuske 2014a),[14] and in a larger sense, to know more about the great spaces of the spatial prehistory of "my" Cuban enslaved people. And second, it meant a world history of slavery as a kind of return to my former involvement in "big" global history at Leipzig (1980–1992). I traveled to Praia in Santiago Island of the Cabo Verde group—one of the earliest islands of the Slavery Atlantic and the European "empire of islands" (Green 2011, 227–45). There during my afternoon run I met, probably in March 2009, a little Black boy who apparently thought I was a crazy tourist from Portugal. He spoke to me, exactly behind the famous Plateau in Praia, in Fala (or Crioulo, the Creole language of the Cabo Verdeans), thinking I could not understand this Portuguese-patois (from a historical standpoint the patois of the enslaved and the Atlantic Creoles—and indeed I did not understand it). But at this moment, it struck me in a flash: this is a descendant of the enslaved or of the Atlantic Creoles (or both), and he and his people are still living, like me and like "my" Cuban ex-slaves, under global capitalism, which at this moment is in one of its worst crises (Cuba still has to survive under global capitalism). Slavery and commodification and the use of human bodies were part of this capitalism. Rather, they were not only part, they were capitalism in its most basic form: corporeal capitalism, using human bodies as currency and for all the other purposes mentioned above. But the commodified bodies had their own cosmopolitism, their transculturation, and their resistance; they even had their own language. Since then, I started thinking: "Slavery equals capitalism," the *capitalism of human bodies*, and I also thought about their enslaved antecedents, about whom I had read so many sources with only a little information about their bodies and, in general, "silence" on their individualities. Their treatment as capital and commodities, as well as workers and servants, or status capital, *was* capitalism, which in the centers of the slavery empires (or formal ex–slavery empires, like Great Britain after 1838) auto-represented itself as "free," "civilized," and progressive. Thus I started to rewrite my two new big projects: first, the history of Atlantic slave trade in a more micro perspective of the ships, captains, crews, Atlantic Creoles, and the enslaved underdeck; second, the world history of slavery, under the concept of *second slavery* (which opened my eyes conceptually to the unification of "modern" slavery and capitalism, Tomich and Zeuske 2008; Zeuske 2014c) and its *Hidden Atlantic* (which I had already begun to work on because of the Atlantic-wide search for Ferrer's second ship, the *Bella Antonia*; Zeuske and García Martínez 2013; Zeuske 2014a). But first of all, and in the background of writing all this,

I began to use the concept of "capital of human bodies" for the world and global history of slaveries (Zeuske 2015a, 2019a).

The problem of lack of historical analysis of the enslaved as actors of slavery and the slave trade (and world capitalism) becomes clearer when we take the perspective of social history and historical social science. Traditional histories of slavery are, in the majority, histories of economic cycles, actors, institutions (as well as law histories), and structures. As such, these histories are mainly narratives with a focus on the institution, the numbers, the slavers, the slave-owners and their personnel, as well as their economic, social, or political activities. When it comes to the three big social groups of the social history of slavery—slave-owners, slave traders, and organizers of slavery and transport, as well as other personnel of slavery (guards, oarsmen, translators, priests, healers/surgeons, cooks, seamen, captains, caravan men, as well as the giant group of middlemen—Atlantic Creoles of the Atlantic and Atlantic Creoles as middlemen in Africa and the Americas), as well as the enslaved (the slaves) themselves, then we have until today, with few exceptions, still a nonhistory of the enslaved (and also a nonhistory of the personnel of slave trade and slavery) (Zeuske 2016c, 65–114). Thus, microhistories of slaves (in slavery and afterward, as ex-slaves), as well as narratives of life histories of the enslaved, are extremely important as part of this big picture. The pioneer, and today also the master of this type of historiography for the Greater Atlantic, the Caribbean, and the entanglements of various slavery and postslavery systems in the American and Atlantic spaces of AAA, is Rebecca J. Scott of the University of Michigan. Her work, of which I can cite here only what is most important for the subject (Scott 1985, 2000, 472–79; Martínez et al. 2003; Scott and Zeuske 2004, 521–45; Scott 2005; Hébrard 2012, 199–220; Scott 2012, 915–24; Scott and Hébrard 2012; Scott 2012, 152–64; 2017, 101–29), initially was inspired by (according to her own statements) the following scholars: the work on individually identifiable life stories of colored and Black actors in the history of Havana and Cuba by Pedro Deschamps (Deschamps Chapeaux 1971; Deschamps Chapeaux and Pérez de la Riva 1974); works by Sidney W. Mintz, notably his eminent book on the Puerto Rican cane worker Taso (Mintz 1960); and one of John Shy's excellent articles on the American anticolonial rebellion as military revolution ("for a model of deep archival research on a single individual, in the context of warfare," Shy 1976, 165–79).[15] In the 1990s, the strongest influence for her was the archival work and fieldwork of the "Cienfuegos trio" in Cienfuegos, the most developed second-slavery region of Cuba (Rebecca J. Scott, Orlando García Martínez, and Michael Zeuske), and Orlando García's knowledge of the archives helped locate the needles in a haystack of notarial records.[16] Added to this were European influences, notably the work of Arlette Farge (1989, 2015) and Scott's collaboration with Jean-Michel Hébrard (e.g., Hébrard 2012, 7–61).[17]

Instead of a Conclusion

This is not a conclusion but a window to the future of more research about the main actors of slaveries and slave trades, as enslaved and as ex-enslaved. The actors traced by Scott (and Hébrard) do not move so much within the hierarchies of given juggernaut institutions (like slavery, imperial or national societies, and from "bottom to top" in ex-slavery societies) or within the great narratives/spaces of slavery, slave trade, abolition/freedom, or revolution/reform, or within the history of great territorial spaces. But they were very mobile and agile in seeking to secure their individual freedom and that of their families and descendants. They did so through great spaces—such as the Atlantic. They were also very cosmopolitan and mobile, as it were, across the narratives, economic areas, or nations or major political events (such as revolutions). They profited from the translocal emancipatory potential of revolutions and, in a sense, subverted the developing national spaces and extended their mobility to the whole of the Atlantic, Caribbean, Central American, North American, and European countries (Scott and Hébrard 2011, 199–220, 2012, 49–64).

In modern history the Slavery Atlantic, in its macro- and its microdimension, was nearly always an *African-Iberian Atlantic* (1400–1900). The Iberian powers maintained their "empires of slaves" (Reséndez 2016, 131–34) with their Atlantic slaveries, but they also developed one of the largest (Brazil) and one of the most "modern" (Cuba) second slaveries and special types of Slavery Capitalism, as well as slavery modernity (Piqueras 2016, 2017, 23–55; Marquese and Salles 2015; Tomich 2018, 477–501), based on *Atlanticization*—that is, Atlantic capital accumulation (Zeuske 2018a, 79–119).The actors from below and all types of dependencies played a very important role in the construction, the development, but also in the destruction of these empires.

Notes

1. I cannot give a straightforward definition of *Slavery Capitalism*. Basically, the dynamics of capitalism in "bourgeois society" consists in the accumulation and investment of capital

to make more capital. *Capitalism* as a concept came into broader use as a concept only around 1900. I build on this concept to construct two usages of *Slavery Capitalism*. The first is based on current debates about nineteenth-century slavery from the perspective of the second slavery. *Second slavery* refers to specific local types of slave societies, which formed as parts of the restructuring of world production and markets by industrial capital, and the modern societies based on them during the nineteenth century. These second-slavery societies are analyzed here also as *Slavery Capitalism*. The second usage of *Slavery Capitalism* derives from a much broader debate about slaves as the "capital of human bodies." This debate is not yet as defined as the second slavery/capitalism of the nineteenth-century debate. This is because it deals with global history and also includes "slaves without slavery" in prehistory, in small societies all over the world, and today. In particular, this debate revolves around prisoners/enslaved people as multidimensional value (in human bodies) in all societies (most notably see Cameron 2018, 151–68). I think this is the more important debate for global history. It includes the first debate in colonial and ex-colonial societies and their mother countries where slave-owners and traders had come to power (more or less), but also Africa and other regions of the two hemispheres.

2. I understand the Atlantic between 1450 and 1900 as the *Slavery Atlantic*, because on it and on its shores Atlantic slavery developed and spread in the form of slave trades and slaveries (see http://www.slavevoyages.org). I also understand it as a Slavery Atlantic because of a hypothesis of mine that the capital of human bodies was the greatest macrovalue transported on it. The value of more or less eleven million enslaved bodies of men, women, and children, with a single price of more or less 300 silver pesos as a *pieza de Indias* (an estimated total of 3,300,000,000 pesos from 1440 to 1900, first of all between Africa and the Americas, was greater than all other commodities/products from Europe—EAA, first of all from Europe to Africa to the Americas, but also greater than AA—from the Americas to Africa, and IPAA—from the Indian Ocean to the Pacific to Africa to the Americas). But my hypothesis goes even beyond that: the macrovalue of the enslaved human bodies from Africa was even greater than the values of precious metals and diamonds (A-EA—from the Americas to Europe and Africa). The problem in this macroestimation concerns the commodities (cash crops) produced *for* and *by* enslaved people in the Americas and transported into the global markets as well as the food necessary for the maintenance of the enslaved and the slave traders on the Atlantic (A = Atlantic food: fish, meat, water, wine/alcohol, vegetable food such as beans, rice, yuca/farinha, bananas, fruits, etc., and drugs like tobacco, kola, etc.) (Zeuske 2021, forthcoming). Usually in the debate on capitalism and slavery, the commodities produced *by* the enslaved are highlighted; I also emphasize the food, animals, wood, tools, infrastructures, and commodities produced, sold, or exchanged as well as used *for* the slave trade, the enslaved, and the ship's crew as well as the transporters and guards in general (etc.).

3. See also, in the course of the history of knowledge, the spatial concept of a "Plantation Atlantic" (Newman 2013) and the spatial concept of a "slavery hinterland" in Central Europe (Brahm and Rosenhaft 2016).

4. See also the database in Zeuske (2019c).

6. For Conneau, see his manuscript after editing by Brantz Mayer (Mayer 1845); and for the original before Mayer's editing, see Theophilus Conneau, *A Slaver's Log Book, or 20 Years' Residence in Africa* (Englewood Cliffs, NJ: Prentice Hall, 1976).

7. The European rulers exchanged the political tranquility of European peoples for colonial/tropical luxury goods (commodities/cash crops) that were produced by enslaved people, with mostly negative trade balances for Europe. I owe the term "*biedermeier* capitalism" to Robin Blackburn.

8. For the global historical relation between captivity and slavery, see Cameron (2016, 2018).

9. Reséndez estimates 2.5–5 million enslaved people beyond the formal forms of slavery of Africans in the America; see Reséndez (2016, appendix 1).

10. For Spanish America a different cycle began with the so-called Bourbon Reforms, which started to liberate the Spanish American slavery elites from state monopolies over the Atlantic slave trade and theoretically also over the direct accumulation of capital of human bodies (the real slave trade was controlled by English, Dutch, and Americans until more or less 1810) (Borucki, Eltis, and Wheat 2015, 433–61). For the larger continental colonies of Spain these reforms came too late; during the Atlantic revolutions they rebelled against the "mother" country (as in the cases of Simón Bolívar and others, Zeuske 2012). For Cuba, where the reforms had already begun in 1763, or, more accurately, for the big Cuban plantation and slave-owners and the big (Spanish) merchants in Cuba, under the pressure of the independence revolutions on the continent and the Napoleonic Wars, the extremely conservative Spanish crown initiated in 1815 a new reform period, providing the most important resources for the capitalist development of the second slavery (land as private property in the sense of "Roman" law, and also the wood on the lands, formerly an important resource—almost only—for the Spanish imperial fleet), enabling the separation of the traditional haciendas (by *agrimensores* [surveyors]), and fostering the total liberation of Atlantic slavery (only for five years, because the British pressed the Spanish crown to take over their British abolition discourses and laws—but disguised as general ideas and policies of Christian civilization—that had formally forbidden the Atlantic slave trade since 1808 [Great Britain] and 1820 [Spain]) (Zeuske 2018b, 212–44). This is linked to the development of the Hidden Atlantic, which since the 1820s was primarily an endeavor of poor, formerly liberal Spanish men (and some others) to reinforce the colonial links and the resting imperial positions of Spain in Cuba and Puerto Rico (Fradera 2005, 17–59). The result was colonial Slavery Capitalism in the so-called *Cuba grande*—the most compact and dynamic Slavery Capitalism of the nineteenth century.

11. See examples from the debate on slavery and capitalism, and on slavery as capitalism: Williams (1994), Anderson and Gallman (1977, 24–46), Wirz (1884), Fogel (1992, 77–99, 2003), Follett (2000, 1–27), Beckert (2014/2004), Johnson (2004, 299–308), Baucom (2005), Rockman (2006a, 2006b, 335–61), Marrero Cruz (2006), Kolchin (2009,

565–80), Martin (2010, 817–66), Post (2011), Johnson (2013), Graden (2014), Grandin (2014), Baptist (2014), Schermerhorn (2014, 897–921; 2015), Marquese and Salles (2015), Muaze and Salles (2015), Nelson (2015, 289–310), Follett et al. (2016), Piqueras (2016, 2017, 23–55), Blackburn (2016, 48–54), Kocka (2017, 55–59), Zeuske (2013a, 2014a, 49–54; 2016b, 96–144; 2018a, 79–119), Beckert and Rockman (2016), Tomich (2016, 2017, 2018, 477–501), Burnard and Garrigus (2016), Rood (2017).

12. Based on these cultural-ethnic markers the buyers expected some predictability of the "character" of the enslaved, and the enslaved themselves used these markers to form their religious networks and their "naciones" in Cuba (and Spanish America as well as Brazil) (Guanche [Pérez] 2009).

13. These markers, which had very different meanings in Africa and in the Atlantic/the Americas (Lovejoy 2010, 99–138), were used in the latter two spaces primarily for the persecution and recognition of slaves who had fled (Maroons or *cimarrones*).

14. Just when I was writing this chapter, I found a new trace; see Archivo Nacional de Cuba (ANC) (1834).

15. Rebecca J. Scott, personal correspondence to author, September 2019.

16. Rebecca J. Scott, personal correspondence to author, September 2019.

17. For the joint works, see above.

References

Archivo Nacional de Cuba (ANC). 1834. *Miscelánea de libros*, t. xxi, leg. 3129, Bi. Expediente de la entrada del bergantín español "Bella Antonia," Havana.

Adelman, Jeremy. 2006. *Sovereignty and Revolution in the Iberian Atlantic.* Princeton, NJ: Princeton University Press.

Alencastro, Luiz Felipe de. 2000. "São Tomé: Laboratório tropical." In Alencastro, *O Trato dos viventes: Formacão do Brasil no Atlantico Sul, seculos 16. e 17.* São Paulo: Companhia das Letras, 63–67.

———. 2006. "Le versant brésilien de l'Atlantique-Sud: 1550–1850." *Annales: Histoire, Sciences Sociales* 61, no. 2: 339–82.

———. 2007. "Gulf of Guinea and São Tomé: A Laboratory for Tropical Slavery." In *Portuguese Oceanic Expansion 1400–1800*, edited by Francisco Bethencourt and Diogo Ramada Curto, 110–12. Cambridge: Cambridge University Press.

Alexandre, Valemtim. 1991. "Portugal e a abolição do tráfico de escravos (1834–1851)." *Análise Social* 25, no. 3: 293–333.

Allen, Richard B. 1999. *Slaves, Freedmen, and Indentured Laborers in Colonial Mauritius.* Cambridge: Cambridge University Press.

———. 2013. "Slave Trading, Abolitionism, and 'New Systems of Slavery' in the Nineteenth-Century Indian Ocean World." In *Indian Ocean Slavery in the Age of Abolition*, edited by Robert Harms, Bernard K. Freamon, and David W. Blight, 183–99. New Haven, CT: Yale University Press.

———. 2014. *European Slave Trading in the Indian Ocean*, 1500–1850. Athens: Ohio University Press.

Anderson, Ralph V., and Robert E. Gallman. 1977. "Slaves as Fixed Capital: Slave Labor and Southern Economic Development." *Journal of American History* 64, no. 1: 24–46.

Appleby, John C. 1996. "English Settlements in the Lesser Antilles during War and Peace, 1603–1660." In *The Lesser Antilles in the Age of European Expansion*, edited by Robert L. Paquette and Stanley Engerman, 86–104. Gainesville: University Press of Florida.

Arango y Parreño, Francisco. 1952. *Obras de D. Francisco de Arango y Parreño*. 2 vols. Havana: Publicaciones de la Dirección de Cultura del Ministerio de Educación (Obras 1).

———. 2005. *Obras: Ensayo introductorio, compilación y notas García Rodríguez*. 2 vols. Havana: Imagen Contemporánea (Obras 2).

Araujo, Ana Lucia. 2012. "Dahomey, Portugal and Bahia: King Adandozan and the Atlantic Slave Trade." *Slavery & Abolition* 33, no. 1: 1–19.

Austen, Ralph A., and Jonathan Derrick. 1999. *Middlemen of the Cameroons Rivers: The Duala and Their Hinterland, c.1600–c.1960*. London: Cambridge University Press.

Bailey, Anne C. 2006. *African Voices of the Atlantic Slave Trade: Beyond the Silence and the Shame*. Boston: Beacon.

Baptist, Edward E. 2014. *The Half Has Never Been Told: Slavery and the Making of American Capitalism*. New York: Basic Books.

Bassi, Ernesto. 2014. "Beyond Compartmentalized Atlantics: A Case for Embracing the Atlantic from Spanish American Shores." *History Compass* 12, no. 9: 704–16.

Baucom, Ian. 2005. *Specters of the Atlantic: Finance Capital, Slavery, and the Philosophy of History*. Durham, NC: Duke University Press.

Beckert, Sven. 2014. "Einleitung." In Beckert, *King Cotton: Eine Geschichte des globalen Kapitalismus*. Munich: Beck, 7–18. (English: Beckert, Sven. 2014. *The Empire of Cotton: A New History of Global Capitalism*. London: Macmillan.)

Beckert, Sven, and Seth Rockman, eds. 2016. *Slavery's Capitalism: A New History of American Economic Development*. Philadelphia: University of Pennsylvania Press.

Belaubre, Christophe, Jordana Dym, and John Savage, eds. 2010. *Napoleon's Atlantic: The Impact of Napoleonic Empire in the Atlantic World*. Leiden: Brill.

Bethencourt, Francisco. 2013. "Iberian Atlantic: Ties, Networks, and Boundaries." In *Theorising the Iberian Atlantic*, edited by Harald E. Braun and Lisa Vollendorf, 15–36. Leiden: Brill.

Blackburn, Robin. 2016. "De la invención del desayuno a la importancia de la ropa interior." In *Esclavitud y capitalismo histórico en el siglo XIX: Brasil, Cuba y Estados Unidos*, edited by José Antonio Piqueras, 48–54. Santiago de Cuba: Casa del Caribe.

Borucki, Alex, David Eltis, and David Wheat. 2015. "Atlantic History and the Slave Trade to Spanish America." *American Historical Review* 120, no. 2: 433–61.

Boubacar, Barry. 1998. *Senegambia and the Atlantic Slave Trade*. Translated by Ayi Kwei Armah. Cambridge: Cambridge University Press.

Brahm, Felix, and Eva Rosenhaft, eds. 2016. *Slavery Hinterland: Transatlantic Slavery and Continental Europe, 1680–1850*. Woodbridge, UK: Boydell.

Brandon, Pepijn. 2015. "Dutch Capitalism and Slavery: New Perspectives from American Debates." *Tijdschrift voor Sociale en Economische Geschiedenis* 12, no. 4: 117–37.

Brooks, George E. 1976a. "A Nhara of the Guinea-Bissau Region: Mãe Aurélia Correia." In *Women and Slavery in Africa*, edited by Claire C. Robertson and Martin A. Klein, 295–319. Madison: University of Wisconsin Press.

———. 1976b. "The Signares of Saint-Louis and Gorée: Women Entrepreneurs in Eighteenth-Century Senegal." In *Women and Slavery in Africa*, edited by Claire C. Robertson and Martin A. Klein, 19–44. Madison: University of Wisconsin Press.

——. 1993. *Landlords and Strangers: Ecology, Society, and Trade in West Africa, 1000–1630*. Boulder, CO: Westview.

Buchanan, Thomas C. 2004. *Black Life on the Mississippi: Slaves, Free Blacks, and the Western Steamboat World*. Chapel Hill: University of North Carolina Press.

Burnard, Trevor, and John D. Garrigus. 2016. *The Plantation Machine: Atlantic Capitalism in French Saint-Domingue and British Jamaica*. Philadelphia: University of Pennsylvania Press.

Burnside, Madeleine, and Rosemary Robotham. 1997. *Spirits of the Passage: The Transatlantic Slave Trade in the Seventeenth Century*. New York: Simon & Shuster.

Caldeira, Arlindo Manuel. 2013a. "Aprender os Trópicos: Plantações e trabalho escravo na ilha de São Tomé." In *Para a história da escravatura insular nos séculos XV a XIX*, edited by Margarida Vaz do Rego Machado, Rute Dias Gregorio, and Susana Serpa Silva, 25–54. Lisbon: CHAM, 2013.

———. 2013b. *Escravos e traficantes no império português: O comércio negreiro português no Atlântico durante os séculos XV a XX*. Lisbon: Esfera dos Livros.

Cameron, Catherine M. 2016. *Captives: How Stolen People Changed the World*. Lincoln: University of Nebraska Press.

——. 2018. "The Nature of Slavery in Small-Scale Societies." In *What Is a Slave Society? The Practice of Slavery in Global Perspective*, edited by Noel Lenski and Catherine M. Cameron, 151–68. Cambridge: Cambridge University Press.

Campbell, Gwyn (ed.). 2004. *The Structure of Slavery in Indian Ocean Africa and Asia*, London; Portland: Frank Cass (Studies in Slave and Post-Slave Societies and Cultures; Series Editor: Gad Heuman).

Candido, Mariana P. 2010. "Different Slave Journeys: Enslaved African Seamen on Board of Portuguese Ships, c. 1760–1820s." *Slavery & Abolition* 31, no. 3: 395–409.

———. 2013. *An African Slaving Port and the Atlantic World: Benguela and Its Hinterland.* New York: Cambridge University Press.

Cantero, Justo G. 1857. *Los Ingenios: Colección de vistas de los principales ingenios de azúcar de la isla de Cuba.* Dibujos de Eduardo Laplante, La Habana; Litografía de Luis Marquier. http://www.gutenberg.org/files/39312/39312-h/39312-h.htm (February 26, 2013). Modern reedition: García Mora, José Luis, and Antonio Santamaría García, eds. *Los Ingenios: Colección de vistas de los principales ingenios de azúcar de la Isla de Cuba.* El texto redactado por Cantero, Justo G. Con las láminas dibujadas del natural y litografiadas por Eduardo Laplante, Madrid.

Cañizares Esguerra, Jorge. 2006. *Puritan Conquistadors: Iberianizing the Atlantic, 1500–1700.* Stanford, CA: Stanford University Press.

Cañizares Esguerra, Jorge, and Benjamin Breen. 2013. "Hybrid Atlantics: Future Directions for the History of the Atlantic World." *History Compass* 11, no. 8: 597–609.

Cañizares, Esguerra, Matt D. Childs, and James Sidbury, eds. 2013. *The Black Urban Atlantic in the Age of the Slave Trade.* Philadelphia: University of Pennsylvania Press.

Cañizares Esguerra, Jorge, and Erik R. Seemann, eds. 2017. *The Atlantic in Global History, 1500–2000.* New York: Routledge.

Carreira, António. 1981. *O tráfico de escravos nos rios de Guiné e Ilhas de Cabo Verde (1810–1850): Subsídios para o seu estudio.* Estudos de Antropologia Cultural, no. 14. Lisbon: Junta de Investigações Científicas do Ultramar, Centro de Estudos de Antropologia Cultural.

Christopher, Emma. 2006. *Slave Ship Sailors and Their Captive Cargoes, 1730–1807.* Cambridge: Cambridge University Press.

Coclanis, Peter A. 2005. "Atlantic World or Atlantic/World?" *William and Mary Quarterly* 63, no. 4: 725–42.

Coelho, Margarida et al. 2008. "Human Microevolution and the Atlantic Slave Trade: A Case Study from São Tomé." *Current Anthropology* 49, no. 1: 134–43.

Coquery-Vidrovitch, Catherine. 2005. *The History of African Cities South of the Sahara: From the Origins to Colonization.* Princeton, NJ: Princeton University Press.

Curto, José C., and Renée Soulodre-La France, eds. 2005. *Africa and the Americas: Interconnections during the Slave Trade.* Trenton, NJ: Africa World Press.

Dal Lago, Enrico. 2012. *American Slavery, Atlantic Slavery, and Beyond: The U.S. "Peculiar Institution" in International Perspective.* Boulder, CO: Paradigm.

de Almeida Mendes, António. 2008. "The Foundations of the System: A Reassessment of the Slave Trade to the Spanish Americas in the Sixteenth and Seventeenth Centuries." In *Extending the Frontiers: Essays on the New Transatlantic Slave Trade Database*, edited by David Eltis and David Richardson, 63–94. New Haven, CT: Yale University Press.

———. 2013. "Les Portugais et le premier Atlantique (XVe-XVIe siècles)." In *Les Territoires de la Méditerranée XIe-XVIe siècle*, edited by Annliese Nef with Damien de Coulon,

Christophe Picard, and Dominique Valérian, 137–57. Rennes, France: Presses Universitaires de Rennes.

DeCorse, Christopher. 2001. *West Africa during the Atlantic Slave Trade: Archaeological Perspectives.* London: Leicester University Press.

Degn, Christian. 1974. *Die Schimmelmanns im atlantischen Dreieckshandel: Gewinn und Gewissen.* Neumünster, Germany: Wachholtz (3rd ed., 2000).

———. 2006. "Schwarze Fracht: Dokumentation und Interpretation." In *Der dänische Gesamtstaat: Ein unterschätztes Weltreich?*, edited by Eva Heinzelmann et al., 37–50. Kiel, Germany: Verlag Ludwig.

Deschamps Chapeaux, Pedro. 1971. *El negro en la economía habanera del siglo XIX.* Havana: UNEAC.

Deschamps Chapeaux, Pedro, and Juan Pérez de la Riva. 1974. *Contribución al la historia de la gente sin historia.* Havana: Ed. de Ciencias Sociales.

Domingues [da Silva], Daniel B. 2017. *The Atlantic Slave Trade from West Central Africa 1780–1867.* Cambridge: Cambridge University Press.

Donoghue, John, and Evelyn P. Jennings, eds. 2015. *Building the Atlantic Empires: Unfree Labor and Imperial States in the Political Economy of Capitalism, ca. 1500–1914.* Leiden: Brill.

Downey, Tom. 2006. *Planting a Capitalist South: Masters, Merchants, and Manufacturers in the Southern Interior, 1790–1860.* Baton Rouge: Louisiana State University Press.

Drescher, Seymour. 2009. *Abolition: A History of Slavery and Antislavery.* Cambridge: Cambridge University Press.

Dubois, Laurent, and Scott S. Julius, eds. *Origins of the Black Atlantic.* New York: Routledge.

Duncan, Thomas B. 1972. *Atlantic Islands: Madeira, the Azores, and the Cape Verdes in Seventeenth-Century Commerce and Navigation.* Chicago: University of Chicago Press.

Eagle, Marc, and David Wheat. 2020. "The Early Iberian Slave Trade to the Spanish Caribbean, 1500–1580." In *From the Galleons to the Highlands: Slave Trade Routes in the Spanish Americas*, edited by Alex Borucki, David Eltis, and David Wheat, 47–52. Albuquerque: University of New Mexico Press.

Eltis, David, and Stanley Engerman, eds. 2011. *The Cambridge World History of Slavery.* Vol. 3. *AD 1420–AD 1804.* Cambridge: Cambridge University Press.

Eltis, David, Paul E. Lovejoy, and David Richardson. 1999. "Slave Trading Ports: Toward an Atlantic-Wide Perspective, 1672–1832." In *Ports of the Slave Trade (Bights of Benin and Biafra)*, edited by Robin Law and Silke Strickrodt, 12–34. Stirling, UK: Centre of Commonwealth Studies, University of Stirling.

Eltis, David, and David Richardson, eds. *Extending the Frontiers: Essays on the New Transatlantic Slave Trade Database.* New Haven, CT: Yale University Press.

Eltis, David, and David Richardson. 2010. *Atlas of the Transatlantic Slave Trade.* New Haven, CT: Yale University Press.

Eltis, David, David Richardson, and Stephen D. Behrendt. "Patterns in the Transatlantic Slave Trade, 1662–1867: New Indications of African Origins of Slaves Arriving in the Americas." In *Black Imagination and the Middle Passage*, edited by Maria Diedrich, Henry Louis Gates, and Carl Pedersen, 1–30. Oxford, UK: Oxford University Press.

Fábregas García, Adela. 2000. "Del cultivo de la caña al establecimiento de las plantaciones." In *História e tecnología do açúcar*, edited by Região Autónoma da Madeira, 59–85. Funchal, Portugal: Centro de Estudos de História do Atlântico.

Farge, Arlette. 1989. *Le goût de l'archive*. Paris: Seuil.

———. 2015. *The Allure of the Archives*. Translated by Thomas Scott-Railton. New Haven, CT: Yale University Press.

Fernández Chaves, Manuel F., and Rafael M. Pérez García. 2010. "La redes de la trata negrera: Mercaderes portugueses y tráfico de esclavos en Sevilla (c. 1560–1580)." In *La esclavitud negroafricana en la historia de España*, edited by Martín Casares and García Barranco, 5–34. Granada: Editorial Comares.

———. 2016. "La élite mercantil judeoconversa andaluza y la articulación de la trata negrera hacia las Indias de Castilla, ca. 1518–1560." *Hispania* 76, no. 253: 385–414.

Ferreira, Roquinaldo. 1995–1999. "Negociantes, fazendeiros e escravos: O tráfico ilegal de escravos no Brasil." *Revista Internacional de Estudos Africanos*, nos. 18–22: 9–28.

———. 2012a. *Cross-Cultural Exchange in the Atlantic World: Angola and Brazil during the Era of Slave Trade*. Cambridge: Cambridge University Press.

———. 2012b. "Rebalancing Atlantic History." In Ferreira, *Cross-Cultural Exchange in the Atlantic World: Angola and Brazil during the Era of Slave Trade*. Cambridge: Cambridge University Press, 242–48.

Florentino, Manolo G. 2004. "Slave Trading and Slave Traders in Rio de Janeiro, 1790–1830." In *Enslaving Connections: Changing Cultures of Africa and Brazil during the Era of Slavery*, edited by José C. Curto and Paul E. Lovejoy, 57–79. New York: Humanity Books.

Fogel, Robert W. 1992. "American Slavery: A Flexible, Highly Developed Form of Capitalism." In *Society and Culture in the Slave South*, edited by J. William Harris, 77–99. London: Routledge.

———. 2003. *The Slavery Debates, 1952–1990: A Retrospective*. Baton Rouge: Louisiana State University Press.

Follett, Richard. 2000. "Slavery and Plantation Capitalism in Louisiana's Sugar Country." *American Nineteenth Century History* 1, no. 3: 1–27.

Follett, Richard, Sven Beckert, Peter A. Coclanis, and Barbara Hahn. 2016. *Plantation Kingdom: The American South and Its Global Commodities*. Baltimore: Johns Hopkins University Press.

Fradera, Josep María. 2005. "Cuba, Puerto Rico y Filipinas: Del Imperio al sistema de tres colonias." In Fradera, *Colonias para después de un imperio*. Barcelona: Edicions Bellaterra, 17–59.

Fragoso, João, Roberto Guedes, and Thiago Krause. 2013. *A América portuguesa e os sistemas atlânticos na Época Moderna*. Rio de Janeiro: Editora FGV.

Franco, José Luciano. 1996. "La oligarquía negrera." In Franco, *Comercio clandestino de esclavos*. Havana: Editorial de Ciencias Sociales, 142–78.

Fuente, Alejandro de la. 2008. *Havana and the Atlantic in the Sixteenth Century*. Chapel Hill: University of North Carolina Press.

Funes, Reinaldo. 2017. "Paisajes de la nueva plantación esclavista azucarera en Cuba: La llanura de Colón." In *Plantación, espacios agrarios y esclavitud en la Cuba colonial*, edited by José Antonio Piqueras, 91–114. Castellón de la Plana, Spain: Publicacions de la Universitat Jaume I/Casa de las Américas.

Fynn-Paul, Jeff, and Damian A. Pargas, eds. 2018. *Slaving Zones: Cultural Identities, Ideologies, and Institutions in the Evolution of Global Slavery*. Leiden: Brill.

Gemery, Henry A., and Jan S. Hogendorn, eds. 1979. *The Uncommon Market: Essays in the Economic History of the Atlantic Slave Trade*. New York: Academic.

Graden, Dale T. 2014. *Disease, Resistance, and Lies: The Demise of the Transatlantic Slave Trade to Brazil and Cuba*. Baton Rouge: Louisiana State University Press.

Grandin, Greg. 2014. *The Empire of Necessity: Slavery, Freedom, and Deception in the New World*. New York: Metropolitan Books.

Green, Tobias. 2011. "Building Slavery in the Atlantic World: Atlantic Connections and the Changing Institution of Slavery in Cabo Verde, Fifteenth–Sixteenth Centuries." *Slavery & Abolition* 32, no. 2: 227–45.

———, ed. 2012a. *Brokers of Change: Atlantic Commerce and Culture in Pre-Colonial Western Africa*. London: British Academy; Oxford, UK: Oxford University Press.

———. 2012b. *The Rise of the Trans-Atlantic Slave Trade in Western Africa, 1300–1589*. Cambridge: Cambridge University Press.

———. 2016. "Beyond an Imperial Atlantic: Trajectories of Africans from Upper Guinea and West-Central Africa in the Early Atlantic World." *Past and Present*, no. 230: 91–122.

Grindal, Peter. 2016. *Opposing the Slavers: The Royal Navy's Campaign against the Atlantic Slave Trade*. London: Tauris.

Guanche [Pérez], Jesús. 2009. *Africanía y etnicidad en Cuba: Los componentes étnicos africanos y sus multiples denominaciones*. Havana: Editorial de Ciencias Sociales.

Hall, Catherine, Nicholas Draper, and Keith McClelland. 2014. "Introduction." In *Legacies of British Slave-Ownership: Colonial Slavery and the Formation of Victorian Britain*, edited by Catherine Hall, Nicholas Draper, and Keith McClelland, 1–32. Cambridge: Cambridge University Press.

Harris, John. 2016. "Circuits of Wealth, Circuits of Sorrow: Financing the Illegal Transatlantic Slave Trade in the Age of Suppression, 1850–1866." *Journal of Global History*, no. 11: 409–29.

Hawthorne, Walter G. 2003. *Planting Rice and Harvesting Slaves: Transformations along the Guinea-Bissau Coast, 1400–1900.* Portsmouth, NH: Heinemann.

———. 2010. *From Africa to Brazil: Culture, Identity, and an Atlantic Slave Trade, 1600–1830.* Cambridge: Cambridge University Press.

Hébrard, Jean-Michel. 2012. "L'esclavage au Brésil: Le débat historiographique et ses racines." In *Brésil: Quatre siècles d'esclavage: Nouvelles questions, nouvelles recherches*, edited by Jean-Michel Hébrard, 7–61. Paris: Karthala & CIRESC.

Heintze, Beatrix. 2002. "Schwarze 'Weiße': Die Ambakisten." In Heintze, *Afrikanische Pioniere: Trägerkarawanen im westlichen Zentralafrika (ca. 1850–1890).* Frankfurt am Main: Verlag Otto Lehmbeck, 155–74.

Hernández González, Manuel. 2006. "La esclavitud en Canarias y su emigración a América." *Esclavos*, Archivo Histórico Provincial de Santa Cruz de Tenerife, 27–39. Santa Cruz de Tenerife: Gobierno de Canarias, Consejería de Educación, Cultura y Deportes. Dirección General del Libro, Archivos y Bibliotecas (Documentos para la Historia de Canarias, vol. 8).

Heywood, Linda, and John K. Thornton. 2007. *Central Africans, Atlantic Creoles, and the Foundations of the Americas, 1585–1660.* Cambridge: Cambridge University Press, 2007.

Hopkin, Daniel, 2016. "Julius von Rohr, an Enlightenment Scientist of the Plantation Atlantic." In *Slavery Hinterland: Transatlantic Slavery and Continental Europe, 1680–1850*, edited by Felix Brahm and Eva Rosenhaft, 133–60. Woodbridge, UK: Boydell.

Horta, José da Silva, and Francisco Freire. 2013. "Os primeiros contactos luso-saarianos: Narrativas europeias quatrocentistas e tradições orais Bidān (Mauritânia)." In *As Lições de Jill Dias: Antropologia, História, África e Academia*, edited by Maria Cardeira da Silva and Clara Saraiva, 37–53. Lisbon: Centro em Rede de Investigação em Antropologia (CRIA).

Ipsen, Pernille. 2015. *Daughters of the Trade: Atlantic Slavers and Interracial Marriage on the Gold Coast.* Philadelphia: University of Pennsylvania Press.

Johnson, Walter. 2004. "The Pedestal and the Veil: Rethinking the Capitalism/Slavery Question." *Journal of the Early Republic* 24, no. 2: 299–308.

———. 2013. *River of Dark Dreams: Slavery and Empire in the Cotton Kingdom.* Cambridge, MA: Belknap Press of Harvard University Press.

Kaye, Anthony. 2014. "The Second Slavery: Modernity in the Nineteenth-Century South and the Atlantic World." In *The Second Slavery: Mass Slaveries and Modernity in the*

Americas and in the Atlantic Basin, edited by Javier Laviña and Michael Zeuske, 174–202. Berlin: LIT Verlag.

Keegan, William F. 1996. "Columbus Was a Cannibal: Myth and the First Encounters." In *The Lesser Antilles in the Age of European Expansion*, edited by Robert L. Paquette and Stanley L. Engerman, 17–32. Gainesville: University Press of Florida.

Klein, Martin A. 2001. "The Slave Trade and Decentralized Societies." *Journal of African History* 42, no. 1: 49–65.

———. 2002. "El comercio atlántico de esclavos en el siglo XIX y el suministro de mano de obra a Cuba y Brasil." In *Azúcar y esclavitud en el final del trabajo forzado: Homenaje a Manuel Moreno Fraginals*, edited by José Antonio Piqueras, 37–49. Madrid: Fondo de Cultura Económica.

Klooster, Wim. 2016. *The Dutch Moment: War, Trade, and Settlement in the Seventeenth-Century Atlantic World.* Ithaca, NY: Cornell University Press.

Klooster, Wim, and Gerd Oostindie. 2018. *Realm between Empires: The Second Dutch Atlantic, 1680–1815.* Ithaca, NY: Cornell University Press; Leiden: Leiden University Press.

Kocka, Jürgen. 2017. "Plantagenwirtschaft und Sklaverei." In Kocka, *Geschichte des Kapitalismus.* Munich: Beck: 55–59.

Kolchin, Peter. 2009. "The South and the World." *Journal of Southern History* 75, no. 3: 565–80.

la Rosa Corzo, Gabino. 2011. *Tatuados: Deformaciones étnicas de los cimarrones en Cuba.* Havana: Fundación Fernando Ortiz.

Laviña, Javier, and José Luis Ruiz-Peinado. 2006. *Resistencias esclavas en las Américas.* Aranjuez, Spain: Doce Calles.

Law, Robin. 1989. "Slave-Raiders and Middlemen, Monopolists and Free Traders: The Supply of Slaves for the Atlantic Trade in Dahomey, c. 1715–1850." *Journal of African History*, no. 30 (1989): 45–68.

Lawrance, Benjamin N. 2013. "'Your Poor Boy No Father No Mother': 'Orphans,' Alienation, and the Perils of Atlantic Child Slave Biography." *Biography* 36, no. 4: 672–703.

Lawrance, Benjamin N. 2014. *Amistad's Orphans: An Atlantic Story of Children, Slavery, and Smuggling.* New Haven, CT: Yale University Press.

———. 2014. "'A Full Knowledge of the Subject of Slavery': The *Amistad*, Expert Testimony, and the Origins of Atlantic Studies." *Slavery & Abolition* 36, no. 2: 298–318.

———. 2014. "La Amistad's 'Interpreter' Reinterpreted: James Kaweli Covey's Distressed Atlantic Childhood and the Production of Knowledge about Nineteenth-Century Sierra Leone." In *Slavery, Abolition and the Transition to Colonialism in Sierra Leone*, edited by Suzanne Schwarz and Paul E. Lovejoy, 215–56. Trenton, NJ: Africa World Press.

Lindsay, Lisa A. 2007. *Captives as Commodities: The Transatlantic Slave Trade.* New York: Prentice Hall.

Lloyd, David, and Peter O'Neill, eds. *The Black and Green Atlantic: Cross-Currents of the African and Irish Diasporas.* Basingstoke, Houndmills, UK: Palgrave Macmillan.

Lobo Cabrera, Manuel. 1985. "Esclavos negros a Indias a través de Gran Canaria." *Revista de Indias* 45, no. 175: 28–50.

Lopes, Carlos, ed. 1993. *Mansas, escravos, grumetes e gentio: Cacheu na encruzilhada de civilações*. Bissau: Instituto Nacional de Estudos e Pesquisa.

Lopes Filho, João. 2006. "Tráfico clandestino." In Lopes Filho, *Cabo Verde: Abolição da escravatura: Subsidios para o estudo*. Praia, Cabo Verde: Spleen Edições, 45–75.

López Mesa, Enrique. 2017. "¿Vega grande o plantación?" In *Plantación, espacios agrarios y esclavitud en la Cuba colonial*, edited by José Antonio Piqueras, 249–66. Castellón de la Plana, Spain: Publicacions de la Universitat Jaume I/Casa de las Américas.

Lovejoy, Paul E., ed. 2000a. *Identity in the Shadow of Slavery*. London: Continuum.

———. 2000b. *Transformations in Slavery: A History of Slavery in Africa*. Cambridge: Cambridge University Press

———. 2010. "Scarification and the Loss of History in the African Diaspora." In *Activating the Past Historical Memory in the Black Atlantic*, edited by Andrew Apter and Lauren Derby, 99–138. Newcastle, UK: Cambridge Scholarly.

———. 2018. "Slavery in Societies on the Frontier of Centralized States in West Africa." In *What Is a Slave Society? The Practice of Slavery in Global Perspective*, edited by Noel Lenski and Catherine M. Cameron, 220–47. Cambridge: Cambridge University Press.

Lovejoy, Paul E., and Benjamin P. Bowser, eds. 2012. *The Transatlantic Slave Trade and Slavery: New Directions in Teaching and Learning*. Trenton, NJ: Africa World Press.

Majewski, John D. 2009. *Modernizing a Slave Economy: The Economic Vision of the Confederate Nation*. Chapel Hill: University of North Carolina Press, 2009.

Mann, Michael. 2005. "Empirische Eilande: Inseln als Laboratorien der europäischen Expansion." *Jahrbuch für Europäische Überseegeschichte*, no. 5: 27–53.

Marques, João Pedro. 1999. *Os sons do silêncio: O Portugal de oitocentos e a abolição do tráfico de escravos*. Lisbon: Imprensa de Ciências Sociais. (English: Marques, João Pedro. 2006. *The Sons of Silence: Nineteenth-Century Portugal and the Abolition of the Slave Trade*. New York: Berghahn Books.)

Marques, Leonardo. 2010. "A participação norte-americana no tráfico transatlântico de escravos para os Estados Unidos, Cuba e Brasil." *Historia: Questões & Debates*, no. 52: 91–117.

———. 2012 "Slave Trading in a New World: The Strategies of North American Slave Traders in the Age of Abolition." *Journal of the Early Republic* 32, no. 2 (Summer): 233–60.

———. 2016. *The United States and the Transatlantic Slave Trade to the Americas, 1776–1867*. New Haven, CT: Yale University Press.

———. 2017. "O tráfico interestadual de escravos nos Estados Unidos em suas dimensões globais, 1808–1860." *Revista Tempo* 23, no. 2: 340–59.

Marquese, Rafael. 2008. "African Diaspora, Slavery, and the Paraiba Valley Coffee Plantation Landscape: Nineteenth Century Brazil." *Review: A Journal of the Fernand Braudel Center*, no. 2 (2008): 195–216.

———. 2009. "Espacio y poder en la caficultura esclavista de las Américas: El Vale do Paraíba en perspectiva comparada." In *Trabajo libre y coactivo en sociedades de plantación*, edited by José Antonio Piqueras, 215–51. Madrid: Siglo XXI de España Editores.

Marquese, Rafael, and Ricardo Salles, eds. 2015. *Escravidão e capitalismo histórico no século XIX: Brasil, Cuba e Estados Unidos*. Rio de Janeiro: Civilização Brasileira.

Marrero Cruz, Eduardo. 2006. "Traficante de esclavos y chinos." In Marrero Cruz, *Julián de Zulutea y Amondo: Promotor del capitalismo en Cuba*. Havana: Ediciones Unión, 46–79.

———. 2007. "La llanura de Colón, emporio azucarero del mundo en el siglo XIX." *Boletín: Archivo Nacional de la República de Cuba*, no. 15: 21–33.

Martin, Bonnie. 2010. "Slavery's Invisible Engine: Mortgaging Human Property." *Journal of Southern History* 76, no. 4: 817–66.

Martínez Heredia, Fernando, Rebecca J. Scott, and Orlando García Martínez. 2003. *Espacios, silencios y los sentidos de la libertad: Cuba 1898–1912*. Havana: Ediciones Unión.

Martínez Shaw, Carlos, and José María Oliva Melgar, eds. 2005. *El sistema atlántico español (siglos XVII–XIX)*. Madrid: Marcial Pons Historia.

Marzagalli, Silvia. 1999. "The French Atlantic." *Itinerario* 23, no. 2: 70–83.

Mayer, Brantz, ed. 1845. *Captain Canot; or, Twenty Years of an African Slaver: Being an Account of his Career and Adventures on the Coast, in the interior, on Shipboard, and in the West Indies*. Reprint, New York: Arno, 1968. (The original before it was edited by Brantz Mayer: Conneau, Theophilus. 1976. *A Slaver's Log Book, or 20 Years' Residence in Africa*. Englewood Cliffs, NJ: Prentice Hall.)

McMichael, Philip. 1991. "Slavery in Capitalism: The Rise and Demise of the U. S. Antebellum Cotton Culture." *Theory and Society* 20, 3: 321–49.

Miers, Suzanne. 2003. *Slavery in the Twentieth Century: The Evolution of a Global Problem*. Lanham, MD: Altamira.

Miller, Christopher L. 2008. *The French Atlantic Triangle: Literature and Culture of the Slave Trade*. Durham, NC: Duke University Press.

Miller, Joseph C. 1997. "O Atlântico escravista: Açúcar, escravos e engenhos." *Afro-Asia*, nos. 19–20 (1997): 9–36.

———. 2012. *The Problem of Slavery as History: A Global Approach*. New Haven, CT: Yale University Press.

Mintz, Sidney W. 1960. *Worker in the Cane*. New Haven, CT: Yale University Press, New Haven.

Mira Caballos, Esteban. 1997. *El indio antillano: Repartimiento, encomienda y esclavitud (1492–1542)*. Seville: Muñoz Moya Editor.

———. 2000. "El proyecto esclavista de Cristóbal Colón." In Mira Caballos, *Indios y mestizos americanos en la España del siglo XVI*. Frankfurt am Main: Iberoamericana Vervuert, 46–48, 141–43.

Moreno Fraginals, Manuel. 1978. "El mercado ilegal de brazos." In Moreno Fraginals, *El ingenio: Complejo económico social cubano del azúcar*, 3 vols. Havana: Editorial de Ciencias Sociales, 1:269–74.

Morgado García, Arturo. 2010. "Guerra y esclavitud en el Cádiz de la modernidad." In *La esclavitud negroafricana en la historia de España*, edited by Aurelia Martin Casares and Margarita García Barranco, 55–74. Alborote, Spain: Editorial Comares.

———. 2013. *Una metropolí esclavista: El Cádiz de la modernidad.* Granada: Editorial Universidad de Granada.

Muaze, Mariana, and Richard Salles, eds. 2015. *O Vale do Paraíba e o Império do Brasil nos quadros da segunda escravidão.* Rio de Janeiro: 7 Letras.

Nelson, Scott R. 2015. "Who Put Their Capitalism in My Slavery?" *Journal of the Civil War Era* 5, no. 2: 289–310.

Nerín, Gustau. 2015. *Traficants d'ànimes: Els negrers espanyols a l'Àfrica.* Barcelona: Raval Edicions SLU, Pòrtic.

Newman, Simon P. 2013. *A New World of Labor: The Development of Plantation Slavery in the British Atlantic.* Philadelphia: University of Pennsylvania Press.

Obenaus, Andreas. 2013. *Islamische Perspektiven der Atlantikexpansion: Der islamische Atlantikraum des mittelalterlichen Abendlandes.* 2 vols. Vienna: Turia & Kant.

O'Malley, Gregory E. 2014. *Final Passages: The Intercolonial Slave Trade of British America, 1619–1807.* Chapel Hill: University of North Carolina Press.

O'Malley, Gregory E., and Alex Borucki. 2017. "Patterns in the Intercolonial Slave Trade across the Americas before the Nineteenth Century" *Revista Tempo* 23, no. 2: 314–38.

Oostindie, Gerd, and Jessica V. Roitman. 2014. "What Is the 'Dutch Atlantic'?" In *Dutch Atlantic Connections, 1680–1800: Linking Empires, Bridging Borders*, edited by Gerd Oostindie and Jessica V. Roitman, 2–10. Leiden: Brill.

Ortega, José Guadalupe. 2006. "Cuban Merchants, Slave Trade Knowledge, and the Atlantic World, 1790s–1820s." *Colonial Latin American Historical Review* 15, 3: 225–51.

Palmer, Bryan D. 2017. "'Mind Forg'd Manacles' and Recent Pathways to 'New' Labor History." *International Review of Social History* 62, no. 2: 279–303.

Perbi, Akosua Adoma. 2002. "Merchants, Middlemen and Monarchs." In *Merchants, Missionaries, and Migrants: 300 Years of Dutch-Ghanaian Relations*, edited by Ineke van Kessel, 33–41. Amsterdam: KIT, 2002.

Pérez Tostado, Igor, and Enrique García-Hernán. 2012. *Irlanda y el Atlántico ibérico: Movilidad, participación e intercambio cultural (1580–1823).* Madrid: Albatros Ediciones.

Phillips Jr., William D. 2011. "Slavery in the Atlantic Islands and the Early Modern Atlantic World." In *The Cambridge World History of Slavery*, vol. 3, *AD 1420–AD 1804*, edited by David Eltis and Stanley L. Engerman, 325–47. Cambridge: Cambridge University Press.

Piqueras, José Antonio. 2011. *La esclavitud en las Españas: Un lazo transatlántico*. Madrid: Catarata.

———, ed. 2016. *Esclavitud y capitalismo histórico en el siglo XIX: Brasil, Cuba y Estados Unidos*. Santiago de Cuba: Casa del Caribe.

———. 2017. "La plantación esclavista en Cuba: Ensayo de conceptualización y Segunda Esclavitud." In *Plantación, espacios agrarios y esclavitud en la Cuba colonial*, edited by José Antonio Piqueras, 23–55. Castellón de la Plana: Publicacions de la Universitat Jaume I/Casa de las Américas.

Post, Charles. 2011. *The American Road to Capitalism*. Chicago: Haymarket Books.

Postma, Johannes Menne. 1990. *The Dutch in the Atlantic Slave Trade 1600–1815*. Cambridge: Cambridge University Press.

Postma, Johannes Menne, and Victor Enthoven, eds. 2003. *Riches from Atlantic Commerce: Dutch Transatlantic Trade and Shipping, 1585–1817*. Leiden: Brill, 2003.

Pritchard, James. 2004. *In Search of Empire: The French in the Americas 1670–1730*. Cambridge: Cambridge University Press.

Ratelband, Klaas. 2003. *Os holandeses no Brasil e na costa Africana: Angola, Kongo e São Tomé, 1600–1650*. Lisbon: Vega.

Rediker, Marcus. 2007. *The Slave Ship: A Human History*. New York: Viking.

Reis, João, Flávio dos Santos Gomes, and Marcus J. M. de Carvalho, 2010. *O alufá Rufino: Tráfico, escravidão e liberdade no Atlântico Negro (c. 1822—c. 1853)*. São Paulo: Companhia das Letras.

Reséndez, Andrés. 2016. *The Other Slavery: The Uncovered Story of Indian Enslavement in America*. Boston: Houghton Mifflin Harcourt.

Rockman, Seth. 2006a. *Scraping By: Wage Labor, Slavery, and Survival in Early Baltimore*. Baltimore: Johns Hopkins University Press.

———. 2006b. "The Unfree Origins of American Capitalism." In *The Economy of Early America: Historical Perspectives and New Directions*, edited by Cathy Matson, 335–61. University Park: Pennsylvania State University Press.

———. 2012. "The Future of Civil War Era Studies: Slavery and Capitalism." *Journal of the Civil War Era*, no. 2. http://journalofthecivilwarera.com/forum-the-future-of-civil-war-era-studies/the-future-of-civil-war-era-studies-slavery-and-capitalism (accessed March 18, 2014).

Rodrigo y Alharilla, Martín. 2007. "Navieras y navieros catalanes en los primeros tiempos del vapor 1830–1870." *Transportes, Servicios y Telecomunicaciones*, no. 13: 62–92.

———. 2013. "De la esclavitud al cosmopolitismo: Tomás Terry Adán y su familia." In *Afroamérica, espacios e identidades*, edited by Javier Laviña, Ricardo Piqueras, and Cristina Mondejar, 93–119. Barcelona: Icaria Editorial.

Rodrigo y Alharilla, Martín, and Lizbeth J. Chaviano, eds. 2017. *Negreros y esclavos: Barcelona y la esclavitud atlántica (siglos XVI–XIX)*. Barcelona: Icaria Editorial.

Rodrigues, Jaime. 2005. *De costa a costa: Escravos, marinheiros e intermediarios do tráfico negreiro de Angola ao Rio de Janeiro.* São Paulo: Companhia das Letras.

Rood, Daniel. 2017. *The Reinvention of Atlantic Slavery: Technology, Labor, Race, and Capitalism in the Greater Caribbean.* New York: Oxford University Press.

Rossum, Matthias van. 2021, forthcoming. "Slavery and Its Transformations: Prolegomena for a Global and Comparative Research Agenda." CSSH.

Rossum, Matthias van, and Karwan Fatah-Black. 2012. "Wat is winst? De economische impact van de Nederlandse trans-Atlantische slavenhandel." *Tijdschrift voor Sociale en Economische Geschiedenis* 9, no. 1: 3–29.

Salvador, José Gonçalves. 1981. *Os magnatas do tráfico negreiro.* São Paulo: Pioneira/Edusp.

Sánchez, Jean-Noël. 2015. "Autour d'une source: De l'esclavage aux Philippines, XVIe-XVIIe siècles." *Source(s): Arts, Civilisation et Histoire de l'Europe* 7, no. 2: 95–172.

Santana Pérez, Germán. 2014. "El África Atlántica: La construcción de la historia atlántica desde la aportación africana." *Vegueta: Anuario de la Facultad de Geografía e Historia,* no. 14, 11–25.

Santos-Granero, Fernando. 2018. "Slavery as Structure, Process, or Lived Experience, or Why Slave Societies Existed in Precontact Tropical America." In *What Is a Slave Society? The Practice of Slavery in Global Perspective,* edited by Noel Lenski and Catherine M. Cameron, 191–219. Cambridge: Cambridge University Press.

Sanz, Vicent, and Michael Zeuske. 2017. "Microhistoria de esclavos y esclavas." In *Millars: Espai i Història* 42, no. 1, edited by Vicent Sanz and Michael Zeuske (número monográfico dedicado a "Microhistoria de esclavas y esclavos"), 9–21.

Sheriff, Abdul. 1987. *Slaves, Spices, and Ivory in Zanzibar: The Integration of an East African Commercial Empire into the World Economy, 1770–1872.* London: James Currey.

Schermerhorn, Calvin. 2014. "Capitalism's Captives: The Maritime United States Slave Trade, 1807–1850." *Journal of Social History* 47, no. 4: 897–921.

Schermerhorn, Calvin. 2015a. *The Business of Slavery and the Rise of American Capitalism, 1815–1860.* New Haven, CT: Yale University Press.

Schermerhorn, Calvin. 2015b. "Slave Trading in a Republic of Credit: Financial Architecture of the United States Slave Market, 1815–1840." *Slavery & Abolition* 36, no. 3: 586–602.

Schnakenbourg, Eric. 2013. "Sweden and the Atlantic: The Dynamism of Sweden's Colonial Projects in the Eighteenth Century." In *Scandinavian Colonialism and the Rise of Modernity: Small Time Agents in a Global Arena,* edited by Magdalena Naum and Jonas M. Nordin, 229–42. New York: Springer

Schneider, Elena. 2015. "African Slavery and Spanish Empire." *Journal of Early American History* 5, no. 1: 3–29.

Schwarz, Suzanne, ed. 2008. *Slave Captain: The Career of James Irving in the Liverpool Slave Trade.* Liverpool: Liverpool University Press.

Scott, Rebecca J. 1985. *Slave Emancipation in Cuba: The Transition to Free Labor, 1860–1899.* Princeton, NJ: Princeton University Press. Reprinted, 2000, Pittsburgh: University of Pittsburgh Press.

———. 2000. "Small-Scale Dynamics of Large-Scale Processes." *American Historical Review* 105, no. 2: 472–79.

———. 2005. *Degrees of Freedom: Louisiana and Cuba after Slavery.* Cambridge, MA: Belknap Press of Harvard University Press (Spanish: Scott, Rebecca J. 2006. *Grados de libertad: Cuba y Louisiana después de la esclavitud.* Havana: Editorial de Ciencias Sociales.)

———. 2011. "Slavery and the Law in Atlantic Perspective: Jurisdiction, Jurisprudence, and Justice." *Law and History Review* 29, no. 4: 915–24.

———. 2012. "Under Color of Law: Siliadin v. France and the Dynamics of Enslavement in Historical Perspective." In *The Legal Understanding of Slavery: From the Historical to the Contemporary*, edited by Jean Allain, 152–64. Oxford, UK: Oxford University Press.

———. 2017. "Reclamando la mula de Gregoria Quesada: El significado de la libertad en los valles del Arimao y del Caunao, Cienfuegos, Cuba (1880–1899)." In *Millars: Espai i Història* 42, no. 1, edited by Vicent Sanz and Michael Zeuske (número monográfico dedicado a "Microhistoria de esclavas y esclavos"), 101–29.

Scott, Rebecca J., and Jean-Michel Hébrard. 2011. "One Woman, Three Revolutions: Rosalie of the Poulard Nation." In *Revolution! The Atlantic World Reborn*, edited by Thomas Bender, Laurent Dubois, and Thomas Richard Rabinowitz, 199–220. London: Antique Collectors Club.

———. 2012. *Freedom Papers: An Atlantic Odyssey in the Age of Emancipation.* Cambridge, MA: Harvard University Press.

Scott, Rebecca J., and Michael Zeuske. 2004. "Le 'droit d'avoir des droits': Les revendications des ex-esclaves à Cuba (1872–1909)." *Annales HSS*, no. 3: 521–45.

Seibert, Gerhard. 2013. "São Tomé & Príncipe: The First Plantation Economy in the Tropics." In *Commercial Agriculture, the Slave Trade and Slavery in Atlantic Africa*, edited by Robin Law, Suzanne Schwarz, and Silke Strickrodt, 54–78. London: James Currey.

Seijas, Tatiana. 2008. "The Portuguese Slave Trade to Spanish Manila: 1580–1640." In *Itinerario: International Journal on the History of European Expansion and Global Interaction*, no. 32: 19–38.

———. 2014. *Asian Slaves in Colonial Mexico: From Chinos to Indians.* New York: Cambridge University Press.

Shumway, Rebecca. 2011. *The Fante and the Transatlantic Slave Trade.* Rochester, NY: University of Rochester Press.

Shy, John. 1976. "Hearts and Minds in the American Revolution: The Case of 'Long Bill' Scott and Peterborough, New Hampshire." In Shy, *A People Numerous and Armed: Reflections on the Military Struggle for American Independence.* New York: Oxford University Press, 165–79.

Silva, Alberto da Costa e. 2004a. "Africa—Brazil—Africa during the Era of the Slave Trade." In *Enslaving Connections: Changing Cultures of Africa and Brazil during the Era of Slavery*, edited by José C. Curto and Paul E. Lovejoy, 21–28. New York: Humanity Books.

———. 2004b. *Francisco Félix de Souza: Mercador de escravos*. Rio de Janeiro: Editora Nova Fronteira/Ed. Uerj.

Silva Jr., Carlos. 2012. "Tráfico, escravidão e comércio em Salvador do século XVIII: A vida de Francisco Gonçalves Dantas (1699–1738)." In *Escravidão e suas sombras*, edited by José Reis and Elciene Azevedo, 143–85. Salvador, Brazil: EDUFBa (Federal University of Bahia Press).

Silva, Daniel B. Domingues da. 2017. "The Slave Trade and the Development of the Atlantic Africa Port System, 1400s–1800s." *International Journal of Maritime History* 29, no. 1: 138–54.

Sluyter, Andrew. 2010. "The Hispanic Atlantic's Tasajo Trail." *Latin American Research Review* 45, no. 1: 98–120.

———. 2012. *Black Ranching Frontiers: African Cattle Herders of the Atlantic World, 1500–1900*. New Haven, CT: Yale University Press.

Solow, Barbara L., ed. 1991. *Slavery and the Rise of the Atlantic System*. Cambridge: Cambridge University Press.

Sosa Rodríguez, Enrique. 1998. *Negreros, catalanes y gaditanos en la trata cubana 1827–1833*. Havana: Fundación Fernando Ortiz.

Soule, Emily B. 2018. "From Africa to the Ocean Sea: Atlantic Slavery in the Origins of the Spanish Empire." *Atlantic Studies* 15, no. 1: 16–39.

Surwillo, Lisa. 2014. *Monsters by Trade: Slave Traffickers in Modern Spanish Literature and Culture*. Stanford, CA: Stanford University Press.

Sweet, James H. 2003. "The Slave Trade in the Portuguese Colonial World, 1441–1700." In Sweet, *Recreating Africa: Culture, Kingship, and Religion in the African-Portuguese World, 1441–1770*. Chapel Hill: University of North Carolina Press, 15–22.

———. 2009. "The Subject of the Slave Trade: Recent Currents in the Histories of the Atlantic, Great Britain, and Western Africa." *Early American Studies* 7, no. 1: 1–45.

Thornton, John K. 1998. *Africa and the Africans in the Making of the Atlantic World, 1400–1880*. Cambridge: Cambridge University Press.

———. 2012. *A Cultural History of the Atlantic World, 1350–1820*. Cambridge: Cambridge University Press.

Tomich, Dale W. 1988. "The 'Second Slavery': Bonded Labor and the Transformations of the Nineteenth-Century World Economy." In *Rethinking the Nineteenth Century: Contradictions and Movement*, edited by Francisco O. Ramírez, 103–117. New York: Greenwood.

———. 2003. "The Wealth of the Empire: Francisco de Arango y Parreño, Political Economy, and the Second Slavery in Cuba." *Comparative Studies in Society and History*, no. 1: 4–28.

———. 2004a. "O Atlântico como Espaço Histórico." Special issue, *Estudos AfroAsiáticos* 26, no. 2: 221–40.

———. 2004b. *Through the Prism of Slavery: Labor, Capital, and World Economy*. Lanham, MD: Rowman & Littlefield.

———. 2015. "Commodity Frontiers, Spatial Economy and Technological Innovation in the Caribbean Sugar Industry, 1783–1878." In *The Caribbean and the Atlantic World Economy: Circuits of Trade, Money and Knowledge, 1650–1914*, edited by Adrian Leonard and David Pretel, 184–216. London: Palgrave Macmillan.

———, ed. 2016. *New Frontiers of Slavery*. Albany: State University of New York Press.

———, ed. 2017. *Slavery and Historical Capitalism during the Nineteenth Century*. Lanham, MD: Lexington Books.

———. 2018. "The Second Slavery and World Capitalism: A Perspective for Historical Inquiry." *International Review of Social History* 63, no. 3: 477–501.

Tomich, Dale W., and Reinaldo Funes Monzote. 2009. "Naturaleza, tecnología y esclavitud en Cuba: Frontera azucarera y Revolución industrial, 1815–1870." In *Trabajo libre y trabajo coactivo ensociedades de plantación*, edited by José Antonio Piqueras, 75–117. Madrid: Siglo XXI de España.

Tomich, Dale W., and Michael Zeuske. 2008. "The Second Slavery: Mass Slavery, World Economy and Comparative Microhistories." *Review: A Journal of the Fernand Braudel Center* 31, no. 3: 91–100.

———, eds. 2009. "The Second Slavery: Mass Slavery, World-Economy, and Comparative Microhistories." Special issue, *Review: A Journal of the Fernand Braudel Center* 31, nos. 2–3.

Turgeon, Laurier. 2009. "Codfish, Consumption, and Colonization: The Creation of the French Atlantic World during the Sixteenth Century." In *Bridging the Early Modern Atlantic World: People, Products, and Practices on the Move*, edited by Caroline A. Williams, 33–56. Farnham, Surrey, UK: Ashgate.

Vansina, Jan. 2005. "Ambaca Society and the Slave Trade, c. 1760–1845." *Journal of African History* 46, no. 1: 1–27.

Vieira, Alberto. 1995. "La isla de Madeira y el tráfico negrero en el siglo XVI." *Revista de Indias* 55, no. 204: 333–56.

———. 2004. "Sugar Islands: The Sugar Economy of Madeira and the Canaries, 1450–1650." In *Tropical Babylons: Sugar and the Making of the Atlantic World, 1450–1680*, edited by Stuart B. Schwartz, 42–84. Chapel Hill: University of North Carolina Press.

Viña Brito, Ana. 2006. "Canarias en el comercio atlántico de esclavos." *Esclavos*, Archivo Histórico Provincial de Santa Cruz de Tenerife, 15–25. Santa Cruz de Tenerife: Gobierno de Canarias, Consejería de Educación, Cultura y Deportes. Dirección General del Libro, Archivos y Bibliotecas (Documentos para la Historia de Canarias, vol. 8).

Vries, Jan de. 2005. "The Dutch Atlantic Economies." In *The Atlantic Economy during the Seventeenth and Eighteenth Centuries: Organization, Operation, Practice, and Personnel*, edited by Peter A. Coclanis, 1–29. Columbia: University of South Carolina Press.

Weaver, Jace. 2014. *The Red Atlantic: American Indigenes and the Making of the Modern World, 1000–1927.* Chapel Hill: University of North Carolina Press.

Weber, Klaus. 2004. *Deutsche Kaufleute im Atlantikhandel 1680–1830: Unternehmen und Familien in Hamburg, Cádiz und Bordeaux.* Munich: C. H. Beck.

Welie, Rik van. 2008. "Slave Trading and Slavery in the Dutch Colonial Empire: A Global Comparison." *New West Indian Guide/Nieuw West-Indische Gids* 82, nos. 1–2: 45–94.

Wheat, David. 2016. *Atlantic Africa and the Spanish Caribbean, 1570–1640.* Chapel Hill: University of North Carolina Press.

Williams, Eric. 1994. *Capitalism and Slavery.* Chapel Hill: University of North Carolina Press. First published 1944.

Wimmler, Jutta. 2012. *Centralized African States in the Transatlantic Slave Trade: The Example of 18th Century Asante and Dahomey.* Graz, Austria: Leykam.

———. 2017. *The Sun King's Atlantic: Drugs, Demons and Dyestuffs in the Atlantic World, 1640–1730.* Leiden: Brill.

Wirz, Albert. 1984. *Sklaverei und kapitalistisches Weltsystem*, Frankfurt am Main: Suhrkamp.

Zeuske. Michael. 2002a. "Hidden Markers, Open Secrets: On Naming, Race Marking and Race Making in Cuba." *New West Indian Guide/Nieuwe West-Indische Gids* 76, nos. 3–4: 235–66.

———. 2002b. "Estructuras e identidad en la 'segunda esclavitud': El caso cubano, 1800–1940." *Historia Crítica: Revista del Departamento de Historia de la Facultad de Ciencias Sociales de la Universidad de los Andes*, no. 24: 125–40.

———. 2004. "Einleitung." In Zeuske, *Schwarze Karibik: Sklaven, Sklavereikulturen und Emanzipation.* Zürich: Rotpunktverlag, 11–41.

———. 2006a. "Atlantik, Sklaven und Sklaverei: Elemente einer neuen Globalgeschichte." *Jahrbuch für Geschichte der Europäischen Expansion*, no. 6: 9–44.

———. 2006b. *Sklaven und Sklaverei in den Welten des Atlantiks, 1400–1940: Umrisse, Anfänge, Akteure, Vergleichsfelder und Bibliografien.* Münster: LIT Verlag.

———. 2010. "Mongos und Negreros: Atlantische Sklavenhändler im 19. Jahrhundert und der iberische Sklavenhandel 1808/1820–1873." *Periplus: Jahrbuch für außereuropäische Geschichte*, no. 20, 57–116.

———. 2012. "Historiography and Research Problems of Slavery and the Slave Trade in a Global-Historical Perspective." *International Review of Social History* 57, no. 1: 87–111.

———. 2013a. "Historiografie und Forschungsprobleme in globalhistorischer Perspektive." In Zeuske, *Handbuch Geschichte der Sklaverei: Eine Globalgeschichte von den Anfängen bis zur Gegenwart*. Berlin: De Gruyter, 27–96.

———. 2013b. "Zentrale Themen und Theorien." In Zeuske, *Handbuch Geschichte der Sklaverei: Eine Globalgeschichte von den Anfängen bis zur Gegenwart*. Berlin: De Gruyter, 51–63.

———. 2014a. *Amistad: A Hidden Network of Slavers and Merchants*. Princeton, NJ: Markus Wiener.

———. 2014b. "Rethinking the Case of the Schooner *Amistad*: Contraband and Complicity after 1808/1820." *Slavery & Abolition* 35, no. 1: 156–64.

———. 2014c. "The Second Slavery: Modernity, Mobility, and Identity of Captives in Nineteenth-Century Cuba and the Atlantic World." In *The Second Slavery: Mass Slaveries and Modernity in the Americas and in the Atlantic Basin*, edited by Javier Laviña and Michael Zeuske, 113–42. Berlin: LIT Verlag.

———. 2015a. "Historiografische Skizze zur Geschichte der Sklavenhändler." In Zeuske, *Sklavenhändler, Negreros und Atlantikkreolen: Eine Weltgeschichte des Sklavenhandels im atlantischen Raum*. Berlin: De Gruyter, 49–54.

———. 2015b. "*Slaving*: Traumata und Erinnerung der Verschleppung." In Zeuske, *Sklavenhändler, Negreros und Atlantikkreolen*, 55–100.

———. 2015c. "Atlantikkreolen, Leben auf und am Atlantik sowie *beyond the Atlantic*." In Zeuske, *Sklavenhändler, Negreros und Atlantikkreolen*, 172–205.

———. 2015d. "Versklavte, Sklavereien und Menschenhandel auf dem afrikanisch-iberischen Atlantik." In Zeuske, *Sklavenhändler, Negreros und Atlantikkreolen*, 296–364.

———. 2015e. "*Atlantic Slavery* und Wirtschaftskultur in welt- und globalhistorischer Perspektive." *Geschichte in Wissenschaft und Unterricht* 66, nos. 5–6: 280–301.

———. 2015f. "The French Revolution in Spanish America: With Some Reflections on Manfred Kossok as Marxist Historian of 'Bourgeois Revolutions.' " *Review: A Journal of the Fernand Braudel Center* 38, nos. 1–2: 99–145.

———. 2016a. "Cosmopolites of the Hidden Atlantic: The 'Africans' Daniel Botefeur and His Personal Slave Robin Botefeur in Cuba/"Cosmopolitas del Atlántico esclavista: Los 'africanos' Daniel Botefeur y su esclavos de confianza Robin Botefeur en Cuba." *Almanack*, no. 12: 129–55.

———. 2016b. "Karl Marx, Sklaverei, Formationstheorie, ursprüngliche Akkumulation und Global South." In *Marx und der globale Süden*, edited by Felix Wemheuer, 96–144. Cologne: PapyRossa Verlag.

———. 2016c. "Die Nicht-Geschichte von Versklavten als Archiv-Geschichte von 'Stimmen' und 'Körpern.' " *Jahrbuch für Europäische Überseegeschichte*, no. 16: 65–114.

———. 2016d. "Coolies—Asiáticos and Chinos: Global Dimensions of Second Slavery." In *Bonded Labour: Global and Comparative Perspectives (18th–21st Century)*, edited by

Sabine Damir-Geilsdorf, Ulrike Lindner, Gesine Müller, Oliver Tappe, and Michael Zeuske, 35–57. Bielefeld: transcript Verlag.

———. 2017. "Microhistorias de vida y Hidden Atlantic: Los 'africanos' Daniel Botefeur y Robin Botefeur en África, en el Atlántico y en Cuba/ Life Microhistories and Hidden Atlantic: The 'Africans' Daniel Botefeur and Robin Botefeur in Africa, the Atlantic, and Cuba." In *Millars: Espai i Història* 42, no. 1, edited by Vicent Sanz and Michael Zeuske (número monográfico dedicado a "Microhistoria de esclavas y esclavos"), 151–91.

———. 2018a. "Drittes Sklavereiplateau (Beginn etwa 1400 n. Chr.)." In Zeuske, *Sklaverei: Eine Menschheitsgeschichte von den Anfängen bis heute*. Stuttgart: Reclam, 79–119.

———. 2018b. "Kein Ende nach dem Ende: Diskurse und Realitäen der globalen Sklaverei seit 1800." In Zeuske, *Sklaverei*, 212–44.

———. 2018c. "Out of the Americas: Slave Traders and the Hidden Atlantic in the Nineteenth Century." *Atlantic Studies* 15, 1: 103–35.

———. 2019a. *Handbuch Geschichte der Sklaverei: Eine Globalgeschichte von den Anfängen bis zur Gegenwart*. Rev. ed., 2 vols. Berlin: De Gruyter.

———. 2019b. "Kolumbus als Sklavenhändler und der Kapitalismus menschlicher Körper." In *Romanistik in Rostock: Beiträge zum 600. Universitätsjubiläum*, edited by Rafael Arnold, Albrecht Buschmann, Steffi Morkötter, and Stephanie Wodianka, 11–36. Norderstedt, Germany: BoD

———. 2019c. "2019 Hidden Atlantic Atlántico oculto (august agosto)." http://www.academia.edu/40119218/2019_Hidden_Atlantic_Atl%C3%A1ntico_oculto (accessed September 7, 2019).

———. 2021, forthcoming. *Der afrikanisch-iberische Atlantik: Eine Handelsgeschichte 1400–1900*.

Zeuske, Michael, and Orlando García Martínez. 2009. "*La Amistad* de Cuba: Ramón Ferrer, contrabando de esclavos, captividad y modernidad atlántica." *Caribbean Studies* 37, no. 1: 97–170.

———. 2013. *La sublevación esclava en la goleta Amistad: Ramón Ferrer y las redes de contrabando en el mundo Atlántico*. Havana: Ediciones UNIÓN.

Chapter 5

The Commodification of Freedom in Cuba during Second Slavery

Henry B. Lovejoy[1]

During the economic and political restructuring of the world-economy in the midst of the Industrial Revolution, new zones of slavery emerged, most especially around the production of cotton in the southern United States, coffee in Brazil, and sugar in Cuba. This period, known as *second slavery*, demonstrates how chattel slavery adapted, transformed, and expanded with the advent of industrial capitalism, modern political regimes, and liberal ideologies (Tomich 2004; Tomich and Zeuske 2008). The reorganization of a major labor force overlapped with the period known as the "Age of Revolution," whereby the intellectual and philosophical movement of the Enlightenment—which advanced ideologies related to reason, liberalism, liberty, independence, and human rights—directly resulted in the transformation from monarchial rule to constitutional states or republics in Europe and the Americas, as well as the formation of states in West Africa as a result of jihad. The concept of the second slavery, however, requires some critique because analysis of the transformation of the global institution of slavery tends to overlook the experiences of the millions of individuals and their descendants who involuntarily became the labor force of large-scale cotton, coffee, and sugar production in the Americas. This chapter, therefore, examines from a microeconomic and personal-finance perspective how an emerging capitalist structure in Cuba meant slave-owners permitted self-manumission programs as a means by which to manage the risk of their human capital, incentivize productivity, and avoid paying for long-term healthcare. As a result, groups of enslaved Africans organized along ethnic lines and incorporated traditional West African savings, credit, and banking institutions to pool their money together in order to buy their freedom, and in some cases, return to Africa.

The case study under analysis relates to a group of seventy self-emancipated Africans and their Cuban-born descendants whom British abolitionists and missionaries documented in England in 1854 and 1855. These families were traveling from Havana, where they had been slaves, to Abeokuta, a city in what is now modern-day Nigeria. The majority of these men, women, and children were "Lucumí," which was a colonial designation that slave traders generally labeled people arriving to Cuba from the Bight of Benin hinterland and who spoke the Yoruba language. This group of Lucumí returned to Africa in two phases, and to avoid being reenslaved, they went via England on British ships. The first group of eleven men, eight women, and four children arrived in Southampton via the island of Saint Thomas in June 1854, where they spent over three weeks before taking another ship to Lagos. The second group of fourteen men, twelve women, and twenty-one children arrived in London in July 1855, and after spending a few days there, they were relocated to Plymouth for over a month, also before going on to Lagos (Anon. (a) 1854; Anon. (b) 1855; Anon. (c) 1855). Lydia Prideaux, a charitable widow from Plymouth, recorded the story of the second group, and out of curiosity she read out a list of names from the first group. Through an interpreter, several people maintained that "they were *all* their friends; some were their Relations." They also stated how they were going to "the 'Land of Lucomi' [by which] they seem to mean the territory behind Lagos to a considerable extent." In Prideaux's attempts to learn more about these former Cuban slaves, she mentioned Abeokuta from another missionary report, at which point people began shouting, " 'Abbeokuta!' 'Oh Abbeokuta.' '*Me* Abbeokuta,' said one; 'Me Abbeokuta,' said another. 'Todos Abbeokuta.' "[2] This reaction implied that in both groups all planned on going to this West African city, which emerged as a major refugee center during the jihad and wars associated with the collapse of the Kingdom of Oyo between 1817 and 1836 (figures 5.1 and 5.2).

This circum-Atlantic movement of people from Africa to Cuba to England and back to Africa raises questions about how a Yoruba-speaking community raised enough money in a slave society to buy their freedom and pay for their voyage home. Most of the forty-three African-born adults in this migration had left

Figure 5.1. Group of *emancipados*, sketched from life. Source: Courtesy of the Hampshire Archives England, 16M97/13/11, 4.

Figure 5.2. The *emancipados* at Plymouth. Source: Courtesy of the Hampshire Archives England, 16M97/13/11, 10.

Africa in the 1820s and 1830s. This chronology demonstrates how people had been enslaved during Oyo's collapse, and before they left the coast of the Bight of Benin they had probably never been to Abeokuta, which formed as a new urban center. During their time in Cuba as slaves, which ranged from about ten to forty years, these friends and families accumulated in excess of $25,000 to pay for their collective freedom and tickets to Africa via England.[3] Their story was even more remarkable considering that the highest wage they could earn was "twelve dollars a week," while average salaries hovered around "seven dollars per week."[4] Regardless, these people rarely received a full income because slave masters were often entitled to or stole any money generated by the people they owned. This chapter provides a close analysis of the individual finances, expenditures, and traditional saving mechanisms that this group of enslaved Africans utilized to raise enough capital to return to West Africa.

More puzzling is the regularity with which masters allowed their slaves to buy their own freedom. In Cuba self-emancipation occurred with considerable regularity during the period of second slavery. Alexander von Humboldt, a Prussian geographer who wrote about his travels to the island in the first decade of the nineteenth century, observed how "nowhere in the world where slavery reigns [were] manumissions as frequent as on the island of Cuba" (1826, 79). By mid-century British abolitionists of the Anti-Slavery Society recognized how Cuban slave-owners provided "slaves certain rights," such as their "right to demand a change of masters, [and] to manumit themselves on payment of a certain sum, fixed by the Government" (Anon. (a) 1854, 234). In this process of gradual self-purchase, called *coartación*, the master and slave agreed upon a manumission price, which sometimes resulted in enslaved people filing lawsuits against their masters, who often tried to set the price higher than market value. Once a price became "fixed," it theoretically could not be adjusted even if the value of a slave increased or decreased thereafter. As soon as an enslaved person made the initial down payment on themselves, they became known as a *coartada/coartado*, and then they paid off the debt toward their freedom in installments. Moreover, if the owners rented or hired out their slave, the *coartada/o* had a right to earn the percentage of the rental fee paid commensurate with the share of themselves they owned (Humboldt 1826; Bergad, Iglesias Garcia, and Carmen Barcia 1995; de la Fuente 2007; Obrando Andrade 2011; Salmoral 1999; Varella 2012).

Arguably, the *coartación* system motivated enslaved people to work harder during their prime working years, while slave-owners reduced the risk of violent resistance with promises of freedom. In addition, unregulated rules and unsupervised loan repayments also meant the masters dictated when an enslaved individual actually became free. As a result, self-manumission generally occurred after prime working years when productivity decreased and healthcare costs steadily increased. Among the returnees to Abeokuta, the cost of freedom "varied from 300 to 1,000 dollars" per adult, and children "had been included in the redemption price of the mothers" (Anon. (c) 1855, 245). In addition, tickets to England cost $100 for adults and $50 for children.[5] In most cases, therefore, the path to freedom, and passage back to Africa, required "more than twenty years labour" (Anon. (b) 1855: 268). While the slave-owning classes benefited from this scheme, the enslaved population recognized how the *coartación* process was a lengthy endeavor, which required strategic financial planning for people earning just fractions of an annual salary between $300 and $650 per year. In this microhistorical case study, evidence affirms how Yoruba, likely from the Egba subgroup, organized along ethnic lines to establish and operate traditional African savings, credit, and banking institutions called *esusu* and *ajo*. In Havana they pooled the little money they could earn, and by engaging in rotating credit and savings associations effectively, these Lucumí raised substantial capital with a little help from the lottery to subsidize their freedom and return home.

Egba in Diaspora

Before discussing the saving mechanisms of enslaved Africans in Cuba, it is necessary to establish when and where these people came from in Africa. Ethnic solidarity played a major role in the ability of these people to raise capital to buy freedom and return to Africa. In Cuba they were classified as "Lucumí," which, as noted, was a colonial designation that relates to "Yoruba." Even though "Yoruba" has been applied retroactively in the historiography, people who call themselves "Yoruba" today never referred to themselves as such before the mid-nineteenth century. They adopted this ethnonym to identify themselves once former slaves and their descendants, especially from Brazil, Cuba, and Sierra Leone, began returning to the Bight of Benin interior (Matory 2005; McKenzie 1997; Peel 2000; Sarracino 1988; Verger 1968, 1977). Within West Africa, speakers of Hausa, Kanuri, Songhay, and by extension Arabic used the term Yarabawa (يرب) to refer to people who spoke the Yoruba language since at least the sixteenth century, if not earlier (Bābā

1615; H. B. Lovejoy and Ojo 2015). In the Americas, people who boarded slave ships came to be known variably as "Lucumí," "Terranova," "Nagô," and eventually "Yoruba" depending on the period and colony in question. And in Freetown during British campaigns to suppress the Atlantic slave trade after 1807, they were also called "Aku" (Falola and Childs 2004; Law 1997; H. B. Lovejoy and Ojo 2015; Peel 2000). As a case in point, British abolitionists and missionaries wrestled with how to refer to these people as a distinct ethnolinguistic group. In 1855 the *Plymouth Herald* published this description of the "Lucumí" in England: "All but one [were] Yorubas, speaking the Aku language, from the Lucome land, behind Lagos, Bight of Benin."[6]

Before Yoruba became a widely accepted term of self-ascription as ethnicity, people who spoke the Yoruba language generally identified with their hometowns, which resided within major political entities such as Oyo, Egba, Ife, Ijebu, or Owu to name but a few. These subgroups continue to be used as a means to differentiate among the diverse people known as "Yoruba" today. Other identifiable characteristics of "Yoruba" identity centered on the worship of a pantheon of gods, called *orisa*. According to the *Encyclopedia of the Yoruba*, there are 401 deities in this pantheon, "although that figure should be viewed as a sacred metaphor and not a scientific fact" (Falola and Akinyemi 2016, 84). Belief tended to focus on one deity within a complex "cluster of sacred symbols" (Pemberton 1977, 5). In Plymouth in 1855, Prideaux observed how the former Cuban slaves were curious about "the difference between the Roman Catholic and the Protestant Religion." One woman wore a necklace of "red and white beads," which symbolized the colors of Sango, the principal deity worshipped within Oyo's sphere of influence (Tishken, Falola, and Akinyemi 2009).[7]

The Kingdom of Oyo dominated the Bight of Benin hinterland in the eighteenth century. Its initial development is usually attributed to the strategic location of its capital, also known as Oyo (or Katunga in Hausa and Kanuri), along major trade routes near the Niger River almost 150 miles inland from the coast. Oyo participated in the trans-savannah trade from Gonja northward to the Hausa states, primarily in cowrie shells, kola nuts, salt, textiles, and slaves; and eventually firearms, iron products, and manufactured goods from Europe. Oyo's sizable military, famous for its cavalry, facilitated commercial expansion and imperial conquest (Law 1977; P. E. Lovejoy 1980). At the kingdom's height ca. 1780, Oyo's population was close to one million people, and the total area was around 18,000 square miles (Law 1977, 90; Lloyd 1971, 3). In comparison, the island of Cuba, which was just over 42,000 square miles, had an approximate population of 275,000 in the late eighteenth century (Kiple 1976, table 1).

The mass arrival of Yoruba speakers to Cuba during the 1820s and 1830s coincided with Oyo's collapse between 1817 and 1836. The kingdom disintegrated because of jihad emanating from the Sokoto Caliphate and a complex series of wars and shifting alliances among Oyo's tributaries and other nontributary kingdoms, whether "Yoruba" or not. Because of the displacement of people in the region, refugee settlements formed new cities, such as Abeokuta. As the frontiers of Sokoto extended more widely, Oyo ended with the abandonment of its capital city by ca. 1836 (Law 1977; P. E. Lovejoy 2016). During this nineteen-year period, an estimated 120,000 people boarded slave ships; 40 percent each went to Brazil and Cuba, another 15 percent went to Sierra Leone, and the remainder scattered throughout the Caribbean (Eltis 2019). Out of an estimated 48,000 enslaved people leaving the Bight of Benin for Cuba between 1817 and 1836, over 35,000 had been directly involved in the jihad and wars associated with Oyo's collapse (H. B. Lovejoy 2018, ch. 6). Among the former Cuban slaves returning to Africa via England in the 1850s, the majority arrived to Cuba in the 1820s and 1830s.

The strong desire of Lucumí in England to identify with Abeokuta requires special consideration. Robin Law has summarized how in the wake of the Muslim uprising in the eastern Oyo town of Ilorin in 1817, Oyo fell into civil war over a constitutional crisis, whereby "its tributaries in the west were falling away." At the same time, another series of wars in the south were being waged to destroy Oyo's main ally, the Kingdom of Owu. After the destruction of Owu in 1822, an Ife and Ijebu alliance invaded and destroyed all the old Egba towns one by one, whereby the Egba "rallied and established a new city at Abeokuta" (1977, 273–75). Before this westward resettlement of refugees, it is worth noting that Egba was not a centralized state, but rather "a loose confederation" of "some 150 small towns and villages [that] came together in the single city of Abeokuta in around 1830" (Law, 137). Initially Egba consisted of three provinces: the Egba Agura (Gbagura), the Egba Alake, and the Egbs Oke Ona. Up until 1830 this confederacy paid tributes to Oyo; hence most Egba revered Sango as their principal deity of worship (see also Ajiṣafẹ 1912; Biobaku 1965; S. Johnson 1921, 17).

Even though members of the first group in Southampton claimed to be "natives of Lagos," much like the definition for "Land of Lucomí" recorded in Plymouth in 1855, references to "Lagos" almost certainly meant the territory behind the port city to a considerable extent. According to Prideaux's report from Plymouth in

1855, these people "wished to go to Lagos, when they could quickly get to their own Country, which they called 'Lucomi.' "[8] Olatunji Ojo has correctly pointed out that after the British occupied Lagos in 1851, many "Yoruba" in diaspora began to idolize the place as "another Freetown," and a "no man's land" where residents were immune to some of the cultural encumbrances associated with towns in the hinterland" (2015, 14). In Southampton, Lorenzo Clarke stated that as "a native of Lagos" he was "brought from Lagos in the brig *Negrito*." In 1832, however, the British captured and escorted this ship to the Anglo-Spanish mixed commission operating in Havana. According to trial records, including the testimony of the ship's captain, the *Negrito* left from the port of Ouidah, not Lagos.[9]

Transcontinental stories about Abeokuta appealed to former slaves and liberated Africans returning to Africa. Clarke stated how he knew he would find his family upon his return "because he has heard of them quite recently through some new slaves" (Anon. (a) 1854, 234–35). Arguably, former Cuban slaves in England wanted to go to Abeokuta because they had heard about it as a refugee settlement. According to Saburi O. Biobaku, the town had an "open-door" policy, and in addition to Egba, Owu formed the second-largest group of people who resettled there (1965, 18). Clarke's deposition from 1854 was especially unique because he recalled that the mixed commission entered his African name "in a book," and a register for 477 Africans removed from the *Negrito* has survived (Anon. (a) 1854, 234–35). Lorenzo's Yoruba name was Ocusona, and he identified as "Lucumí Elló," which was a colonial reference to Oyo.[10] Several Yoruba speakers have interpreted this transliterated African name to conclude independently from one another that it translates in Yoruba as Okusono, which means "death has created beauty." This particular name revealed a more precise ethnic dimension because Egba and Ijebu subgroups use "oku" only as a prefix in personal names (Nwokeji and Eltis 2002).[11] This evidence demonstrates how Okusono was more likely than not Egba for two main reasons: (1) Ijebu historically never paid tributes to Oyo, while Egba did, and (2) most of the Lucumí passing through England were on their way to Abeokuta, which predominantly developed as an Egba town. Although it will remain a matter of interpretation, Okusono, among the others documented in England, in all likelihood identified as Egba, and possibly from the Gbagura province, which is "said to have been founded by immigrants from Oyo" (Ajișafẹ 1912, 11; Law 1977, 137). This evidence therefore affirms that the majority of these seventy Lucumí returnees were of Egba origins.

Yoruba Rotating Credit and Savings Associations

Enslaved Africans in colonial Cuba raised capital using traditional savings, credit, and banking institutions to buy their freedom and return to Africa. According to Toyin Falola and Akanmu Adebayo, the study of banking in colonial and postcolonial Africa continues to "avoid dealing with traditional financial institutions under the pretext that they were, strictly speaking, not *banks*." This point of view has popularized a misguided preconception that Africans never produced surplus wealth, and the capital they could accumulate "was *kept* (as distinct from *saved*) in pots and buried in the ground, thus putting the money away from any possibility of its being put to immediate economic use by others" (2000, 127). Regardless of this prejudiced point of view, people from the Bight of Benin hinterland who spoke the Yoruba language had at least two traditional institutions for accumulating wealth: *esusu* and *ajo* (Adebayo 1992, 1994; Falola 1995; Ojo 2008). Although they were not structured in the same way as modern banks, people in the past had faith in these financial institutions, in part because they were "culturally rooted" (Barrow 1978; Bonnett 1981; Hossein 2014; Katzin 1958; Levin 1973; Maynard 1996; Warner-Lewis 1996).

By definition, *esusu* is a rotating credit and savings association, which continues to be found in almost every culture worldwide (Geertz 1962, 263, 201–2; Low 1995). In the most basic schema: Ten people meet once a week to contribute one dollar to a collective fund. Every week one of the members receives the entire pool of money, and the cycle continues until each member puts in ten dollars and each member receives a single ten-dollar payout over a ten-week period. As Shirley Ardener describes, the first recipient of the pool becomes a debtor until the end of the rotation, the last to receive the fund is a creditor, and the other members shift between being creditors and debtors depending on their place in the rotation. Each association differs in size, structure, membership, as well as economic impact (1964, 201–2). In comparison, *ajo* operated where members paid a fixed sum of money to a collector at regular intervals. They could draw out their contributions at any time, but usually at the end of an agreed period. The main difference between the two is that in *ajo* "the contributor could draw his/her money at short notice, unlike the *esusu* where he/she had to wait his/her turn" (Falola and Adebayo 2000, 131).

Although the origins of *esusu* and *ajo* in Yoruba-speaking territories cannot be known with any certainty, these financial institutions likely emerged alongside the monetization of economies in the Bight of Benin hinterland. Many diverse groups of people in this region used cowrie shells as "a sophisticated form of currency" (M. Johnson 1970, 17). As Jan S. Hogendorn and Marion M. Johnson have summarized:

> Cowrie-money was not really primitive at all. It seems so only to eyes grown so familiar to dates, faces, and nationalities stamped on coins that they can conceive of no alternative. It was a "general-purpose money" that served as medium of exchange, unit of account, store of value, and standard for deferred payment. For a very long period of time, the shells were actually better suited to transactions of extremely low value than were metallic coins, because it was all but impossible to mint a coin with worth as low as an individual cowrie. . . . The shells were used for large transactions as well, up to half a million sometimes changing hands at one time. (1986, 1–3)

By 1800 cowries circulated more widely in foreign markets than the dollar, peso, and pound combined. These shells were found in places all around the Indian Ocean littoral, along the Ganges River, and across West Africa. Harvested from the lagoons of the Maldive Islands, Arab maritime traders initially brought the shells to North Africa for export across the Sahara. And then, European trading companies carried them to Europe's capital cities as ballast, before reexporting them to the coast of West Africa, along with other goods, to barter for people.

Counting cowries led to the development of a "great variety" of numeration systems "geared to the needs of non-literate but intensely commercial peoples" (Hogendorn and Johnson 1986, 1–3). Cardinal numbers in the Yoruba language likely emerged before the arrival of cowries. Counting mostly consists of "multiples or compounds." For example, the Yoruba word for the number 110 is expressed as an equation "20 × 6 – 10;" or the word for "2,500" is "200 × 13 – 100" (Adebayo 1994, 380–87; Armstrong 1962; S. Johnson 1921, i–iv). The development of this complicated enumeration system, possibly alongside the expansion of cowrie currency, illustrates the history of a "great deal of mathematical talent and interest" (Zaslavsky 1970, 81). Simply put, counting and exchanging large quantities of cowries required complex math, which suggests many enslaved Yoruba speakers in diaspora were able to manage their finances to obtain freedom. Moreover, Adebayo has argued that the monetization of "pre-colonial Yoruba economies" also developed advanced banking institutions that "were increasing in complexity by the beginning of the 19th century" (1994, 399).

The bureaucracy of *esusu* or *ajo* was as simple and as complex as required. Crowther explained in Abeokuta in the 1850s that *esusu* "members may consist of men and women, but most commonly each sex form separate clubs of themselves."[12] Likewise, Robert Campbell, a missionary, stated that these financial institutions were "formed chiefly by women" (1859–1860, 200). In 1900 Ajayi Kolawole Ajiṣafẹ was among the first scholars to publish a set of rules and regulations about these traditional financial institutions (1900, 45–46). By 1952 William Bascom elaborated how the term *esusu* referred to the fund, not the members. He detailed their foundation and operation whereby "anyone who wishes to do so may found an *esusu* group, provided that others are willing to entrust their money . . . [thus] the founder becomes the head." Membership was called a "hand or branch" (*owo*), and one person could control more than one "hand"; or if need be, more than one person could pay into a single "hand." In other words, complex *esusu* consisted of different levels whereby the collectors could "delegate considerable authority to the heads" for collecting and making payments; and in many cases *esusu* leaders did not know the identity of all the members, since they dealt "only with the heads of subgroups." The larger *esusu* consisted of multiple subgroups or "roads" or "paths" (*ona*). People kept track of the cycle and their contributions by "marking a line for payment on the wall of their rooms" (1952, 63–69). The penalties for default were settled through appeals to the *orisa*, such as Sango, the god of thunder known to kill thieves and cheaters with lightning; hence the proverb: "He who collects the pool (*esusu*) in turn but does not make a contribution: same as thief" (Owomoyela 2005, 284–85).

Traditional banking systems were ubiquitous among Egba. In 1842 Anglican catechists opened a mission in Abeokuta, and two years later they began documenting *esusu* and *ajo* in association with Egba. Samuel Ajayi Crowther, a Liberated African taken to Sierra Leone, compiled the first dictionary of the Yoruba language. Therein he translated the phrase *itadogun li ajo Egba*, meaning "a round of seventeen is the meeting [*ajo*] of the Egba." He elaborated on its meaning, whereby: "There are many savings clubs among the Egba: the members meet to deposit their contributions (called Esu [*esusu*]) . . . the interval is seventeen days; hence the proverb" (1843, 62–63). In 1845 Henry Townsend from Exeter, who visited the town of Osiele a few miles east of Abeokuta, reported how local Egba farmers were holding regular meetings where money was "collected and put together, and committed to the care of a trustworthy member" (Serrett Barber 1857, 109). By 1861 Charles Gollmer, a German missionary, described how "there were around

300 saving clubs in Abeokuta alone."[13] Traditional financial institutions played a major role in the accumulation of capital during the urbanization of major West African cities (Little 1971, 51–52).

Rotating credit and saving associations were not exclusive to Egba but widespread throughout the Bight of Benin hinterland. By 1856 Crowther expanded upon his previous dictionary entry that the "saving club" was "universal in the Yoruba country."[14] By late century Samuel Johnson observed that "*Esusu* is a universal custom for the clubbing together of a number of persons for monetary aid, [which] enables a poor man to do something worthwhile where a lump sum is required" (1921, 119). Comparable financial institutions existed among neighboring ethnolinguistic groups, such as Nupe (where they were called *dashi*), Hausa (*adashi*), Dahomey (*ndjonu*), Porto Novo (*tontines*), Ibibio (*osusu*), and Igbo (*isusu*). It is therefore a matter of interpretation whether or not rotating credit and saving associations developed independently in Yoruba-speaking territories or were borrowed from elsewhere. In either case, *esusu* and *ajo* were widespread across West Africa in the late eighteenth century (Amogu 1956; Austin 1993; Bascom 1952; Ardener 1953; Falola and Adebayo 2000; Jeffreys 1951; Nadel 1942; Nwabughuogu 1984; Tardits 1958).

Because of the Atlantic slave trade and British campaigns to abolish it, *esusu* and *ajo* spread to Sierra Leone, the Caribbean, and Brazil, especially during Oyo's collapse. In Freetown in 1843, Robert Clarke, a missionary, described how "Akoos, who form a great proportion of the liberated Africans, are pre-eminently distinguished for their love of trading, and occasionally amass large sums" (1843, 40). In Cuba rotating credit and saving institutions continue to exist as *esusu* among people who worship *orisa*, although they are known commonly as a "little cow" (*vaquita*) (Valdés Jané et al. 1997, 1–10).[15] After 1833 British and Spanish officials from the Havana mixed commission resettled over two thousand Yoruba speakers involved in the collapse of Oyo to British Caribbean colonies (H. B. Lovejoy 2016). Alfred Burdon Ellis, a lieutenant colonel of the First Battalion of the West India Regiment, noticed in the late nineteenth century the existence of "*Esu* societies, or subscription clubs, which are general amongst the Yoruba tribes, and still exist, under the same name, among the negroes of Yoruba descent in the Bahamas" (1894, 150). By the 1940s Melville and Frances Herskovits identified the continuation of *esusu* in a northern village on the island of Trinidad, and remarked that "persons from Barbados and Guiana who live in [Trinidad] told me of its form in their homes, where it is known as 'a meeting' and 'boxi money,' respectively"

(1947, 292). In Brazil, where tens of thousands of people from the Bight of Benin hinterland went directly as slaves, gradual self-purchase occurred similar to what happened in Cuba. João José Reis and Beatriz Gallotti Mamigonian argue that "manumission societies called *juntas de alforria*, also organized along ethnic lines [and they were] run similarly to a Yoruba *esusu* society" (2004, 89–90).

The Lucky Lucumí

Most of the former Egba slaves who went to Abeokuta via England bought their freedom through gradual self-purchase (*coartación*), which was also tied into the common practice where enslaved people could request to change masters (*pedir papel*). Alejandro de la Fuente demonstrates that these "rights" never appeared in early Castilian codes of law but "emerged as a pragmatic response to the frequent litigation initiated by slaves themselves." Owing to the high number of successful cases, these practices "fell into the category of customary rights, at best, and were quite vulnerable to the whim of individual masters" (2007, 661–62). Claudia Varella has since added that this practice occurred most frequently among the lower strata of urban slave-owners and existed as a dishonest dependency relationship whereby the owners frequently stole from the people they owned (2012, 203–4). Amazingly, enslaved Africans and their descendants in Cuba sometimes had the opportunity to challenge this corruption by filing lawsuits through a public advocate (*síndico procurador*). Even British abolitionists and missionaries in England remarked how these customary practices were "worthy of notice, and go to show, that if the slave population were not constantly recruited by new importations . . . slavery in Cuba must die out within a given time, dependent upon the extent to which the slaves availed themselves of their rights, and upon their ability to do so" (Anon. (a) 1854, 234).

The lengthy and drawn-out process of *coartación* required an agreement between a creditor, i.e., the master, who did not have to honor the agreement with the debtor, i.e., the enslaved. In Plymouth in 1855, Prideaux reported the dishonesty regarding how a former Cuban slave purchased his freedom over a thirteen-year period. Luis Llopar, who was a successful "master mason," reportedly earned twelve dollars a week and paid 1,000 dollars for his freedom. Llopar paid his master according to these installments as a *coartado*.

Table 5.1. Installments Luis Llopar Paid for His Freedom in Cuba during the Nineteenth Century

Salary paid to owner (weekly)	Years	Credit to freedom	Total paid to owners	Personal income (weekly)	Personal income (total)
$6.00	2	$200.00	$624.00	$6.00	$624.00
$5.50	2	$400.00	$572.00	$6.50	$676.00
$5.00	3	$200.00	$780.00	$7.00	$1,092.00
$4.00	6	$200.00	$1,248.00	$8.00	$2,496.00
Total	**13**	**$1,000.00**	**$3,224.00**		**$4,888.00**

Llopar, who had at least two masters, paid "a heavy premium for his good conduct" because he "had marks of merit" as an engineer (Anon. (c) 1855, 245). Under this arrangement he surely calculated his financial loses. After all, he paid over three times the agreed-upon value to his masters, who likely stole money over the short term, but eventually allowed freedom to occur so as to avoid supporting Llopar after his prime working years and into his old age.

Other members of the group of Lucumí who went to Southampton provided clues regarding their gradual path to self-liberation. Manuel Vidau, who was "the leader of the party," described how he was about twenty years old when he was "taken prisoner at Lagos in a war, and thence shipped to Havannah, in 1834." In Cuba Vidau made about "400 cigars a day" as a slave, and if he did not "work well," he was "stripped, tied down, and flogged." In the early 1840s Vidau changed masters and was allowed "to hire himself out to work . . . [where he] used to earn six and seven dollars a week making cigars, and [out of which] he paid his owner(s) four dollars and a half." Upon entering the cash economy, with about 1–2 dollars a week of personal income, Vidau began saving via *esusu* or *ajo*. Ca. 1847 he "joined thirty-nine others in a lottery-ticket [where they] drew a prize of sixteen thousand [pesos], which they divided equally, [with Vidau] getting four hundred" (Anon. (a) 1854, 239).

Lucumí in Cuba organized an *esusu* or *ajo* to pool money to buy a series of lottery tickets so as to increase their chances of winning. Other former slaves in England participated in this scheme. From the Southampton group,

Lorenzo Clarke, aka Okusono, "drew a prize of three hundred dollars," which was later stolen by his master. Miguel Marino "saved some money . . . and drew a prize of one thousand dollars" (Anon. (a) 1854, 235). And within the Plymouth group, the majority of people bought their freedom through "their labour," apart from "the four exceptions [where] it was gained by the lottery."[16] Other Lucumí winners preferred to remain in Cuba. Carl Ritter, a Prussian diplomat and abolitionist, interviewed Triumfo Souchay Lucumí on a plantation to the west of Havana in 1853, who explained, "I used some lottery winnings to buy my freedom" (1853, 12). Buying lottery tickets involved teams of collectors, and subcollectors sold tickets at various offices located around the island. Prizes ranged from as high as $100,000 to as low as a refund on the cost of a single ticket. The colonial Cuban lottery functioned as a raffle with upward of fifteen "ordinary draws" per year with 30,000 tickets at 8 dollars each, and three "big extraordinary" draws per year of 21,500 tickets at 16 dollars each. With a population of close to a million people on the island, there was therefore a very low and limited supply of tickets per game (Kiple 1976, table 1). However, each ticket cost too much for the average salary of a single enslaved African. As a result, these lucky Lucumí pooled their money together and likely won fourth place.[17] How they collected the prize remains unclear, but María Luísa Macorra, who went to Southampton, served as a domestic slave for a man who "kept a lottery-office." Her owner, however, "was a very bad master," and she "exercised her right to demand that he should sell her" (Anon. (a) 1854, 236). Perhaps this woman organized an *esusu* to play the lottery, and she learned enough from her master about how, when, and where to collect the prize.

In Havana a great number of *esusu* or *ajo* likely operated through Lucumí socioreligious brotherhoods or mutual-aid societies, called *cabildos de nación.* Since the sixteenth century, these legally sanctioned and church-sponsored societies were ubiquitous in the island's largest urban centers. By the mid-eighteenth century there was an extensive network of twenty-one *cabildos* operating in Havana, and that number expanded through the nineteenth century (Carmen Barcia 2009).[18] Pedro Deschamps Chapeaux described how these "socio-religious organizations were the African's representative institution in Cuba" (1968, 50). Rafael L. López Valdés adds how *cabildos* evoked "the African origin of their members" (1958, 5–10). According to Jane Landers, Lucumí *cabildos* were "interceding in work agreements, holding money for enslaved brothers, and making *coartación* payments" (2010, 171). Matt D. Childs has argued that "the Yoruba in West Africa, for example, operated mutual-aid societies [*cabildos de nación*] as early as the eighteenth century through the Ajo and Esusu saving institutions" (2012b, 182).

Oddly enough, evidence related to the winning of the lottery provides the clearest indication that Egba organized *esusu* along ethnic lines. In 1851 Fredrika Bremer, a Swedish traveler in Cuba, noted that:

> The slave knows, generally, that he can purchase his own freedom, and he knows also the means for the acquisition of money. The lottery is, in Cuba, one of the principal means for this purpose among the negro slaves, and they understand how to calculate their chances wisely. For instance, several individuals of a certain nation will unite for the purchase of a quantity of tickets, the numbers of which follow in close succession. Out of a total of consecutive numbers, one or two will commonly draw a prize, which, according to agreement, belongs to the nation, and is divided amongst all the members. In this way, I have heard that the Luccomée nation lately obtained at Havannah a prize of eleven thousand dollars, a portion of which, it is said, has been applied to purchase the freedom of slaves of their nation. . . . The [Lucumí] nation is regarded as rich, in consequence of the great prizes which it has won in the lottery, and this wealth it is said to apply to a good use—the purchasing the freedom of slaves of this tribe.
>
> These Cabildos [mutual-aid societies] are governed, as I already said, by queens, one or two, who decide upon the amusements, give tone to the society, and determine its extension. They possess the right of electing a king, who manages the pecuniary affairs of the society, and who has under him a secretary and master of the ceremonies. (1853, 3:143, 185)

The name of this Lucumí mutual-aid society was the "Cabildo de Señora Santa Bárbara de la nación Lucumi Alagua" (1853, 3:181–85). A decade earlier colonial authorities recorded the location of this Lucumí *cabildo*, which they called "Bragurá Santa Barbara."[19] The terms "Bragurá," "Alagua," or both could represent the Gbagura province in Egba territory. Moreover, Santa Bárbara equated with Sango, whose colors of red and white were worn by a woman in Plymouth in 1855 (Herskovits 1937, 640).[20]

Conclusion: Returning to Africa

The surplus wealth circulating around the Atlantic World during the period of second slavery trickled down into communities of enslaved Africans. Over time these people utilized traditional West African credit and saving institutions to raise substantial amounts of capital to purchase their freedom and return to their homelands. This chapter has examined one case study whereby groups of Egba managed the risk of operating *esusu* or *ajo* successfully to buy freedom and return to Africa. In this case study, the trust required to ensure that participants made scheduled payments in these rotating credit and savings associations revolved around ethnic solidarity of people involved in Oyo's collapse. These people made collective payments in order to buy freedom, lottery tickets, and passages back to Africa.

Slave-owners in Cuba permitted the people they owned to accumulate wealth, buy their freedom, and even return to Africa so as to incentivize their labor force to work as hard as possible during their prime working years and reduce the costs of long-term healthcare. The *coartación* system of gradual self-purchase mitigated risk for slave-owners, who worried about productivity and slave resistance. Allowing enslaved people to buy their freedom slowly over time resulted in better productivity of their labor force. After all, the slaves almost certainly worked harder knowing that their efforts would result in emancipation. This strategy also paid dividends for the owner, who more often than not granted freedom once the productivity of an aging person declined later in life.

One of the challenges of "second slavery" is that this framework is generally presented at a systemic, macrohistorical level. Incorporating microhistorical perspectives, which in this chapter involved personal finances and traditional saving mechanisms of groups of enslaved Egba in Cuba, demonstrates how the surplus wealth of sugar production trickled into all levels of society. The industrialized institution of slavery was therefore not simply an archaic system that became obsolete with advancing free-market economies, human rights, and liberalism. Rather, the slave system in Cuba expanded during the initial years of abolitionism and continued to adapt as the worldview of eradicating slavery gradually changed over a *longue durée*. Amid the rise of capitalism, slavery simultaneously became more intense and open, which in turn changed the spaces of agency among enslaved populations to generate personal wealth. By commodifying freedom within systems of gradual self-purchase, slave-owners exploited the prime working years of the people they enslaved while avoiding long-term healthcare costs of the people they owned. Meanwhile enslaved Africans and their descendants could buy their own freedom, and in the more exceptional cases, return home.

Notes

1. I would like to thank Ann Carlos and Pamela Laird for helping conceptualize this chapter in earlier drafts. I am truly grateful to Marial Iglesias Utset who has shared with me digital copies of primary sources she collected in England. I also want to thank Catherine Coquery-Vidrovitch, her husband Michel, and their children, who looked after and played with me when I lived in France as a child.

2. Hampshire Archives England (HAE), 16M97/13/11, "Manuscript account by Lydia Prideaux of Plymouth recounting the stay of a group of emancipated Havana slaves in Plymouth workhouse on their way home to West Africa," November 1855. The list of names Prideaux read referred to Anon (a) 1854.

3. For clarity, the prices stated herein are nominal values as they appear in British and Spanish primary sources, which often shifted between dollars, pesos, and pounds sterling. Since it is next to impossible to know fluctuating exchange rates in any given month or year leading up to the 1850s, Prideaux approximated "four or five hundred Dollars" as being equal to "80£ or 100£" (see HAE, 16M97/13/11, "Manuscript account by Lydia Prideaux," 10). Otherwise, Laird W. Bergad, Fe Iglesias García, and María del Carmen Barcia have shown that the "peso was generally on par with the U.S. dollar during the nineteenth century, until 1860 when the U.S. temporarily abandoned the gold standard" (1995, 22). As a frame of reference, the dollar and peso were almost one-to-one, while five dollars/pesos equaled about a pound. Henceforth, dollars are used because the key primary sources from which this economic data derives used the dollar as the main currency. To simplify currency exchanges, I have converted pesos or pounds to dollars for consistency.

4. HAE, 16M97/13/11, "Manuscript account by Lydia Prideaux," 10.

5. HAE, 16M97/13/11, "Manuscript account by Lydia Prideaux," 11.

6. Prideaux compiled this list included in HAE, 16M97/13/11, "Manuscript account by Lydia Prideaux," 31. The same list was republished in Anon. (b) 1855: 273.

7. HAE, 16M97/13/11, "Manuscript account by Lydia Prideaux," 17–18.

8. HAE, 16M97/13/11, "Manuscript account by Lydia Prideaux," 3.

9. Refer to *Voyages* (ID #1266); National Archives, England (NA), FO 84/128, "Abstract of the Evidence in the Case of the Brig Negrito," November 21, 1832, f. 285–89.

10. NA, FO 313/58, "Cargamento del Bergantin Mercante Español Negrito," January 5, 1833, f. 135, register #185.

11. Emails with Andrew Apter, June 11, 2010; Toyin Falola, June 11, 2010; and Ademola Omobewaji Dasylva, June 24–27, 2010.

12. CMS, CA2 O 31/78, "Correspondence from Samuel Crowther to T. J. Hutchinson," September 10, 1856.

13. Church Missionary Society (CMS), CA2 O 43/63, "Gollmer," June 4, 1861; cf. Shields (1997, 126).

14. CMS, CA2 O 31/78, "Correspondence from Samuel Crowther to T. J. Hutchinson," September 10, 1856.

15. Pers. comm., Francis Martinez Otero, July 15, 2017.

16. HAE, 16M97/13/11, "Manuscript account by Lydia Prideaux," 10.

17. For information on Cuba's lottery, see "Renta de Lotería: Real Ordenanza de 1 de Junio de 1836," in José María Zamora y Coronado, ed., *Biblioteca de legislación ultramarina en forma de diccionario alfabético . . .* , vol. 3 (Madrid: Alegria y Charlain, 1844), 290–309; "Orden del gobierno, autorizando á los particulares para revender billetes de la real lotería," November 21, 1855, in Félix Erenchun, ed., *Anales de la isla de Cuba: Diccionario administrativo, economico, y legislativo . . .* , vol. 2 (Havana: Imprenta de la Antilla, 1859), 2163; "Real órden, apropando el aumento del número de billetes y premios de lotería," October 29, 1858, in ibid., 2164–65; "Circular del Sr. administrador general de loterías, prohibiendo á los colectores conbrar una suma mayor de la señalada en los billetes," May 10, 1860, in ibid., 2165.

18. Archivo General de las Indias (AGI), SD 515/51, "Inventario de los cabildos," 1755.

19. Archivo Nacional de Cuba (ANC), GSC 1677/83995, "Lucumí Bragurá Santa Barbara," 1834.

20. See also HAE, 16M97/13/11, "Manuscript account by Lydia Prideaux," 17–18.

References

Anon. (a). 1854. "Cuban Slaves in England." *Anti-Slavery Reporter* 2, no. 10. London: Peter Jones Bolton, 234–39.

Anon. (b). 1855. "The Emancipados and Their Fatherland." *Church Missionary Intelligencer*, vol. 6. London: Church Missionary Society, 267–79.

Anon. (c). 1855. "The Yoruba Mission." *Church Missionary Intelligencer*, vol. 6. London: Church Missionary Society, 243–53.

Adebayo, Akanmu. 1992. "Pre-Colonial Institutional Frameworks for Moneylending and Loan Repayment among the Yoruba." *Paideuma*, no. 38: 163–76.

———. 1994. "Money, Credit, and Banking in Precolonial Africa: The Yoruba Experience." *Anthropos* 89, no. 4: 379–400.

Ajiṣafẹ, Ajayi Kọlawọlẹ. 1900. *The Laws and Customs of the Yoruba People*. Abeokuta: Fola Bookshops.

———. [1912] 1964. *History of Abẹokuta*. Abeokuta: Fola Bookshops.

Amogu, Okwara O. 1956. "Some Notes on Savings in an African Economy." *Social and Economic Studies* 5, no. 2: 202–9.

Ardener, Shirley G. 1953. "The Social and Economic Significance of the Contribution Club among a Section of the Southern Ibo." Annual Conference, West African Institute of Social and Economic Research, Ibadan.

———. 1964. "The Comparative Study of Rotating Credit Associations." *Journal of the Royal Anthropological Institute*, no. 94: 201–29.

Armstrong, Robert G. 1962. *Yoruba Numerals*. Ibadan: Oxford University Press.

Austin, Gareth. 1993. "Indigenous Credit Institutions in West Africa, c. 1750–c. 1960." In *Local Suppliers of Credit in the Third World, 1750–1960*, edited by Gareth Austin and Kaoru Sugihara, 93–159. Houndmills, Basingstoke, UK: Macmillan.

Bābā, Aḥmad. [1615] 2000. *Mi'rāj al-Ṣu'ūd: Ajwibat Aḥmad Bābā ḥawla al-istirqāq*. Rabat: Ma'had al-Dirāsāt al-Ifrīqīyah.

Barrow, Christine. 1978. "Meetings: A Group Savings Arrangement in Barbados." *Bulletin of the African Studies Association of the West Indies*, no. 8: 32–40.

Bascom, William. 1952. "The *Esusu*: A Credit Institution of the Yoruba." *Journal of the Royal Anthropological Institute*, no. 82: 63–69.

Bergad, Laird W., Fe Iglesias Garcia, and María del Carmen Barcia. 1995. *The Cuban Slave Market, 1790–1880*. Cambridge: Cambridge University Press.

Biobaku, Saburi O. 1965. *The Egba and Their Neighbours, 1842–1872*. Oxford, UK: Clarendon.

Bonnett, Aubrey W. 1981. *Institutional Adaptation to West Indian Immigrants to America: An Analysis of Rotating Credit Associations*. Washington, DC: University Press of America.

Bremer, Fredrika. 1853. *The Homes of the New World: Impressions of America*. Vol. 3, translated by Mary Howitt. New York: Harper & Brothers.

Campbell, Robert. [1859–1860] 1969. "A Pilgrimage to My Motherland: An Account of a Journey among the Egbas and Yorubas of Central Africa, 1859–1860." In *Search for a Place: Black Separatism and Africa, 1860*, edited by M. R. Delaney and Robert Campbell, 149–250. Ann Arbor: University of Michigan Press.

Carmen Barcia, Maria del. 2009. *Los ilustres apellidos: Negros en la Habana colonial*. Havana: Editorial de Ciencias Social.

Childs, Matt D. 2012a. "Gendering the African Diaspora in the Iberian Atlantic: Religious Brotherhoods and the *Cabildos de Nación*." In *Women in the Iberian Atlantic*, edited by Sarah E. Owens and Jane Mangan, 230–62. Baton Rouge: Louisiana State University Press.

———. 2012b. "Slave Culture." In *The Routledge History of Slavery*, edited by Gad Heuman and Trevor Burnard, 170–86. London: Routledge.

Clarke, Robert. 1843. *Sierra Leone: A Description of the Manners and Customs of the Liberated Africans*. London: James Rigway.

Crowther, Samuel. 1843. *Vocabulary of the Yoruba Language*. London: Church Missionary Society.

Curtin, Philip. 1967. "The Life of Joseph Wright: A Native of Akoo." In *Africa Remembered: Narratives by West Africans from the Era of the Slave Trade*, edited by Philip Curtin, 317–33. Madison: University of Wisconsin Press.

de la Fuente, Alejandro. 2007. "Slaves and the Creation of Legal Rights in Cuba: *Coartación* and *Papel*." *Hispanic American Historical Review* 87, no. 4: 659–92.

Deschamps Chapeaux, Pedro. 1968. "Cabildos: Solo para esclavos." *Cuba* 7, no. 69: 50–51.

Ellis, Alfred Burdon. 1894. *The Yoruba-Speaking Peoples of the Slave Coast of West Africa: Their Religion, Manners, Customs, Laws, Language, etc.* London: Chapman & Hall.

Eltis, David, dir. *Voyages: The Trans-Atlantic Slave Trade Database*. http://www.slavevoyages.org (accessed 2019).

Falola, Toyin. 1995. "Money and Informal Credit Institutions in Colonial Western Nigeria." In *Money Matters: Instability, Values, and Social Payments in the Modern History of West African Communities*, edited by Jane I. Guyer, 162–87. Portsmouth, UK: Heinemann.

Falola, Toyin, and Akanmu G. Adebayo. 2000. *Culture, Politics, and Money among the Yoruba*. New Brunswick, NJ: Transaction.

Falola, Toyin, and Akintunde Akinyemi, eds. 2016. *Encyclopedia of the Yoruba*. Bloomington: Indiana University Press.

Faloloa, Toyin, and Matt D. Childs, eds. 2004. *The Yoruba Diaspora in the Atlantic World*. Bloomington: Indiana University Press.

Falola, Toyin, and Ann Genova, eds. 2005. *Òrìṣà: Yoruba Gods and Spiritual Identity in Africa and the Diaspora*. Trenton, NJ: Africa World Press.

Fyle, C. Magbaily. 2004. "The Yoruba Diaspora in Sierra Leone's Krio Society." In *The Yoruba Diaspora in the Atlantic World*, edited by Toyin Falola and Matt D. Childs, 366–82. Bloomington: Indiana University Press.

Geertz, Clifford. 1962. "The Rotating Credit Association: A 'Middle Rung' in Development." *Economic Development and Cultural Change* 10, no. 3: 241–63.

Guyer, Jane I. 2004. *Marginal Gains: Monetary Transactions in Atlantic Africa*. Chicago: University of Chicago Press.

Herskovits, Melville J. 1937. "African Gods and Catholic Saints in New World Negro Belief." *American Anthropologist*, no. 39: 635–43.

Herskovits, Melville J., and Frances S. Herskovits. 1947. *Trinidad Village*. New York: Alfred A. Knopf.

Hogendorn, Jan S., and Marion M. Johnson. 1986. *The Shell Money of the Slave Trade*. Cambridge: Cambridge University Press.

Hossein, Caroline Shenaz. 2014. "The Politics of Resistance: Informal Banks in the Caribbean." *Review of Black Political Economy* 41, no. 1: 85–100.

Humboldt, Alexander von. [1826] 2011. *Political Essay on the Island of Cuba.* Edited by Vera M. Kutzinski and Ottmar Ette, translated by J. Bradford Anderson, Vera M. Kutzinski, and Anja Becker. Chicago: University of Chicago Press.

Jeffreys, M. D. W. 1951. "Le associazoni 'Osusu' nell'Africa occidentale." *Revista di etnografia* 5, no. 1: 3–12.

Johnson, Marion. 1970. "The Cowrie Currencies of West Africa: Part I." *Journal of African History* 11, no. 1: 17–49.

Johnson, Samuel. 1921. *The History of the Yorubas from the Earliest Times to the Beginning of the British Protectorate.* London: Routledge & Sons.

Katzin, Margaret Fisher. 1958. "'Partners,' an Informal Savings Institution in Jamaica." *Social and Economic Studies*, no. 8: 436–40.

Kiple, Kenneth F. 1976. *Blacks in Colonial Cuba, 1774–1899.* Gainesville: University Presses of Florida.

Landers, Jane. 2010. *Atlantic Creoles in the Age of Revolution.* London: Harvard University Press.

Law, Robin. [1977] 1991. *The Ọyọ Empire, c. 1600–c. 1836: A West African Imperialism in the Era of the Atlantic Slave Trade.* Brookfield, VT: Gregg Revivals.

Levin, Daniel. 1973. "Susu and Investment: A Pilot Survey of Indigenous Security Institutions in Trinidad." MA diss., M. A. Fletcher School of Law and Diplomacy, Tufts University.

Little, Kenneth. 1971. *West African Urbanization: A Study of Voluntary Associations in Social Change.* Cambridge: Cambridge University Press.

Lloyd, Peter C. 1971. *The Political Development of Yoruba Kingdoms in the Eighteenth and Nineteenth Centuries.* Occasional Paper 31, Royal Anthropological Institute, i–55.

López Valdés, Rafael L. 1985. *Componentes africanos en el etnos cubano.* Havana: Editorial de Ciencias Sociales.

Lovejoy, Henry B. 2016. "The Registers of Liberated Africans of the Havana Slave Trade Commission: Implementation and Policy, 1824–1841." *Slavery & Abolition* 37, no. 1: 23–44.

———, dir. *Liberated Africans.* http://www.liberatedafricans.org (accessed 2018).

———. 2018. *Prieto: Yoruba Kingship in Colonial Cuba during the Age of Revolutions.* Chapel Hill: University of North Carolina Press.

Lovejoy, Henry B., and Olatunji Ojo. 2015. "'Lucumí' and 'Terranova' and the Origins of the Yoruba Nation." *Journal of African History* 56, no. 3: 353–72.

Lovejoy, Paul E. 1980. *Caravans of Kola: The Hausa Kola Trade, 1700–1900.* Zaria: Ahmadu Bello University Press.

———. 2006. "The Context of Enslavement in West Africa: Aḥmad Bābā and the Ethics of Slavery." In *Slaves, Subjects, and Subversives: Blacks in Colonial Latin America,* edited by Barry Robinson and Jane Landers, 9–38. Albuquerque: University of New Mexico Press.

———. 2016. *Jihād in West Africa during the Age of Revolutions*. Athens: Ohio University Press.

Low, Alaine. 1995. *A Bibliographical Survey of Rotating Savings and Credit Associations*. Oxford, UK: Oxfam.

Matory, J. Lorland. 2005. *Black Atlantic Religion: Tradition, Transnationalism, and Matriarchy in the Afro-Brazilian Candomblé*. Princeton, NJ: Princeton University Press.

Maynard, Edward S. 1996. "The Translocation of a West African Banking System: The Yoruba *Esusu* Rotating Credit Association in the Anglophone Caribbean." *Dialectical Anthropology* 21, 1: 99–107.

McKenzie, Peter. 1997. *Hail Orisha! A Phenomenology of a West African Religion in the Mid-Nineteenth Century*. Leiden: Brill.

Mintz, Sidney, and Richard Price. 1976. *An Anthropological Approach to the Afro-American Past: A Caribbean Perspective*. Philadelphia: Institute for the Study of Human Issues.

Nadel, Siegfried Frederick. 1942. *A Black Byzantium: The Kingdom of Nupe in Nigeria*. London: Oxford University Press.

Nwabughuogu, Anthony I. 1984. "The Isusu: An Institution for Capital Formation among the Ngwa Igbo; Its Origin and Development to 1951." *Africa* 54, no. 4: 46–58.

Nwokeji, G. Ugo, and David Eltis. 2002. "The Roots of the African Diaspora: Methodological Considerations in the Analysis of Names in the Liberated African Registers of Sierra Leone and Havana." *History in Africa*, no. 29: 365–79.

Obrando Andrade, Rafael Ángel. 2011. "Manunisión, coartación y carta de venta: Tres de los mecanismos legales de obtención de la libertad para los esclavos negros en la América Española." *Revista de historia de América* 145: 103–25.

Ojo, Olatunji. 2008. "The Organization of the Atlantic Slave Trade in Yorubaland, ca. 1777 to ca. 1856." *International Journal of African Historical Studies* 41, no. 1: 77–100.

———. 2015. "Amazing Struggle: Dasalu, Global Yoruba Networks, and the Fight against Slavery, 1851–1856." *Atlantic Studies* 12, no. 1: 5–25.

Olupona, Jacob K., and Terry Rey, eds. 2008. *Òrìṣà Devotion as World Religion: The Globalization of Yoruba Religious Culture*. Madison: University of Wisconsin Press.

Otero, Solimar. 2010. *Afro-Cuban Diasporas in the Atlantic World*. Rochester, NY: University of Rochester Press.

Owomoyela, Oyekan. 2005. *Yoruba Proverbs*. Lincoln: University of Nebraska Press.

Peel, J. D. Y. 2000. *Religious Encounter and the Making of the Yoruba*. Bloomington: Indiana University Press.

Pemberton, John. 1977. "A Cluster of Sacred Symbols: Oriṣa Worship among the Igbomina Yoruba of Ila-Ọrangun." *History of Religions* 17, no. 1: 1–28.

Reis, João José, and Beatriz Gallotti Mamigonian. 2004."Nagô and Mina: The Yoruba Diaspora in Brazil." In *The Yoruba Diaspora in the Atlantic World*, edited by Toyin Falola and Matt D. Childs, 77–110. Bloomington: Indiana University Press.

Ritter, Carl. 1853. "Mittheilungen über einige westafricanische Stämme in Cuba, gesamelt von Hesse." In *Monatsberichte über die Verhandlungen der Gesellschaft für Erdkunde zu Berlin*, edited by T. E. Gumprecht, 12–16. Berlin: Bei Simo Schropp.

Salmoral, Manuel Lucena. 1999. "El derecho de la coartación del esclavo en la América Española." *Revista de Indias* 59, no. 216: 357–73.

Sarracino, Rodolfo. 1988. *Los que volvieron a África*. Havana: Editorial de Ciencias Sociales.

Serrett Barber, Mary Anne. 1857. *Oshielle: Or, Village Life in the Yoruba Country*. London: J. Nisbet.

Shields, Francine. 1997. "Palm Oil and Power: Women in the Era of Economic and Social Transition in 19th Century Yorubaland (South-Western Nigeria)." PhD diss., University of Stirling.

Tardits, Claude. 1958. *Porto-Novo: Les nouvelles générations africaines entre leurs traditions et l'occident*. Paris: Mouton.

Tishken, Joel, Toyin Falola, and Akintunde Akinyemi, eds. 2009. *Ṣàngó in Africa and the African Diaspora*. Bloomington: Indiana University Press.

Tomich, Dale W. 2004. *Through the Prism of Slavery: Labor, Capital, and World Economy*. Lanham, MD: Rowman & Littlefield.

Tomich, Dale W., and Michael Zeuske. 2008. "Introduction, the Second Slavery: Mass Slavery, World-Economy, and Comparative Microhistories." *Review* 31, no. 2: 91–100.

Valdés Jané, Ernesto, Omar García Ruiz, Michael Hernández López, and Julio Valdés Jané, eds. 1997. *Documentos para la historia de Osha Ifá en Cuba: Tratado enciclopédico de caminos: Obara*. Havana: Proyecto Orunmila.

Varella, Claudia. 2012. "The Price of 'Coartación' in the Hispanic Caribbean: How Much Freedom Does the Master Owe to the Slave?" *International Journal of Cuban Studies* 4, no. 2: 200–210.

Verger, Pierre Fatumbi. [1968] 1976. *Trade Relations between the Bight of Benin and Bahia from the 17th to the 19th Century*. Translated by Evelyn Crawford. Ibadan: Ibadan University Press.

———. 1977. "America Latina en África." In *África en América Latina*, edited by Moreno Fraginals, 363–77. Madrid: UNESCO.

Warner-Lewis, Maureen. 1996. *Trinidad Yoruba: From Mother Tongue to Memory*. Tuscaloosa: University of Alabama Press.

Zaslavsky, Claudia. 1970. "Mathematics of the Yoruba People and of Their Neighbors in Southern Nigeria." *Two-Year College Mathematics Journal* 1, no. 2: 76–99.

Chapter 6

Atlantic Slavery, African Landscapes

Change and Transformation in the Era of the Atlantic World

Christopher R. DeCorse

Drawing on historical and archaeological data, this chapter interprets sociocultural and socioeconomic transformations in West Africa within the context of the expanding world-economy. Beginning in the fifteenth century, maritime exchange intricately linked Africa, Europe, and the Americas and engendered dramatic changes for all of the societies involved. The advent of European commerce, the Atlantic slave trade, abolition, and colonial rule each heralded new patterns of exchange and cultural interactions that reflected global economic patterns as well as African cultural, social, and political structures.

The archaeological record offers unique insight into these transformations. Understanding Africa's intersection with the early modern world is constrained by the lack of information on Africa's pre-Atlantic past, as well as the more recent history of many portions of the continent. Researchers have turned to multiple strands of evidence to understand the transformations in African societies during the past five centuries (e.g., Falola and Jennings 2003; Mitchell and Lane 2013; Ogundiran and Falola 2007; Philips 2007; Reid and Lane 2004). While there are scattered Arabic sources on the West African savanna and Sahel dating back to the first millennium AD and European accounts for the portions of the coast begin in the fifteenth century, these sources are incomplete and restricted in their coverage. Oral traditions have been usefully exploited in some areas. However, in many contexts, they provide limited information and their interpretation can be methodologically challenging. As a consequence of these lacunae, interpretations of the African past are in many instances shallow; understanding of the entanglements, transformations, and consequences is limited both spatially and temporally.

The archaeological record thus provides a key source of information, in many instances the only source of information, on the transformations of the past millennium, perceived materially in changes in settlement patterns, settlement organizations, and artifact inventories. The archaeological record extends our view back in time, placing the African-European entanglements within the deeper African past. Archaeology also expands our view of the pre-Atlantic and Atlantic landscapes beyond the settlements, polities, and European trading enclaves of the coast into hinterland areas that were largely left undescribed in written sources until the late nineteenth and twentieth centuries. This chapter contextualizes the changes and transformations of the early modern world within the *longue durée* of the West African past. It considers how transformations within West Africa reflect change and alteration in the wider world-system, as well as the varied local economic, political, and cultural formations that shaped European-indigene interactions and economic relations. In doing so it seeks to understand how African societies intersected with, and in part shaped, the contours of the early modern world. These transformations are considered chronologically, moving from the opening period of African-European exchanges and concluding with the advent of European colonization in the nineteenth century.

West Africa before the Europeans

Before European contact and the advent of the Atlantic System, West African societies were interconnected in a variety of sociopolitical systems and economic networks.[1] West Africa is larger than the continental United States, encompassing a variety of environmental and geographic zones, and resource areas (e.g., Casey 2003; Mendonsa 2002). The region's sociopolitical formations have been equally diverse, ranging from relatively decentralized societies to state-level polities. Archaeological data has provided an increasingly complex view of West Africa's pre-Atlantic past. Although the paucity of archaeological work limits understanding of the culture histories of many areas, it is clear that West Africa was well settled by agricultural communities long before European contact in the fifteenth century.

Ongoing research in the eastern forests continues to document evidence for the construction of earthwork systems during the first and early second millennia AD. These are massive settlement sites encircled by ditches and embankments; monumental works indicative of sociopolitical complexity. There is also substantial evidence for iron smelting, sophistical brass casting, and indigenous glass production (e.g., Babaloa et al. 2017; Ogundiran 2005). In the Republic of Benin, the Late Iron Age underpinnings of historically known polities have been extended back into the first millennium AD (e.g., Monroe 2017; Randsborg and Merkyte 2011). Research in the southern Ghanaian forest has also revealed widespread settlement during the first millennium and early second millennium AD, including earthworks, dense scatters of ceramics, stone beads, iron slag, and gold artifacts (e.g., Chouin and DeCorse 2010; DeCorse 2005). Although poorly studied archaeologically, the western forests of Guinea, Sierra Leone, Liberia, and Côte d'Ivoire were also likely thoroughly settled by iron-using agricultural populations well before the second millennium AD (e.g., Coon 1968; DeCorse 2012). To the north, in the Senegambia, the coast was linked with the polities of the interior through trade routes and the Senegal and Gambia river systems. Thousands of tumuli, megaliths, and settlement sites provide evidence for nascent complexity and interregional exchange beginning in the second millennium BC (e.g., Deme and McIntosh 2006; Gokee 2016; Holl and Bocoum 2017; MacIntosh, MacIntosh, and Bocoum 2016; Richard 2015).

These societies intersected intra- and extraregionally in varied ways. The West African forests were not an impenetrable barrier.[2] Historically documented riverine trade, use of the coastal estuaries, and routes through the forest likely reflect exchange networks that had persisted for millennia (see discussions in Brooks 1993, 49–96; Green 2012, 31–68; Hawthorne 2003, 27–54; Kea 2004; Rodney 1970, 1–65). On the Lower Guinea Coast, the lagoonal systems behind the coast (Law 1983) likely facilitated the movement of people and goods long before the opening of the Atlantic trade. The societies of the coastal forests were also linked to the societies and states of the southern Saharan margins. If not in direct contact, the tendrils of the trans-Saharan trade documented in Arabic sources beginning in the first millennium AD extended south of the savanna and Sahel linking the societies of sub-Saharan and northern Africa (Garrard 1980, 6–33; Gokee 2016, 23–42; Kea 2004; Levtzion and Hopkins 1981). Prestige or elite goods, such as brass and copper alloy vessels, glass, and carnelian beads, may have made up the majority of long-distance trade materials reaching West Africa. These items have been recovered archaeologically and found curated in ritual contexts in the southern forests (e.g., Silverman 2015). West African gold was a major focus of trade and is likely represented in North African coinage beginning in the first millennium AD (Garrard 1980, 6–7). It is likely that less elite goods such as iron, cloth, kola, foodstuffs, and especially salt also widely circulated, but these items have poor documentary and archaeological visibility. In a similar vein, the extent of the trade in slaves before European contact is difficult to assess. Slaves from sub-Saharan Africa are, however, referred to in Arabic accounts and, as discussed below, slaves were traded from the onset of European trade (Chouin and Lasisi 2019; Lovejoy 2012; Rodney 1969).

These data collectively put aside notions that the African coast and forest hinterlands were only thinly occupied by hunting and gathering populations before the arrival of the Europeans in the fifteenth century and that sociopolitical complexity was largely a consequence of the emerging Atlantic economy.[3] More significant than the evidence of trade connections are the collective data on settlement patterns and site densities indicative of autochthonous state formation in West Africa during the first and early second millennia AD. Although existing networks would be refocused, altered, and in some instances dramatically reformed during the Atlantic period, arriving Europeans took advantage of productive and exchange systems that had been established in the preceding millennia.

Opening Encounters

Iberian traders explored the West African coast beginning in the fifteenth century and the margins of European expansion were soon marked by Portuguese forts, factories, and trading enclaves (e.g., Blake 1967, 1977; Brooks 2003; Cortesão, Teixeira da Mota, and Sjöfararen 1960; DeCorse 2020; Green 2012; Morgan 2009; Parry 1990, 40–46; Pereira 1967; Thornton 2012, 60–99). Portuguese colonies were established on the African-Atlantic islands of the Madeiras, Canaries, and Cabo Verde during the fifteenth century. Portuguese and Luso-African trading enclaves were also established on the Upper Guinea Coast, and plantations dependent on enslaved African labor were established on Cabo Verde during the 1460s (Green 2012, 95–119). The Portuguese established Castelo São Jorge da Mina (now known as Elmina Castle), their West Africa headquarters, in coastal

Ghana in 1482. With Elmina (see figure 6.1) and forts at Shama (São Sebastião) and Axim (São Antonio) as well as smaller outposts, the Portuguese attempted to restrict African trade with other European nations (DeCorse 2010; Rodney 1965; Vogt 1979). The cultural encounters in these early sites were important in shaping the contours of the early Atlantic World and in shaping later African-European interactions. These Portuguese trading enclaves were also of continued importance in the Atlantic slave trade. Indeed, the social and economic relations that unfolded provided a template for Iberian colonial projects in the Americas (Thomas 1997, 87–113; Wheat 2016, 104–18).

West African gold was a major focus in the opening phase of the European trade. If Christian conversion provided a nominal rationale, the impetus for the initial exploration of the West African coast was equally economic. As Wallerstein (2011a, 38–51) underscores, Iberian expansion of the fifteenth century was not a sudden outthrust but rather a continuation of European expansion—expansion into marginal lands, unsettled territories, and the Atlantic islands—that had begun in the preceding centuries. And bullion was needed to fuel this expansion. The Portuguese attempted

Figure 6.1. Elmina Castle in coastal Ghana, founded by the Portuguese in 1482. The current layout is largely the same as it was when the fort was captured by the Dutch in 1637. Source: Photograph by Christopher R. DeCorse.

to find inroads into the gold sources of Bambuk and Bure in the African interior through the rivers of the Senegambia and other portions of the coast. However, the most readily available source of gold was the region demarcated by Assine in Côte d'Ivoire and in Keta in modern-day Ghana. Portuguese ships were trading on the coast of Ghana by the 1470s if not earlier (Pereira 1967, 118; cf. Cortesão, Teixeira da Mota, and Sjöfararen 1960, xxxi; de Oliveira Marques 1972, 135). The region became known as Mina or "the Mine" and later as the Gold Coast.

One of the major consequences of the European trade was the linking of exchange systems that had previously been unconnected. The Portuguese and later European traders were adept at inserting themselves into existing trade networks and finding new markets (e.g., DeCorse 2019). While gold was an important focus of trade from the onset, a wide range of other commodities were important. The Portuguese and later European traders sought goods from different areas that could be exchanged on other parts of the coast. Initially, European trade did not so much restructure existing African networks as utilize and intensify them. Cotton from Cabo Verde, kola from Guinea-Bissau, and iron from Sierra Leone were purchased for trade elsewhere in West Africa, and caravels brought slaves from the Bight of Benin for sale to African merchants at Elmina (e.g., Brooks 1993, 127–28; 2003, 74–76; Chouin and Lasisi 2019; Rodney 1969, 1970, 72–74; Vogt 1971).

Significantly, this initial period of African-European interactions—the initial contacts and development of trade in the fifteenth and sixteenth centuries—is poorly perceived archaeologically (DeCorse 2020). The Portuguese and other Europeans arriving on the coast were interested in trade, not in settlement or colonization (Brooks 2003, 27; Chouin and DeCorse 2018; Gijanto 2017, 40–54; Green 2012, 115; Thomas 1997, 48–86). The number of Europeans living on the West African coast was limited, numbering only in the hundreds.[4] While there were Portuguese and *lançado* (Cabo Verdeans of mixed ancestry) settlements on the Upper Guinea Coast and rivers (the area of modern Guinea north to the Senegambia), these were small trading enclaves. European activities were also constrained by African customs and norms. Europeans were dependent on the African communities with whom they interacted for provisions and protection, as well as trade. In many areas, gifts or ground rent was given to African rulers for the right to conduct trade or occupy the land on which European outposts were located.

The Portuguese forts at Elmina and Axim are the most substantial, surviving monuments to Africa's early intersection with the Atlantic World. However, the majority of the smaller Portuguese outposts, factories, and trading enclaves that undoubtedly dotted the coast from the Senegambia to Cameroon have been obliterated by time and development.[5] More pointed than the ephemeral footprint of Portuguese trading enclaves is the limited indication of change in African social and economic organization in the fifteenth and sixteenth centuries—or at least the material indicators of change. Comprehensive data for all of West Africa are hardly at hand. However, West African archaeological sites of the century of initial encounter evince little if any material of European origin and African settlement patterns are comparable to those of the preceding centuries.

That is not to say change did not occur. New opportunities arose, new polities emerged, and others were transformed. For example, the African settlement of Elmina was likely subservient to the neighboring polity of Eguafo at the time of European contact. However, with the founding of Castelo São Jorge da Mina, the town became increasingly independent and acted with the Portuguese in military engagements, eventually emerging as an independent polity (DeCorse 2001, 38–43; 2008, 2020). Eguafo, Fetu, and other states that predated European contact also expanded in the course of the sixteenth century. In the Niger Delta, small coastal settlements that had been at the margins of the forest states of the interior also grew in size and importance (Law 1991). Changes arising in the societies along the savanna-Sahel margins as a result of the long-standing intersections with the trans-Saharan trade also continued. However, the dramatic urbanization, increasing multifunctionality within principal towns, and shifts in wider settlement patterns associated with the emerging Atlantic World would culminate in the succeeding centuries. In the wider hinterlands the settlement patterns of the previous millennia persisted. European trade materials of the fifteenth through the mid-seventeenth century are virtually absent from West African artifact assemblages.

The Atlantic Slave Trade

The growth of the Atlantic slave trade was dramatic. By 1625—a century and a half after the founding of São Jorge da Mina—fewer than five hundred thousand enslaved Africans had likely reached the Americas.[6] Another twelve million would follow in the next two and half centuries. The primary reason for this shift was the expansion of the slave-based plantation economies of the Americas. Enslaved Africans were being brought to the Spanish Caribbean beginning in the opening decades of the sixteenth century, and the trade in slaves was well established by

1600 (Knight 1993; Thomas 1997, 89–149). It was, however, with the expansion of Brazilian sugar production and the foundation of new plantation colonies in other parts of South America, the Caribbean, Mesoamerica, and North America that the need for labor—enslaved labor—expanded dramatically.[7] The Atlantic was increasingly interlinked economically. The European nations that established colonies in the Americas also vied to carve out trading enclaves in West Africa. As is the case with various post-Iberian European colonial projects in the Americas and in Asia, the majority of European forts that dot the West African coast were built between 1650 and 1800.[8] Although gold, ivory, dyewoods, and other materials remained important trade items, the principal purpose of these outposts was the holding of captive Africans and the provisioning of slave ships.

Through political machinations, forts, and the use of force, the Portuguese had attempted to maintain a monopoly of the European trade in West Africa. In part, they succeeded and there was a half century of quiet consolidation. Portuguese were, however, purveyors rather than producers of goods, and they were ill prepared productively or institutionally to deal with other European competitors (Wallerstein 2011a, 165–221). They were initially challenged by the French and, especially, the Dutch. By the end of the seventeenth century the Dutch controlled the major Portuguese forts in coastal Ghana, while the French, Swedes, Danes, English, Brandenburgers, and Coorlanders had also established forts in West Africa (see figure 6.2; DeCorse 2010, 2016a; Lawrence 1963). In coastal Ghana—the Gold Coast—slaves replaced gold as the focus of trade by the end of the seventeenth century (Bean 1974; Elbl 1997; Eltis 1994; Shumway 2011, 51–52; van den Boogaart 1992). Importantly, there was also a shift in African perceptions of the value of gold vs. slaves at the opening of the eighteenth century, gold dust becoming the universal form of money among the Akan (Spicksley 2013). This rush for trading enclaves and forts was the first European "scramble" for Africa; the next would come at the end of the nineteenth century and would have dramatically different objectives, contours, and methods.

Here it should be noted that the European forts and castles of the West African coast were first and foremost emporiums, their *raison d'être* trade. While texts sometimes refer to European "rule" or European "settlements" before the late nineteenth century, these were not colonial projects. With few exceptions, most notably the Portuguese forts, the European outposts were established by private trading companies. Although important *foci* of economic and cultural entanglement, the European garrisons consisted of small numbers of men who were largely dependent on the African societies in which they lived for supplies as well as for

Figure 6.2. Eighteenth-century map of West and Central Africa with flags marking the locations of the principal forts of different European nations. The inset, dating ca. 1773, shows the detail of coastal Ghana. Source: National Archives UK, Ref. MPK45.

Figure 6.3. Bunce Island in the Sierra Leone Estuary, first established in the 1670s, emerged as a major center of the British slave trade on the Upper Guinea Coast during the eighteenth century. The island represents the development of the slave trade into an efficient commercial network. Source: Photograph by Christopher R. DeCorse.

the maintenance of trade relations (Chouin and DeCorse 2018; DeCorse 2018; Shumway 2011, 61–64; Sparks 2014). Neither were Africans naive players in these coastal entanglements; often African rulers displayed an astute understanding of European politics and alliances.

Materially, the new entanglements of the Atlantic slave trade are seen in a variety of ways. The most striking monuments to this refocusing of interest are the European forts and castles that dot the West African coast. Yet the distribution of these surviving fortified European emporiums of West Africa represents neither the full extent of the Atlantic slave trade nor its impacts. The major forts and ports of trade represent only a small subset of European mercantile interests. Apart from the factories and trading enclaves that dotted the coast from the Senegambia to Cameroon, the Europeans maintained active trade in many areas where no permanent outposts were established and trade was conducted directly from ships (see Thomas 1997, 388–93). The major forts such as São Jorge, Cape Coast Castle (the British headquarters in Ghana), and Christiansborg (the Danish headquarters in Accra) were places where enslaved Africans from disparate areas were held to await transportation to the Americas.

Yet the distribution of the European outposts does little more than hint at the social, political, and economic impacts of the slave trade in the wider hinterlands from which enslaved Africans were taken (DeCorse 1991, 2016b; Kea 1982; Monroe and Ogundiran 2012). The European forts and trading posts were points of contact between foreign traders, interior polities, and the various networks linking them. Towns and polities that lay beyond the range of the forts' and castles' immediate influences have often not been examined or contextualized in terms of their Atlantic contexts and trajectories. However, the distribution of these settlements, and their rise and demise, are indicative of significant changes in political economy and associated sociopolitical organizations.

These changes in settlement organization and patterns are not unique to the Atlantic period. Such changes occurred in earlier periods and these are similarly indicative of societal transformations. They are, however, illustrative of the types of material expressions associated with the vicissitudes of the Atlantic period. Their temporalities and geographical distribution are distinct from earlier patterns and they present an internal frontier of the expanding global economy. Among the most visible changes in some areas are the appearance of fortified towns and movement to more inaccessible, easily defended locations that were refugia in areas raided for slaves (see figure 6.4). These are dramatically illustrated in the *tata* strongholds

Figure 6.4. House ruins in the hilltop settlement of Yagala Old Town, northern Sierra Leone. Such inaccessible locations provided natural protection against slave raiding. Source: Photograph by Christopher R. DeCorse.

of Senegal and in the hilltop and fortified towns of Guinea, Sierra Leone, and Liberia (e.g., DeCorse 2012; Thiaw 2012). However, the transformations in African societies and their material expressions were not unitary in nature. The responses were shaped by local histories, adaptations, and accommodations.

There is a pattern of increasing urbanism, concomitant with depopulation in other areas.[9] This pattern is well documented historically and archaeologically in coastal Ghana. Some settlements on the coast and in the coastal hinterland, such as Eguafo and Elmina, clearly predate European contact but expanded with the advent of the Atlantic trade. Before European contact in the late fifteenth century, the population of the central Ghanaian coast occupied small villages, mainly focused on lagoonal resources (DeCorse 2001, 18–20, 2005; DeCorse and Spiers 2009; Spiers 2012). With the advent of the Atlantic trade, populations became increasingly concentrated in larger settlements associated with European trade entrepôts and the centers of the hinterland polities, which also expanded in size and importance. This pattern of growth in hinterland centers that were nodes of the slave trade is illustrated by many examples in West Africa (e.g., Law 2004, 18–49; Kelly 1997; Monroe 2011, 2017; Norman 2012; Ogundiran 2012; Richard 2012).

These shifts minimally represent population relocation, that is, spatial adaptations within particular historical and societal contexts. However, evidence for increasing urbanism is significant as it is one of a suite of attributes, which also includes agricultural intensification, surplus production, specialization, and social stratification, that have often been used by social scientists to assess sociopolitical complexity. These changes in African settlement organization and patterns also represent the restructuring of political economies and associated changes in sociopolitical organization. New political alliances were formed and manipulated by emerging polities and merchant elites able to take advantage of the new frontiers of opportunity afforded by the Atlantic trade, particularly the trade in slaves. The Eguafo Kingdom already existed when the Europeans arrived on the coast in the late fifteenth century and it was one of several of the polities in coastal Ghana that first traded with the Portuguese (Blake 1967, 86; Chouin 1998, 2009; Hair 1994, 39; Spiers 2007, 29–32; 2012). However, in the succeeding centuries there were dramatic changes in the spatial arrangement of the titular capital and in the polity's size, changes that hint at wider sociopolitical transformations. As a result of its intermediary position between the coast and hinterland, Eguafo played a key role in the coastal trade, especially during the seventeenth and eighteenth centuries; a period that coincides with the dramatic expansion of the slave trade.

The increasing population in Eguafo was likely coupled with wide-ranging transformations in sociopolitical organization, including changes in political structures, new forms of social control, and the emergence of more centralized political hierarchies. At its apogee in the seventeenth century, Eguafo's influence extended from the Pra River Basin in the west to the Sweet River in the east.[10] The population of the capital itself grew in size, resulting in the abandonment of the old hilltop settlement in favor of the valley below. The kingdom had a military that may have been organized around a series of satellite towns within its core. It could also levy taxes on traders who passed through from the north to trade with Europeans on the coast. This was also a trend in other hinterland polities such as Fetu (Deffontaine 1993).

Completely new polities also emerged. In coastal Ghana, settlements located adjacent to European trading enclaves such as Annamaboe, Elmina, Cape Coast, and Komenda became the focal points of increasing trade, craft production, and specialization, and they emerged as independent or semi-independent polities (Shumway 2011; Sparks 2014). Elmina, likely a part of Eguafo in the fifteenth century, emerged as an independent polity with the advent of the Atlantic trade (DeCorse 2001, 38–40; 2008). Initially political authority was diffuse, with power shared between different quarters of the settlement. The position of king, as a title, only appears in the eighteenth century. Elmina emerged as the center of the Edina state, which extended its authority over the towns and villages of the surrounding hinterland. A variety of informal crosscutting links served to unify the settlement. These included intermarriage, the general importance of trade, economic competition with surrounding Fante groups, and Akan culture. It was, however, the traditional, African crosscutting means of sociopolitical organization that provided cohesiveness in the settlement's internal political organization and relationships with neighboring polities. Although Elmina and other emerging city-states in the central Ghanaian coast employed political structures found in interior Akan polities, they also incorporated new features such as *asafo* military and social organizations (DeCorse 2001, 40–41).

Transformations in sociopolitical organization can similarly be charted in other parts of West Africa. These coastal nodes—ports of the slave trade and associated inland polities—dotted the West African coast and its hinterlands (e.g., Daaku 1970; Gijanto 2017; Kea 1982; Law 1991, 2004; Law and Strickrodt 1999; Monroe 2011; Norman 2012; Thomas 1997, 332–69). This is dramatically illustrated in the growth of historically known states such as Niumi on the Gambia River,

Asante in Ghana, the Kingdom of Dahomey in Benin, and the city-states in the Bight of Benin. The temporal and geographic contours of these polities can be traced in settlement size and organization, and in associated dependent settlements.

West Africa in the Age of Abolition

The British Act for the Abolition of the Slave Trade was passed in 1807, taking effect the following year. However, it prohibited the slave trade only within the British Empire. Slavery and the slave trade continued through the century (Anstey 1975; Eltis 1987; Lovejoy 2012; Thomas 1997, 562–790). The Slavery Abolition Act of 1833 and related legislation abolished slavery throughout most of the British colonies. In the United States, slavery formally ended only with the Thirteenth Amendment in 1865, while Brazil's Lei Aurea, "the Golden Law," was passed in 1888. Although the post-1807 nineteenth-century slave trade is often referred to as the "illegal" slave trade, this British-centric vantage at best refers to only a subset of the regions, peoples, and institutions involved. As Tomich (2004, 2016, 2018) underscores, slavery in the era of abolition was re-formed in the context of nineteenth-century industrialization and world-economic expansion. This "second slavery" was marked by the restructuring of world markets, decolonization, and the emergence of new, postcolonial states, along with liberal conceptions of politics and economy.

In the Americas, the second slavery was characterized by the emergence of new zones of slave commodity production, particularly the cotton, sugar, and coffee plantations of the Southern United States, Cuba, and Brazil. In West Africa, changes in the economic organization of the slave trade and the associated sociopolitical organizations were equally dramatic. The places that had been the foci of the slave trade throughout the seventeenth and eighteenth centuries—Gorée Island in Senegal, James Fort in the Gambia, Bunce Island in Sierra Leone, the European forts and castles of coastal Ghana and Benin—were now economic liabilities, their raison d'être gone. The outposts of the private companies were nationalized, and treaties between European nations sought to secure revenue through tariffs and duties on goods traded within spheres of influence. There were also increasing claims for territorial rights beyond the confines of the small coastal enclaves where European powers had previously operated. However, these efforts were largely unsuccessful.[11]

Some of the early forts and port settlements remained important commercial centers. Places such as Cape Coast in coastal Ghana were used as bases for the British West Africa Squadron. However, no longer needed to secure trade against other European nations or as bases to hold slaves, many of the forts of the seventeenth and eighteenth centuries were left unstaffed and abandoned. The African settlements associated with these early emporiums also declined. Elmina and Eguafo were gradually passed by, diminishing in size and importance until by the early twentieth century they were little more than villages. In the course of the nineteenth century, the Ghanaian coastal hinterland was gradually repopulated with smaller villages and farming hamlets.

Yet demand for slaves continued, and consequently new areas and new structures of slave procurement emerged (Thomas 1997, 709–90). However, in many instances the same populations continued to serve as reservoirs for slaves for both the Atlantic trade and African states. For example, in Sierra Leone, despite the prohibition of the slave trade and the decline of the slave-trading center of Bunce Island, the slave trade remained significant and, in fact, expanded during the nineteenth century.[12] In northern Sierra Leone, slave raiding remained a threat throughout the nineteenth century (e.g., Fyle 1979, 117–24; Jackson 1977, 2; Lipschutz 1973, 62–79). Fulbe polities from the north raided Susu, Limba, and Yalunka and Koranko settlements. While some slaves were held by African states, others found their way to new Atlantic outlets in coastal lagoons and estuaries in Sierra Leone and Guinea. The zones of slave-trade procurement played out differently across the West African hinterland (e.g., Lovejoy 2012; Swanepoel 2005, 2009, 2011).

New ports—or at least sheltered harbors—had to be sought to service the Atlantic trade. In contrast to the European forts and outposts of the preceding centuries, smaller settlements and emporiums managed by Africans were the focus of trade (Thomas 1997, 712–14). In these locations slaves were often held in barracoons, simple fenced and uncovered enclosures of sticks and brambles. In Sierra Leone, for example, the infamous British trading fort on Bunce Island in the Sierra Leone Estuary had been positioned at the point farthest upstream that could be navigated by European slave ships. With abolition and the abandonment of Bunce as a slave-trading site, the trade moved into other areas less easily monitored by the British West Africa Squadron.

In the nineteenth century, the Rio Pongo on the Atlantic Coast in modern Guinea became the focus of the slave trade (see figure 6.5; Mouser 2003, 2011,

Figure 6.5. The capture of a slave ship on the Rio Pongo by the HMS *Linnet*, 1853. Source: From the *Illustrated London News*, June 18, 1853. Collection of Christopher R. DeCorse.

2015). Located in the network of small tributaries, they afforded sheltered anchorages. They were at times established near existing African settlements, but in other cases settlements developed in association with the trading posts (Kelly 2019; Kelly and Fall 2015). In contrast to forts, fortified outposts, and slave ports that had typified the preceding century, these trading settlements were relatively small, including warehouses for storing goods and housing for the merchant. Personal and family ties between Africans, European traders, and an emerging class of Atlantic Creoles facilitated trade. Slaves were obtained from hinterland sources hundreds of miles to the west in the Fuuta Jalon, and from areas that had likely long supplied slaves to Bunce Island and traders in the Sierra Leone Estuary (DeCorse 2012). Archaeological and historical research has shown these small trading enclaves of the Rio Pongo to have been remarkably cosmopolitan. Some families sent their children to Sierra Leone and Europe for their education, while the sites produced a variety of imported goods (Kelly 2019, 311).

Conclusion

The trade in slaves, and responses to it, continued to shape sociopolitical developments in West Africa through the nineteenth century. Paradoxically, abolition helped lay the foundation for European colonization. Increasing European perceptions of political authority and economic gain became the rationale for territorial claims that would typify the end of the nineteenth century. The language of abolition was embedded in arguments to aid Africans in their development, the introduction of "legitimate trade," and missionization. Ultimately, the commercial value of the West African trade would be important in justifying colonial expansion in the last decades of the nineteenth century.[13]

From the onset, the nineteenth century was marked by much more overt European involvement in African affairs and the authority of African leaders and states was increasingly challenged (e.g., DeCorse 2001, 28–31; Dike 1966, 10–18; M. Klein 1998). There were expressly colonial experiments beginning in the first decades of the nineteenth century. Denmark, which had retained its trade forts in costal Ghana, moved beyond these small coastal emporiums and established a number of plantations in the Accra plains (see figure 6.6; Bredwa-Mensah 2004; Breuning-Madsen et al. 2002; DeCorse 1993). These endeavors were, however, economically and politically infeasible. Denmark sold all of its forts in coastal Ghana to Britain in 1850, and they were subsequently incorporated into the Gold Coast Colony.

Figure 6.6. The ruins of the Danish plantation house of Daccubie in southern Ghana, a failed colonial project of the early nineteenth century. Source: Photograph by Christopher R. DeCorse.

In Sierra Leone, the short-lived Province of Freedom had been founded in 1787 as a settlement for freed slaves, nominally under the protection of the British government (Peterson 1969). Having been reorganized under the Sierra Leone Company, a chartered company of private merchants, the settlement was a dismal failure. The slave trade was prohibited from the onset and, although the settlement was expected to be economically self-sustaining, there was little income from any other source. The company subsequently requested that Parliament assume responsibility, and Sierra Leone became the first British colony in West Africa on January 1, 1808 (Peterson 1969, 36). Initially confined to the Freetown settlement and the Western Peninsula, this became the first British colony of the British West African settlements, which would eventually include the Gambia, Ghana, and Nigeria.

The closing decades of the nineteenth century saw a second scramble for Africa, the first having been marked by the European forts of the slave trade. European mercantile aims culminated in the Berlin Conference of 1884–1885 (Pakenham 1991). European trade and colonization in Africa were regulated, and Britain, France, Belgium, Portugal, Germany, and Spain delineated colonial territories. Africa provided a source of both raw materials and markets for European manufactures; trade agreements and diplomacy secured these markets rather than fortified outposts. While this scramble can be seen as a continuation of European commercial interests in Africa of the previous centuries, the boundaries, institutional frameworks, and conceptualizations of nineteenth- and twentieth-century imperialism were distinct. The areas of early commercial interest and slave trade did not neatly overlap the European colonial enterprises of the late nineteenth and twentieth centuries.

The past millennium witnessed dramatic changes in West African societies. Situating the intersections of the past five hundred years within the contexts of the deeper African past complicates our understanding of these changes and delineates the varied ways in which Africa intersected with, and in part fashioned, the social, political, and cultural entanglements of the early modern world. African-European interactions were shaped by the capitalist world-economy in distinctive, local ways. Materially these intersections are seen in changes in settlement patterns, settlement organizations, and artifact inventories. The foci of European trade, the rise and demise of African polities, the distribution of fortified-town sites in the West African hinterlands are equally linked to global-local relations. The colonial and postcolonial periods are similarly marked by their own social, political, and economic reformations reflecting their distinct historical relations to global patterns, and marked by their own material transformations. This perspective pushes the interpretation of the archaeological record beyond local site-specific questions and affords a means of placing the observed changes within wider historical processes.

Notes

1. The focus of this discussion is on West Africa, here considered to extend from southern Mauritania in the West to Cameroon in the East. The coastal environs of this region were a major focus of early African-European interaction and an important area in the Atlantic slave trade. Central Africa and other portions of the continent were equally engaged with the emerging world-economy but are beyond the focus of this chapter.

2. It has been suggested that the African forests were not occupied until the advent of iron technology used in land clearing (Bailey et al. 1989; cf. Casey 2003; Chouin and DeCorse 2010).

3. This evidence is contrary to some historical studies that have often portrayed the West African forests as having been thinly settled before the early modern period, the genesis of complexity a consequence of the trade and economic transformations during the Atlantic period, particularly the ability to control and manipulate the slave trade (e.g., Wilks 1993, 2005; Shumway, 2011; cf. Chouin and DeCorse 2010; DeCorse 2014).

4. Boxer (1972, 20) estimates that during the sixteenth century the total number of Portuguese serving in overseas posts scattered across Africa, South America, India, and Asia was less than ten thousand individuals. On the lower Guinea Coast the major headquarters generally had a garrison consisting of a few dozen.

5. The Portuguese were active in many portions of the coast that had no substantial outposts or forts but were rather places of trade and watering sites, such as those on Goree Island, the Sierra Leone Estuary, eastern Ghana at Accra, and Benin (Blake 1977, 100–105; DeCorse 2010). The limited archaeological evidence for early Portuguese-African interactions in many areas can be dramatically contrasted with Kongo Kingdom sites in Central Africa. See Clist, de Maret, and Bostoen (2018).

6. Estimates of the number of enslaved Africans taken to the Americas are often placed at around twelve million, but some assessments are as much as three or four million higher (e.g., Curtin 1969; Eltis 2001; Inikori 1982; H. S. Klein 2010; Thomas 1997). Also see the Trans-Atlantic Slave Trade Database, http://www.slavevoyages.org/.

7. See Solow (1993); Thomas (1997, 210–61). An excellent collection of essays on the growth, contours, and complexities of Caribbean slavery is presented in Shepard and Beckles (2000).

8. The success of these imperial projects in both the Americas and Africa was highly varied, and some were much more successful than others. The British, French, and to a lesser extent the Netherlands and Denmark were more successful. For the economic context of the growth and development of American plantation economies, see Wallerstein 1980 (103–4, 156–75).

9. See Coquery-Vidrovitch (2005, 169–208) for discussion of general trends. Increasing urbanism, and the presumed, associated transformations in sociopolitical organization, have often been cited as evidence regarding the consequences of the slave trade on African societies. However, as Manning (1990, 12–15) has pointed out, generalizing impacts belies the complexity of the cultural, political, and economic entanglements that occurred.

10. The more centralized authority of individual rulers within the Eguafo Kingdom was circumscribed by a council of other chiefs, elders, and other crosscutting social groups (see Chouin 1998; Spiers 2012).

11. Coombs (1963, 14–49) notes that by the mid-nineteenth century neither the Dutch nor the British possessions on the Gold Coast were self-supporting.

12. The slave trade reached it apogee in southern Sierra Leone during the nineteenth century (Jones 1983, 37–38).

13. The economic basis of abolition has been widely treated (e.g., Eltis 1987; Williams 2014; also see Wallerstein 2011b). The more general points here are that the trade in enslaved Africans continued through the nineteenth century and that both abolition and European colonialism brought their own distinctive shifts in African economic, political, and social systems.

References

Anstey, Roger. 1975. *The Atlantic Slave Trade and British Abolition, 1760–1810*. London: Macmillan.

Babaloa, Abidemi Babatunde, Susan Keech McIntosh, Laure Dussubieux, and Thilo Rehren. 2017. "Ile-Ife and Igbo Olokun in the History of Glass in West Africa." *Antiquity* 91, no. 357: 732–50.

Bailey, Robert C., Genevieve Head, Mark Jenike, Bruce Owen, Robert Rechtman, and Elzbieta Zechenter. 1989. "Hunting and Gathering in Tropical Rain Forest: Is It Possible?" *American Anthropologist* 91, no. 1: 59–82.

Bean, Richard. 1974. "A Note on the Relative Importance of Slaves and Gold in West African Exports." *Journal of African History* 15, no. 3: 351–56.

Blake, John William. 1967. *Europeans in West Africa, 1450–1560*. London: Hakluyt Society.

———. 1977. *West Africa: Quest for God and Gold, 1454–1578*. London: Curzon.

Boxer, C. R. 1972. *Four Centuries of Portuguese Expansion, 1415–1825*. Berkeley: University of California Press.

Bredwa-Mensah, Yaw. 2004. "Global Encounters: Slavery and Slave Lifeways on Nineteenth Century Danish Plantations in the Gold Coast (Ghana)." *Journal of African Archaeology* 2, no. 2: 203–27.

Breuning-Madsen, Henrik, Theodore W. Awadzi, Yaw Bredwa-Mensah, Henry Mount, and Berman Hudson. 2002. "The Danish Plantations of the Former Gold Coast Colony of Ghana: Why Did They Fail?" *Soil Survey Horizons* 43, no. 1: 1–8.

Brooks, George E. 1993. *Landlords and Strangers: Ecology, Society, and Trade in Western Africa, 1000–1630*. Boulder, CO: Westview.

———. 2003. *Euroafricans in Western Africa*. Athens: University of Ohio Press.

Casey, Joanna. 2003. "The Archaeology of West Africa from the Pleistocene to the Mid-Holocene." In *Under the Canopy: The Archaeology of Tropical Rain Forests*, edited by J. Mercader, 35–65. New Brunswick, NJ: Rutgers University Press.

Chouin, Gérard. 1998. *Eguafo: Un royaume africain "au cœur françois" (1637–1688)*. Paris: AFERA Éditions.

———. 2009. "Forests of Power and Memory: An Archaeology of Sacred Groves in the Eguafo Polity, Southern Ghana (c. 500–1900 A.D.)." PhD diss., Syracuse University.

Chouin, Gérard, and Christopher R. DeCorse. 2010. "Prelude to the Atlantic Trade: New Perspectives on Southern Ghana's Pre-Atlantic History (800–1500)." *Journal of African History*, no. 51: 123–45.

———. 2018. "Atlantic Intersections: African-European Emporia in Early Modern West Africa." In *Trade and Colonization in the Ancient Western Mediterranean: The Emporion, from the Archaic to the Hellenistic Period*, edited by Éric Gailledrat, Michael Dietler, and Rosa Plana-Mallart, 253–65. Montpellier, France: Presses universitaires de la Méditerranée.

Chouin, Gérard L., and Olanrewaju Blessing Lasisi. 2019. "Crisis and Transformation in the 'Slave Rivers' at the Dawn of the Atlantic Trade." In *Power, Political Economy, and Historical Landscapes of the Modern World*, edited by Christopher R. DeCorse, 285–306. Albany: State University of New York Press.

Clist, Bernard, Pierre de Maret, and Koen Bostoen, eds. 2018. *Une archéologie des provinces septentrionales du royaume Kongo*. Oxford, UK: Archaeopress.

Coombs, Douglas. 1963. *The Gold Coast, Britain and the Netherlands, 1850–1874*. Oxford, UK: Oxford University Press.

Coon, Carleton S. 1968. *Yengema Cave Report*. Philadelphia: University Museum, University of Pennsylvania.

Coquery-Vidrovitch, Catherine. 2005. *The History of African Cities South of the Sahara: From the Origins to Colonization*. Translated by Mary Baker. Princeton, NJ: Markus Weiner.

Cortesão, Armando, Avelino Teixeira da Mota, and Henrik Sjöfararen. 1960. *Portugaliae monumenta cartographica*. 6 vols. Lisbon: Comemoracoes do V Centenario da Morte do Infante d. Henrique.

Curtin, Philip D. 1969. *The Atlantic Slave Trade*. Madison: University of Wisconsin Press.

Daaku, Kwame Yeboa. 1970. *Trade and Politics on the Gold Coast 1600–1720*. London: Oxford University Press.

de Oliveira Marques, A. H. 1972. *History of Portugal*. Vol. 1. *From Lusitania to Empire*. New York: Columbia University Press.

DeCorse, Christopher R. 1991. "West African Archaeology and the Atlantic Slave Trade." *Slavery & Abolition* 12, no. 2: 92–96.

———. 1993. "The Danes on the Gold Coast: Culture Change and the European Presence." *African Archaeological Review*, no. 11: 149–73.

———. 2001. *An Archaeology of Elmina: Africans and Europeans on the Gold Coast, 1400–1900*. Washington, DC: Smithsonian.

———. 2005. "Coastal Ghana in the First and Second Millennia AD: Change in Settlement Patterns, Subsistence and Technology."*Journal des Africanistes* 75, no. 2: 43–52.

———. 2008. "Varied Pasts: History, Oral Tradition, and Archaeology on the Mina Coast." In *Place, Event, and Narrative Craft: Method and Meaning in Microhistory*, edited by James Brooks, Christopher R. DeCorse, and John Walton, 77–93. Santa Fe, NM: School of Advanced Research.

———. 2010. "Early Trade Posts and Forts of West Africa." In *First Forts: Essays on the Archaeology of Proto-Colonial Fortifications*,. edited by Eric Klingelhofer, 209–33. Leiden: Brill.

———. 2012. "Fortified Towns of the Koinadugu Plateau: Northern Sierra Leone in the Atlantic World." In *Landscapes of Power: Regional Perspectives on West African Polities in the Atlantic Era*, edited by Cameron Monroe and Akin Ogundiran, 278–308. New York: Cambridge University Press.

———. 2014. "Postcolonial or Not? West Africa in the Pre-Atlantic and Atlantic Worlds." Keynote Address, 50th Anniversary of the African Studies Center, University of Ibadan.

———. 2016a. "Tools of Empire: Trade, Resources and the British Forts of West Africa." In *Building the British Atlantic World, 1600–1850*, edited by Bernard L. Herman and Daniel Maudlin, 165–87. Chapel Hill: University of North Carolina Press.

———, ed. 2016b. *West Africa during the Atlantic Slave Trade: Archaeological Perspectives*. New York: Bloomsbury.

———. 2018. "Landlords and Strangers: British Forts and Their Communities in West Africa." In *British Forts and Their Communities: Archaeological and Historical Perspectives*, edited by Christopher R. DeCorse and, 206–30. Gainesville: University Press of Florida.

———, ed. 2019. *Power, Political Economy, and Historical Landscapes of the Modern World: Interdisciplinary Perspectives.* Albany: State University of New York Press.

———. 2020. "Contact, Colonialism, and the Fragments of Empire: Portugal, Spain, and the Iberian Moment in West Africa." In *The Global Spanish Empire: Five Hundred Years of Place Making and Pluralism*, edited by Christine Beaule and John G. Douglass, 31–54. Tucson: University of Arizona Press.

DeCorse, Christopher R. and Sam Spiers. 2009. "A Tale of Two Polities: Socio-Political Transformation on the Gold Coast in the Atlantic World." *Australian Journal of Historical Archaeology*, no. 27: 29–42.

Deffontaine, Yann. 1993. *Guerre et societe au royaume de Fetu, Ghana: 1471–1720.* Paris: Karthala.

Deme, Alioune, and Susan Keech McIntosh. 2006. "Excavations at Walaldé: New Light on the Settlement of the Middle Senegal Valley by Iron-Using Peoples." *Journal of African Archaeology* 4, no. 2: 317–47.

Dike, K. Onwuka. 1966. *Trade and Politics in the Niger Delta, 1830–1885.* Oxford, UK: Clarendon.

Elbl, Ivana. 1997. "The Volume of the Early Atlantic Slave Trade, 1450–1521." *Journal of African History* 38, no. 1: 31–75.

Eltis, David. 1987. *Economic Growth and the Ending of the Atlantic Slave Trade.* New York: Oxford University Press.

———. 1994. "The Relative Importance of Slaves and Commodities in the Atlantic Trade of Seventeenth-Century Africa." *Journal of African History* 35, no. 2: 237–49.

———. 2001. "The Volume and Structure of the Transatlantic Slave Trade: A Reassessment." *William and Mary Quarterly* 58, no. 1: 17–46.

Falola, Toyin, and Christian Jennings, eds. 2003. *Sources and Methods in African History: Spoken, Written, Unearthed.* Rochester, NY: University of Rochester Press.

Fyle, C. Magbaily. 1979. *Almamy Suluku of Sierra Leone, c. 1820–1906: The Dynamics of Political Leadership in Pre-Colonial Sierra Leone.* Ibadan: Evans Brothers.

Garrard, Timothy F. 1980. *Akan Weights and the Gold Trade.* London: Longman.

Gijanto, Liza. 2017. *The Life of Trade: Events and Happenings in Nuimi's Atlantic Center.* New York: Routledge.

Gokee, Cameron. 2016. *Assembling the Village in Medieval Bambuk.* Bristol, CT: Equinox.

Green, Toby. 2012. *The Rise of the Trans-Atlantic Slave Trade in Western Africa, 1300–1589.* New York: Cambridge University Press.

Hair, Paul E. H. 1994. *The Founding of the Castelo de São Jorge da Mina: An Analysis of the Sources.* Madison: African Studies Program, University of Wisconsin.

Hawthorne, Walter. 2003. *Planting Rice and Harvesting Slaves: Transformations along the Guinea-Bissau Coast, 1400–1900.* Portsmouth, NH: Heinemann.

Holl, Augustin F. C., and Hamadi Bocoum. 2017. *Megaliths, Cultural Landscape and the Production of Ancestors.* Saarbrücken, Germany: Editions universitaires europeennes.

Inikori, J. E., ed. 1982. *Forced Migration: The Impact of the Export Slave Trade on African Societies.* New York: Africana.

Jackson, Michael. 1977. *The Kuranko: Dimensions of Social Reality in a West African Society.* London: C. Hurst.

Jones, Adam. 1983. "From Slaves to Palm Kernels: A History of the Galinhas Country (West Africa), 1730–1890." *Studien zur Kulturkunde*, no. 68. Wiesbaden: Franz Steiner Verlag.

Kea, Ray. 1982. *Settlements, Trade, and Politics in the Seventeenth-Century Gold Coast.* Baltimore: Johns Hopkins University Press.

———. 2004. "Expansions and Contractions: World-Historical Change and the Western Sudan World-System (1200/1000 B.C.–1200/1250 A.D.)." *Journal of World-Systems Research* 10, no. 3: 723–816.

Kelly, Kenneth G. 1997. "The Archaeology of African-European Interaction: Investigating the Social Roles of Trade, Traders, and the Use of Space in the Seventeenth- and Eighteenth-Century Hueda Kingdom, Republic of Bénin." *World Archaeology* 28, no. 3: 351–69.

———. 2019. "Nineteenth-Century Coastal Guinea: Manifestations of the 'Illegal' Slave Trade in a Local System." In *Power, Political Economy, and Historical Landscapes of the Modern World*, edited by Christopher R. DeCorse, 285–306. Albany: State University of New York Press.

Kelly, Kenneth, and Elhadj Ibrahima Fall. 2015. "Employing Archaeology to (Dis)Entangle the Nineteenth-Century Illegal Slave Trade on the Rio Pongo, Guinea." *Atlantic Studies* 12, no. 3: 317–35.

Klein, Herbert S. 2010. *The Atlantic Slave Trade.* Cambridge: Cambridge University Press.

Klein, Martin. 1998. *Slavery and Colonial Rule in French West Africa.* New York: Cambridge University Press.

Knight, Franklin W. 1993. "Slavery and Lagging Capitalism in the Spanish and Portuguese American Empires, 1492–1713." In *Slavery and the Rise of the Atlantic System*, edited by Barbara L. Solow, 62–74. New York: Cambridge University Press.

Law, Robin. 1983. "Trade and Politics behind the Slave Coast: The Lagoon Traffic and the Rise of Lagos, 1500–1800." *Journal of African History*, no. 24: 321–48.

———. 1991. *The Slave Coast of West Africa, 1550–1750: The Impact of the Atlantic Slave Trade on an African Society.* Oxford, UK: Oxford University Press.

———. 2004. *Ouidah: The Social History of a West African Slaving "Port" 1727–1892.* Athens: Ohio University Press.

Law, Robin, and Silke Strickrodt, eds. 1999. *Ports of the Slave Trade (Bights of Benin and Biafra).* Papers presented at a conference of the Centre of Commonwealth Studies,

University of Stirling, June 1998. Stirling, UK: Centre of Commonwealth Studies, University of Stirling.

Lawrence, A. W. 1963. *Trade Castles and Forts of West Africa.* London: Jonathan Cape.

Levtzion, N., and Hopkins, J. F. P. 1981. *Corpus of Early Arabic Sources for West African History.* New York: Cambridge University Press.

Lipschutz, Mark Ross. 1973. "Northeast Sierra Leone after 1884: Responses to the Samorian Invasions and British Colonialism." PhD diss., University of California, Los Angeles.

Lovejoy, Paul E. 2012. *Transformations in Slavery: A History of Slavery in Africa.* New York: Cambridge University Press.

MacIntosh, Roderick J., Susan MacIntosh, and Hamady Bocoum. 2016. *The Search for Takrur: Archaeological Excavations and Reconnaissance along the Middle Senegal Valley.* New Haven, CT: Yale Peabody Museum.

Manning, Patrick. 1990. *Slavery and African Life: Occidental, Oriental, and African Slave Trades.* Cambridge: Cambridge University Press.

Mendonsa, Eugene. 2002. *West Africa: An Introduction to Its History, Civilization, and Contemporary Situation.* Durham, NC: Carolina Academic Press.

Mitchell, Peter, and Paul Lane. 2013. *The Oxford Handbook of African Archaeology.* Oxford, UK: Oxford University Press.

Monroe, Cameron. 2011. "Urbanism on West Africa's Slave Coast: Archaeology Sheds New Light on Cities in the Era of the Atlantic Slave Trade." *American Scientist 99*, no. 5: 400–409.

———. 2015. "Power and Landscape in Southern Benin: Commercial Entanglement and the Question of Scale in the Archaeology of Atlantic West Africa." In *Preserving African Cultural Heritage: Proceedings of the 13th Panafrican Archaeological Association for Prehistory and Related Studies*, edited by Ibrahima Thiaw and Hamady Bocoum, 385–96. *Mémoires d l'IFAN-Cheikh Anta Diop*, no. 93. Dakar: IFAN-Cheikh Anta Diop.

———. 2017. "'Elephants for Want of Towns': Archaeological Perspectives on West African Cities and Their Hinterlands." *Journal of Archaeological Research*, DOI: http://doi.org/10.1007/s10814-017-9114-2.

Monroe, Cameron, and Akin Ogundiran, eds. 2012. *Landscapes of Power: Regional Perspectives on West African Polities in the Atlantic Era.* New York: Cambridge University Press.

Morgan, Philip. 2009. "Africa and the Atlantic, c. 1450 to c. 1820." In *Atlantic History: A Critical Appraisal*, edited by Jack P. Greene and Philip D. Morgan, 223–48. New York: Oxford University Press.

Mouser, Bruce. 2003. "Continuing British Interest in Coastal-Conakry and the Fuuta Jaloo Highlands (1790–1850)." *Cahiers d'Etudes africaines* 43, no. 4: 761–90.

———. 2011. "The Rio Pongo Crisis of 1820 and the Search for a Strategy for the Anti-Slavery Squadron off West Africa." *The Mariner's Mirror* 97, no. 3: 145–62.

———. 2015. "US Slave Trading on the Rio Pongo: Evidence from the Capture and Trial of the Spitfire of New Orleans, 1845." *The Mariner's Mirror* 101, no. 1: 21–37.

Norman, Neil L. 2012. "From the Shadow of an Atlantic Citadel: An Archaeology of the Huedan Countryside." In *Landscapes of Power: Regional Perspectives on West African Polities in the Atlantic Era*, edited by Cameron Monroe and Akin Ogundiran, 142–68. New York: Cambridge University Press.

Ogundiran, Akin, ed. 2005. *Precolonial Nigeria: Essays in Honor of Toyin Falola*. Trenton, NJ: Africa World Press.

———. 2012. "The Formation of an Oyo Imperial Colony during the Atlantic Age." In *Landscapes of Power: Regional Perspectives on West African Polities in the Atlantic Era*, edited by Cameron Monroe and Akin Ogundiran, 222–52. New York: Cambridge University Press.

Ogundiran, Akin, and Toyin Falola, eds. 2007. *Archaeology of Atlantic Africa and the African Diaspora*. Bloomington: Indiana University Press.

Pakenham, Thomas. 1991. *The Scramble for Africa: 1876–1912*. New York: Random House.

Parry, J. H. 1990. *The Spanish Seaborne Empire*. Berkeley: University of California Press.

Pereira, Duarte Pacheco. 1967. *Esmerado de situ orbis*. Translated by George H. Kimble. Nendeln, Liechtenstein, the Netherlands: Kraus Reprint.

Peterson, John. 1969. *Province of Freedom: A History of Sierra Leone, 1787–1870*. Evanston, IL: Northwestern University Press.

Philips, John. 2007. *Writing African History*. Rochester, NY: University of Rochester Press.

Randsborg, Klavs, and Inga Merkyte, eds. 2011. *Benin Archaeology: The Ancient Kingdoms*. Oxford, UK: Wiley-Blackwell.

Reid, Andrew M., and Paul J. Lane, eds. 2004. *African Historical Archaeologies*. New York: Springer.

Richard, François G. 2012. "Political Transformations and Cultural Landscapes in Senegambia during the Atlantic Era: An Alternative View from the Siin (Senegal)." In *Landscapes of Power: Regional Perspectives on West African Polities in the Atlantic Era*, edited by Cameron Monroe and Akin Ogundiran, 78–114. New York: Cambridge University Press.

———. 2015. "The Politics of Absence: The *Longue Durée* of State-Peasant Dynamics in the Siin, Senegal." In *Materializing Colonial Encounters: Archaeologies of African Experience*, edited by François G. Richard, 229–61. New York: Springer.

Rodney, Walter. 1965. "Portuguese Attempts at Monopoly on the Upper Guinea Coast, 1580–1650." *Journal of African History* 6, no. 3: 307–22.

———. 1969. "Gold and Slaves on the Gold Coast." *Transactions of the Historical Society of Ghana*, no. 10: 13–28.

———. 1970. *A History of the Upper Guinea Coast*. New York: Monthly Review.

Shepard, Verene, and Hilary McD. Beckles, eds. 2000. *Caribbean Slavery in the Atlantic World*. Oxford, UK: Jame Currey.

Shumway, Rebecca. 2011. *The Fante and the Transatlantic Slave Trade*. Rochester, NY: University of Rochester Press.

Silverman, Raymond A. 2015. "Material Biographies: Saharan Trade and the Lives of Objects in Fourteenth and Fifteenth-Century West Africa." *History in Africa*, no. 42: 375–95.

Solow, Barbara, ed. 1993. *Slavery and the Rise of the Atlantic System*. New York: Cambridge University Press.

Sparks, Randy. 2014. *Where the Negroes Are Masters: An African Port in the Era of the Slave Trade*. Cambridge: Harvard University Press.

Spicksley, Judith. 2013. "Pawns on the Gold Coast: The Rise of Asante and Shifts in Security for Debt, 1680–1750." *Journal of African History*, no. 54: 147–75.

Spiers, Sam. 2007. "The Eguafo Kingdom: Investigating Complexity in Southern Ghana." PhD diss., Syracuse University.

———. 2012. "The Eguafo Polity: Between the Traders and Raiders." In *Landscapes of Power: Regional Perspectives on West African Polities in the Atlantic Era*, edited by Cameron Monroe and Akin Ogundiran, 115–41. New York: Cambridge University Press.

Swanepoel, Natalie. 2005. "Socio-Political Change on a Slave-Raiding Frontier: War, Trade and 'Big Men' in Nineteenth Century Sisalaland, Northern Ghana." *Journal of Conflict Archaeology*, no. 1: 264–93.

———. 2009. "Every Periphery Is Its Own Center: Sociopolitical and Economic Interactions in Nineteenth-Century Northwestern Ghana." *International Journal of African Historical Studies* 42, no. 3: 411–32.

———. 2011. "Different Conversations about the Same Thing? Source Materials in the Recreation of a Nineteenth-Century Slave-Raiding Landscape, Northern Ghana." In *Slavery in Africa: Archaeology and Memory*, edited by Paul J. Lane and Kevin C. MacDonald, 167–97. Proceedings of the British Academy, no. 168. Oxford, UK: Oxford University Press.

Thiaw, Ibrahima. 2012. "Atlantic Impacts on Inland Senegambia: French Penetration and African Initiatives in Eighteenth- and Nineteenth-Century Gajaaga and Bundu (Upper Senegal River)." In *Landscapes of Power: Regional Perspectives on West African Polities in the Atlantic Era*, edited by Cameron Monroe and Akin Ogundiran, 49–77. New York: Cambridge University Press.

Thomas, Hugh. 1997. *The Slave Trade: The Story of the Atlantic Slave Trade, 1440–1870*. New York: Touchstone.

Thornton, John K. 2012. *A Cultural History of the Atlantic World, 1250–1820*. New York: Cambridge University Press.

Tomich, Dale. 2004. "The 'Second Slavery': Bonded Labor and the Transformation of the Nineteenth-Century World Economy." In *Through the Prism of Slavery: Labor, Capital, and World Economy*, edited by Dale Tomich, 56–71. Lanham, MD: Rowman & Littlefield.

———, ed. 2016. *New Frontiers of Slavery*. Albany: State University of New York Press.

———. 2018. "The Second Slavery and World Capitalism: A Perspective for Historical Inquiry." *História Social*, no. 90: 149–64.

van den Boogaart, Ernst. 1992. "The Trade between Western Africa and the Atlantic World, 1600–90: Estimates of Trends in Composition and Value." *Journal of West African History* 33, no. 3: 369–85.

Vogt, John. 1971. "The Early Sao Tome-Principe Slave Trade with Mina, 1500–1545." *International Journal of African Historical Studies* 6, no. 3: 453–67.

———. 1979. *Portuguese Rule on the Gold Coast 1469–1682*. Athens: University of Georgia Press.

Wallerstein, Immanuel. 1980. *The Modern World-System*. Vol. 2. *Mercantilism and the Consolidation of the European World-Economy, 1600–1750*. New York: Academic.

———. 2011a. *The Modern World-System*. Vol. 1. *Capitalist Agriculture and the Origins of the European World-Economy in the Sixteenth Century*. Berkeley: University of California Press.

———. 2011b. *The Modern World-System*. Vol. 4. *Centrist Liberalism Triumphant, 1789–1914*. Berkeley: University of California Press.

Wheat, David. 2016. *Atlantic Africa and the Spanish Caribbean, 1570–1640*. Chapel Hill: University of North Carolina Press.

Wilks, Ivor. 1993. *Forests of Gold: Essays on the Akan and the Kingdom of Asante*. Athens: Ohio University Press.

———. 2005. "The Forest and the Twis." *Transactions of the Historical Society of Ghana*, New Series, no. 8: 1–81.

Williams, Eric. 2014. *The Economic Aspect of the Abolition of the West Indian Slave Trade and Slavery*. Edited by Dale W. Tomich with an introduction by William Darity. New York: Rowman & Littlefield.

Chapter 7

The Cultivation System in Java, Second Slavery in Brazil, and the World Coffee Economy (ca. 1760–1860)

Rafael Marquese

The Origins of *Brazil and Java*

On August 4, 1883, after a six-year experience as an employee of the Department of Interior in Batavia, Java, thirty-eight-year-old Dutch agronomist Karel Frederik van Delden Laërne received direct orders from the minister of the colonies. He was to leave Indonesia immediately and head to the Empire of Brazil. The new era of steamships, telegraph communication, and the opening of the Suez Canal allowed Laërne to reach Rio de Janeiro (via Lisbon) in just fifty days. The Brazilian railroad system also allowed him to perform his mission in a relatively short time. Between the months of September 1883 and April 1884, he toured coffee zones of three Brazilian provinces—Rio de Janeiro, Minas Gerais, and São Paulo—interviewing authorities, brokers, bankers, and coffee planters. Of particular note was his visit to more than forty large plantations, where he was able to gather detailed information on the composition of the labor force, the financial status of each of them, their technical standards, and soil productivity—in sum, all that concerned the labor process and coffee production. Laërne's capacity for hard work was very impressive. After returning to the Netherlands in April 1884, his long report was finalized in less than six months. In 1885 the report was published simultaneously in Dutch, English, and French (Laërne 1885).

The main objective of the whole enterprise was to evaluate the inner secrets of the coffee colossus of the nineteenth century, the only space that managed to overcome the Javanese production in the world market. In the early 1880s the Dutch colony faced a difficult situation, marked by both the impasse of the compulsory labor regime of its native population in the government crops and the new coffee-rust disease (caused by the fungus *Hemileia vastatrix*) (McCook 2006). Laërne had to investigate how Brazil had achieved its prominent market position and what were its possibilities for future growth, comparing them step-by-step with those of Java. It seemed as if Brazil had all the advantages: soil productivity was higher, the enslaved workers produced more coffee per capita than the Indonesian peasants, and, thanks to a newly built railroad system, vast new lands were now open to coffee production. The only problem Brazil faced was the crisis of slave labor: as Laërne noted, "there are very many mines of prosperity in Central Brazil, which would yield rich returns if they could only be worked. But all progress is arrested now by want of labourers" (1885, 372).

But there was no clear prediction, in 1884, of how the impasse over the continuity of Brazilian slavery would be solved. In Laërne's opinion, it was likely that Brazil would follow the path of post-1838 Jamaica (the general decline of agricultural exports as a result of emancipation) because of Brazilian planters' stubborn reliance on slave labor. That was where the Dutch agronomist saw an opportunity for the recovery of the Dutch East Indies in the world coffee market. Peasant production under the compulsion of the Dutch colonial state had been essential between the 1830s and 1860s, but now, in the 1880s, this prior arrangement represented an obstacle to the growth of the Javanese coffee economy. To overcome the negative legacies of the Cultivation System, it was necessary to stimulate the technical and productive development of the Javanese coffee sector through incentives to plantation agriculture by private investors, including foreign entrepreneurs. (This is what explains the immediate translation of the book into English and French.)

Laërne's expectations, however, proved unfounded in the short term. The abolition of slavery in Brazil came soon, in 1888, and Brazilian coffee planters successfully faced the crisis of slave labor by resorting to an unprecedented scheme of subsidized mass immigration of Italian peasants (Holloway 1984). The coffee crisis in Java deepened, and only after World War I was Indonesia able to recover its production levels of the 1880s (Dumont Villares 1927, 2:31–148). Perhaps this error of judgment determined the apparent failure of Laërne's book shortly after its publication in 1885. But if it failed as a work of practical instruction for coffee planters at the end of the nineteenth century, in the next century it became one of the main historical sources about slavery in Brazil. The enormous historical and statistical work done by Laërne, who compiled multiple sources published in several countries and languages, also become an obligatory reference for all those working with the history of coffee in Latin America, Asia, and Africa. Laërne's book is crucial for understanding cultural transfers and the formation of the global economy in the long nineteenth century.

Given the facilities of electronic databases, one can easily find copies of the book on the web. The available information, however, ends there. We do not know exactly how Laërne did his training. His father had been a senior official in the Dutch state of Indonesia, the founder of the New Guinea colony, and a resident of Menado. Laërne had a long life, dying only in 1940, also in Indonesia. What was his intellectual background and his professional trajectory before going to Brazil? What did he do after the Brazilian experience? These questions, which evidently deserve a careful investigation, will not be answered here. This is a task for a solid critical edition.

What interests me in this chapter is the broader question concerning the origins of the coffee economy in Brazil and Java, the two largest producers in the nineteenth century, the comparison of which was the purpose of Laërne's trip in 1883–1884. In other words, my objective is to examine the profound reconfiguration of the global coffee economy that occurred at the turn of the nineteenth century, a transformation that crystallized in the early 1840s with the consolidation of Brazil and Java's position in the world market. First, I will present some general data on the global coffee production from 1760 to 1860 and identify the general trends in the composition of supply and consumption. Then I will describe how the rise of coffee in Brazil and Java resulted from the unified process of crisis of the Iberian and Northwestern Atlantic Systems, whose epicenter lies in the French Revolution and the Haitian Revolution. My final remarks indicate the common ground—albeit seemingly quite disparate—of the slave and peasant labor regimes in Brazil and Java, respectively, after 1820. My argument is that second slavery in Brazil and the Cultivation System in Java are closely intertwined.

Global Coffee Production and Consumption, 1760–1860

Let us begin with some of the major changes that occurred in the world coffee economy between 1760 and 1860 and then examine the role played in these transformations by the historical forces of the French Revolution, the Haitian

Revolution, and the Napoleonic Wars. Table 7.1 summarizes the available data on world coffee exports until these events.

As Steven Topik (2004) warns us, all coffee statistics until the end of the nineteenth century are quite imprecise. For instance, there is no exact estimate of the amount produced in Yemen; Michel Tuchscherer (2003, 55) suggests that it remained stable at relatively high levels, around twelve thousand tons throughout the eighteenth century. In this sense, what is presented in the table should be taken only as a simple approximation of the order of numbers, notably the total volume, calculated on the assumption that the relative positions remained unchanged for the whole period. Despite their imprecision, these figures emphasize, first, the rapid growth of world coffee production in the four decades until the outbreak of the French Revolution, and second, the complete reversal of positions between the slave colony of Saint-Domingue and the peasant zone of Yemen. The Arab product, exported through Moka, dominated world production until the mid-eighteenth century. The accelerated growth of the French Caribbean colony after the beginning of the Seven Years' War changed the profile of the global coffee economy. Between 1755 and 1790, while other producers remained relatively stagnant, coffee production in Saint-Domingue grew tenfold, and, in doing so, it increased the total world supply two and a half times. In 1755, Yemen controlled almost half of the market; in 1790, this position belonged to Saint-Domingue.

The growth of coffee production in the French colony was founded on the intensification of the transatlantic slave trade. In this period it is estimated that

Table 7.1. Estimates of Coffee Exports in Metric Tons, 1755–1790

	Java	**Suriname**	**Saint-Domingue**	**Martinique**	**Yemen**	**Total**
1755	1.512	2.423	3.150	5.517	12.000	26.950
			12%		**45%**	**100%**
1764	1.731	6.160	6.750	3.157	12.000	32.700
			21%		**37%**	**100%**
1774	2.284	7.615	18.000	6.771	12.000	51.600
			35%		**23%**	**100%**
1790	1.678	5.143	34.650	4.404	12.000	69.400
			50%		**17%**	**100%**

about five hundred thousand enslaved Africans were disembarked in Saint-Domingue (http://www.slavevoyages.org). As a vector of demand, coffee seems to have had more weight than the sugar economy. The slave population of the "pearl of the Antilles," as Saint-Domingue was known at the time, jumped from 265,000 in 1767 to 480,000 slaves in 1791, without a noticeable rise in sugar production—a modest increase from 62,000 to 68,000 tons (Watts 1992, 331, 369). Proportionally, the number of slaves allocated to coffee production increased more than the number of slaves employed in the sugar plantations. Further, the proportional amount of colonial coffee reexported by France—the consumer market of the French colonial product was not in its metropolis but in the urbanized areas of the Baltics and Germany—was also higher than that of sugar (88.9 percent vs. 69.4 percent in 1789) (Tarrade 1972, 753; de Vries 2008, 183; Carmagani 2012, 191).

Global coffee production was relatively stagnant between 1790 and 1825, despite the dramatic rise in prices that occurred with the Haitian Revolution (Posthumus 1946, 1:75–79). In the vacuum created by the massive slave rebellion, new coffee producers such as Jamaican and Cuban planters appeared on the world market, but the bans caused by war and military blockades on a planetary scale combined with the very nature of the coffee agronomic cycle (newly planted bushes take five years to come into full production) prevented a quick recovery of the previous supply. Between 1815 and 1825 (the decade immediately following the Congress of Vienna), the world's coffee production was only 20 percent higher than it had been in 1790. From 1825 onward, however, there was an explosive growth in coffee production. In 1840 the total amount produced worldwide was about 200,000 tons, a volume that rose to more than 330,000 tons in 1860. This was largely the result of two novelties in the geographical composition of coffee supply: the emergence of the Dutch colony of Java (in the eighteenth century, under the command of the Dutch East India Company or VOC, the island had been a marginal coffee zone) and, above all, of the Empire of Brazil as the major world producers of coffee. The total amount produced by the Caribbean macroregion, marked by considerable changes in the relative position of the volume coming from its diverse political units (Haiti, Cuba, Jamaica, Puerto Rico, Venezuela, Guyana), remained stable throughout this period (Samper and Fernando 2003, 412–39).

Brazil and Java showed continuous growth curves, but Brazil's advantage is noticeable. Brazil's linear growth trend was the same as that of world production. After 1815 Brazil defined the pace of the transformation of the global coffee market, occupying a place that between 1755 and 1790 had belonged to Saint-

Domingue. In fact, the growing supply of coffee from the French colony after the Seven Years' War was directly related to what Jan de Vries (2008) has called the "industrious revolution." There was in this period a clear popularization of coffee consumption in some of the great urban centers of Western Europe; the beverage was becoming a sort of "luxury of the poor" in these places. Take, for instance, the case of the Netherlands, the European region that until the outbreak of the British Industrial Revolution was the most urbanized and had the highest relative number of wage laborers in its working classes. In the 1780s the spread of coffee consumption through the social fabric of Dutch cities and countryside implied an annual per capita consumption of about 2.8 kilograms. This volume, however, was still lower than what the Viennese consumed at that time (5 kilograms per capita), but higher than Parisian consumption (1.9 kilograms) and well above the European average (420 grams) (de Vries 2008, 152–61).

The high level of Dutch consumption as the "first modern economy"—according to the title of Jan de Vries and Ad van der Woude's book (1995)—depended on the increasing and low-cost supply of New World slavery areas, foreshadowing what was going to happen during the nineteenth century. The transition from the eighteenth-century coffee economy to that of the nineteenth century meant, above all, the transition from a relatively restricted consumer market to a mass market. On the basis of this transformation there were correlated processes of population and urban growth associated with the Industrial Revolution, although Great Britain did not participate as a major market for coffee. Because of policy choices made in the eighteenth century dictated by the interests of the British East India Company, the country became a captive market for Eastern tea; Britain's large colonies in Asia—India and Ceylon—never became leading coffee-producing zones comparable to Brazil or Java (Smith 1996).

The great nineteenth-century innovation in the realm of consumption was the North American market. By the mid-nineteenth century, the United States already accounted for almost 25 percent of the global demand for coffee. Such a transformation was driven by four factors. First, coffee had been associated with the new national ethos since the birth of the republic. Here it is enough to recall the role that the rejection of the East India Company's mercantilist policy favoring tea played in catalyzing the anti-British sentiments in 1773. Second, the growing role that the independent United States played as buyers of Caribbean coffee (whether for reexport or for home consumption) between 1783 and 1812 also derived from the deep prior involvement of North American merchants with the

Caribbean trade (McDonald and Topik 2013). Third, the North American coffee market was exempt from import tariffs from 1832, a direct result of the free-trade economic platform advocated by the cotton slaveholding interests of the Southern states (Parron 2015). Tax free, coffee became cheaper for US consumers, for which the growing Brazilian supply was decisive (Marquese 2013a). Finally, accelerated demographic growth (based on both high fertility rates and the massive influx of immigrants) and equally increasing income constantly widened the domestic market throughout the nineteenth century (Marquese and Tomich 2009).

Although growing, European demand was less elastic than that of North America. In comparative terms, European consumers were more demanding about the final quality of the product. In these markets Java did better than Brazil. From the point of view of European consumers, the old position of the former French colony was inherited by Java rather than Brazil. Known for its better quality, and therefore more expensive, the Javanese product, reexported by the Netherlands, tended to control Europe's consumer markets (especially in Germany), while the low-quality, cheaper Brazilian product indisputably dominated the US market, which had the fastest growth rates both in absolute (total imports) and relative numbers (per capita consumption). In 1850, 45 percent of Brazilian exports were shipped to the US; 90 percent of the coffee the US imported came from Brazil (Thurber 1884; Carvalho Franco 1983; Schivelbusch 1993; Schneider 1992; Topik 2003; Cunha 1992, 283–91).

The Age of Revolution and the Rise of Coffee in Brazil and Java

In the immediate conjuncture of 1790–1815, the historical forces unleashed by the revolutionary wave in the Atlantic were absolutely crucial to the changes observed in the world coffee market. Of course, the collapse of Saint-Domingue, the largest coffee producer of the eighteenth century, was a direct result of the unified revolutionary process in France and the Caribbean in the 1790s, and the failure of Napoleon Bonaparte to reinstitute black slavery and colonialism in French Saint-Domingue after 1802 (Dubois 2004). But on the other hand, the rise of the two largest nineteenth-century coffee zones was also an outcome of the very same cluster of events that followed 1789. In other words, the emergence of Brazil and Java as the major actors in the world coffee market has some of its foundations in the reorganization of the economy and the global politics produced by the French Revolution, the Napoleonic Wars, and the post–Congress of Vienna era. It is worth examining this matter in its "local" aspect, that is, from the historical trajectories of the Portuguese and Dutch Empires between the 1790s and 1820s.

The year 1808 represented the turning point in the making of the Brazilian coffee economy. The economic and political reorganization around the commercial hub of Rio de Janeiro, the new headquarters of the Portuguese Empire after the flight of the Portuguese royal family to Brazil, notably activated the flow of mercantile activities throughout the Center-South region, since the eighteenth century the most dynamic of Portuguese America. In the context of the closure of European continental markets as a result of Napoleonic policy, the opening of ports to "friendly nations"—that is, British merchants—gave a crucial outlet to the Portuguese colonial product and, more important, established once and for all free trade with the world market for Brazilian planters. Before 1815 this measure brought few results in terms of raising Brazilian coffee exports, but with the return of the peace to Europe it proved to be crucial in stimulating local producers. The other aspect of the boost to coffee cultivation brought by the elevation of Rio de Janeiro to the headquarters of the Portuguese Empire in 1808 lies in the transatlantic slave trade. Since the end of the seventeenth-century wars against the Dutch, the slave-trade business in the Portuguese Atlantic had been managed from the American ports. During the gold cycle of the eighteenth century, Rio de Janeiro stood out—followed by Bahia—as the main gateway for enslaved Africans destined for the highlands of Minas Gerais. Agricultural diversification in Center-South Brazil in the late eighteenth century kept the demand for slaves high. However, after 1808 it almost doubled: in the decade before the arrival of the royal family, about 117,000 Africans were disembarked as slaves in Rio de Janeiro; in the 1810s that number jumped to 225,000 (Marquese and Tomich 2009).

This growing labor supply was channeled largely to the expansion of the coffee frontier. The region where this occurred was previously relatively unoccupied owing to the policy of forbidding settlement imposed by Portugal during the peak of the gold-mining economy. In fact, the territorial funds of the Paraíba Valley, not very far from the port of Rio de Janeiro, remained blocked to the plantation economy for a long time. The turning point came precisely in the first two decades of the nineteenth century, when the Bragantine crown promoted an aggressive policy of occupation of this area through the granting of extensive tracts to private planters (the so-called sesmarias) and the reduction or simply the extermination of the

Indian populations that still lived in the zone. Given the geoecological conditions of the Paraíba Valley region, coffee soon proved to be the ideal product to be exploited by the slaveholders who were investing there (Marquese and Salles 2015).

The political changes that Brazil underwent after the return of peace to Europe established the institutional conditions for the definitive takeoff of its coffee economy. Contrary to the expectations of the European powers gathered in the Congress of Vienna in 1814, in the following year the court of Portuguese king D. João chose to remain in Brazil, elevating it to the status of the United Kingdom of Portugal and the Algarve and thus showing without halftones the full commitment of the Portuguese crown to the enslaving platform of the local businessmen. At the time of the imperial crisis of 1820–1822, this pact between the Braganças and the coffee planters was once more reaffirmed, now under the aegis of a new independent empire ruled by a constitutional regime. Despite the political mishaps of the 1820s, which would soon lead to the resignation of Dom Pedro I from the Brazilian throne in the name of his five-year-old son, it can be said that the Empire of Brazil was born under the sign of a close alliance between the new coffee zone of the Vale do Paraíba and the new constitutional monarchy (Marquese and Salles 2015).

If the starting point of all these transformations—the flight of the Portuguese royal family to Brazil—must be understood from the perspective of longer-term tendencies that began to operate in the mid-seventeenth century (such as the structural fragility of Portugal within the European interstate system, internal doubts about the convenience of the Portuguese diplomatic alliance with Britain, and previous plans to move the royal family to Brazil in the event of a serious threat to the Bragança crown in Europe), its immediate reasons reside in the post-1789 European conjuncture. Between 1793 and 1796, Portugal belonged to the wide range of alliances of the European *ancien régime* against revolutionary France. In 1796, in view of the agreement between the Directory and Bourbon Spain, Portugal returned to its secular neutrality policy. In 1801, after a short war against Spain, two separate platforms were set up in Lisbon to meet the challenges posed by Bonaparte's aggressive policy: the first arguing for an alignment with the Spanish Bourbons and the French emperor; the second, for keeping the historical alignment with Great Britain. The Continental Blockade and the ultimatum given to the regent D. João pushed him to the British solution and, therefore, to the escape route toward Brazil (Slemian and Pimenta 2008).

In sum, all these processes that help explain the takeoff of the Paraíba Valley as a major coffee-plantation zone clearly have as their point of departure the chain of events opened by the Atlantic revolutionary processes that unfolded in the Haitian Revolution, the rise and fall of Bonaparte, and in the post–Congress of Vienna political and economic world order. This very same chain of events also paved the way for the rise of coffee in the Dutch East Indies. The Age of Revolution played an absolutely central role in the process that turned eighteenth-century Java, with relatively strong and autonomous local powers in relation to the Dutch East India company (VOC, itself a political and business body with great autonomy in relation to the United Provinces of the Netherlands), into a new type of colony, subjected directly to the harsh yoke of the new United Kingdom of the Netherlands in the nineteenth century.

The Netherlands, France, Britain, and their overseas possessions formed an articulated historical bloc, with common temporal rhythms and multiple reciprocal determinations since the turn of the seventeenth century. In a coauthored book I have called this historical structure the Northwestern European Atlantic System, whose crisis began with the results of the Seven Years' War (Marquese, Parron, and Berbel 2016, 13–60). I cannot examine here all the details of that crisis but only briefly point out how the key episodes of the dissolution of the United Provinces of the Netherlands and of the VOC were directly associated with the wider context of the breakdown of British colonial relations in the North Atlantic and the dynamics of the French Revolution.

At the turn to the eighteenth-century, after a long period of enormous financial and military success (1602–1680) in which it came to a certain extent to embody the power and opulence of the Netherlands, the VOC entered a new phase in which the abundance of capital in the metropolis allowed the maintenance of continuous rates of growth of its operations in Asia, but without substantial additional returns. What happened with coffee is quite significant for this second moment of the VOC. In the 1700s and 1710s, strong price hikes and difficulties in purchasing the product in Yemen stimulated the Northwestern European powers to seize the secrets of coffee production. The initial results were very promising, as the VOC quickly set up its coffee economy in western Java. However, this success, coupled with the quite simultaneous founding of the coffee slave plantations in Surinam and Martinique, caused coffee prices to plummet in European markets between 1725 and 1738 (Posthumus 1946, 1:75). The response of the VOC's top managers was conservative. Treating coffee as if it were a spice, the Amsterdam Board of Directors forced the artificial downturn of the prices paid to the Javanese rulers in Batavia, banned new plantings, and ordered the destruction of the surplus coffee trees (Knaap 1986, 46; Breman 2015, 64–68). The comparative profitability of products carried by the VOC's vessels throughout the eighteenth century—always unfavorable to coffee—indicated the structural limit to the expansion of Javanese coffee cultivation in the old Dutch regime. In fact, the difficulties encountered with coffee expressed in some ways the VOC's new situation, characterized by continuous stagnation, in which the dividends paid to its many investors in the Netherlands gradually decapitalized it. In the words of historians Jan de Vries and Ad van der Woude (1995, 449), whom I follow in this analysis, "the era of profitless growth had given way to the era of the unprofitable giant."

Despite the VOC's enormous capital stock in the late eighteenth century, the company no longer functioned efficiently. Its stock prices were steadily dropping, but investors continued to put faith in the company by understanding it as the financial mainstay of the republic. Everything changed with the outbreak of the Fourth Anglo-Dutch War, directly motivated by the tensions of the American Revolution. In the early years of the British imperial conflict, the Netherlands sought to remain officially neutral but traded with the American rebels and opened their credit portfolio for French military spending. Britain's answer was brutal. In the war of 1780–1784, British naval power imposed heavy defeats on the Netherlands. The VOC was the main victim: its fleet was halved, its power in Asia declined notably, and above all its financial situation became unsolvable. Between 1784 and 1790 in the midst of the so-called Patriotic Revolution of 1785–1787—directly inspired by the successes of the American Revolution (Palmer 2014, 311–33; Schama 1977)—the United Provinces of the Netherlands rescued the VOC with direct subsidies and loan guarantees. Without any chance of success for this financial operation, the destinies of one and the other were inextricably linked (de Vries and van der Woude 1995, 456; Israel 1995, 1098–1130; Boxer 1965, 124–25).

With the victory of the republic in France in 1792, the so-called Dutch Patriot leaders of 1785–1787 who had been exiled returned as liberators, overthrowing the regime that had been in power in the Netherlands since the late sixteenth century. The new political unit that emerged, the Batavian Republic founded in 1795, which was responsible for the dissolution of the VOC in 1800 and for the formal incorporation of all its Asian territories, was an early ally of the French Directory and, subsequently, of Bonaparte. This happened, however, in the context of the erosion of the Dutch positions in the Indian Ocean. Still in 1795, in response to the new alliance of the Batavian Republic and the French Republic, Britain conquered the Cape colony in southern Africa and the island of Ceylon in the Indian subcontinent (Schrikker 2007, 129–58). At first Java was out of the British orbit, but it would soon fit into London's imperial calculations as Bonaparte began to intervene more directly in the Dutch affairs.

In 1806, as part of the broader strategy of the Continental Blockade (the Dutch ports were one of the main entrances for the British product into Germany), the same strategy that would force the Portuguese royal family to flee to Brazil, the Batavian Republic disappeared. In its place the French emperor imposed the constitutional monarchy of the Kingdom of Holland, having for its sovereign Luis Bonaparte, his own brother. The new regime outlined new guidelines for Java. As in Brazil, 1808 also represented for Java a decisive step in the making of its nineteenth-century coffee economy. The incorporation of the Kingdom of Holland into the Napoleonic Empire began the chain of events that would transform the relations of the metropolis and the Indonesian space. The first governor-general of this new stage, Herman Willem Daendels, was the only field marshal of the Napoleonic army who had not been born in France. Founded on the principles of the French revolutionary order, during his short government (1808–1811) he profoundly modified the nature of the political relations between the Dutch colonial powers and the Javanese courts of Surakarta and Yogyakarta (Rickfels 2001,145–46; Carey 2010, 172–76).

Formally incorporated into the French Empire in 1810, with the dissolution of the Kingdom of Holland, Java became a priority target for Britain in the Indian Ocean theater. A great expedition landed at Batavia in 1811 under the civil command of Thomas Raffles, whose platform for reorganizing the Javanese powers was rather close to that of Daendels. The British conquered Yogyakarta in 1812, and many of the lands of neighboring sultanates were directly expropriated. Raffles's administration, following the general guidelines of Daendels, introduced a system of "land rent" that would lay the basis for the later monetarization of the Javanese economy; he converted the peasant villages into the primary units of colonial administration; he began to treat Javanese native officials as part of the governmental bureaucratic machine. Many of these reforms remained only on paper, but their principles would help guide forthcoming renewed Dutch colonialism. In 1816 Java returned to Dutch hands as a result of the deliberations of the Congress of Vienna in the same movement that had led to the creation of the new United Kingdom of the Netherlands under the regime of a constitutional monarchy. On the other side of the world, the profound change of the peasant and aristocratic way of life in the interior of Java was already producing great discontent, without the Dutch state being able to obtain, at that moment, a significant fiscal harvest (Rickfels 2001, 147–54; Carey 2010, 176–80).

In the Daendels and Raffles administrations and the post-Vienna European order reside the foundations of the war that would break out in Java in 1825. This extremely violent conflict, which caused the deaths of about two hundred thousand people in just five years, represented both the culmination of a crisis that had begun in the 1780s and the starting point of the new nineteenth-century Dutch colonialism, in which the imposition of the so-called Cultivation System on the colonial space led to the definitive "peripheralization" of Java (Fasseur 1999, 13–55; Wallerstein 1989, 130–31) and the consolidation of the new liberal monarchical order in the metropolitan space, largely supported by the intensive economic exploitation of Java (van Zanden and van Riel 2004, 121–87).

In summary, the events that occurred with the Portuguese Empire in Brazil and with the Dutch Empire in Java, seemingly very distant from one another, were in fact connected to the unified historical process of crisis of the Iberian Atlantic System and the Northwestern European Atlantic System, itself part of the general crisis of the Old Regime accelerated by the French Revolution and the Napoleonic Wars. Likewise, the construction of the new labor regimes in the Brazilian and Javanese coffee economies also answered to a unified bundle of historical forces.

Second Slavery and the Cultivation System

In the post-1815 world order, shaped by the free market, industrialization, urbanization, and new patterns of mass consumption in the North Atlantic and Continental Europe, the advancement of Brazil and Java as the major global coffee producers depended entirely on an innovative restoration, given a new content, of their former forms of compulsory labor. The *second slavery*, a concept originally proposed by Dale Tomich (2004) and that I have been employing to illuminate the dynamics of the coffee economy, society, politics, and culture in the Paraíba Valley (Marquese 2004, 259–98; 2008, 2010, 2013b), is a clear manifestation of that. The second slavery in the Brazilian coffee fields was—in remarkable synchrony with the Dutch colonial experience—the mainstay of the construction of a new liberal monarchical order in Brazil (Parron 2011; Salles 2013).

The Cultivation System was in itself a recomposition, on an enlarged scale, of forms of surplus extraction from the Javanese peasantry designed by the VOC for the western part of Java over which the company had had stable control (Priangan and Ciberon, but not the Mataram Kingdom). After successfully acclimatizing coffee on the island, in the 1710s and 1720s the VOC forced local powers to offer their product at fixed prices that were well below current values in Europe, and whose resale generated considerable gains to the company. The local authorities, in turn, forced their subjects to cultivate the article on a small scale, retaining much of peasants' income as taxes. As can be seen in table 7.1, the size of the whole operation was always reduced, and throughout the nineteenth century Java was never able to produce more than 2,500 tons of coffee per year (Rickfels 2001, 100–111; Elson 1994, 24–25; Clarence-Smith 1994, 241–43; Breman 2015, 64–66).

The model, however, would be fruitful in the nineteenth century. The Kultuur Stelsel or Cultivation System consisted simply of a readjustment of the VOC's past practices to the new circumstances in Java after the war of 1825–1830 when Holland began to exercise effective control over the whole island. In this new pattern of colonial exploitation, designed by Johannes van den Bosch and deployed as soon as he took office as governor-general of Java in 1830, Indonesian peasants were compelled to pay land taxes through a system of coerced farming. Daendels's (1808–1811) and Raffles's (1811–1816) goals would finally begin to pay off. According to Van den Bosch's scheme, Java peasants had to allocate a given area of their communities to produce items as determined by the colonial government, providing them at fixed prices to the official stores. In view of its easy links to the peasant mode of life (family units were unsupervised in the production process, and they managed cultivating and processing completely autonomously), coffee became the backbone of the system and the main source of income for the colonial state. The Netherlands also profited from the Nederlandsche Handelmaatschappij, a quasi-monopolist company that sent the coffee bought in Java to the metropolis for auction sales at values well below those current in the world market (Fasseur 1992, 26–55).

The distinctions between the second slavery in Brazil and the Cultivation System in Java are undeniable. Brazilian production was highly elastic throughout the nineteenth century; the Javanese production, after reaching a seventy-thousand-ton level in 1840, no longer grew. Up to 1850 the foundations of Brazilian elasticity resided in the process of mass enslavement of Africans (1,200 million slaves landed in the ports of Center-South Brazil between 1808 and 1850), and after that in a huge domestic slave trade (220,000 slaves were sold to the coffee provinces between 1850 and 1881). These slaves toiled on plantations whose spatial scale was much greater than that of their eighteenth-century Caribbean counterparts, and where the search to improve the processing of coffee beans went hand in hand with the need to extract more labor from the slaves (Marquese 2009a, 2009b). Java's inelastic production stemmed from the functioning of the Cultivation System, grounded in the preexisting demographic base of the island. The Dutch colonial administrations never intervened in the labor and production processes, which remained in full control of the peasant households. Unlike Brazil, coffee processing in Java was done manually. To summarize these differences in one sentence: the Paraíba Valley was a reinvention of Saint-Domingue on a giant scale, and Java was a reinvention of Yemen.

The tremendous success of the Paraíba Valley in the early 1820s established one of the immediate conditions for the creation of the Cultivation System in Java. Restoring the income of the Dutch state was an urgent task in 1830. The liberal economic policies of colonial exploitation in Java, implemented in 1816 after its return to Dutch rule, had been unable to increase the colonial product; the conquest war between 1825 and 1830 consumed an enormous amount of money, and at its end the United Kingdom of the Netherlands began to face Belgian secession, fighting it unsuccessfully for the rest of the 1830s. At this moment Java was seen as "the cork on which the Netherlands floats," that is, the only possible solution to the bankrupt status of the monarchy, and Java was basically the coffee economy.

Between 1827 and 1829, when he was commissioner-general in the slave colony of Surinam, Van den Bosch noted that, given Java's system of free labor and its geographical distance from the consumer markets of the North Atlantic, it would never be able to compete with the slave zones of the New World. The effectiveness of the latter was evident in the increasingly massive Brazilian coffee harvests, which toppled coffee prices on the world market in the 1820s. In a memorial presented to King William in 1829 before moving to Java as its new governor-general, Van den Bosch claimed that only with compulsory labor such as the VOC's old model would it be possible to rebuild the island's coffee economy in the adverse world market conditions created by the Brazilian product (Fasseur 1992, 23–25). At the end of the day, slave labor at Paraíba Valley determined the working conditions of the global coffee market in the post-Napoleonic era.

References

Boxer, Charles R. 1965. *The Dutch Seaborne Empire, 1600–1800*. London: Penguin Books, 1965.

Breman, Jan. 2015. *Mobilizing Labour for the Global Coffee Market: Profits from an Unfree Work Regime in Colonial Java.* Amsterdam: Amsterdam University Press.

Carey, Peter. 2010. "Revolutionary Europe and the Destruction of Java's Old Order, 1808–1830." In *The Age of Revolutions in Global Context, c. 1760–1840*, edited by David Armitadge and Sanjay Subrahmanyam, 167–88. London: Palgrave-Macmillan.

Carmagani, Marcelo. 2012. *Las islas del lujo: Productos exóticos, nuevos consumos y cultura económica europea, 1650–1800.* Mexico, DF: El Colegio de México.

Carvalho Franco, Maria Sylvia de. 1983. *Homens livres na ordem escravocrata.* São Paulo: Kairós.

Clarence-Smith, William Gervase. 1994. "The Impact of Forced Coffee Cultivation on Java, 1805–1917." *Indonesia Circle*, no. 64: 241–64.

Cunha, Mauro Rodrigues da. 1992. "Apêndice estatístico." In *150 anos de café*, edited by Edmar Bacha and Robert Greenhill, 283–391. Rio de Janeiro: Marcellino Martins & E. Johnston.

de Vries, Jan. 2008. *The Industrious Revolution: Consumer Behaviour and the Household Economy, 1650 to the Present.* Cambridge: Cambridge University Press.

de Vries, Jan, and Ad van der Woude. 1995. *The First Modern Economy. Success, Failure, and Perseverance of the Dutch Economy, 1500–1815.* Cambridge: Cambridge University Press.

Dubois, Laurent. 2004. *Avengers of the New World: The Story of the Haitian Revolution.* Cambridge, MA: Harvard University Press.

Dumont Villares, Jorge. 1927. *O café: Sua produção e exportação.* 2 vols. São Paulo: Instituto do Café do Estado de São Paulo.

Elson, Robert. 1994. *Village Java under the Cultivation System, 1830–1870.* Sydney: Asian Studies Association of Australia in association with Allen & Unwin.

Fasseur, Cornelis. 1992. *The Politics of Colonial Exploitation: Java, the Dutch, and the Cultivation System.* Ithaca, NY: Southern Asia Program, Cornell University.

González Fernandéz, Doria. 1989. "Acerca del mercado cafetelero cubano durante la primeira mitad del siglo XIX." *Revista de la Biblioteca Nacional José Martí*, no. 2: 151–76.

Holloway, Thomas H. 1984. *Imigrantes para o café: Café e sociedade em São Paulo, 1886–1934.* Rio de Janeiro: Paz & Terra.

Israel, Jonathan. 1995. *The Dutch Republic: Its Rise, Greatness, and Fall, 1477–1806.* Oxford, UK: Oxford University Press.

Knaap, G. J. 1986. "Coffee for Cash: The Dutch East India Company and Its Expansion of Coffee Cultivation in Java, Ambon and Ceylon, 1700–1730." In *Trading Companies in Asia, 1600–1800*, edited by J. van Goor, 33–49. Utrecht: HES.

Laërne, K. F. van Delden. 1885. *Brazil and Java: Report on Coffee-Culture in America, Asia, and Africa.* London: W. H. Allen.

Marquese, Rafael de Bivar. 2004. *Feitores do corpo, missionários da mente: Senhores, letrados e o controle dos escravos nas Américas, 1660–1860.* São Paulo: Companhia das Letras.

———. 2008. "African Diaspora, Slavery, and the Paraiba Valley Coffee Plantation Landscape: Nineteenth Century Brazil." *Review: A Journal of the Fernand Braudel Center* 31, no. 2: 196–216.

———. 2009a. "A ilustração luso-brasileira e a circulação dos saberes escravistas caribenhos: A montagem da cafeicultura brasileira em perspectiva comparada." *História, Ciências, Saúde—Manguinhos* 16, no. 4: 855–80.

———. 2009b. "Espacio y poder en la caficultura esclavista de las Américas: El Valle del Paraíba en perspectiva comparada, 1750–1850." In *Trabajo libre y trabajo coactivo en sociedades de plantación*, edited by José Antonio Piqueras, 215–52. Madrid: Siglo XXI.

———. 2010. "O Vale do Paraíba cafeeiro e o regime visual da segunda escravidão: O caso da fazenda Resgate." *Anais do Museu Paulista* 18, no. 1: 83–128.

———. 2013a. "Estados Unidos, Segunda Escravidão e a Economia Cafeeira do Império do Brasil." *Almanack*, no. 5: 51–60.

———. 2013b. "Capitalismo, Escravidão e a Economia Cafeeira do Brasil no longo século XIX." *Saeculum* (UFPB), no. 29: 289–321.

Marquese, Rafael, Tâmis Parron, and Márcia Berbel. 2016. *Slavery and Politics: Brazil and Cuba, 1790–1950.* Albuquerque: New Mexico University Press.

Marquese, Rafael, and Ricardo Salles. 2015. "A cartografia do poder senhorial: Cafeicultura, escravidão e a formação do Estado Nacional brasileiro, 1822–1848." In *O Vale do Paraíba e o Império do Brasil nos quadros da Segunda Escravidão*, edited by Mariana Muaze and Ricardo Salles, 98–126. Rio de Janeiro: 7 Letras.

Marquese, Rafael, and Dale Tomich. 2009. "O Vale do Paraíba escravista e a formação do mercado mundial do café no século XIX." In *O Brasil Imperial*, vol. 2, *1831–1870*, edited by Keila Grinberg and Ricardo Salles, 339–83. Rio de Janeiro: Civilização Brasileira.

May, Louis-Philippe. 1972. *Histoire Économique économique de la Martinique (1635–1763).* Fort-de-France: Société de Distribution distribution et de Cculture.

McCook, Stuart. 2006. "Global rust Rust bBelt: *Hemileia Vastatrix* and the eEcological iIntegration of wWorld cCoffee pProduction since 1850." *Journal of Global History* 1, no. 2: 177–195.

McDonald, Michelle Craig, and Steven Topik. 2013. "Why Americans Drink Coffee: the The Boston Tea Party or American Slavery?" In: *Coffee: A Comprehensive Guide to the Bean, the Beverage, and the Industry*, 234–47. Boulder, CO: Rowman & Littlefield, 234–247.

Palmer, Robert R. 2014. *The Age of Democratic Revolution: A Political History of Europe and America, 1760–1800.* Princeton, NJ: Princeton University Press.

Parron, Tâmis. 2011. *A política da escravidão no Império do Brasil, 1826–1865.* Rio de Janeiro: Civilização Brasileira.

———. 2015. "*A política da escravidão na era da liberdade: Brasil, Estados Unidos e Cuba, 1787–1846.*" PhD diss., Dissertation, Universidade deUniversity of São Paulo.

Posthumus, N. 1946. *Inquiry into the History of Prices in Holland.* 2 vols. Leiden: E. J. Brill.

Rickfels, M. C. 2001. *A History of Modern Indonesia since c. 1200.* London: Palgrave-Macmillan.

Salles, Ricardo. 2013. *Nostalgia Imperial: Escravidão e formação da identidade nacional no Brasil do Segundo Reinado.* Rio de Janeiro: Ponteio.

Samper, Mario, and Radin Fernando. 2003. "Historical Statistics of Coffee Production and Trade from 1700 to 1960." In: *The Global Coffee Economy in Africa, Asia, and Latin America, 1500–1989*, edited by W. G. Clarence-Smith and S. Topik, 411–62. Cambridge: Cambridge University Press.

Schama, Simon. 1977. *Patriots and Liberators: Revolution in the Netherlands, 1780–1815.* New York: Oxford University Press.

Schivelbusch, Wolfgang. 1993. *Tastes of Paradise: A Social History of Spices, Stimulants, and Intoxicants.* New York: Vintage Books.

Schneider, Jürgen. 1992. "The Effects on European Markets of Imports of Overseas Agriculture: The Production, Trade and Consumption of Coffee (15th to late 18th Century)." In *Economic Effects of the European Expansion, 1492–1824*, edited by José Casas Pardo, 283–306. Stuttgart: Franz Steiner Verlag.

Schrikker, Alicia. 2007. *Dutch and British Colonial Intervention in Sri Lanka, 1780–1815: Expansion and Reform.* Leiden: Brill.

Slemian, Andréa, and João Paulo Pimenta. 2008. *A corte e o mundo: Uma história do ano em que a família real portuguesa chegou ao Brasil.* São Paulo: Alameda.

Smith, S. D. 1996. "Accounting for Taste: British Coffee Consumption in Historical Perspective." *Journal of Interdisciplinary History* 27, no. 2: 183–214.

Tarrade, Jean. 1972. *Le commerce colonial de la France a la cin de l'Ancien Régime: L'évolution du régime de 'l'Exclusif' de 1763 à 1789.* 2 vols. Paris: PUF.

Thurber, Francis Beatty. 1884. *Coffee, from Plantation to Cup: A Brief History of Coffee Production and Consumption.* New York: American Grocer.

Tomich, Dale. 2004. *Through the Prism of Slavery: Labor, Capital, and World Economy.* Boulder, CO: Rowman & Littlefield.

Topik, Steven. 2003. "The Integration of the World Coffee Market." In *The Global Coffee Economy in Africa, Asia, and Latin América, 1500–1989*, edited by W. G. Clarence-Smith and S. Topik, 21–49. Cambridge: Cambridge University Press.

Topik, Steven. 2004. "The World Coffee Market in the Eighteenth and Nineteenth Centuries, from Colonial to National Regimes." Working Papers of the Global Economic History Network, no. 4, London School of Economics.

Trouillot, Michel-Rolph. 1982. "Motion in the System: Coffee, Color, and Slavery in Eighteenth-Century Saint-Domingue." *Review: A Journal of the Fernand Braudel Center* 5, no. 3: 331–88.

Tuchscherer, Michel. 2003. "Coffee in the Red Sea Area from the Sixteenth to the Nineteenth Century." In *The Global Coffee Economy in Africa, Asia, and Latin América,*

1500–1989, edited by W. G. Clarence-Smith and S. Topik, 50–66. Cambridge: Cambridge University Press.

van Zanden, Jan Luiten, and Arthur van Riel. 2004. *The Strictures of Inheritance: The Dutch Economy in the Nineteenth Century.* Princeton, NJ: Princeton University Press.

Wallerstein, Immanuel. 1989. *The Modern World-System III: The Second Era of Great Expansion of the Capitalist World-Economy, 1730–1840s.* New York: Academic.

Watts, David. 1992. *Las Indias Occidentales: Modalidades de desarrollo, cultura y cambio medioambiental desde 1492.* Madrid: Alianza Editorial.

Chapter 8

African Businesswomen in the Age of Second Slavery in Angola

Mariana P. Candido

Influenced by Catherine Coquery-Vidrovitch's scholarship on women and economic changes within Africa, this study explores the role of African women in mid-nineteenth-century Angola (Coquery-Vidrovitch 1994, 1997, 1975; Coquery-Vidrovitch and Lovejoy 1985). Although the slave trade was outlawed in the colony of Angola in 1836, trade in human beings continued, in part to attend to the demand for labor in newly installed farms. In fact, similar to Cuba, Brazil, and the Gold Coast, Benguela and its surrounding areas became new zones of slavery as part of the reorganization of the world economy during the nineteenth century (Ferrer 2008, 2014; Karasch 1987; Mann 2010). After the ban on slave exports, West Central Africans and Portuguese colonial officers began looking for new economic activities and shifted their focus and energy to trade in commodities as legitimate commerce expanded in Benguela. Looking at the case of Teresa Ferreira Torres Barruncho, I examine the mechanisms that African women employed to accumulate property, including human beings, a process that Coquery-Vidrovitch has analyzed earlier and linked to inequality in power based on inheritance practices that did not favor female heirs (1994, 29–37).

In dialogue with Coquery-Vidrovitch's scholarship, I examine how African women achieved new social and economic positions in the colonial setting, accumulating dependents and goods. Teresa Ferreira Torres Barruncho amassed many enslaved dependents and land, and she became the most important cotton producer and exporter of the 1860s (Alexandre and Dias 1998, 450). She married at least three times, challenged local rulers' land claims, and controlled more than three hundred slaves on one of her farms. The concentration of dependents, including those who were enslaved, consolidated wealth in fewer hands and altered notions of land access and rights. This study emphasizes African women's role as active agents of change on the coast and in the interior of Benguela during this time of economic transformation, and their extensive use of the kinship and economic networks that already existed (Schmidt 1992; Zimba 2003, 120–33; A. Jones 1995; White 1981; Havik 2016). By focusing on one African woman I reconstruct the life experience of a historical actor whose agency reveals the intricacies of gender, race, colonialism, slavery, and early capitalism in the second half of nineteenth-century Angola. Examining Teresa Ferreira Torres Barruncho's story is an effort to place African women at the center of historical narratives about the end of the slave trade, second slavery, and the plantation economy as entrepreneurs rather than as enslaved labor.

Benguela in the Age of Second Slavery

Despite the 1836 ban, in the 1840s caravans continued to arrive from the interior to engage in the profitable illegal slave trade that operated in Equimina, Cuio, and many of the smaller natural ports south of Benguela.[1] After 1850 when the Brazilian government enforced legislation that banned the import of enslaved Africans, the number of people retained in captivity increased in Benguela, leading by 1860 to a ratio of four enslaved people to each free person (Domingues da Silva 2017, 30–37). Illegal embarking continued to operate, such as the case of the schooner *Laura*, caught in 1854 with more than 150 captives on board near Equimina south of Benguela (Candido 2018, 215–41).[2] Besides the external market, slavery was central to the organization and functioning of the colonial towns in West Central Africa and enslaved men and women performed most productive tasks, from cultivating, preparing, and selling food to offering services in the port, such as shoemakers, washers, and sailors, as well as domestic tasks associated with housekeeping and tending children. Enslaved people labored within the urban limits but also on the surrounding farms and sugarcane, coffee, and cotton plantations. In a context of economic transformation, African women emerged as major entrepreneurs and mobilized efforts to acquire more enslaved people or freed individuals to work on farms and in houses (Clarence-Smith 1979; Freudenthal 2005; Ferreira 2013; Vos 2014, 2010).

For most of the nineteenth century enslaved people represented half or more of Benguela's population. In 1804 the number totaled around 1,118 enslaved individuals. The number reached its peak in 1860 after the official ban of slave exports and the closure of the Brazilian market, when around 4,300 people were in captivity as can be seen in figure 8.2.

The case of Benguela reveals that the nineteenth century was not the age of emancipation, liberty, and democratic revolution framed by Robert Palmer and, more recently, Janet Polasky (Palmer 1969; Polasky 2015). Instead it was a period when slavery expanded and became vital to economic production in this region (Scott and Hébrard 2012; Tomich and Zeuske 2008; Lovejoy 2016; Greene 2017). Indeed, slavery was central to the organization and functioning of colonial towns in West Central Africa such as Benguela and Luanda (see figure 8.1). Bondage was also widespread within local states, with elite and nonelite members securing unfree dependents who could increase production and prestige.

The enslaved population of Benguela was predominantly female, as can be seen in figure 8.3. Only in the first decade of the nineteenth century and in 1850 and 1860 were more men enslaved than women. People were bought and sold in markets, public auctions, taverns, and along the docks, despite the lack of a centralized system of human-property registrations until the 1850s. Slavery remained legal in Portuguese overseas territories until 1878, although a series of metropolitan decrees between 1854 and 1858 began to slowly restrain it, a process that Paul Lovejoy and Jan Hogendorn call the slow death of slavery (1993; Candido 2018, 215–41). Although the 1869 decree officially abolished slavery, it still required that the newly freed slaves, called *libertos*, continue to work for their former masters for periods of seven to nine years or until 1878, when the status of *liberto* was revoked.[3] After 1869 the category *slave* disappears from the census, giving the illusion that all people who lived in territories under Portuguese control were free and masking the fact that slavery remained alive (Allina 2012). By 1878 the census listed only free people, a total of 4,298, implying that in Benguela everyone enjoyed the same degree of freedom.

It was in this context of expanding slavery that wealthy Benguela residents consolidated control over land and human beings, claiming property rights. The end of slave exports in the 1820s and 1830s accelerated competition for land access in

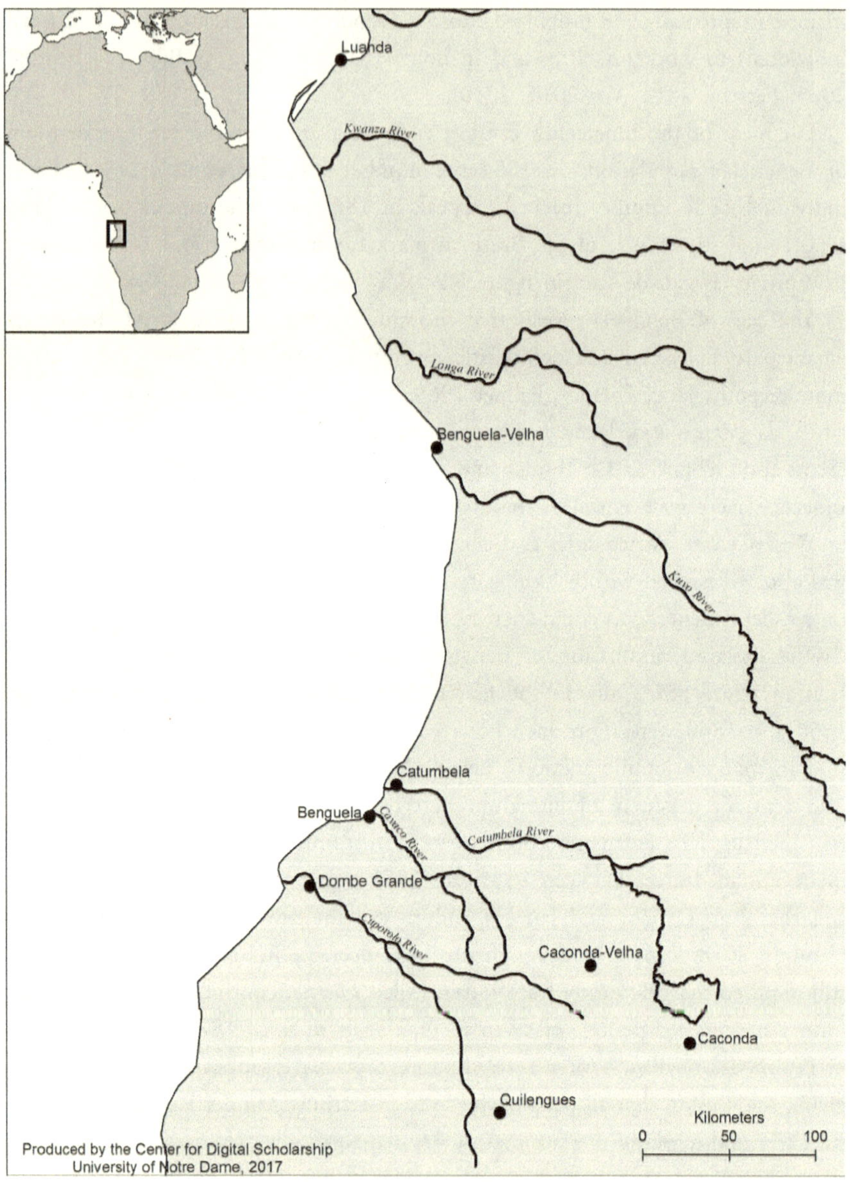

Figure 8.1. West Central Africa. Source: GIS Library, University of Notre Dame.

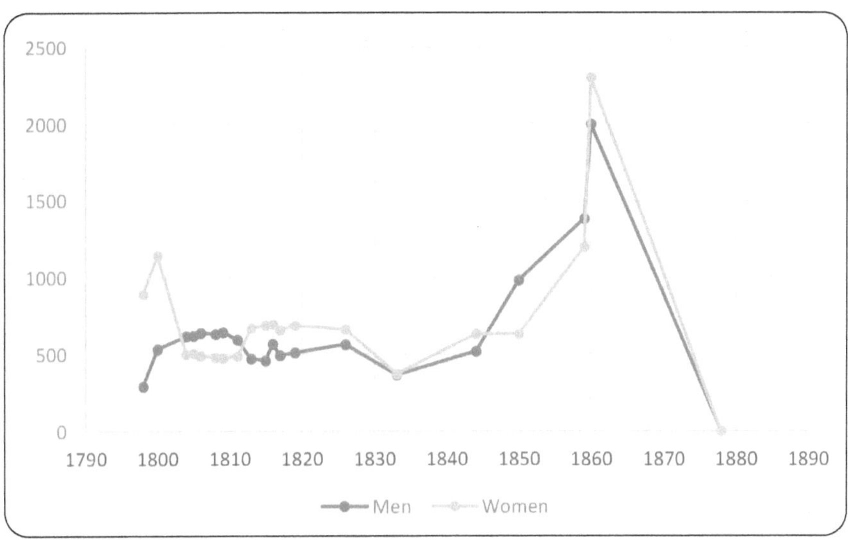

Figure 8.2. Population of Benguela by legal status. Sources: Compiled by author from data in AHU, Angola, 1 sec., cx. 88, d. 46; ANA, Cod. 442, fl 161v–162; AHU, Angola, 1 sec., cx. 113, d. 6; AHU, Angola, 1 sec., cx. 116, d. 87; AHU, Angola, 1 sec., cx. 118, d. 21; AHU, Angola, 1 sec., cx. 120 d. 21; AHU, Angola, 1 sec., cx. 121, d. 32; AHU, Angola, 1 sec, cx, 124, d. 8; AHU, Angola, 1 sec., cx. 127, d. 59; AHU, Angola, 1 sec., cx. 131 d. 45; AHU, Angola, 1 sec., cx 133, d. 32; AHU, Angola, 1 sec., cx. 136, d. 19; AHU, Angola, 1 sec., cx. 138, d. 1; AHU, Angola, 1 sec., cx 156 d. 16; AHU, Angola, 1 sec., cx, 176, d. 17; Lopes de Lima, p. 4-A; *Almanak estatístico da província de Angola*, p. 9; ANA, cx 5568; AHU, Pasta 48.

and around Benguela, resulting in changes regarding use and access to public land. In the 1820s and 1830s local rulers started to lose the use of the land they had occupied for decades, under the contention that this was unproductive or unoccupied land. Curiously, a series of African women managed to secure landed property at the expense of local rulers. Some were single, but most African women who received land were married to Portuguese- or Brazilian-born men (Candido 2015a; Pantoja 2001).

The Emergence of Teresa de Jesus as an Entrepreneur

Marriages between indigenous elite women and European traders were common in the Atlantic World, as cases from the Americas and African coast reveal. These

Figure 8.3. Enslaved population of Benguela by gender. Sources: Compiled by author from data in AHU, Angola, 1 sec., cx. 88, d. 46; ANA, Cod. 442, fl 161v–162; AHU, Angola, 1 sec., cx. 113, d. 6; AHU, Angola, 1 sec., cx. 116, d. 87; AHU, Angola, 1 sec., cx. 118, d. 21; AHU, Angola, 1 sec., cx. 120 d. 21; AHU, Angola, 1 sec., cx. 121, d. 32; AHU, Angola, 1 sec, cx, 124, d. 8; AHU, Angola, 1 sec., cx. 127, d. 59; AHU, Angola, 1 sec., cx. 131 d. 45; AHU, Angola, 1 sec., cx 133, d. 32; AHU, Angola, 1 sec., cx. 136, d. 19; AHU, Angola, 1 sec., cx. 138, d. 1; AHU, Angola, 1 sec., cx 156 d. 16; AHU, Angola, 1 sec., cx, 176, d. 17; Lopes de Lima, p. 4-A; *Almanak estatístico da província de Angola*, p. 9; ANA, cx 5568; AHU, Pasta 48.

associations facilitated cross-cultural commercial interactions and brought connections and advantages to both partners. Since the early seventeenth century, sexual and domestic relationships between Ndombe and Luso-African women and Portuguese men played a crucial role in expanding colonialism beyond the urban settlements and facilitating the interiorization of the Atlantic slave trade. By the nineteenth century several powerful families lived in Benguela, and it was common for Ndombe women and European traders to engage in long-term relationships, often legitimized in the local Catholic church, that offered advantages to those involved. Women and men chose their marital partners carefully to improve their social position and boost their economic and political power. In many cases this increased with the adoption of the husband's last name, especially if he was a foreigner (Scully 2005; Ipsen 2013; Jean-Baptiste 2014; A. M. Caldeira 2007;

Rodrigues 2015; Candido 2017; Oliveira 2018; Everst 2012; Kriger 2019). Teresa de Jesus, later identified as Teresa Barruncho, was not the only businesswomen to successfully secure a place as a commercial player. Her case reveals the rise of merchant women who accumulated economic and social power and, as Coquery-Vidrovitch stressed decades ago, shows how the experiences of African women in the past were plural and more complex than often thought (1994, 57–60). Teresa, as well as other women who lived in West Central Africa, were active agents in the social and economic changes that occurred at this time (Pantoja 2000; Oliveira 2015, 2016a; Candido 2014, 2015b, 2017).

In the earliest record I was able to locate related to Teresa Barruncho, she was identified as Teresa de Jesus, originally from Novo Redondo. The document in question was her second marriage certificate, in which Teresa de Jesus indicated that before 1840 she was married to António Joaquim Ferreira Torres, a Luanda merchant who maintained strong links to Brazil. After her first marriage Teresa incorporated Antonio Joaquim's last names, signing as "Dona Teresa de Jesus Ferreira e Torres."[4] Teresa was able to sign her own name, a surprising event in a town with no schools and where both men and women had limited literacy. In Angola the ability to read and write was, as Pedro da Paixão Franco declares, "a privilege bigger than having the title of baron or viscount" (quoted in Pacheco 2000, 30). Before the 1830s Luanda and Benguela merchants were involved in the trade in human beings, and many couples operated as business partners, connecting the coast to inland markets. Caravans arrived in Benguela from markets controlled by African rulers, as well as from places controlled by Portuguese forces such as Caconda (Candido 2007, 2013, 160–85).

Teresa remarried after the death of her first husband in 1840. In 1841 she married José Luis da Silva Viana from Viana do Minho, Portugal, and added his last name to hers. Her new husband was surveyor of the municipal chamber, a position that gave him legal authority over business development. Their wedding was a major event in Benguela, bringing together the top commercial traders and colonial officers, including the governor of the port, João Jacinto Tavares.[5] The 1840s was a period of economic reorganization after the 1836 ban on slave exports. Although illegal slave trade continued to operate, local merchants began securing land to diversify their investment in commercial agriculture, employing the enslaved men and women who could no longer be sent to the Americas (Freudenthal 2005; Ferreira 2011, 2013; Oliveira 2016b; Domingues da Silva 2017).

Teresa's second husband, Viana, prospered with the expansion of agriculture, importing cattle from Dombe Grande and selling them in Benguela. Travelers such as George Tams and Antonio Caldeira noted his wealth and prosperity in their written accounts. Viana maintained business links with several important agents and hosted caravan merchants in his house, including Swahili traders from Zanzibar. He eventually became governor of Benguela in the late 1840s (Tams 1850, 1, 144; C. J. Caldeira 1852, 174; Ferreira 2006, 689). Although the sources are silent on the nature of the trade in which Viana was involved, it is easy to imagine that he continued to buy and sell human beings despite the abolition of slave exports. The slave trade was the most profitable business, and Benguela merchants resisted colonial efforts to bring it to an end. In fact, in 1854 Viana and another Benguela-based trader, Ignácio Teixeira Xavier, were caught smuggling slaves. In the operation 194 slaves were apprehended, indicating the direct involvement of former colonial officers in the slave trade's survival.[6] Viana died sometime before 1855.[7] I have not been able to find his burial record, but I have located Teresa's request to place a tombstone marker at the site of her deceased husband's burial site. She also presented legal proceedings to inherit the estate of José Luis da Silva Viana as his legitimate natural heir, protecting the interests of her children.[8]

The Portuguese legal system recognized the inheritance rights of wives, allowing them to receive real estate and manage the family assets. This seems to have been the path to consolidating Teresa's wealth. She acquired property in the form of real estate and human beings, in a process similar to that for other African women before her (Pantoja 2001, 35–49; A. M. Caldeira 2007; Dantas 2014; Rodrigues 2014, 2015). The marriage brought prosperity to Teresa. Under the name D. Teresa de Jesus Ferreira Torres Viana, she employed itinerant merchants, *caixeiros*. One such merchant was Manoel Rodrigues Silva Rego from Portugal, who conducted business on her behalf between markets in the interior and Benguela.[9] In 1854 the British explorer David Livingstone noted that "none of these gentlemen [living in the interior] had Portuguese wives. They usually come to Africa in order to make a little money, and return to Lisbon. Hence, they seldom bring their wives with them, and never can be successful colonialists in consequence. It is common for them to have families by native women" (Livingstone 1857, 235). These women's cooperation or lack thereof could favor or damage the social standing and economic power of their partners. Wives such as Teresa facilitated hospitality, diplomacy, and business deals, and helped establish contacts with local merchants, foreign agents, and colonial administrators. These links could aid their own access to land and business, even after the departure or death of their partners (Sheldon 2002, 7–8; H. Jones 2013, 34–39).

The burial of one her slaves indicates that by the late 1850s Teresa had married for the third time.[10] She had dropped the last name Viana for Barruncho. In 1856 Vicente Ferrer Barruncho, the new governor of Benguela, arrived in town; his relationship with Teresa may have evolved shortly after.[11] Governor Barruncho was particularly interested in the development of agriculture around Benguela. In an 1856 report a few months after his arrival in Benguela, he described the region of Dombe Grande as "excellent for agriculture. It could be even better if the heathens [*gentio*] were not so devoted to their customs and habits and neglectful of hard labor[;] all the flour consumed in Benguela comes from this location." One example of the prosperity he offered was the Equimina farm, owned by Ignácio Teixeira Xavier, whom he described as an entrepreneur and persevering. In Equimina, Governor Barruncho argued, "the establishment produced *aguardente*, but not sugar . . . and sugarcane, labor was employed in the production of manioc, potato [*sic*] and corn. . . . I saw how the slaves are well employed and treated. Only 46 slaves were used, which included carpenters and a blacksmith. In the production of orchil weed, 63 slaves are employed. In the coast town of Lucira, Teixeira Xavier employs 52 of his slaves in fishing."[12] The governor suggested that Benguela residents should copy Teixeira Xavier's business model, employing slaves and free labor for the advancement of plantation agriculture. Teixeira Xavier had had previous commercial alliances in slave contraband with José Luis da Silva Viana, Teresa's second husband.

Barruncho's suggestions agreed with Portuguese policies. With the end of transatlantic slave exports the Portuguese administration encouraged diversification of the economy, favoring the export of local staples such as orchil (a red or violet dye obtained from certain lichens). However, his model entrepreneur, Teixeira Xavier, was repeatedly accused of exporting slave labor and using his plantations as a facade for his illegal business. This case shows how legitimate trade in raw materials and tropical goods developed hand in hand with illegal slave exports. The governor of Angola, José Sobrinho Coelho do Amaral, accused Governor Barruncho of involvement in the illegal slaving scheme, suggesting that Teixeiro's legal activity camouflaged contraband trade in slaves.[13] The trader John Monteiro, who visited Benguela a few years later, argued that "only a very large number of cruisers on the Angolan coast could have prevented the shipment of slaves, as every man and woman, white or black, was interested in the trade, and a perfect system of communication existed from all points, overland and by sea" (1876, 267). Thus Barruncho was an authority involved in slave exports despite the crown's legislation suppressing it.

By the early 1860s, after two marriages and four decades operating as a merchant, Teresa had become the companion of the most important authority in Benguela, the governor. The adoption of a new last name shows that she reinvented herself, changing what in the European world was considered one's most basic self-perception, one's name. She bolstered her personal history and her status by making use of a legal path, belonging to the Catholic Church and claiming this new identity in baptismal records. Teresa was recognized as Governor Barruncho's wife in official records.

Although the sources provide little information on her role as wife, Teresa was very likely responsible for translation and social connections. She helped the governor entertain guests, among them important Atlantic traders and local merchant elites. She was a key factor in helping her newly arrived husband forge commercial alliances. Marriage to Barruncho gave Teresa visibility in the colonial archive. Among the more than 2,100 court cases available at the Tribunal Província de Benguela, Teresa initiated eight legal proceedings and was the defendant in six cases between 1856 and 1880. In many of these cases Teresa used the colonial courts to collect debts or inheritance of her deceased husbands, registered the sale of property, and justified control over an enslaved man.[14]

African Women and New Business Opportunities

The expansion of commercial agriculture offered new economic opportunities for Benguela residents who were able to mobilize resources and labor in response to the international demand for cotton, sugarcane, and rubber during the nineteenth century (Freudenthal 2005; Ferreira 2013; Candido 2015a; Vos 2018; Oliveira 2021). Teresa Barruncho recognized the economic changes and the new business opportunities that were available. While it is tempting to stress the role of men in her economic consolidation, it is important to stress that single African women also engaged in commerce. In Teresa's case, her social and economic standing made her an attractive partner to foreign men such as José Luis da Silva Viana and Vicente Barruncho, who could rely on her business contacts and her knowledge of trade routes, local politics, and market operations. Marriages and relationships expanded networks, based on mutual acquaintances and shared interests (Coquery-Vidrovitch 1994, 33–37; Crais and Scully 2010, 107–9). Through the colonial sources it is possible to identify an African woman who had economic control of her life. By utilizing her relationships, Teresa de Jesus, whether known as Teresa de Jesus Ferreira Torres Viana or later Teresa Barruncho, explored economic opportunities that brought her financial autonomy. Each new relationship produced additional economic power and social capital. Associating with the governors Viana and Barruncho brought material advantages, including access to land. In 1861 the Overseas Secretary authorized a concession of 9,259 hectares to Teresa.

She also acquired land from smaller landowners, such as impoverished Brazilian and Portuguese immigrants who had received land a few years earlier but had no financial assistance in establishing their plantations. The colonial government misappropriated land to distribute to the recently arrived immigrants. Reports indicate that during the 1860s the landscape was transformed by the expansion of agriculture and plantation economy: "The great plains that used to be covered by dense woods and served as refuge for wild animals are now clear of trees, and almost all of the land along the coast is now plantations of cotton and sugar cane."[15] The distribution of land to settlers with no financial resources resulted in frequent failures, and eventually that land was transferred into fewer hands, including those of Teresa. In the 1860s Teresa incorporated the lands of the *soba* Kipumu at the Luacho in the Dombe Grande. The *soba* were local rulers such as Kipumu, who complained to the administration that he paid taxes for his communal lands, yet the colonial government labeled the lands as vacant and expropriated them to Teresa's benefit. On these newly acquired lands Teresa set up farms dedicated to the cultivation of sugarcane and cotton. By 1861 she had three different plantations in the Dombe Grande. As a result Teresa became the leading exporter of cotton, wax, and orchil weed from the port of Benguela (Freudenthal 2005, 213; Alexandre and Dias 1998, 450).[16]

The outbreak of the Civil War in the United States in 1861 affected the availability of cotton for European industry and drove cotton prices up. The textile industries in Europe searched for new sources of cotton, and Angola was one of the options (Henderson 1934, 48–49; Clarence-Smith 1979; Pitcher 1991). Teresa was able to take advantage of the international context to expand her business. She owned land and mobilized free and enslaved people to work on dike construction to irrigate her manioc fields around the Dombe Grande. Teresa also took advantage of policies offered by the colonial government, such as the tax-exempt distribution of seeds to farmers and access to slave and free-labor schemes very similar to the apprenticeship programs in Brazil and the Caribbean (Menezes 1876, 81–82; Freudenthal 2005, 127–33; Clarence-Smith 1979; Pitcher 1991, 48–49).

Besides relying on the Angolan colonial state to provide her with land to establish cotton plantations, Teresa secured support for acquiring seeds and the labor of freed people.[17] She also used the court system to challenge private ownership and claim better resources to invest in agriculture. In 1864 she challenged the land concessions that a business partner of her former husband António Joaquim Ferreira Torres had received in the 1850s. In 1859 Torres's business partner, Amaral, received land measuring 2 *léguas*, or 8.4 kilometers, by 1 *légua* on land located between the São Francisco River and Luache and declared to be empty, where he intended to establish cotton and sugarcane plantations with Torres. The land was given to Amaral as *aforamento*, that is, transferred in perpetuity through the payment of an annual tax. Facing a series of difficulties in launching his plantation, in 1862 Amaral requested exemption from his official duties at the Benguela customs office to focus on his agricultural enterprise. The partnership with Ferreira Torres did not last, which compromised any attempt by Amaral to carry out his agricultural plan. Amaral lacked the manpower since Torres owned most of the enslaved people who would clear the land and cultivate the soil. Amaral had twelve enslaved people, mostly women, which was not enough labor for the vast piece of land.[18] Witnesses brought in to testify in Amaral's favor stated that the land extension required at least two hundred people to work the fields, and the few enslaved men Amaral owned were occupied "cutting wood and building furniture to attend to the demand of the residents of Dombe and Cuio."[19] In 1864 Teresa challenged Amaral's rights to the property, arguing that he did not have the means to cultivate the land and his plots were preventing the expansion of her cotton production. The Conselho Ultramarino (Overseas Council) intervened and ruled that Amaral could maintain ownership of the cultivated land plus land four times its size. The remainder would then be seized by the state and offered to Teresa to expand her agricultural production.[20]

Women such as Teresa who maintained strong links with the administration benefited from colonialism. Through their relationships they accumulated land and dependents, and they invested in legitimate trade, the new focus of the colonial state, though relying heavily on slave labor (Freudenthal 2005, 298n241).[21] While some Africans lost access to land, such as the case of the ruler of Kipumu, some women capitalized on the changes in the mid-nineteenth century. In 1863 alone

Teresa Barruncho exported over 1,354 *arrobas* of cotton and hence was a major cotton supplier to the colonial state.[22] Unlike in other regions, in Benguela women competed with men for control over land and economic power (Clark 1980, 363; Mamdani 1996, 146–47). For example, among the thirteen cotton-plantation owners in Dombe Grande in 1864 there were three women—Dona Teresa Ferreira Torres Barruncho, Isabel António de Luz Abreu, and Dona Maria Dias de Jesus, as can be seen in table 8.1.

Teresa's land accumulation provided economic resources that further expanded her wealth. She lent money to local traders such as Agostinho Antonio Ramos, a resident of Cuio. In his 1862 will Ramos declared that he owed 40$000 réis to Teresa Ferreira Torres Barruncho and the same amount to Joaquim Ferreira, a resident of Novo Redondo, and that both "had documents."[23] The Rio de Janeiro trader Tomé Ribeiro Antunes had accumulated debts with her during his stay in Benguela. He died in her house in 1867, unable to pay back a cash advance. As a result, after a two-year legal case Teresa acquired Antunes's farm and his slaves as collateral.[24] Antunes was not the only foreign trader to die at her house; in 1875 Luis Bernardo de Carvalho from Braga in Portugal also died there.[25] These cases

Table 8.1. Cotton Plantations in Dombe Grande, 1864

Growers	**Location**	**Year established**	**Number of cotton plants**	**Number of enslaved people**
Tomé Ribeiro Antunes	Mama	1863	41,000	120
Francisco Marcelino Galvão	Tumbo	1864	1,000	40
João Esteves de Araújo	Luaxe	1862	40,000	100
Manuel da Costa Souza	Luaxe	1862	20,000	60
José Joaquim Geraldo do Amaral	Luaxe	1862	20,000	48
D. Teresa Ferreira Torres Barruncho	Luaxe	1862	NA	439
D. Isabel António da Luz Abreu	Dombe	1863	NA	74
João Henriques Teixeira	Mama	1863	12,000	48
D. Maria Dias de Jesus	Dombe	1862	20,000	46
Custódio José de Sousa Veloso	Dombe	1863	16,600	62
José Manuel Ribeiro	Dombe	1863	1,356	50
Francisco Pacheco de Sousa e Silva	Dombe	1864	3,000	30
Casal de Inácio Teixeira Xavier	Equimina	1863	4,000	200

indicate Teresa's ability to host travelers and entertain and nurse them, though sometimes unsuccessfully, while they were in Benguela.

In the 1870s Teresa's agrarian expansion consolidated her position as the largest cotton producer and exporter of Benguela. Her agricultural wealth also allowed her to establish a commercial enterprise, the Sociedade Teresa Barruncho. The work connected with that company meant she traveled regularly between Benguela, Dombe Grande, and Lisbon.[26] The cotton was transported from Dombe Grande to the port of Benguela on the backs of free and enslaved blacks. Although some were paid for their role as porters, the bulk of the profit stayed in the hands of the estate owner, in this case Teresa Barruncho.[27] The colonial documents are silent on the people who inhabited the land, the Ndombes. Pushed away from the bay where Benguela was founded in the early seventeenth century, the Ndombe chiefs had moved to the arid lands in what became known as Dombe Grande, where important cassava cultivation supplied Benguela with much-needed cassava flour.[28]

Teresa's Wealth and Color

Teresa's business and marriage meant that she traveled between Benguela and Lisbon in the 1860s and 1870s. Her husband, Vicente Barruncho, recorded in his 1865 will that the couple was residing in Lisbon at 15 Junqueira Street. It was an upscale neighborhood dotted with nineteenth-century mansions and farmhouses (Queiroz Vellozo 1869, 95). Barruncho named "his legitimate spouse, the honorable Dona Teresa de Jesus Ferreira Torres Barruncho" as his natural heir, suggesting that they had eventually married though I have been unable to locate a marriage record. After his death on December 3, 1874, she inherited his assets, which were not identified in his will.[29] None of the primary sources in Angola nor Barruncho's will refer to Teresa's skin color. In an empire obsessed with color classification and blood purity, the silence around her color classification is curious (Candido 2015b, 2015c).

Despite her residence in Lisbon, Teresa Barruncho continued to be one of the major businesspeople in Benguela. In the 1870s she brought some of her freed people to be baptized at the church at Dombe Grande near her farms. The parish records list their names, including Agostinho, Damázia, and João, all young adults who lived on her properties. Since slavery had been outlawed in Angola in 1869 all were listed as freed people, yet the names of the former owners were recorded.

As can be seen in table 8.2, in the 1870s a small number of residents controlled most of the freed labor at Dombe Grande. Both Manuel de Paula Barbosa and

Table 8.2. Baptisms in Dombe Grange, 1874–1875

Former Owners	Freed people
Manuel de Paula Barbosa	56
D. Teresa Jesus Ferreira Torres Barruncho	44
Martinho Lopes Cordeiro	9
Farm Santa Teresa	9
Luis Bernardo Tavano	8
D. Isabel António da Luz Abreu	5
Two Residents	3
Eight Residents	2
Thirty Residents	1
Total	**184**

Teresa owned vast amounts of land. Other powerful residents, such as Martinho Lopes Cordeiro, Luis Bernardo Tavano, and D. Isabel António da Luz Abreu, registered between five and nine freed people. Thirty residents each brought a single *liberto* to be baptized between November 1874 and January 1875. Freed people moved between the houses and farms of Portuguese settlers and African subjects as loans, pawns, and favors. In some instances the refusal to return *libertos* in time or as requested led to court challenges that reveal the arbitrariness and lack of individual liberty that these individuals endured.

Teresa's will provides few clues about her role as a businesswoman or even how she was perceived in Lisbon. She died in Lisbon in 1881, leaving one-third of her assets to her daughter, Teresa de Jesus da Silva Viana Costa; another third to her son, João Luis da Silva Viana; and the remaining third to be divided among her grandchildren.[30] She apparently lived in Lisbon for some time, considering that in 1880 she sold some of her property in Catumbela and was identified as a Lisbon resident.[31] However, her will does not identify assets in Angola.

Final Remarks

In 1994 Catherine Coquery-Vidrovitch published her influential *Les Africaines: Histoires des femmes d'Afrique subharianne du XIXe au XIXe siècle,* which pushed research into new topics and resulted in new studies. Important research has shed light on the economic role of merchant women and elsewhere, yet few historians have investigated and written about African women's lives before the twentieth century. This study is inspired by Coquery-Vidrovitch's scholarship on women and their importance in matters relating to labor, economic change, and power.

In Angola, as elsewhere along the Atlantic coast, women acted as intermediaries and traders. The expansion of agriculture relying on enslaved labor was central to official Portuguese economic policy after the 1830s. Most of those cultivating sugarcane, cotton, and coffee in Angola were women. Besides enslaved female labor, women also operated as entrepreneurs, investing in commercial agriculture such as in the case of Teresa de Jesus, later Teresa Barruncho. Her association with foreign men makes her visible in the colonial archive, showing that her capital and work propelled her economic role.

Teresa's case reveals how the expansion of slavery in the second half of the nineteenth century was linked to the use of enslaved labor but also to that of freed people. Recent studies have indicated that women participated in the abolitionist movement and emancipation in Cuba and Brazil, but we still know little about women's participation in the expansion of slave labor in the second half of the nineteenth century. Like Teresa, other African women shifted their economic interests from slave trading to slave production in Benguela, and in the process they acquired private property. Following Catherine Coquery-Vidrovitch's footsteps, this study aims to bring attention to the role of women and the gendered nature of access to land and accumulation of wealth in Angola during the nineteenth century.

Notes

1. Arquivo Nacional de Angola (hereafter ANA), Codice (Cod.) 455, E-4-3, fl. 117–177v, September 7, 1845. For other cases see ANA, Cod. 326, fl. 8, December 12, 1846; fl. 53, August 29, 1848; and fl. 56, October 10, 1848.

2. ANA, cx. 1341, doc. "To the regent of Dombe Grande from Casimiro Simões Margioli, the secretary of Benguela," February 16, 1854.

3. Arquivo Histórico Ultramarino (AHU), DGU, 1112, "Extinção da condição de servil e regulamento do trabalho nas colônias," 1875–1877.

4. Bispado de Luanda (BBL), Casamento, Benguela, 1806–1853, fl. 41v, May 27, 1841. It is not clear if her first husband was the same Luanda merchant Joaquim Ferreira Torres identified by Roquinaldo Ferreira in Ferreira (2007, 107).

5. BL, Casamento, Benguela, 1806–1853, fl. 41v, May 27, 1841. For more on Jose Luis Viana's position, see Casamento, Benguela, 1806–1853, fl. 54–54v, October 22, 1848; and AHU, Angola, Correspondência dos Governadores, Pasta 15, doc. August 22, 1849.

6. Tribunal da Comarca de Benguela (TCB), "Translado de uns autos de tomada e apreensão, exame, avaliação e depósito de uns escravos, em que são apreensores o capitão de fragata e comandante da estação naval portuguesa João Máximo da Silva Redovalho, sua oficialidade e tripulação, os quais escravos pertencem a Jose Luís da Silva Viana e Ignacio Teixeira Xavier," 1854.

7. Biblioteca da Província de Benguela (BPB), "Termo de Terreno," fl. 55 and 55v, July 2, 1855.

8. TCB, "Autos do Concelho de Família do Casal de Jose Luiz da Silva Viana, Requerente D. Teresa de Jesus Ferreira Torres Viana," 1859.

9. BL, Benguela, Óbito, 1858–1868, fl. 6v, January 17, 1859.

10. BL, Benguela, Óbito, 1858–1868, fl. 24, October 21, 1860.

11. AHU, Angola, Correspondência dos Governadores, Pasta 16, d. 725, December 20, 1856; Arquivo Nacional da Torre do Tombo (ANTT), Registro Geral das Mercês, D. Pedro V, livro 5, fl. 230v., March 7, 1856.

12. Boletim Oficial do Governo Geral da Província de Angola (BOGGPA), n. 585, December 13, 1856, pp. 3–6, November 26, 1856. Orchil weed is a lichen from which violet dyestuff color is obtained. For more on the importance of orchil weed in Benguela, see Santos (1986, 75); Wissenbach (2011).

13. AHU, Angola, Correspondência dos Governadores, pasta 22A, doc. July 15, 1856; see also BOGGPA, 1865, n. 585, December 13, 1856, pp. 3–6.

14. An inventory of the court cases accessible at the Tribunal da Comarca de Benguela will be available soon.

15. AHU, Correspondência dos Governadores, Pasta 38, December 21, 1868, "Relatório do Governo de Benguela referente a 1864–68."

16. BOGGPA, 1862, n. 894, November 22, 1862, fl. 333–4; BOGGPA, 1864, n. 6, February 6, 1864, fl. 55.

17. Sá da Bandeira, *Synopse dos trabalhos do Conselho Ultramarino* (Lisbon: Imprensa National, 1857), 62; AHU, Angola, Correspondência dos Governadores, Pasta 38, December 21, 1868, "Relatório do Governo de Benguela referente a 1864–68."

18. AHU, SEMU, DGU, Consultas do Conselho Ultramarino, cx. 36, doc. 1651, September 2, 1862; AHU, SEMU, DGU, Consultas do Conselho Ultramarino, cx. 39, doc 1812, "Consultando novamente sobre um Aforamento de terrenos em Benguela a José Joaquim Geraldo do Amaral, guarda mor da alfandega da dita cidade 1864," doc. 5, "Auto de investigação," September 18, 1861.

19. AHU, SEMU, DGU, Consultas do Conselho Ultramarino, cx. 39, doc. 1812, September 18, 1861.

20. AHU, SEMU, DGU, Consultas do Conselho Ultramarino, cx. 39, doc. 1812, April 19, 1864.

21. AHU, Correspondência dos Governadores, Pasta 38, December 21, 1868, "Relatório do Governo de Benguela referente a 1864–68."

22. BOGGPA, n. 6 1864, February 6, 1864, pp. 55–56; Sá da Bandeira, *Synopse*, 62.

23. ANA, cx. 5251, Dombe Grande, "Junta da Fazenda Pública de Benguela [Luis Teodoro França] to Chefe do concelho do Dombe Grande," July 1, 1862.

24. BL, Óbito, Benguela, 1858–1868, July 2,1867, fl. 77V; BOGGPA, 1869, n. 33, August 14, 1869, fl. 395. I want to express my thanks to Vanessa Oliveira for sharing her copy of this document with me.

25. BL, Óbito, Benguela, 1874–1876, fl. 21, July 13,1876.

26. BL, Dombe Grande, Batismo, 1874–1875, fl. 5–6, November 11, 1874.

27. AHU, Angola, Correspondência dos Governadores, Pasta 38, December 21, 1868, "Relatório do Governo de Benguela referente a 1864–68."

28. *Relatório dos Governadores da Províncias Ultramarinas: Relatório do Governador Geral da Província de Angola, 1887* (Lisbon: Imprensa Nacional, 1889), 42.

29. ANTT, Feitos Findos, Registro Geral dos Testamentos, Belém, L. 23, cx. 94, fl. 5, December 3, 1874.

30. ANTT, Feitos Findos, Registro Geral dos Testamentos, Belém, L. 31, cx, 95, April 23, 1881.

31. TCB, "Autos civis, Declaração de venda de propriedade de casas, Dona Teresa Ferreira Torres Barruncho vs Custódio José de Souza."

References

Alexandre, Valentim, and Jill Dias. 1998. *O Império africano*. Lisbon: Estampa.

Allina, Eric. *Slavery by Any Other Name: African Life under Company Rule in Colonial Mozambique*. Charlottesville: University of Virginia Press, 2012.

Brooks, George E. 1976. "The Signares of Saint-Louis and Gorée: Women Entrepreneurs in Eighteenth Century Senegal." In *Women in Africa: Studies in Social and Economic Change*, edited by Nancy Hafkin and Edna Bay, 19–44. Stanford, CA: Stanford University Press.

———. 1983. "A Nhara of Guine-Bissau Region: Mãe Aurélia Correia." In *Women and Slavery in Africa*, edited by Claire C. Robertson and Martin A. Klein, 295–317. Madison: University of Wisconsin Press.

Caldeira, Arlindo Manuel. 2007. "Mestiçagem, estratégias de casamento e propriedade feminina no arquipélago de São Tomé e Príncipe nos séculos XVI, XVII e XVIII." *Arquipélago História*, 2nd série, 11–12: 49–72.

Caldeira, Carlos José. 1852. *Apontamentos d'uma viagem de Lisboa á China e da China a Lisboa.* Lisbon: G. M. Martins.

Candido, Mariana P. 2007. "Merchants and the Business of the Slave Trade at Benguela, 1750–1850." *African Economic History*, no. 35: 1–30.

———. 2013. *An African Slaving Port and the Atlantic World: Benguela and Its Hinterland.* New York: Cambridge University Press.

———. 2014. "Trade Networks in Benguela, 1700–1850." In *Networks and Trans-Cultural Exchange: Slave Trading in the South Atlantic, 1590–1867,* edited by David Richardson and Filipa Ribeiro da Silva, 143–63. Leiden: Brill.

———. 2015a. "Women, Family, and Landed Property in Nineteenth-Century Benguela." *African Economic History* 43, no. 1: 136–61.

———. 2015b. "African Women in Ecclesiastical Documents, Benguela, 1760–1860." *Social Sciences and Missions* 28, nos. 3–4: 235–60.

———. 2015c. "Engendering West Central African History: The Role of Urban Women in Benguela in the Nineteenth Century." *History in Africa*, no. 42: 7–36.

———. 2017. "As comerciantes de Benguela na virada do século XVIII: O caso de dona Aguida Gonçalves." In *Laços Atlânticos: África e africanos durante a era do comércio transatlântico de escravos,* edited by Carlos Liberato, Mariana P. Candido, Paul E. Lovejoy, and Renée Soulodre-LaFrance, 231–58. Luanda: Ministério da Cultura/ Museu Nacional da Escravatura.

———. 2018. *Fronteiras da escravidão: Escravatura, comércio e identidade em Benguela, 1750–1850.* Benguela: Universidade Katyavala Bwila/Ondjiri.

Clarence-Smith, W. G. 1979. *Slaves, Peasants, and Capitalists in Southern Angola, 1840–1926.* New York: Cambridge University Press.

Clark, Carolyn M. 1980. "Land and Food, Women and Power, in Nineteenth Century Kikuyu." *Africa: Journal of the International African Institute* 50, no. 4: 357–70.

Coquery-Vidrovitch, Catherine. 1975. "Research on an African Mode of Production." *Critique of Anthropology* 2, nos. 4–5: 38–71.

———. 1994. *Les Africaines: Histoire des femmes d'Afrique noire du XIXe au XXe siècle.* Paris: Editions Desjonquères.

———. 1997. "Histoire des femmes d'Afrique." *Clio*, no. 6: 7–13.

Coquery-Vidrovitch, Catherine, and Paul E. Lovejoy, eds. 1985. *The Workers of African Trade.* Beverly Hills, CA: Sage.

Crais, Clifton, and Pamela Scully. 2010. *Sara Baartman and the Hottentot Venus: A Ghost Story and a Biography.* Princeton, NJ: Princeton University Press.

Dantas, Mariana L. R. 2014. "Succession of Property, Sales of Meação, and the Economic Empowerment of Widows of African Descent in Colonial Minas Gerais, Brazil." *Journal of Family History* 39, no. 3: 222–38.

Domingues da Silva, Daniel B. 2017. *The Atlantic Slave Trade from West Central Africa, 1780–1867.* Cambridge: Cambridge University Press.

Everst, Natalie. 2012. "A Motley Company: Differing Identities among Euro-Africans in Eighteenth-Century Elmina." In *Brokers of Change: Atlantic Commerce and Cultures in Precolonial Western Africa,* edited by Toby Green, 53–69. Oxford, UK: British Academy/Oxford University Press.

Ferreira, Roquinaldo. 2006. "Biografia, mobilidade e cultura atlântica: A micro-escala do tráfico de escravos em Benguela, séculos XVIII–XIX." *Tempo* 10, no. 2: 23–49.

———. 2007. "Atlantic Microhistories: Mobility, Personal Ties, and Slaving in the Black Atlantic World (Angola and Brazil)." In *Cultures of the Lusophone Black Atlantic,* edited by Nancy Prisci Naro, Ro Sansi-Roca, and D. Treece, 99–127. New York: Palgrave Macmillan.

———. 2011. "A supressão do tráfico de escravos em Angola (ca. 1830-ca. 1860)." *História Unisinos* 15, no. 1: 3–13.

———. 2013. "Agricultural Enterprise and Unfree Labour in Nineteenth Century Angola." In *Commercial Agriculture, the Slave Trade and Slavery in Atlantic Africa,* edited by Robin Law, Suzanne Schwarz, and Silke Strickrodt, 225–42. Woodbridge, UK: James Currey.

Ferrer, Ada. 2008. "Cuban Slavery and Atlantic Antislavery." *Review: A Journal of the Fernand Braudel Center* 31, no. 3: 267–95.

———. 2014. *Freedom's Mirror: Cuba and Haiti in the Age of Revolution.* New York: Cambridge University Press.

Freudenthal, Aida. 2005. *Arimos e fazendas: S transição agrária em Angola, 1850–1880.* Luanda: Chá de Caxinde.

Greene, Sandra E. 2017. *Slave Owners of West Africa: Decision Making in the Age of Abolition.* Bloomington: Indiana University Press.

Havik, Philip J. 2016. "Gender, Land, and Trade: Women's Agency and Colonial Change in Portuguese Guinea (West Africa)." *African Economic History* 43, no. 1: 162–95.

Henderson, W. O. *The Lancashire Cotton Famine 1861–65.* Manchester: Manchester University Press, 1934.

Ipsen, Pernille. 2013. "'The Christened Mulatresses': Euro-African Families in a Slave-Trading Town." *William and Mary Quarterly* 70, no. 2: 371–98.

———. 2015. *Daughters of the Trade: Atlantic Slavers and Interracial Marriage on the Gold Coast.* Philadelphia: University of Pennsylvania Press.

Jean-Baptiste, Rachel. 2014. *Conjugal Rights: Marriage, Sexuality, and Urban Life in Colonial Libreville, Gabon.* Athens: Ohio University Press.

Jones, Adam. 1995. "Female Slave-Owners on the Gold Coast: Just a Matter of Money?" In *Slave Cultures and the Cultures of Slavery*, edited by Stephan Palmié, 100–111. Knoxville: University of Tennessee Press.

Jones, Hilary. 2013. *The Métis of Senegal: Urban Life and Politics in French West Africa.* Bloomington: Indiana University Press.

Karasch, Mary C. *Slave Life in Rio de Janeiro, 1808–1850.* Princeton, NJ: Princeton University Press, 1987.

Kriger, Colleen E. 2019. "From Child Slave to Madam Esperance: One Woman's Career in the Anglo-African World, c. 1675–1707." In *African Women in the Atlantic World: Property, Vulnerability and Mobility, 1680–1880*, edited by Mariana P. Candido and Adam Jones, 171–89. Woodbridge, UK: James Currey.

Livingstone, David. 1857. *Missionary Travels and Researches in South Africa.* London: J. Murray.Lovejoy, Paul E. 2016. *Jihād in West Africa during the Age of Revolutions.* Athens: Ohio University Press.

Lovejoy, Paul E., and Jan S. Hogendorn. 1993. *Slow Death for Slavery: The Course of Abolition in Northern Nigeria, 1897–1936.* Cambridge: Cambridge University Press.

Mamdani, Mahmood. 1996. *Citizen and Subject: Contemporary Africa and the Legacy of Late Colonialism.* Princeton, NJ: Princeton University Press.

Mann, Kristin. 2010. *Slavery and the Birth of an African City: Lagos, 1760–1900.* Bloomington: Indiana University Press.

Monteiro, Joachim John. 1876. *Angola and the River Congo.* New York: Macmillan.

Neto, Maria da Conceição. "De escravos a serviçais, de serviçais a contratados: Omissões, percepções e equívocos na história do trabalho africano na Angola colonial." *Cadernos de Estudos Africanos*, no. 33 (2017): 107–29.

Oliveira, Vanessa S. 2015. "The Gendered Dimension of Trade: Female Traders in Nineteenth Century Luanda." *Portuguese Studies Review* 23, no. 2: 93–121.

———. 2016a. "Mulher e comércio: A participação feminina nas redes comerciais em Luanda (século XIX)." In *Angola e as angolanas: Memória, sociedade e cultura*, edited by Selma Pantoja, Edvaldo Bergamo, and Ana Claudia da Silva, 133–52. São Paulo: Intermeios.

———. 2016b. "Slavery and the Forgotten Women Slave Owners of Luanda (1846–1876)." In *Slavery, Memory, Citizenship*, edited by Paul E. Lovejoy and Vanessa S. Oliveira, 129–47. Trenton, NJ: Africa World Press.

———. 2018. "Donas, pretas livres e escravas em Luanda (séc. XIX)." *Estudos Ibero-Americanos* 44, no. 3: 447–56.

———. 2021. *Slave Trade and Abolition: Gender, Commerce, and Economic Transition in Luanda.* Madison: University of Wisconsin Press.

Pacheco, Carlos. 2000. "Leituras e bibliotecas em Angola na primeira metade do século XIX." *Locus (Juiz de Fora)* 6, no. 2: 21–41.

Palmer, Robert Roswell. 1969. *The Age of the Democratic Revolution: The Challenge*. Princeton, NJ: Princeton University Press.

Pantoja, Selma. 2000. "Quintandas e quitandeiras: História e deslocamento na nova lógica do espaço em Luanda." In *África e a instalação do sistema colonial (c. 1885–c. 1935): Actas da III Reunião Internacional de História de África*, edited by Maria Emília Madeira Santos, 175–86. Lisbon: Centro de Estudos de História e Cartografia Antiga.

———. 2001. "Donas de 'arimos': Um negócio feminino no abastecimento de gêneros alimentícios em Luanda (séculos XVIII e XIX)." In *Entre Áfricas e Brasis*, edited by Selma Pantoja, 35–49. Brasilia: Paralelo.

Pitcher, M. Anne. "Sowing the Seeds of Failure: Early Portuguese Cotton Cultivation in Angola and Mozambique, 1820–1926." *Journal of Southern African Studies* 17, no. 1 (1991): 43–70.

Polasky, Janet L. 2015. *Revolutions without Borders: The Call to Liberty in the Atlantic World*. New Haven, CT: Yale University Press.

Queiroz Vellozo, Eduardo Pereira. 1869. *Roteiro das ruas de Lisboa e immediações*. Lisbon: Typographia Portugueza.

Rodrigues, Eugénia. 2014. *Portugueses e africanos nos Rios de Sena: Os prazos da coroa em Moçambique nos séculos XVII e XVIII*. Lisbon: Imprensa Nacional-Casa da Moeda.

———. 2015. "Women, Land, and Power in the Zambezi Valley of the Eighteenth Century." *African Economic History* 43, no. 1: 19–56.

Santos, Maria Emília Madeira. 1986. *Viagens e apontamentos de um portuense em Africa: Diário de António Francisco Ferreira da Silva Porto*. Coimbra, Portugal: Universidade de Coimbra.

Schmidt, Elizabeth. 1992. *Peasants, Traders, and Wives: Shona Women in the History of Zimbabwe, 1870–1939*. Portsmouth, NH: Heinemann.

Scott, Rebecca J., and Jean M. Hébrard. 2012. *Freedom Papers: An Atlantic Odyssey in the Age of Emancipation*. Cambridge, MA: Harvard University Press.

Scully, Pamela. 2005. "Malintzin, Pocahontas, and Krotoa: Indigenous Women and Myth Models of the Atlantic World." *Journal of Colonialism and Colonial History* 6, no. 3, 10.1353/cch.2006.0022.

Sheldon, Kathleen E. 2002. *Pounders of Grain: A History of Women, Work, and Politics in Mozambique*. Portsmouth, NH: Heinemann.

Tams, Georg. 1850. *Visita ás possessões portuguezas na costa occidental d'Africa: Com uma introducção e annotações*. Porto: Typographia do Calvário.

Tomich, Dale, and Michael Zeuske. 2008. "Introduction, the Second Slavery: Mass Slavery, World-Economy, and Comparative Microhistories." *Review: A Journal of the Fernand Braudel Center* 31, no. 2: 91–100.

Vos, Jelmer. 2010. "Child Slaves and Freemen at the Spiritan Mission in Soyo, 1880–1885." *Journal of Family History* 35, no. 1: 71–90.

———. 2014. "Work in Times of Slavery, Colonialism, and Civil War: Labor Relations in Angola from 1800 to 2000." *History in Africa* 41, no. 1: 363–85.

———. 2018. "Coffee, Cash, and Consumption: Rethinking Commodity Production in the Global South." *Radical History Review*, no. 131: 183–88.

White, E. Frances. 1981. "Creole Women Traders in the Nineteenth Century." *International Journal of African Historical Studies* 14, no. 4: 626–42.

Wissenbach, Maria Cristina Cortez. 2011. "As feitorias de urzela e o tráfico de escravos: Georg Tams, José Ribeiro dos Santos e os negócios da África centro-ocidental na década de 1840." *Afro-Ásia*, no. 43: 43–90.

Zimba, Benigna de Jesus Lurdina Mateus Lisboa. 2003. *Mulheres invisíveis: O género e as políticas comerciais no sul de Moçambique, 1720–1830.* Maputo: Promédia.

Chapter 9

The "Second Slavery" in Africa

Migration and Political Economy in the Nineteenth Century

Patrick Manning

In studies of African population and migration from the fifteenth to the twentieth century, estimates for the nineteenth century have emerged as a set of problems of particular interest and complexity. For the era before 1800, the retention of captives in Africa was overwhelmingly as a by-product of the export slave trade; as a result, the number of enslaved people in Africa was relatively modest, and it grew at roughly the same rate as the export slave trade (Manning et al. 2014–2015, 2014, 2010, 1990). During the nineteenth century, however, waves of enslavement developed in many parts of Africa, and such enslavement had steadily less and less to do with the export slave trade, especially as the latter declined sharply after 1850.[1]

For the past several decades of active research on African enslavement, it has been understood that continental enslavement grew significantly during the nineteenth century, only to decline (but not to disappear) with European colonization as the twentieth century opened. There were some very rough estimates of the overall magnitude of African slavery during the 1980s (Manning 1981; Inikori 1982; Lovejoy 1989). Thereafter, efforts to trace the magnitude of slave population have taken place at regional and local levels but not at a continental level because of the overall shortage and inconsistency of records. Yet the regional studies have accumulated impressively with time, and there is now a stronger base for assembling them and beginning to build a continental interpretation.

In addition to these advances in the supply of data on African enslavement, the demand for data on African enslavement has also grown as part of the expanded collection of data on early modern population and economies. The debates on global economic and demographic history are bringing steadily more insistent questions on where Africa fit into the global picture at regional and continental levels.[2] As a result, it is now clear that the estimation of African population and migration for the nineteenth century requires explicit and quantitative estimates of the number of people captured and held in slavery for each African region and over time.[3]

This preliminary review of enslavement within nineteenth-century Africa is mainly qualitative, with only a few estimates of the numbers and proportions of people enslaved at the aggregate level. Even at the introductory level of this qualitative approach, it seems clear that there was an African "second slavery," roughly parallel in time to the nineteenth-century expansions in enslavement in the Americas, in North Africa and the Middle East, and in South and Southeast Asia. Given the size of Africa and its continental population of roughly 140 million (and a population of roughly 110 million in regions in which people were captured), it is likely that the number of persons living in slavery in Africa exceeded that of any of the other regions, especially for the period after 1850 and perhaps even before that date (Manning 2014, 132).

While the literature confirms the demographic significance of nineteenth-century African slavery, that same literature has been vague on the political economy or the "business model" of such enslavement. What ambitions and benefits set the initiative and the timing of those who seized, sold, and exploited so many people as slaves? How does this pattern fit with broad changes in African economies and with shifting patterns of the global economy? Individual authors have offered insights of interest, but there is not yet a general discussion.[4]

This chapter presents an introductory overview of two big questions. First, it sketches narratives, both regional and continental, of the rise and decline of enslavement in nineteenth-century Africa. I assemble these narratives from major regional accounts of enslavement. I proceed in counterclockwise direction around the continent, beginning in Southeast Africa and ending up in West Central Africa. The chronology is not deeply specific—I start in 1780 and end in 1900, separating the periods before and after 1850 rather clearly, and at times divide the first half-century period into segments at 1820 and the second half century at 1880. In the course of the narrative I ask, especially, when and how big were the changes in levels of enslavement?

Second, the chapter offers initial speculations as to the motives, functions, and consequences of the expanded enslavement as it is presented in the narrative. Most broadly, this is the question of the "business model" of Africa's second slavery—its socioeconomic design and profitability. This broad question breaks down into specific questions such as:

- What were the ties of continental enslavement to external markets—both the demand for slaves and the demand for slave-produced goods such as palm oil, cloves, peanuts, cotton, and leather goods?
- In what instances were slave systems largely independent of external links?
- Were expanding slave systems tied to an expanding local elite? If so, what was the reason for elite expansion at this time?
- Did markets for land grow along with the growth in enslavement?
- What was the impact of enslavement on longer-term economic stability and growth?

Southeast Africa

By the 1780s, French planters on the Mascarenes were greatly expanding slave purchases from Southeast Africa and Madagascar (Allen 2014, 72–84). In 1790 the Kingdom of Imerina unified, exporting slaves in exchange for arms to facilitate expansion. But the export of slaves seems also to have increased the size of the enslaved population held in Imerina. Then, from 1820 to 1825, Imerina first halted slave exports in alliance with Britain; then Imerina broke the alliance, setting up an autarkic regime, during the period 1825–1850. Enslavement expanded in the era of autarky to serve the Merina elite; at the same time, corvée labor (*fanampoana*) was required for plantation labor. Campbell cites an estimate that, in 1817, one-third of the Merina population was in slavery, and half of those were captives rather than born into slavery. The slave population remained stable after 1830. Female slaves were highly valued; highland women were prized in the Muslim Comoros. But Imerina occupied only one-third of Madagascar. To the west, the Sakalava kingdoms participated in exchange of slaves and provisions with

Mozambique. Campbell estimates that, from 1801 to 1891, 290,000 captives were exported from Madagascar; and that, from 1820 to 1891, 400,000 were imported to Madagascar. With the French conquest, 500,000 slaves were liberated in 1896, comprising 20–26 percent of Madagascar's population.[5] The 1899 French census showed 778 males per 1,000 females on the island.

East Africa

Export slave trade from the Swahili coast to the Persian Gulf expanded from about 1780. Clove plantations on Zanzibar and then Pemba began in roughly 1810; the volume of output and enslavement grew to the 1860s, then declined in the 1870s and 1880s (Sheriff 1987). Sheriff shows annual exports of some seventeen thousand captives from Kilwa in the 1860s, mostly to Zanzibar, with some redistribution to Pemba and the mainland. Thus, market-oriented enslavement was intense in those areas to the end of the century. Ivory trade drawing on the interior—the Great Lakes and the upper Congo Valley—expanded from the 1850s. One has a sense of substantial interior transformations resulting from ivory trade, but we have little detail on the number enslaved (Farrant 1975).

Bunyoro

Bunyoro was the leading kingdom of the Great Lakes region in the eighteenth century. Its political influence expanded late in the century, accompanied by growing enslavement; there seem to have been few external links to this enslavement (Doyle 2007, 235–45). From the 1820s the Egyptian-based Turkiyya forces expanded into the Upper Nile region, seizing and purchasing slaves. A description of Bunyoro for the nineteenth century shows two castes: elite cattle-keepers and a lower agricultural caste. Slaves and lower-caste people were not well distinguished from each other in such reports. But elite families gained in independence from the monarchy and were able to win control of more slaves. Nyoro tradition included three categories of slaves: those in society without masters, war captives, and slaves purchased from neighboring states. Female slaves could be married without bridewealth, and they were reputed to have higher fertility than Nyoro wives. From the 1840s to 1870, Bunyoro suffered at the hands of expanding Buganda. From 1871, however, King Kabaleega centralized Bunyoro and reversed the terms of the relationship with Buganda. As for the export slave trade from Bunyoro, one may say that it grew from 1780 to 1820, declined from 1820 to 1850, rose from 1850 to 1880, and declined in the 1890s.

Nile Valley

Taqali, a Muslim-ruled state in the Nuba hills of Kordofan, was populated mainly by independent farmers. In the last half of the eighteenth century, merchants from Sinnar (to the northeast) and Dar Fur (northwest) came to Kordofan. In 1820–1821, Muhammad Ali's Turco-Egyptian army defeated Sinnar and the Fur governors of Kordofan, opening an era of slave raiding in which Turkiyya soldiers and merchants went even into the Congo watershed, collecting slaves. The Taqali Kingdom held out in its hills yet suffered from Turkiyya slave raids (Ewald 2000). In 1883 the Turkiyya outpost in Kordofan fell to the Mahdiyya, which had arisen in 1881 under the leadership of Muhammad Ahmad. The Mahdiyya ruled the whole region until 1898, collecting many captives and exploiting them within their

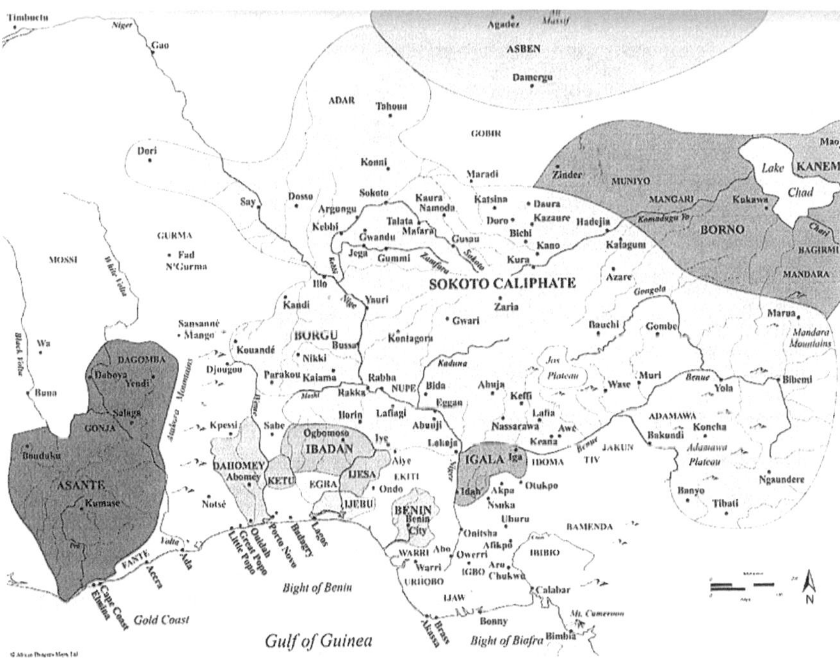

Figure 9.1 Central Sudan and the Bights. Source: Courtesy of Henry B. Lovejoy, *African Diaspora Maps*, 2016.

Sudanese realm. Land ownership was a key factor in Taqali and throughout the region. It seems that the number of enslaved held in Taqali did not grow greatly, though the number of captures was significant and the slave population of the overall region grew to a high level, especially during the Mahdiyya. As for the export slave trade from Taqali, it grew from 1820 to 1850 then leveled off; those enslaved from 1883 to 1898 were held within the region.

Central Sudan

The jihad led by Usuman dan Fodio, 1804–1808, brought the creation of the Sokoto Caliphate, which rapidly expanded eastward into Adamawa. Enslavement rose rapidly with conquest and continued thereafter; captives were seized from within the realm of the caliphate and were mostly settled on lands in the caliphate. (See Figure 9.1 for a map of the caliphate and surrounding regions.) The caliphate maintained an elaborate hierarchy and considerable stability to the 1890s, enabling institutionalization of textile and leather industries. Surrounding the substantial cities of the caliphate were plantations for production of grains. Paul Lovejoy argues that there was an effort to enslave but keep slaves in the caliphate rather than send them across the Atlantic (Lovejoy 1978). He estimates a slave population of 1.25–2.5 million in 1900, 25–50 percent of the total population. As for the export slave trade from the Sokoto Caliphate, it grew from 1780 to 1820, selling more to the north and across the desert than to the Atlantic (Lovejoy 1989). Export slave trade to the Atlantic expanded from the 1820s and halted by 1850; trade to the north declined in the 1870s.

Western Sudan

Atlantic exports of slaves from Senegambia fell below five thousand per decade in the 1830s; slave exports from Sierra Leone did not fall to that level until the 1850s (Manning and Liu 2020). The Inner Delta state of Masina under Shehu Ahmadu lasted from 1818 to 1862 and thus had half a century to institutionalize itself. There was less time for stabilization in the regime of Umar (who led in conquests from 1860 to his death in 1864, though his son sustained the regime into the 1890s). Time was even shorter for Samori Touré, who founded a kingdom in Guinea in the 1880s and moved it to the east under attacks from the French until 1898. Martin Klein estimates the level of enslavement in the Western Sudan at 1.7 million in 1900 (1998). The proportion enslaved ranged from 20 percent in Haut-Sénégal-Niger (Umar's realm) to 50 percent in Guinée (Samori's realm). Senegal and Gambia became regions in which many slaves were settled down to grow peanuts for export, increasingly under the Mourides of Ahmadou Bamba from 1883. There may have been time for stabilization of institutions of slavery in the realm of Ahmadu in Masina (and perhaps earlier in the Bambara state of Segu), but the shifts in enslavement in late nineteenth-century Western Sudan appear to have been chaotic (Klein 1998; Meillassoux 1986).

West African Coast

As the border state of Ilorin rebelled against the Oyo Empire in 1823 and became an emirate within the Sokoto Caliphate, Oyo's eventual collapse brought a long series of wars among Yoruba-speaking peoples. These wars brought the period of greatest export of Yoruba slaves, from the 1820s to the 1850s; yet war and enslavement continued in the region to 1893. The Kingdom of Dahomey continued slave raiding up to 1890, exporting slaves across the Atlantic to the 1860s, but also settled large numbers of slaves from the 1820s on, including for production of palm oil for export (Manning 1982, 45–50, 335–39). For coastal Fante and inland Asante, slave exports virtually ended in 1808. Asante sustained enslavement, and it conquered Fante from 1807 to the 1820s. Rebecca Shumway notes that Fante elites turned away from slaveholding from the 1820s to the 1850s—but when the British lost interest in Fante allies, Fante elites again invested in slaves.[6] For the Bight of Benin, export slave trade persisted, although at a slightly reduced level, until it declined sharply in the 1850s and ended by 1880.

West Central Africa

Nineteenth-century Atlantic exports of captives grew to a very high level—from the 1820s through 1840s to Brazil, and to Cuba in the 1850s (Manning and Liu 2018). West Central Africa had low levels of population density, large distances for travel of captives, and its regions extended all the way to such other regions of heavy enslavement as Southeast Africa, West Africa, the Nile Valley, and North Central Africa. It is certain that regional population declined significantly during the nineteenth century.[7] Cotton plantations are known for Angola, especially during the US Civil War, but otherwise not much is known about enslavement. The actions of the Congo Free State from 1885 and of the expanding Angolan colony clearly involved enslavement. As for West Central Africa, slave exports reached very high levels up to 1850.

Quantitative Summary

For a continental population of 140 million, or roughly 110 million in the area susceptible to enslavement, 20 percent enslavement would mean 20 million in slavery. (For the United States in 1860 the slave population was 4 million, some 13 percent of the total US population.) It is certain that there had been a huge expansion in Africa's enslaved population since 1750. The total population of the continent changed little, so the 1750 population of enslaved would have been 5 million (assuming a 5 percent proportion) or 3 million (assuming a 3 percent proportion). African slave populations of 3 to 5 million would have been roughly equal to the expatriate slave population in the Americas and Eurasia.

Implications: African Slavery in the World Economy

The interpretation of slavery in the Americas, sustained by slave trade from Africa, has focused on its place within the capitalist economy of the Atlantic and the modern world-system. The debate of the 1970s and 1980s on the profitability of the slave trade, while somewhat inconclusive, was carried out within that framework (Solow and Engerman 1987). Can this market- and export-focused logic be extended to African enslavement of the nineteenth century—that is, was African slavery primarily commercial in motivation? If so, was it tied to the world economy overall, to the capitalist economy based in Europe, or to African economic aims? Alternatively, did a different political economy arise in nineteenth-century Africa, emphasizing social rather than economic benefits of holding slaves?

Indeed, we do find links to intercontinental slave trade in almost all the cases of expanding African slavery—even in Bunyoro, Taqali, and the Sokoto Caliphate. (Trade in slave-produced goods took place in Zanzibar, Sokoto, and along the West African coast but not necessarily elsewhere.) At the same time, the apparent expansion of elite strata in the nineteenth century and their interest in holding slaves to relieve them of work suggests that another motivation—more about social status than about economic profit—was at least supplementary to capitalism and perhaps independent of it. During the seventeenth and eighteenth centuries, African enslavement expanded in a regular relationship with the expansion of overseas slave trade—roughly equal numbers of captives maintained in Africa and sent overseas. In the nineteenth century, however, captives maintained in Africa were far more numerous than those sent overseas, and the ups and downs of continental enslavement did not fit neatly with overseas trade.

The rise and decline of large-scale enslavement on the African mainland was a relatively rapid set of transformations, rarely longer than a century. At the same time, such an expansion in enslavement must have brought implications—presumably negative—for the long-term stability and growth of African economies. Up to the present, however, the "second slavery" has hardly been given any consideration in Africa's economic history. For instance, Nathan Nunn and Leonard Wantchekon, working in the "reversal of fortune" paradigm, have completed widely cited analyses of the impact of slave trade on West Africa but have limited their analysis to a two-point study, comparing volumes of eighteenth-century slave trade to twentieth-century economic and social indicators (Nunn and Wantchekon 2011). It seems reasonable to argue that nineteenth-century enslavement might also have been significant in the long-term trajectory of West African social change. The relationship between slavery and land tenure may be important in helping determine whether slavery was focused on continental or external interests. Was it the case that a land market expanded in nineteenth-century Africa as slaveholders sought properties on which to settle the laborers they controlled? A parallel question may be posed for the end of the second slavery. Of those who had been enslaved during the nineteenth century and who gained some measure of freedom in the twentieth century, how many were able to gain access to or ownership of land? That is, how many former slaves were able to establish an existence as peasants?

The African slave system of the nineteenth century was ephemeral, constrained by shortages in the number of prospective captives and ultimately by imperial European restrictions on enslavement. A class of slave merchants rose and fell, followed by the rise and fall of classes of landowners and slave-owners. Classes of slaves emerged but later became serfs, peasants, or townspeople. While we have yet to develop detailed regional and continental narratives of the transformations in African slavery, the following milestones stand out, at least in approximate terms:[8]

1650—Slave exports to Americas began to exceed slave exports to Mediterranean, Arabia, and Indian Ocean
1700—Slave population in Americas exceeded that in Africa and in the East
1780—Slave population in the East grew until 1870, then declined
1850—Slave population in Africa exceeded that in Americas and in the East
1880—African slave population began to decline
1930—Slavery was declared by colonial rulers to have ended in Africa, though it had not in fact ended (Lugard 1933)

Based on this preliminary survey, it appears that a second slavery arose or accelerated at much the same time in a wide range of tropical and subtropical regions, from the 1820s—in the Americas, Africa, the Middle East and North Africa, Southeast Asia, and perhaps India (Tomich and Zeuske 2008; Ewald 2000; Beemer 2013). Before leaping to conclusions, however, we must compare descriptions of the various regional processes so as to confirm or reject the similarity of their timing and institutional character. If it does turn out to be the case that these expansions of slavery are similar in timing or closely linked, that would raise the issue of a possible common causation. Based on the levels of description that are available at present, it seems certain that the relevant factors included more than simple movements of prices and trade flows linked directly to Europe. What was the demography of enslavement—age and sex composition of captives, mortality rates in capture and in slave status? To the degree that there was emancipation or escape, what were the next steps of ex-slaves? I would venture that we should be on the lookout for types of global interaction that are as much social as economic in nature. They would need to be conveyed at some level by processes moving from region to region.

Notes

1. Research continues to advance knowledge on the volume and timing of Africa's export slave trade. For the Indian Ocean, see Allen (2014); for the Atlantic, see new estimates based on Eltis (http://www.slavevoyages.org) in Manning and Liu (2018).

2. Recent meetings of the World Economic History Congress (Kyoto 2015, Boston 2018) have included significant attention to population and economic data worldwide, including Africa. For details of programs, see http://www.ieha-wehc.org/congresses.html. A 2013

conference at the International Institute of Social History in Amsterdam included historical presentations on population worldwide. For methods of comparing rates of migration, see also Lucassen and Lucassen (2014).

3. Various estimates are ongoing, aimed at simulating free and slave populations and migrations for nineteenth-century Africa.

4. Meillassoux (1986) is an example of a work that sought to generalize from a single regional experience.

5. Campbell (2005, 114–17) disagrees with the earlier estimates of Maurice Bloch, halving them.

6. Rebecca Shumway, pers. comm., March 7, 2018.

7. Decomposing Eltis's consolidated reporting category of "West Central Africa" for slave exports into subgroups for captives dispatched from north and south of the Congo River shows that, especially in the nineteenth century, Angola was the source of over two-thirds of slave exports from West Central Africa overall. This result reaffirms the likelihood that nineteenth-century population declined in Angola (Eltis, "Slave Voyages"; Manning, Zhang, and Yi 2014–2015, 145).

8. Existing narratives include Lovejoy (2012) and Manning (1990); see also Coquery-Vidrovitch (2018).

References

Allen, Richard B. 1999. *Slaves, Freedmen, and Indentured Laborers in Colonial Mauritius.* Cambridge: Cambridge University Press.

———. 2014. *European Slave Trading in the Indian Ocean, 1500–1850.* Athens: Ohio University Press, 2014.

Alpers, Edward A. 1975. *Ivory and Slaves: Changing Pattern of International Trade in East Central Africa to the Later Nineteenth Century.* Berkeley: University of California Press.

Beemer, Bryce. 2013. "The Creole City in Southeast Asia: Slave Gathering Warfare and Culture Exchange in Burma, Thailand, and Manipur, 1752–1885." PhD diss., University of Hawaii.

Campbell, Gwyn. 2005. *An Economic History of Imperial Madagascar, 1750–1895: The Rise and Fall of an Island Empire.* Cambridge: Cambridge University Press.

Coquery-Vidrovitch, Catherine. 2018. *Les routes de l'esclavage: Histoire des traites africaines VIe-XXe siècle.* Paris: Albin Michel.

Doyle, Shane. 2007. "Bunyoro and the Demography of Slavery Debate." In *Slavery in the Great Lakes Region of East Africa*, edited by Henri Médard and Shane Doyle, 231–51. Oxford, UK: James Currey.

Eltis, David et al. "Slave Voyages." http://www.slavevoyages.org.

Ewald, Janet J. 1990. *Soldiers, Traders, and Slaves: State Formation and Economic Transformation in the Greater Nile Valley, 1700–1885.* Madison: University of Wisconsin Press.

———. 2000. "Crossers of the Sea: Slaves, Freedmen, and Other Migrants in the Northwestern Indian Ocean, c. 1750–1914." *American Historical Review* 105, no. 1: 69–91.

Farrant, Leda. *Tippu Tip and the East African Slave Trade.* New York: St. Martin's, 1975.

Inikori, J. E., ed. 1982. *Forced Migration.* London: Hutchinson, 1982.

Klein, Martin A. 1998. *Slavery and Colonial Rule in French West Africa.* Cambridge: Cambridge University Press.

Lovejoy, Paul E. 1978. "Plantations in the Economy of the Sokoto Caliphate." *Journal of African History*, no. 19: 341–68.

———. 1979. "The Characteristics of Plantations in the Nineteenth-Century Sokoto Caliphate (Islamic West Africa)." *American Historical Review* 84, no. 5: 1267–92.

———. 1989. "The Impact of the Slave Trade on Africa: A Review of the Literature." *Journal of African History* 30, no. 3: 365–94.

———. 2012. *Transformations in Slavery: A History of Slavery in Africa.* 3rd ed. Cambridge: Cambridge University Press.

———. 2016. *Jihad in West Africa during the Age of Revolutions.* Athens: Ohio University Press, 2016.

Lovejoy, Paul E., and Jan S. Hogendorn. 1993. *Slow Death for Slavery: The Course of Abolition in Northern Nigeria, 1897–1936.* Cambridge: Cambridge University Press.

Lucassen, Jan, and Leo Lucassen. 2014. "Measuring and Quantifying Cross-Cultural Migrations: An Introduction." In *Globalising Migration History: The Eurasian Experience (16th–21st Centuries)*, edited by Jan Lucassen and Leo Lucassen, 3–54. Leiden: Brill.

Lugard, Frederick. 1933. "'Slavery in All Its Forms.'" *Africa*, no. 6: 1–14.

Manning, Patrick. 1981. "The Enslavement of Africans: A Demographic Model." *Canadian Journal of African Studies* 15, no. 3: 499–526.

———. 1982. *Slavery, Colonialism and Economic Growth in Dahomey, 1640–1960.* Cambridge: Cambridge University Press.

———. 1986. "Slave Trade, 'Legitimate Trade,' and Imperialism Revisited: The Control of Wealth in the Bights of Benin and Biafra." In *Africans in Bondage: Studies in Slavery and the Slave Trade*, edited by Paul E. Lovejoy, 203–33. Madison: University of Wisconsin Press.

———. 1990. *Slavery and African Life: Occidental, Oriental, and African Slave Trades.* Cambridge: Cambridge University Press.

———. 2010. "African Population: Projections, 1851–1961." In *The Demographics of Empire: The Colonial Order and the Creation of Knowledge*, edited by Karl Ittmann, Dennis D. Cordell, and Gregory Maddox, 245–75. Athens: Ohio University Press.

———. 2014. "African Population, 1650–2000: Comparisons and Implications of New Estimates." In *Africa's Development in Historical Perspective*, edited by Emmanuel Akyeampong, Robert Bates, Nathan Nunn, and James Robinson, 131–52. Cambridge: Cambridge University Press.

Manning, Patrick, and Yu Liu. 2020. "Research Note on Captive Atlantic Flows: Estimating Missing Data by Slave-Voyage Routes." *Journal of World-Systems Research* 26, no. 1: 103–25.

Manning, Patrick, Scott Nickleach, Bowen Yi, and Brian McGill. 2014–2015. "Demographic Models for Projecting Population and Migration: Methods for African Historical Analysis." *Journal of World-Historical Information* 2–3, no. 1: 23–39.

Manning, Patrick, Yun Zhang, and Bowen Yi. 2014–2015. "Volume and Direction of the Atlantic Slave Trade, 1650–1870: Estimates by Markov Chain Monte Carlo Analysis." *Journal of World-Historical Information* 2–3, no. 2: 127–49.

Meillassoux, Claude. 1986. *Anthropologie de l'esclavage: Le ventre de fer et de l'argent.* Paris: Presses Universitaires de France.

Nunn, Nathan, and Leonard Wantchekon. 2011. "The Slave Trade and the Origins of Mistrust in Africa." *American Economic Review*, no. 101: 3221–52.

Sheriff, Abdul. 1987. *Slaves, Spices, and Ivory in Zanzibar: Integration of an East African Commercial Empire into the World Economy, 1770–1873.* London: James Currey.

Solow, Barbara, and Stanley L. Engerman, eds. 1987. *British Capitalism and Caribbean Slavery: The Legacy of Eric Williams.* Cambridge: Cambridge University Press.

Tomich, Dale, and Michael Zeuske. 2008. "Introduction, the Second Slavery: Mass Slavery, World-Economy, and Comparative Microhistories." *Review: A Journal of the Fernand Braudel Center* 31, no. 2: 91–100.

Chapter 10

African Enslavement and the East India Articles

Two Captive-Labor Regimes in the Western Indian Ocean ca. 1750–1900[1]

Janet J. Ewald

In 1876 in the Red Sea port of Jeddah a bondsmen, Murjan, worked on a harbor boat.[2] Murjan had arrived in Jeddah from his home in the upper Nile Basin, swept up along with likely more than 1.6 million other captives who, between about 1770 and 1880, embarked from the Indian Ocean coast of Africa for destinations in the Mascarene Islands, Southwestern and Southern Asia, and the Americas (Allen 2014, 16–18; Lovejoy 2011, 46, 137–38, 148).[3] In the nineteenth century, slave exports from Indian Ocean Africa grew in both numbers of captives who embarked and the area of hinterland traversed by slave-trading routes (Manning 1990, 18; Lovejoy 2011,148). This expansion of enslavement occurred during an age of simultaneous abolitionist sentiment and industrial development.

Industrialization played a part in Murjan's enslavement, while British antislavery impulses facilitated his manumission. In Jeddah the harbor boat on which Murjan worked serviced steam vessels. He turned to the British consul for intervention in gaining manumission, as did other enslaved Africans in Jeddah (Miers 1989, 102–28). As a freedman, Murjan disappeared from documentation. We can, however, speculate that he joined the many other freedmen who labored in ports and at sea, on board vessels powered by wind or steam.

Some freedmen entered another captive-labor force: a group of seafarers, mainly Indian, serving on British commercial steam liners under a uniquely restrictive maritime labor contract. Known as East India Articles (EIA), these contracts applied only to non-European mariners who joined vessels in Indian ports. They required that they be returned to those ports—where, significantly, low wages prevailed.[4] The EIA trapped Indian and African seafarers in a pool of cheap maritime labor. The required return to port of entry applied to no other seafarers on British vessels. Freedmen under EIA endured a second captivity. They labored solely below deck, working with coal in the stokehole and bunkers.[5] Their low-paid, dangerous work supplied the furnaces with coal, the source of energy that propelled the vessel. The low wages of all EIA mariners, but especially the coal workers, subsidized the costly development of industrial maritime transport in the Indian Ocean.

In addition to the labor of freedmen, synchronicity linked post-1770 enslavement and the EIA. Each regime of captive labor bore antecedents; each began to take shape in the late eighteenth century; each culminated during the industrialized nineteenth century. For centuries before 1770, enslaved Africans had crossed the northwestern Indian Ocean. But the trade, although constant, was largely opportunistic with irregular fluctuations. It rose and fell according to the coincidence of a supply of captives in Indian Ocean Africa and a transoceanic demand for them (Eaton 2005,105, 128; 2006, 115–35).[6] Sometime before 1615, captains of East India Company cargo ships began to hire Indian sailors, or *lascars*, for their homeward voyages in order to replace men who had died, deserted, or been impressed into naval vessels (see figure 10.1) (Strachan and Penrose 1971, 44, 109).[7] Lascars negotiated for wages, which were sometimes higher than those of European seafarers.[8] Lascars and Company officials agreed that the Company should provide its Indian seafarers with passage back to their home ports.

The transformations in enslavement and maritime labor emerged in an environment undergoing a set of processes that had begun around 1750, within and beyond the Indian Ocean. Nineteenth-century industrialization gave new dynamism to enslavement and spurred the creation of a captive maritime labor force. The late eighteenth-century emergence and entanglement with industrialization, evident in both post-1770 Indian Ocean enslavement and the formation of the EIA, resonate with scholarship about the second slavery in the Atlantic (Tomich 1988, 103–18; Tomich and Zeuske 2008, 91–100).[9]

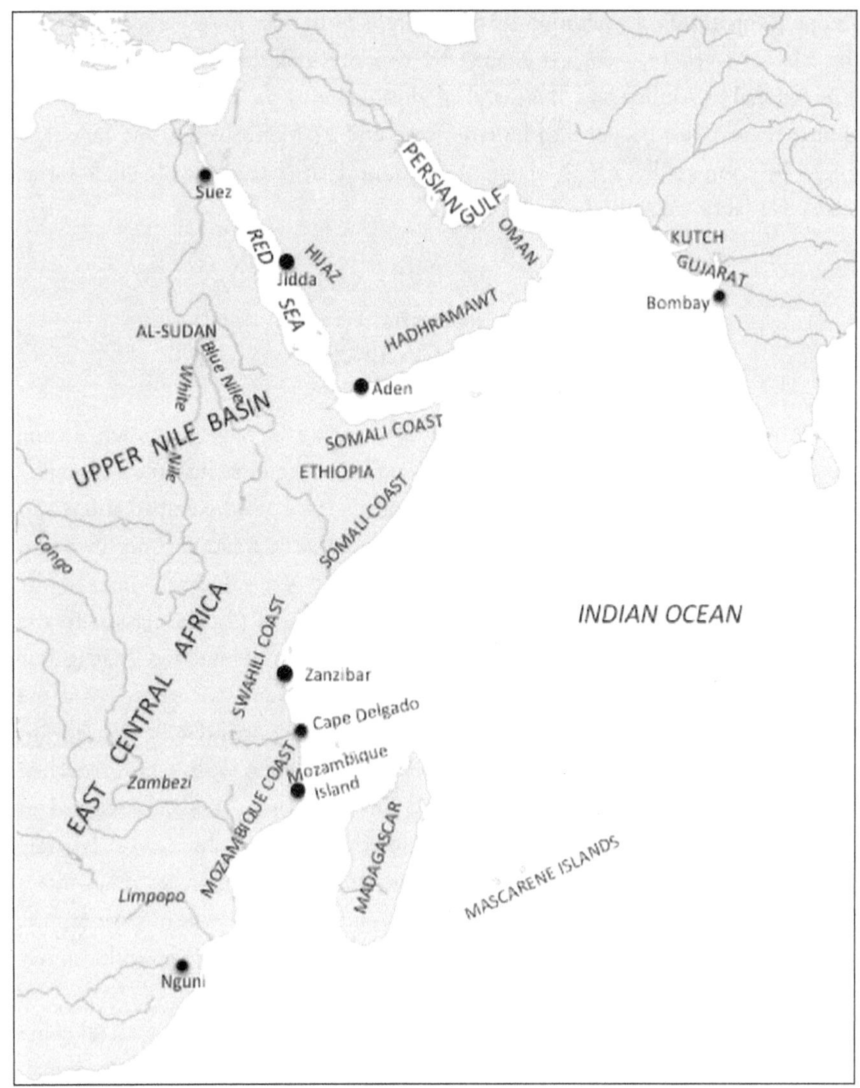

Figure 10.1. East Central Africa and Indian Ocean.

But what does this synchronicity mean for how we think about enslavement in the Atlantic and Indian Oceans, as well as the relationship of enslavement to other captive-labor regimes, such as the EIA? This requires putting the two enslavements and the various other forms of captive labor into a multidirectional conversation.

I hope to open this conversation by tracing how both post-1770 enslavement and the EIA emerged in a context shaped by two previous decades of regional and interregional dynamics and then peaked during industrialization. Does such an approach yield new insight into Indian Ocean and Atlantic slaveries, and how they might be connected? Does it allow us to connect enslavement with other forms of captive labor, such as the EIA?

African Enslavement in the Northwestern Indian Ocean ca. 1750–1880

For purposes of considering post-1750 African Indian Ocean enslavement in the framework of the second slavery, I have redrawn the conventional historical geography of African Indian Ocean enslavement. Based on the sites of slave embarkations and disembarkations, this geography divides the African slave trade into northwestern and southwestern circuits (Campbell 1989:, 1–26).[10] Cape Delgado marked the African coastal divide between the two circuits. South of Cape Delgado, in the southwestern circuit, captives embarked from the Mozambique and Madagascar coasts for European holdings in the Mascarene Islands and, increasingly, for the plantations of the second slavery in the Americas. In the northwestern circuit, captives embarked from the Muslim-ruled African Indian Ocean coast, which stretched from the Red Sea through the Somali and Swahili coasts. They disembarked in Muslim domains in Southwestern and Southern Asia. The absence of dynamic and large-scale plantation development in the Asian slave-importing zones leaves historians with a puzzling question: What accounts for the growth in slave exports to Muslim domains beginning around 1770 and peaking in the nineteenth century (Sheriff 1987, 35–41)? [11]

I redraw this geography in two ways: mutually incongruent, but each allowing insights into enslavement in Indian Ocean Africa. Both challenge the conventional, transcontinental geography of the African slave trade. The first redrawing, which informs most of the following section, takes as a single, albeit internally differentiated, unit all of East Africa where enslavement increased after 1770, regardless of where captives disembarked. It includes the mainland coast and hinterland from the Red Sea through Mozambique, as well as Madagascar. I show how this region experienced a set of common processes during the late eighteenth and early nineteenth centuries (Alpers 1973, 80–124; Allen 2014, 101; Vernet 2011,

477–521).[12] The Cape Delgado divide simply did not map onto the large, shared hinterland of the eastern mainland coast where captives might be funneled to either the Swahili or Mozambique coast. The Upper Nile experienced a similar set of dynamics, although it lay beyond the interconnecting zone of Madagascar and the eastern central mainland.

The second redrawing, which appears in the final section about enslavement, rejects the continental division between an "internal" African slave trade and an "external" slave trade to Asia. Instead I locate as a single zone of slave imports the almost contiguous, long-interacting ocean littoral of the northwestern Indian Ocean, from western India through the Swahili coast (Pearson 1985, 1–8; 2006).[13] This Asian and African littoral imported slaves; people generally did not become slaves there.

The chapter pays considerable attention to the hinterlands of East Central Africa and the Upper Nile, where people both became enslaved and labored as slaves. I do not deny the importance of a demand for captive labor from beyond the hinterlands. But to attribute to that demand the power of conjuring up slaves, ready for export to the northwestern Indian Ocean littoral or overseas, elides the processes in the hinterland that produced slaves: uprooting people, by armed seizure or other means; commodifying them; and inserting them into commercial networks. These processes were deeply connected to forces from the outside but not inevitably driven by them. Nor were the forces from beyond the hinterland, which stimulated enslavement, necessarily or entirely a demand for captive labor.

I will now consider the origins of African Indian Ocean enslavement during the last half of the eighteenth century; proceed to the impact of industrialization on enslavement; and reconsider how nineteenth-century enslavement expanded in the littoral of the northwestern Indian Ocean.

Early Growth of African Enslavement, ca. 1750–1820

Over the last half of the eighteenth century, three interacting processes created the conditions for the growth of post-1770 African enslavement. Far less dramatic than the late eighteenth-century Atlantic political and industrial revolutions, which underlay the second slavery, they also began to unfold earlier. The earliest apparent development was capital accumulation in the hands of regional entrepreneurs: first Indians and then Europeans. Closely related to private capital accumulation, after about 1750 European metropolitan governments—that is, Portugal with its overseas administrative arm, the Estado da India; France and England with their chartered companies—reworked their arrangements with the agencies that represented their sovereignty in the Indian Ocean. Although the substance of the changes took various forms, they all involved greater political supervision from the metropolis and the encouragement of private enterprise. Finally, in the last quarter of the eighteenth century and again in 1820, new states consolidated on the Swahili coast, the central highlands of Madagascar, and the Sudanese Nile Valley. Although the political economies of these states differed radically, they all encouraged enslavement. I first take up these processes in Madagascar and the eastern central mainland, and then in the Upper Nile Basin. I argue that the three processes created conditions for a flourishing ivory trade, followed by a demand for captives in the Mascarene Islands that stimulated enslavement.

Around 1750 Gujarati merchants, having accumulated capital from the recently booming production of cotton textiles, invested in trade with Africa: specifically, tusks of mainland elephants in exchange for cotton cloth (Nadri 2008, 461, 467–73; 2009, 63, 88). The Gujarati entrepreneurs benefited from emerging new political economies on the African coast. Lisbon-based reforms detached Mozambique from the Estado da India and opened the colony's trade to private entrepreneurs (Machado 2014, 8, 29–30; Newitt 1995, 29–30). Gujarati Hindu merchants availed themselves of the new opportunity, making Mozambique Island the most important ivory entrepôt in Indian Ocean Africa for several decades (Alpers 1975, 177–78). In Oman the end of civil war in 1749 had led to a revival of shipping and entrepôt trade, and consequently a renewal of activity in the mainland coast of East Africa (Risso 1986, 41–42, 46–47, 75, 77, 84–85, 118–30). Omani aristocrats and their followers settled north of Portuguese territory, and Gujarati merchants accompanied them. Together, Omanis and their Indian trading partners gradually built a commercial empire based on the offshore island of Zanzibar. The geography of trade routes and customs zones, rather than tribute payments and military outposts, defined the extent and intensity of Omani imperial control in Africa.

Traders from the African hinterland quickly extended their already established regional trade networks, bringing ivory to the coast and shifting their destinations to whatever port on the Swahili or Mozambique coast offered the best conditions (Alpers 1975, 70–71, 134–35, 157–61; Machado 2014, 185–86). They had good reasons to pursue the ivory trade so actively. Elephant tusks did not command high value in African communities; but the novel, patterned Indian cloth did. Cloth represented an important good in socioeconomic transactions, such as marriage and patronage, which exchanged potential or immediate rights over people for valued items: cloth, cattle, iron hoes, beads, etc. As attire, cloth also conveyed power and cosmopolitanism (Prestholdt 2004, 257–60, 63, 773; 2008, 88–89; Glassman 1994, 36–38, 45, 54).[14] Young men in particular were eager to obtain cloth, which would enhance their social status and opportunities for marriage. They attached themselves to men who organized hunting and trading parties.

In addition to elephant tusks, African traders from the interior carried with them a variety of regional products that they bought and sold en route as well as on the coast. These goods included slaves: mainly war captives, famine refugees, and others who had become detached, by various means, from their natal communities. African trading parties thus carried slaves as well as ivory to the coast.

Until perhaps the early 1830s, African traders and hunters based in the hinterland dominated the routes that brought ivory and associated goods to the eastern central mainland—with an important exception. Along the Zambezi River and its tributaries, landed estates (*prazos*) formed the nodes of trading networks. The prazos combined elements of earlier arrangements made between African chiefs and Muslim traders with elements of Portuguese feudal law and Estado practices in India. As new prazos took shape, their holders increasingly became people of mixed Indian, African, and Portuguese descent. Inherently unstable, prazos continued to evolve, disintegrating and coalescing. All prazo-holders, however, commanded armed forces, consisting largely of slaves, fugitives, and other dependents (Newitt 1973, 1–4, 54–59, 66–67; 1995, 218–42; Isaacman 1972, 75–94).

The ivory trade, whether conveyed along the prazos or by trading parties from the interior, cultivated the market for imported cloth in the African hinterland and provided commercial infrastructures that quickly accommodated new overseas demands for captives. Such a demand arrived around 1770 from the Mascarene Islands. For almost a century the French had imported captives into the Mascarenes, particularly from Madagascar but also from the mainland coast. The ca. 1770 demand, however, was far greater and far more aggressively pursued by French traders (Allen 2014, 10–11, 18, 63–107).

The new Mascarene demand for captives arose when, in 1767, the French government dissolved the Compagnie des Indes, thus unleashing the entrepreneurial energies of its former employees who held both capital resources and knowledge of the region. But why, precisely, did these entrepreneurs purchase African captives (Vaughan 2005, 64)? No dynamic plantation complex yet demanded captive labor

(Campbell 2003, 69–70; Allen 1999, 12–13; Vaughan 2005, 257).[15] What, then, did slaves do if they weren't working on plantations? This echoes the question about nineteenth-century enslavement in the northwestern Indian Ocean and is thus worth considering. Although enslaved Africans had arrived in the Mascarenes since the 1600s, enslavement expanded precipitously with a commercial boom and the greater engagement of the French government. The island of Mauritius became a major entrepôt in the trade of the western Indian Ocean as well as the site of a large French naval establishment. These activities called for vast inputs of labor to build and maintain maritime and land infrastructures; sustain commerce and shipping (stevedoring, porterage, seafaring); and, more generally, provide the services that supported the swollen population. Enslaved Africans provided most of this labor (Vaughan 2005, 40–41, 69, 71, 74–79, 172). They were also commodities for speculation. Merchants in the Mascarenes profited from buying, selling, and renting out slaves (Vaughan 2005, 79).

In Madagascar, where the absence of elephants had prevented the ivory trade, the French demand for captives and the formation of an expansionary Merina Kingdom in the interior reinforced each other. In 1777 a former Compagnie translator-turned-merchant trekked inland and opened direct commercial ties to a region of small, competitive, highland polities. By 1782 one aristocrat-merchant gained the edge over his competitors by protecting highlanders loyal to him and profiting from the sale of war captives (Larson 2000, 147–56, 161–62). Even after the Merina king banned slave exports from his realm, people in other parts of Madagascar continued the export trade. In addition, all regions of Madagascar, including the Merina Kingdom, continued to import captives from Mozambique, some of them for reexport to the Mascarenes. The sustained Madagascar demand for captives provided a significant market for enslaved mainlanders (Campbell 2005, 239–41).

The post-1770 increase in slave exports from Madagascar was far exceeded by exports from the mainland—the Swahili and Mozambique coasts alike (Allen 2014, 68). But the flows of slave exports from the Swahili and Mozambique coasts gradually diverged. The consolidation of the Omanis on the Swahili coast encouraged exports to the northwest. In contrast, French vessels, at first rarely and sporadically but increasingly with the sugar boom in Saint-Domingue, began to carry captives, usually from the Mozambique coast, to the Americas.[16]

The Atlantic second slavery reached Indian Ocean Africa in 1793 when 276 captives on the Mozambique coast were forced onboard a Rhode Island ship bound for Cuba.[17] Almost all of the captives from Indian Ocean Africa who arrived in the Americas during the second slavery had embarked from the Mozambique coast.[18] Certainly the labor demands of the second slavery fueled the growth of slave exports from the Mozambique coast. Yet slave ships bound for the Atlantic would not have called at the Mozambique coast unless they knew that they would find an abundance of enslaved Africans at prices low enough to compensate for the long voyage around the southern tip of Africa. That abundance, I argue, resulted from the processes set in motion around 1750 and then stimulated by the rise in the demand for ivory from industrialized Europe and North America.

Enslavement increased rapidly in the Upper Nile Basin at the hands of state violence and accumulation of merchant capital. In 1820 the Ottoman governor of Egypt invaded al-Sudan, partly to gain slave recruits for his newly organized army. Until around 1840 Egyptian troops launched large-scale annual slave raids in the borderlands of the conquest state. These expeditions moved up the headwaters of the Blue Nile into the southern and eastern borderlands of highland Ethiopia; retreated; but opened the region to predatory warlords from al-Sudan who engaged in extensive slave raiding. At the same time, other regions below the Ethiopian plateau suffered first from raiding by local kingdoms and then from the violent consolidation of the Ethiopian Empire after 1870 (James 1978, 37–38; Triulzi 1981; Fernyhough 1989, 103–11).

In the conquest state in al-Sudan, a violent but cash-strapped regime simultaneously nurtured merchant accumulation of capital and enslavement. The perpetually underfinanced regime compensated its troops by paying them in the fruits of their labor: that is, the captives they produced. Traders followed the expeditions, buying at low prices the many captives and refugees not suitable for the army, thus priming the pump of the slave trade and the exploitation of captive labor (Ewald 1990, 56, 163–64). Captives from both the borders of the Ottoman al-Sudan and the Ethiopian plateau fed the long-standing routes that carried slaves across the desert to Egypt or the Red Sea/Gulf of Aden to Arabia.

After about 1820 in the eastern central hinterland, and 1839 in the Upper Nile Basin, a newly voracious demand for ivory impelled the frontiers of enslavement farther into the interior: upstream along the Zambezi Valley and Nile tributaries, especially those of the White Nile; westward across the eastern central hinterland. What gave the new ivory trade such energy to expand, and such a capacity to extract captives from African communities? The next section tackles this question.

Industrialization, the Ivory Trade, and the Height of Enslavement, ca. 1820–1880

This section argues, first, that industrialization endowed the ivory trade with new dynamism. The rapid expansion of the ivory trade, in turn, contributed to deracination, which made people vulnerable to enslavement and set in motion commodification, by which uprooted people could be exchanged for currency and prestige goods. I further suggest that the explosive production of slaves encouraged the exploitation of bondspeople in the hinterland as well as in the slave-importing littoral of the northwestern Indian Ocean. That demand, of course, further encouraged the production and exchange of captives.

Two aspects of industrialization endowed it with the dynamism to move rapidly into the hinterland and, directly or indirectly, encourage enslavement: the consumer market in industrialized societies and the industrial production of goods for export. In Europe and North America industrial wealth created a consumer class, ranging from the middling sort to the very wealthy, with an appetite for discretionary goods and the cash to purchase them. African ivory was made or incorporated into many such discretionary items, from piano keys to knickknacks. In exchange for elephant tusks, African hunters and traders received mass-produced goods, inexpensive at the point of production: cloth; beads; firearms, ammunition, and gunpowder; metal wire, etc. In the hinterland these items were valued as prestige goods; some of them also served as commodity currencies. They both endowed and conveyed power.

Conditions on the world market impelled the expansion of ivory-trading networks deep into the Upper Nile Basin and the hinterland of the eastern central coast. The demand for ivory, as well as the prices that it commanded, steeply increased just after 1820 (Sheriff 1987, 87–89; Gray 1961, 28). At the same time, the price of the US-manufactured white cotton cloth (*merkani*), one of the main items exchanged for ivory, declined (Sheriff 1987, 89). Profit margins were so high that financiers found it relatively cheap to fund large trading parties for long-distance treks into the interior, where they purchased elephant tusks. Paying caravan wageworkers at least partly in kind—that is, in inexpensive trade goods—also kept costs of trade low.

The highest profit margins accrued to financiers with the easiest access to industrially produced commodities. This, in turn, favored traders based on the Indian Ocean coast or in the northern Nile Valley. Around 1830 on the Swahili coast, caravans that consisted of men from all around the northwestern Indian Ocean littoral, as well as from the African hinterland, began to move into the interior.

The Omani customs system gave tusks brought by coast-based caravans a financial edge over those supplied by hinterland-based trading parties (Sheriff 1987, 125). In 1839 merchant parties, which included not only Sudanese and Egyptians but also other Ottoman subjects and Europeans, began to voyage down the White Nile and its tributaries, pushing commercial networks into the Upper Nile Basin (Gray 1961, 16–22). In Zambesia prazo-holders, the descendants of eighteenth-century Luso-Indian adventurers and African women, accumulated territory and wealth from trade (Newitt 1973, 234–74; 1995, 298–316).

But how did this ivory trade, whose financiers and leading merchants sought tusks and not captives, carry enslavement along with it? The ivory trade exacerbated the violence of deracination and encouraged commodification: the two processes that produced slaves. It must be noted that these processes reinforced each other. That is, the opportunity to exchange captives for commodity currency or prestige goods encouraged the violent deracination of raiding and kidnapping.

Deracination

Deracination was coerced uprooting, whether by the overt violence of warfare and kidnapping or "silent violence," which originally applied to famine that threatened to kill (de Waal 1989, 62–65, 73–77).[19] Here I apply the term *silent violence* not only to famines but also to other processes that uprooted people against their will. A debtor might be obligated to send a member of his household to the household of his creditor, as collateral or as a worker whose labor would clear the debt, or both; likewise for payment of compensation and fees. Associated with both droughts and sociopolitical breakdowns, famines created debt relations and put people on the move in search of sustenance. The southern part of the region was also invaded by militaristic Nguni peoples from Southeast Africa (Newitt 1995, 253–64; Iliffe 1979, 54–58, 70–71; Roberts 1973, 119–27, 142–49). These forms of violence, augmented by the violence attendant on the ivory trade, uprooted people and made them vulnerable to commodification and enslavement.

The structures of the ivory trade—that is, commercial settlements and trading parties—encouraged or generated the overt violence that uprooted people. The levels and sites of violence emanating from the ivory trade varied according to the organization of the trade. Caravans based on the eastern central coast generally did not exert violence when they trekked across the hinterland. The presence or promise of valuable imports, however, created competition among hinterland leaders, which sometimes broke out into armed violence that did not directly involve trading parties (Roberts 1973, 127, 198–201, 207, 209, 211–14). Permanent or semipermanent merchant settlements in the hinterland behind the commercial frontier encouraged the formation of a local class of merchants and exacerbated political rivalries, which might become violent and involve coastal merchants (Iliffe 1979, 48–66, 74–77; Sheriff 1987, 179–95). On the frontiers of commercial networks forged by coastal caravans, however, violence became pervasive when merchant-warriors built garrison-like outposts, commanded armies consisting of slave soldiers, and extracted tribute from local people.

After mid-century the domains of merchant-warriors mapped as a rough crescent across East Africa: its north-south spine along both sides of the Congo watershed; its southwestern and northwestern arms along, respectively, the Zambezi and the tributaries of the White Nile. In East Central Africa, a motley group of men from prazos, caravans, and hinterland entrepôts—some with close ties to Indian financiers on the coast; others, bondsmen who served as porters or soldiers—founded conquest states (Sheriff 1987, 182–90; Iliffe 1979, 46, 48; Roberts 1970, 50, 57; St. John 1970, 218–29, 225; Gordon 2009, 928, 934–36; Tippu Tip 1974, passim). Upstream along the Zambezi, they presided over the creation of innovative but distinctly African polities where people forged new identities (Isaacman and Isaacman 2004, 197–280). The White Nile ivory traders voyaged upstream and then along the Bahr al-Ghazal on vessels, protected by armed soldiers including Sudanese slave-soldier veterans of the Egyptian army. When on land, they fortified their outposts; slave soldiers extorted tribute from the countryside and raided for more slaves (Ewald 1990, 166–67, 169–72).

Whatever the source of their deracination—a slave raid, flight from famine or threat of attack, transfer as a debt pawn or compensation—uprooted people sought to form fresh roots; that is, to establish themselves in a household or community. The fortunate among them managed to become valued members of secure households. The unfortunate found themselves as peripheral, less valued dependents in households that faced various kinds of insecurity: food shortages, an importunate creditor, etc. These uprooted people were particularly vulnerable to commodification, which eventually manifested itself in sale.

Commodification

The ivory trade most obviously encouraged the commodification of people by offering easily accessible markets for captives. Trading parties and caravans on the move were mobile markets, casting a network of sites for exchange across the hinterland. Wageworkers in coastal-based caravans, who received their pay in the form of commodities, traded for captives as well as other local produce. The caravans—along with prazos, trade entrepôts, and the frontier settlements of warrior-merchants—infused imported, factory-produced commodity currencies, some of them also prestige goods, into hinterland communities.

The influx of imported commodity currencies restructured exchange. It stimulated standardizing, and making fungible, units of value (Wright 1993, 22). A certain quantity of one commodity currency became regarded as equivalent to a certain quantity of another commodity currency: so many measures of grain for so many beads; so many beads for so many pieces of cloth; so many pieces of cloth for a slave; so many slaves for a gun (Roberts 1973, 207). The qualities of commodities influenced their value: the price of cloth and beads varied according to current local fashions; the price of captives varied according to age, gender, and health. Captive children served as small change in the hierarchy of currencies (Morton 2009, 55).

Imported commodity currencies insinuated themselves into the political economies and social transactions of hinterland communities. People of all political and social standings needed commodity currencies, or the prestige goods that commodity currencies purchased, in order to gain or regain rights over people: that is, patronage and marriage, or return of a debt pawn, or ransom of a kidnapped child (Kilekwa 1937, 10; Sheriff 1987, 182).[20] The use of commodity currencies in social transactions thus encouraged both the violence of seizing people and the commodification of already uprooted, low-status dependents. People who held rights over captives or dependents exchanged them for the commodity currency requisite for a social transaction. Sometimes uprooted and low-status dependents went through a number of these transactions. Many of them ended up by entering the commercial networks that moved them toward the coast.

Unquantifiable thousands of slaves never arrived at the shores of the Indian Ocean but remained in the hinterland (Larson 2000, 270–75).[21] As an abundant side product of a more profitable endeavor, enslaved people were relatively accessible and cheap. Moreover, they functioned in multiple possible ways. Along the frontiers, bondsmen filled the armies of warlords and bondswomen performed the work of social as well as biological reproduction. In commercial entrepôts behind the frontier, they filled private entourages, produced food, and performed household tasks, including maintenance of the standards of hospitality deemed necessary for the households of merchants, or men who wanted to become merchants (Sheriff

1987, 179–80). In local households, slaves could be put to work in a variety of household productive and reproductive tasks, deployed as debt pawns and compensation payments, or sold. Hinterland communities thus developed their own demands for captives, which further encouraged enslavement.

Slave Labor on the Littoral of the Northwestern Indian Ocean, 1820–1880

Along the littoral of the northwestern Indian Ocean, in territories free from British rule, the availability of captives encouraged their exploitation, which in turn nurtured a market for more captives. On the Swahili coast in the early 1820s, entrepreneurs perhaps used a temporary surplus of captives on the island of Zanzibar to establish plantations of cloves, a crop new to the region (Cooper 1977, 43–44; Sheriff 1987, 60). The plantations thrived and cloves soon joined ivory as Zanzibar's main exports. Other entrepreneurs invested in plantations on the Swahili littoral, growing not only cloves but also coconut, grains, oilseed crops, and sugar for local consumption and regional trade (Glassman 1994, 81–84; Cooper 1977, 80–113). The Swahili plantation complex in turn fueled the demand for captives from the hinterland. In Oman, the labor of enslaved Africans expanded the cultivation of dates on the coastal plain; they appear, however, to have been inserted into earlier patterns of date production (Hopper 2015, 51–79). Only on the Swahili coast did enslavement open new lands to a new form of production—one of the distinguishing features of the second slavery in the Atlantic.

The clove and date plantations of, respectively, Zanzibar and Oman were emblematic of the other productive labor of slaves. Bondspeople on the littoral, including its adjacent waters, produced discretionary goods for export to industrialized nations and, especially but not exclusively for cloves, to India. Enslaved men dove for pearls and pearl shells in the Red Sea and the Persian Gulf. On the Swahili coast, bondspeople dug for copal, the fossilized resin that was used as an ingredient in varnish for wooden furniture and carriage wheels. All of these slave-produced commodities needed initial processing, packing, and transport to waterfronts, work also performed by bondspeople.

The rapid growth of commerce and port populations, as well as plantation agriculture, in the mid-nineteenth-century northwestern Indian Ocean littoral relied on the labor of enslaved Africans (Sheriff 1987, 109; Burton 1872, 1:81; Ochsenwald 1984, 17).[22] As had their counterparts in the Mascarenes, bondsmen on the Swahili coast worked in skilled and unskilled labor of all sorts. Wageworkers and bondsmen were so available in Zanzibar that affluent and the humble free people alike purchased captives in order to collect the wages that they earned, or to rent them out to other employers. Hadhrami immigrant porters used their wages to purchase bondsmen and put them to work at porterage or other tasks related to the commerce of the city. Slave-ownership thus became the route out of performing heavy labor to organizing and supervising workers (Christie 1876, 330).

Bondsmen particularly provided overland and maritime transport labor. Enslaved men who had spent some time on the Swahili coast joined caravans headed for the interior. Their owners exercised rights to a portion of their earnings (Baldock 1963, 99–103; Glassman 1994, 61–62, 74–75). Bondsmen also served on sailing ships, especially those of the Omani merchant marine. In contrast to British Indian Ocean territories, in the Muslim domains of the Indian Ocean the early decades of steam transportation likely had limited impact on the labor of bondsmen. But the opening of the Suez Canal in 1869, and consequent flood of commercial steam vessels into the Indian Ocean, created a precipitous demand for labor in the port of Jeddah. Steam vessels needed new port facilities as well as harbor services such as those provided by Murjan. In addition, the availability of steam transportation contributed to the surge in the numbers of Muslim pilgrims arriving in the Hijaz in the 1870s. During two pilgrimage seasons, incoming pilgrims temporarily more than doubled the population of the Hijaz, which itself was in the process of doubling (Ochsenwald 1984, 61). Both the government and private citizens of the Hijaz launched construction projects, the latter to profit from renting newly built accommodations to pilgrims. Enslaved Africans, especially from the Upper Nile Basin, performed much of this work (Hurgronje 1931, 11–12).

Bondsmen in the ports and on the vessels of the northwestern Indian Ocean had long formed a seafaring proletariat along with freedmen and legally free men; some of the latter were bound by debt especially in pearl diving. Bondsmen exercised considerable mobility within ports, between the littoral and the African hinterland, and among ports along the littoral. They stretched, but did not necessarily sever, the ties of bondage; slave-owners often acquiesced to or even encouraged these loose bonds. Other bondspeople received manumission from their owners. Sometimes they remained as clients and employees of their former owners, sometimes not. Many other bondspeople, however, fled their owners for reasons that ranged from physical brutality to difficult working conditions to a desire for a life beyond their owners' purview.

Some escaped or manumitted bondsmen found their way, or were taken, to British territories and enclaves: India, Aden, and ocean vessels. Their status as ex-slaves put them under the firm wing of British "protection." British officials often directed them to the new industrial-port and maritime work involving coal. By 1840 Britons in the Indian Ocean identified African port and maritime workers, almost all of them ex-slaves, as "seedies" (Yule and Burnell 1968, 806). About twenty years later the term was extended to include freedmen who labored with coal on British commercial steam liners.

Captive Labor at Sea: The Development and Application of East India Articles, ca. 1770–1880

The cooperation between government officials in India and the entrepreneurs of industrial transportation in the Indian Ocean channeled freedmen into steam liners, where they joined a largely Indian labor force under EIA. Although the EIA proved admirably suited to the needs of liners for a cheap, disciplined labor force, their deeper origins go back to the late eighteenth century. In the early nineteenth century—in the midst of war and xenophobia, followed by a wave of conservatism—Parliament passed laws that transformed the right to a return to India, which lascars had demanded, into a ban on their remaining in England. Decades later those laws were ensconced in the EIA, which became vital to British steam liners in the Indian Ocean. Among a host of benefits, the EIA solved a problem faced by entrepreneurs of steam: how to incorporate an industrial workforce into ocean transportation. Industrial capital did not create the EIA, but industrial capitalists adopted already existing regulations and practices and shaped them to their needs.

Setting the Foundations for the EIA, ca. 1770–1823

The same processes that created the conditions for post-1770 enslavement also came into play in setting the foundations for the EIA. In the late eighteenth century, the accumulation of private capital intertwined with changes in relations between the East India Company and metropolitan government. Company officials had long relied on British private traders and shippers, based in India, to carry regional products to Indian ports, where Company vessels laded them for transport to the UK. In the 1770s the so-called country traders expanded their activities (Bulley 2000, 5). Also in the 1770s, Parliament passed the first of a series of India Acts that increased government supervision over the Company's affairs. To placate the Company for the impending passage of the India Act of 1784, Parliament lowered duties on tea. As a result, the country trade between India and China boomed (Bulley 2000, 101, 151; Keay 1994, 384–85, 390–91).

In 1795, during the wartime shipping shortage, the British government disrupted this maritime regime by allowing country ships to carry private cargo to London. Unlike Company-chartered cargo ships, which only sometimes employed lascars as a minority of their crew, country ships recruited their entire crew from Asian and African seafarers, with British captains and a few British officers. On the London-bound country ships, the non-European crew suffered terrible mortality and likely frequent brutality (Hunter 1804, unpaginated table).[23] When they arrived in London, groups of lascars protested their lack of pay, often publicly, to Company and other authorities. The war-stressed London public was generally hostile and sometimes openly aggressive toward the seafarers who had brought rice and other vital commodities to the port.

For its part, the directors of the Company deployed the lascars of the country ships in their arguments against allowing private trade between England and India. The directors depicted lascars on country ships as both endangered and dangerous: on voyages, physically and mentally weak; in London, hapless prey for the worst elements of society; returned to India, prone to erode their countrymen's respect for the British.[24] The Company's overall argument about the evils of private trade from India did not carry the day; in 1813 it formally lost its monopoly over the India trade. Parliament, however, absorbed the point about lascars—but without distinguishing country-ship lascars from those on Company-chartered ships.

Between 1802 and 1823 Parliament passed legislation that first made lascars and "native" seafarers from the Indian Ocean into a special category, neither foreign nor British subjects, and then required that they return to their homeports in Asia. The 1823 law also gave British officials in India the authority to regulate the labor of non-European seafarers who joined vessels in Indian ports: that is, to subject them to special contracts on terms that did not apply to other seafarers.[25]

Officials in India devised such a contract in 1850, as part of the Registry of Merchant Seamen Act, during an era when Parliament passed a wave of repressive legislation concerning seafarers (Fink 2011, 29–30). The contract mandated that non-Europeans, who enlisted in ports in the Company's domain, return to their port of enlistment. It also stipulated cheaper diet and smaller shipboard accommodations for nonwhite seafarers.[26] Although enacted when privately owned steam vessels maintained a very limited presence in the northwestern Indian Ocean, these contracts became vital to British steam-liner companies in the region.

Industrialization at Sea, ca. 1830–1900

African freedmen first worked with coal under the employment of the government: the Bombay-based Indian Navy (IN), which managed the early decades of industrial maritime transportation in the region. The IN found it difficult to recruit men from Indian seafaring communities even for deck work, much less work with coal below deck or in port.[27] But freedmen, devoid of roots in Indian communities and usually brought to Bombay on British vessels, were more easily enlisted. Freedmen almost always served in the stokeholes of IN vessels.[28] The IN divided stokehole work into two categories, a division not always made on early steamers. Indians and African freedmen shoveled coal into the furnaces and maintained the required level of flame; African coal trimmers performed the more onerous job of carrying coal to the furnaces, where they cut it into pieces. Coal trimmers earned less than firemen or Indian deck crew.[29] The low pay of coal trimmers thus subsidized the higher wages of Indian seafarers, which likewise subsidized highest wages earned by Britons. Because of the proximity of coal dust and fumes in bunkers, whether at sea or in port, freedmen coal workers performed the most dangerous work for the IN. In the 1840s they labored on a decrepit ("crazy condition") ship in Aden's harbor, which served as the IN's coal depot. After two instances of spontaneous combustion, a major fire broke out in the hold of the ship. The official report of the fire included reassurances that the disaster had not prevented the steady coaling of an IN vessel; it did not mention that freedmen and lascars had perished.[30]

The government likely directed freedmen to the coaling operations of the first commercial British steam-liner company in the Indian Ocean, the Peninsular and Oriental (P&O), which arrived in 1842 and made its Asian headquarters in Bombay. As had the IN, the P&O employed freedmen in its coaling operations in Aden. In the early 1840s freedmen worked around the clock to load coal onto P&O vessels. Supposedly one coaler died for every hundred tons of coal loaded (Griffith and Griffith 1845, 1:19, 21).

Before the opening of the Suez Canal, the P&O and the British India (BI) steamship company, which had established itself at Calcutta in 1856, used geography to justify keeping Asian and African seafarers in the low-wage labor market of the Indian Ocean. The expense, especially for fuel, of the long voyage around the Cape of Good Hope necessitated two separate fleets for each liner company: one circulating in the Indian Ocean, manned largely by Africans and Indians under British officers, the other in the Mediterranean/Atlantic, manned by Europeans. (A land journey across Egypt linked the two.) The low wages of the African and Indian seafarers once again subsidized higher wages for Europeans. The wage differential was particularly useful below deck because European stokehole workers demanded high wages. Moreover, captains and shipowners regarded European stokehole workers, often identified as Irish, as discipline problems. The absence of labor unions and presence of imperial authority, embodied on board by the "indirect rule" of Indian or African work supervisors, made nonwhite coal workers subject to tight discipline, as well as cheap.

When the Suez Canal opened, the EIA became vital to the survival of the P&O and the BI. In order to compete with the other liners that now voyaged into the Indian Ocean, the two companies seized on their one great advantage: a large, inexpensive labor force. BI and P&O liners voyaging between the UK and Asia thus enlisted two sets of crew. The majority consisted of EIA mariners who joined the vessels in India, under EIA. All of the officers, some deck crew, and more service workers joined in the UK. Freedmen dominated the stokeholes of the P&O, representing 20 percent of firemen and 90 percent of trimmers. Although EIA seafarers seldom died on board their vessel, coal trimmers died in higher proportion than firemen or deck crew.[31] The statistics on shipboard deaths do not reveal the likely many more men who suffered illnesses from coal dust and injuries from burns or falls that disabled and even eventually killed them after their maritime service had ended.[32]

Other British liner companies that called at Indian Ocean ports soon began hiring EIA seafarers. Even though they never hired as numerous or as high a proportion of EIA crew as the BI and the P&O, mariners under those restrictive articles formed an increasingly important segment of the British merchant marine. When the British government began to count EIA seafarers in 1888, they represented 7.5 percent of all seafarers on board all British merchant vessels; by 1900, 14.5 percent; by 1938, 26 percent (Tabili 1994, 46).[33] They served almost entirely on steam vessels, although sailing ships remained through the nineteenth century.

Moreover, within steam vessels they clustered in stokeholes. In 1901 EIA mariners represented slightly over a third of the firemen and coal trimmers in the stokeholes of *all* British foreign-going steam vessels, including those that never called in the Indian Ocean.[34] Freedmen, however, apparently disappeared from stokeholes around 1900, for reasons that I cannot fully explore here. Nonetheless, the freedmen on EIA who pioneered stokehole work in the early decades of the development of industrial transportation in the Indian Ocean represent the convergence between two different regimes of captive labor—enslavement and the EIA—that emerged under conditions shaped by some of the same late eighteenth-century shifts and flourished under the impact of industrialization.

Conclusion

I opened this chapter by noting the synchronicity among the Atlantic second slavery, post-1770 African enslavement in the western Indian Ocean, and early nineteenth-century legislation that provided a legal foundation for the EIA. In addition, all three captive-labor regimes later entangled with industrialization. The chapter suggested that a three-way conversation among the captive-labor regimes might give meaning to the observations about synchronicity and industrialization. The dialogue constructed in this chapter engaged the two Indian Ocean captive-labor regimes. What has that dialogue yielded?

Beginning ca. 1750, within and beyond the western Indian Ocean, an overlapping set of changes established the conditions for the transformation of both enslavement and the employment of Indian Ocean mariners on British vessels. The relevant shifts were threefold: state formation in Africa; capital accumulation in the hands of private entrepreneurs, first largely Indians and then Europeans; and the reworking of relations between metropolitan European governments and the institutions that represented their sovereignty in the western Indian Ocean. All of these changes put in place the infrastructures for enslavement, which began to expand around 1770. In the 1770s, too, the activities of private British entrepreneurs in the Indian Ocean trade and shipping, as well as of parliamentary supervision of the East India Company, both accelerated. During the wartime shipping crisis of 1794, Parliament allowed private Indian-based ships with majority-Indian crew to carry cargo to the UK. The agitation of the Company, as well as public xenophobia, then led to legislation that created the foundations for the EIA. The final piece of legislation was enacted in 1823 amid the general conservative backlash after the war and the more specific fear of vagrants and outsiders.

The forces of industrialization pushed enslavement to its peak after the 1820s and gave new significance to the early nineteenth-century maritime legislation, especially after the opening of the Suez Canal in 1869. In industrialized societies, the combination of a burgeoning consumer demand for discretionary goods made with ivory and the low-cost, factory production of commodities highly valued by Africans gave a powerful new impetus to the ivory trade. As hosts carry symbiotic parasites, the networks of the ivory trade carried enslavement with them. The impact of prestige goods/commodity currencies on the social transactions of hinterland communities, already stressed by droughts and Nguni invasions, nurtured deracination and commodification of the unfortunate and vulnerable. Enslaved Africans who reached the Afro-Asian littoral of the northwestern Indian Ocean worked to sustain expanding commerce and burgeoning populations: transport on land and sea; constructing urban and port infrastructures; maintaining standards of living desired by affluent and even not so affluent households; producing discretionary goods for long-distance export and food for local consumption or regional trade. After the Suez Canal opened in 1869, the sudden and enormous increase in steam vessels, especially in the northwestern Indian Ocean, called on the labor of bondsmen, freedmen, and free men. In contrast, beginning in the 1790s, most of the enslaved Africans who arrived at the Portuguese-ruled Mozambique coast embarked for the American plantations of the second slavery, which served and were served by an industrial complex.

The African freedmen and Indian sailors on EIA who served on British steam liners provided the cheap labor that the entrepreneurs of steam deemed essential for profits. Before the opening of the Suez Canal, the entrepreneurs of steam used geography more than the EIA to prevent Indian and African seafarers from reaching UK ports, where wages were high. But the Suez Canal removed the land barrier between the Indian Ocean and the Mediterranean. Owners and managers then turned to the EIA, devised well before widespread maritime industrialization, to capture Indian and African workers in a labor pool characterized by imperial control and low wages.

Attention to synchronicity of origins and engagement with industrialization reveals post-1770 enslavement and the EIA, two quite different captive-labor regimes, as manifestations of similar historical shifts that transcended boundaries of oceans and continents. The territorial and maritime reach of these shifts was vast.

Nonetheless particular processes, in particular places, inflected the development of the captive-labor regimes. The impact of rapid and often violent commercialism on the dynamics of African political economies, sometimes also under the onslaught of droughts, Nguni invasions, and colonial rule, structured how hinterland people interacted with the expanding networks of the ivory trade, and thus the nature and scope of enslavement.

This chapter opened a dialogue between two captive-labor regimes, African enslavement and the EIA, that emerged from a similar field of forces in the late eighteenth- and early nineteenth-century Indian Ocean. The second slavery in the Atlantic shared the synchronicity of post-1770 African Indian Ocean enslavement but remained largely silent. It is my hope that this chapter will encourage a fuller conversation with the second slavery as well as with other captive-labor regimes that spanned oceans.

Notes

1. By *captive labor* I mean people whose physical mobility was so constrained that they were trapped in work sites where they suffered extreme vulnerability to their employers' demands, among them: low or no remuneration; dangerous conditions, including overwork and sexual exploitation; and harsh discipline. Captive labor thus included not only slaves but also workers immobilized by other forms of legal status, such as prisoners and workers under restrictive contracts such as articles of indenture or the East Indian Articles of maritime engagement.

I use the term *enslavement* to cover three major processes: the production of slaves by violent seizure or other methods (especially debt); commercialization of slaves, or the slave trade; and exploitation of slaves, or slave labor in its broadest sense.

2. National Archives, UK, Foreign Office [FO] 84/1482, Slave Trade Department, Turkey, Deposition of Murjan, December 11, 1876, enclosed in Wylde to Derby, February 11, 1877.

3. Statistics for exports from the eastern central mainland into the Atlantic, 1771–1900, come from the Trans-Atlantic Slavery Voyage Database, http://www.slavevoyages.org/estimates/kQWSyWy4.

I used Lovejoy's (2011) estimates of the eighteenth- and nineteenth-century slave trade of the northwestern Indian Ocean. For the thirty-year span 1771–1800, I extrapolated Lovejoy's annual eighteenth-century averages. This almost certainly resulted in an underestimation of the late eighteenth-century exports because other evidence suggests a subsequent increase in overseas slave exports.

4. IOR V/11/2147, *Bombay Gazetteer*, July 11, 1850, 802–4.

5. Memorial University, St. John's, Newfoundland, Maritime History Archives, Crew Lists and Agreements for Peninsular and Oriental Company and British India Company. The vessels and their registration numbers in the sample are: *Africa* (08108), *Agra* (68002), *Almora* (68055), *Arcot* (63809), *Assam* (73581), *Assyria* (67980), *Ava* (68060), *Bengal* (87424), *Bokhara* (68397), *Brindisi* (81478), *Canara* (71637), *China* (27199), *Chyebassa* (71666), *Ellora* (80437), *Kaisar-i-Hind* (76182), *Mirzapore* (65604), *Parramatta* (87377), *Patna* (63826), *Rohilla* (81780), *Rome* (81820), *Siam* (73596), *Umballa* (81645).

6. Eaton's biography of Malik Ambar (Eaton 2005) and his article on military slavery in the Deccan, 1450–1650 (Eaton 2006) describe what was perhaps the largest single wave of African slave exports to Asia before 1770. It resulted from warfare in both Ethiopia, which produced slaves, and the Deccan, which imported slaves.

7. Although seafarers died, or deserted East India Company vessels as soon as they arrived in the Indian Ocean, impressment into the Royal Navy did not become significant until the mid-eighteenth century. It peaked during the late eighteenth- and early nineteenth-century wars with France.

8. British Library, India Office Records [IOR], ships' journals, logs, and related records, 1702–1856, L/MAR/B/624F(1), Admiral Walton; /24FF(1), Asia 2; /122H(1), Benjamin 3; /308Q(1), Calcutta 1; /483E(1), Northington; /462/K(1), Ponsborne; /293FF(1),Walpole 2.

9. Although Tomich first applied the term *second slavery* to Atlantic slavery in 1988, it did not appear more widely in Anglophone scholarship until the early 2000s (Tomich 1988; Tomich and Zeuske 2008).

10. Gwyn Campbell identified the southern circuit as an important part of the slave trade of the eastern central mainland coast.

11. My work relies a great deal on the work of the previous generation of African historians, including Abdul Sheriff's (1987) pathbreaking research on the slave and ivory trade from the Swahili coast. Nonetheless, I depart from his view that the lack of a demand for "productive"—i.e., plantation—slaves resulted in low exports from the Swahili coast to the Asian littoral of the northwestern Indian Ocean. On the other hand, his statement that the commercial boom during the Napoleonic Wars led to an increase in the exploitation of slave labor accords with my argument about the increase of commerce and slave exports in the mid- and late nineteenth century.

12. More than forty years ago, Edward A. Alpers (1970) revealed the importance of Mascarene-based French traders in stimulating slave exports from the Swahili coast. Recently, Richard B. Allen (2014) and Thomas Vernet (2011) have illustrated Alpers's argument.

13. Downplaying continents as distinct, "natural" regions draws on Lewis and Wigen (1997). M. N. Pearson wrote two seminal articles on the coast, which he renamed the littoral, as a coherent historical region (Pearson 1985, 2006).

14. For a broader discussion of commodity currencies and prestige goods in part of Africa that shares many similarities with East Central Africa, see Miller (1988, 40–70).

15. Coffee cultivation on Ile de Bourbon, renamed Réunion, declined between 1740 and the 1790s, interrupted only by a brief surge of production after the dissolution of the Compagnie.

16. Only about 12 percent of the slaves who voyaged to the Americas, 1772–1792, embarked at the Swahili coast. *Trans-Atlantic Slave Voyages*, http://www.slavevoyages.org/voyages/3TcEHKqV, Southeast Africa, 1772–1792, for specific sites of embarkation and number of voyages; http://www.slavevoyages.org/estimates/hCBNo2tf, Southeast Africa, 1772–1792, for estimates of numbers of captives embarked and disembarked.

17. *Trans-Atlantic Slave Voyages*, http://www.slavevoyages.org/voyages/aGRYOVDk.

18. Ninety-five percent of captives from Southeast Africa after 1793 embarked from the Mozambique Coast, http://www.slavevoyages.org/voyage/database#searchId=L9c82unN.

19. Michael Watts gave the term *silent violence* wide currency when he used it in the title of his book *Silent Violence: Food, Famine, and Peasantry in Northern Nigeria* (1983).

20. Kilekwa (1937) relates a particularly poignant example of how deeply the need for cloth had penetrated into local communities.

21. I agree with Pier M. Larson (2000) about the importance of what he calls "intracontinental enslavement." I query, however, the supposed continental boundaries in the northwestern Indian Ocean.

22. Zanzibar's external trade increased fivefold during the first half of the nineteenth century. The populations of Zanzibar and the three Hijazi cities (Jeddah, Mecca, and Medina) each doubled: the former, between 1837 and 1857; the latter, over the last half of the nineteenth century.

23. Hunter (1804, unpaginated table); IOR, Home Miscellaneous, H/501 Committee of Shipping, "Inquiry into the Union," April–June 1802.

24. United Kingdom, Parliamentary Papers, House of Commons Papers, 7:122 (1801). *Papers relating to Private Trade of East India Company between India and Europe, 1797–1801*, "Report of the Special Committee," 35–36, http://parlipapers.proquest.com/parlipapers/docview/t70.d75.1801-000138?accountid=10598.

25. Great Britain, *The Statutes of the United Kingdom of Great Britain and Ireland . . . from A. D. 1801, 41 George III to 1868–1869, 32 & 33 Victoria*, 29 vols. (London: G. Eyre and A. Strahan), 1804–69, 42 Geo. 3, c. 61 (1802), vol. 1, 392, http://hdl.handle.net/2027/nyp.33433035285216; 54 Geo. 3, c. 134 (1814), vol. 5, 856–57, http://hdl.handle.net/2027/nyp.33433035256027; 4 Geo. 4, c. 80 (1823), vol. 9, 416–18, http://hdl.handle.net/2027/msu.31293007782539.

26. IOR V/11/2147, *Bombay Gazetteer*, July 11, 1850, 802–.

27. IOR, Bombay Proceedings and Consultations, Marine Committee, P/412/63, Superintendent, Indian Navy, to Secretary to Government, March 26, 1838.

28. IOR, Bombay Proceedings and Consultations, Marine Committee, P/413/26, Acting Marine Superintendent to Secretary to Government, June 10, 1845, enclosing statement of the crews and disposition of the vessels of the Indian Navy.

29. IOR, Miscellaneous Maritime Records, L/MAR/C/581, Reports of Committees concerning Steam Navigation, Proposed establishment of the HC vessels of war on the Indian Naval Establishment, 1837–1838; IOR, Bombay Proceedings and Consultations, Marine Committee, P/412/15, Consultation, August 18, 1830; P/413/6, Minutes, April 21, 1841; P/413/7, Minutes, September 9, 1841; Minutes, November 4, 1841.

30. IOR, Bombay Proceedings and Consultations, Marine, P/412/74, Marine Superintendent to Secretary to Government, May 27, 1840; P/413/25, from the Military Auditor General to Secretary to Government, January 29, 1845; P/413/27, from Senior Naval Officer, Aden to Marine Superintendent, April 8, 1845; from Assistant Political Agent, Aden, to Commander T[?] G. Canless, March 30, 1845.

The only report of the deaths that I could find appeared in the *Bombay Gazette*, IOR V/11/2148, 20:41, October 2, 1851, in a list of deceased IN seafarers whose estates (such as they were) remained unclaimed—among them two freedmen and a lascar from the *Charger*.

31. The Crew Lists and Agreements for 149 voyages recorded that about 3.2 percent of EIA seafarers died during voyages. Among coal trimmers, however, 4 percent died before being discharged. Interestingly, firemen bore the lowest proportion of deaths, 1 percent, while 2.4 percent of deck crew died during the voyage.

32. Causes of death appear in the records held by the Caird Library of the National Maritime Museum [CLNMM], Peninsular and Oriental Steamship Company [P&O], Death Book, 88/3, Madras, May 17, 1859, and June 29, 1866; Peshawur, April 25, 1874. CLNMM, Nautical Reports, 40/10, January 1862–February 1864, Simla; 40/11, January 1864–May 1866, Carnacitc and Golconda; 40/20, May 1884–July 1886, Tasmania; 40/22, July 1888–September 1890, Venetia and Parramatta; 40/23, October 1890–March 1893, Britannia, Peshawur, Kaisar-i-Hind, and Gwalior; 40/27, April 1899–September 1901, Assaye and Egypt.

33. Great Britain, Board of Trade [BT], *Report of the committee appointed . . . to inquire into certain questions affecting the mercantile marine* (London: Wyman and Sons, 1903), Appendix M, nos. 1–3 (handed in by Malan), 116–21.

34. Great Britain, BT, *Report of the committee*, Appendix M, nos. 1–3 (handed in by Malan), 116–21.

Sources Cited

Unpublished Sources

British Library, India Office Records [BLIOR].
Bombay Gazette, V/11/2147, V/11/2148.

Bombay Proceedings and Consultations, Marine Committee, P/412/63, P/413/26.
Minutes of the East India Company's Directors and Proprietors, Court Book B/123, B/124.
Miscellaneous Maritime Records, L/MAR/C/581.
Memorial University, St. John's, Newfoundland, Maritime History Archives [MUMHA]

Crew Lists and Agreements

National Archives, United Kingdom.
Foreign Office, Slave Trade Department, Turkey, FO 84/1482.
National Maritime Museum, Caird Library [NMMCL].
Peninsular and Oriental Steamship Company Death Book, 88/3.
Peninsular and Oriental Company Steamship Nautical Reports [PONR], 40/10, 40/11, 40/20, 40/22, 40/23, 40/27.

References

Allen, Richard B. 1999. *Slaves, Freedmen, and Indentured Laborers in Colonial Mauritius.* Cambridge: Cambridge University Press.

———. 2014. *European Slave Trading in the Indian Ocean, 1500–1850.* Athens: Ohio University Press.

Alpers, Edward A. 1970. "The French Slave Trade in East Africa, 1721–1810." *Cahiers d'Études africaines* 10, no. 37: 80–124.

———. 1975. *Ivory and Slaves: Changing Patterns of International Trade in East Central Africa to the Later Nineteenth Century.* Berkeley: University of California Press.

Baillie, Donald. 1957. *A Sea Affair.* London: Hutchinson.

Bain, John. *Life of a Scottish Sailor or Forty Years' Experience of the Sea.* Nairn, UK: George Bain/Inverness, UK: Melven Brothers, 1897.

Baldock, W. F. 1963. "The Story of Rashid Bin Hasani of the Bisa Tribe, Northern Rhodesia." In *Ten Africans*, edited by Margery Perham, 81–119. 2nd ed. Evanston, IL: Northwestern University Press.

Bulley, Anne. 2000. The *Bombay Country Ships, 1790–1833.* Richmond, Surrey, UK: Curzon.

Burton, Richard B. 1872. *Zanzibar: City, Island and Coast.* 2 vols. London: Tinsley Bros. Reprint, 1967, 1:81.

Campbell, Gwyn. 1989. "The East African Slave Trade, 1861–1895: The Southern 'Complex.'" *International Journal of African Historical Studies* 22, no. 1: 1–26.

———. 2003. "The Origins and Development of Coffee Production in Réunion and Madagascar, 1711–1972." In *The Global Coffee Economy in Asia, Africa, and Latin*

America, 1500–1989, edited by William Gervase Clarence-Smith and Steven Topik, 67–119. Cambridge: Cambridge University Press.

———. 2005. *An Economic History of Imperial Madagascar, 1750–1885: The Rise and Fall of an Island Empire*. Cambridge: Cambridge University Press.

Christie, James. 1876. *Cholera Epidemics in East Africa*. London: Macmillan.

Cooper, Frederick. 1997. *Plantation Slavery on the East Coast of Africa*. New Haven: Yale University Press.

de Waal, Alexander. 1989. *Famine That Kills: Darfur, Sudan, 1984–1985*. Oxford, UK: Clarendon.

Eaton, Richard. 2005. *Social History of the Deccan, 1300–1761: Eight Indian Lives*. Cambridge: Cambridge University Press.

———. 2006. "The Rise and Fall of Military Slavery in Deccan, 1450–1650." In *Slavery and South Asian History*, edited by Richard Eaton and Indrani Chatterjee, 115–35. Bloomington: Indiana University Press.

Ewald, Janet J. 1990. *Soldiers, Traders, and Slaves: State Formation and Economic Transformation in the Greater Nile Valley, 1700–1885*. Madison: University of Wisconsin Press.

Fernyhough, Timothy. 1989. "Slavery and the Slave Trade in Southern Ethiopia in the 19th Century." In *The Economics of the Indian Ocean Slave Trade in the Nineteenth Century*, edited by William Gervase Clarence-Smith, 103–30. London: Frank Cass.

Fink, Leon. 2011. *Sweatshops at Sea: Merchant Seamen in the World's First Globalized Industry, from 1812 to the Present*. Chapel Hill: University of North Carolina Press.

Glassman, Jonathon. 1994. *Feasts and Riot: Revelry, Rebellion, and Popular Consciousness on the Swahili Coast, 1856–1888*. Portsmouth, NH: Heinemann.

Gordon, David. 2009. "The Abolition of the Slave Trade and the Transformation of the South-Central African Interior during the Nineteenth Century." *William and Mary Quarterly* 66, no. 4: 915–38.

Gray, Richard. 1961. *History of the Southern Sudan, 1839–1889*. London: Oxford University Press.

Great Britain. 1804–1869. *The Statutes of the United Kingdom of Great Britain and Ireland . . . from A. D. 1801, 41 George III to 1868–1869, 32 & 33 Victoria*. 29 vols. London: G. Eyre and A. Strahan. 42 Geo. 3, c. 61 (1802), vol. 1, 392, http://hdl.handle.net/2027/nyp.33433035285216; 54 Geo. 3, c. 134 (1814), vol. 5, 856–57, http://hdl.handle.net/2027/nyp.33433035256027; 4 Geo. 4, c. 80 (1823), vol. 9, 416–18, http://hdl.handle.net/2027/msu.31293007782539.

Great Britain, Board of Trade. 1903. *Report of the committee appointed . . . to inquire into certain questions affecting the mercantile marine*. London: Wyman and Sons, Appendix M, nos. 1–3 (handed in by Malan), 116–21.

Griffith, George Darby, and Mrs Griffith. 1845. *A Journey across the Desert, from Ceylon to Marseilles*. 2 vols. London: Henry Colburn.

Hood, W. H. 1903. The *Blight of Insubordination: The Lascar Question, and Rights and Wrongs of the British Shipmaster, Including the Mercantile Marine Committee Report.* London: Spottiswood.

Hopper, Matthew S. 2015. *Slaves of One Master: Globalization and Slavery in Arabia in the Age of Empire.* New Haven, CT: Yale University Press.

Hunter, William. 1804. *An Essay on the Diseases Incident to Indian Seamen, or Lascars, on Long Voyages.* Calcutta: Printed at the HC's Press.

Hurgronje, C. Snouck. 1931. *Mekka in the Latter Part of the Nineteenth Century: Daily Life, Customs and Learning.* Translated by J. H. Monahan. Leiden: Brill.

Iliffe, John. 1979. *A Modern History of Tanganyika.* Cambridge: Cambridge University Press.

Isaacman, Allen F. 1972. *Mozambique: The Africanization of a European Institution, the Zambesi Prazos, 1750–1902.* Madison: University of Wisconsin Press.

Isaacman, Allen F., and Barbara S. Isaacman. 2004. *Slavery and Beyond: The Making of Men and Chikunda Ethnic Identities in the Unstable World of South-Central Africa, 1750–1920.* Portsmouth, NH: Heinemann.

James, Wendy. 1978. *Kwanim Pa, the Making of the Uduk People: An Ethnographic Study of Survival in the Sudan-Ethiopian Borderlands.* Oxford, UK: Clarendon.

Keay, John. 1994. *The Honorable Company: A History of the English East India Company.* New York: Macmillan.

Kilekwa, Petro. 1937. *Slave Boy to Priest: The Autobiography of Petro Kilekwa.* London: University Missions to Africa.

Larson, Pier M. 2000. *History and Memory in the Age of Enslavement: Becoming Merina in Highland Madagascar, 1770–1822.* Portsmouth, NH: Heinemann.

Lewis, Martin W., and Karen E. Wigen. 1997. *Myth of the Continents: A Critique of Metageography.* Berkeley: University of California Press.

———. "A Maritime Response to the Crisis in Area Studies." 1999. *Geographical Review* 89, no. 2: 161–68.

Lovejoy, Paul E. 2011. *Transformations in Slavery.* 3rd ed. Cambridge: Cambridge University Press.

Machado, Pedro. 2014. *Ocean of Trade: South Asian Merchants, Africa and the Indian Ocean, c. 1750–1840.* New York: Cambridge University Press.

Manning, Patrick. 1990. *Slavery and African Life: Occidental, Oriental, and African Slave Trades.* New York: Cambridge University Press.

Miers, Suzanne. 1989. "Diplomacy versus Humanitarianism: British and Consular Manumission in Hijaz, 1921–1936." *Slavery & Abolition* 10, no. 3: 102–28.

Miller, Joseph C. 1988. *Way of Death: Merchant Capital and the Angolan Slave Trade, 1730–1830.* Madison: University of Wisconsin Press.

Morton, Fred. 2009. "Small Change: Children in the Nineteenth-Century East African Slave Trade." In *Children in Slavery through the Ages*, edited by Gwyn Campbell, Suzanne Miers, and Joseph C. Miller, 55–70. Athens: Ohio University Press.

Nadri, Ghulam A. 2008. "Exploring the Gulf of Kachh: Regional Economy and Trade in the Eighteenth Century." *Journal of the Economic and Social History of the Orient* 51, no. 3: 460–86.

———. 2009. *Eighteenth-Century Gujarat: The Dynamics of Its Political Economy, 1750–1800.* Leiden: Brill.

Newitt, M. D. D. 1973. *Portuguese Settlement on the Zambesi: Exploration, Land Tenure and Colonial Rule in East Africa.* New York: Africana.

Newitt, Malyn. 1995. *A History of Mozambique.* Bloomington: Indiana University Press.

Ochsenwald, William. 1984. *Religion, Society and the State in Arabia: The Hijaz under Ottoman Control, 1840–1908.* Columbus: Ohio State University Press.

Page, Melvin E. 1974. "The Manyema Hordes of Tippu Tip: A Case Study in Social Stratification and the Slave Trade in Eastern Africa." *International Journal of African Historical Studies* 7, no. 1: 69–84.

Pearson, M. N. 1985. "Littoral Society: The Case for the Coast." *The Great Circle,* no. 1: 1–8.

______. 2006. "Littoral Society: The Concept and the Problems." *Journal of World History* 17, no. 4: 353–73.

Prestholdt, Jeremy. 2004. "On the Global Repercussions of East African Consumerism." *American Historical Review* 109, no. 3: 755–81.

———. 2008. *Domesticating the World: African Consumerism and the Genealogies of Globalization.* Berkeley: University of California Press.

Risso, Patricia. 1986. *Oman and Muscat: An Early Modern History.* New York: St. Martin's.

Roberts, Andrew. 1970. "Nyamwezi Trade." In *Pre-Colonial African Trade: Essays on Trade in Central and Eastern Africa before 1900,* edited by Richard Gray and David Birmingham, 37–74. London: Oxford University Press.

———. 1973. *A History of the Bemba: Political Growth and Change in North-Eastern Zambia before 1900.* Madison: University of Wisconsin Press.

Sheriff, Abdul. 1987. *Slaves, Spices, and Ivory in Zanzibar.* Athens: Ohio University Press.

St. John, Christopher. 1970. "Kazembe and the Tanganyika-Nyasa Corridor, 1800–1890." In *Pre-Colonial African Trade: Essays on Trade in Central and Eastern Africa before 1900,* edited by Richard Gray and David Birmingham, 202–30. London: Oxford University Press.

Strachan, Michael, and Boies Penrose, eds. 1971. *The East India Company Journals of Captain William Keeling and Master Thomas Bonner, 1615–1617.* Minneapolis: University of Minnesota Press.

Tabili, Laura. 1994. *"We Ask for British Justice": Workers and Racial Difference in Late Imperial Britain.* Ithaca: Cornell University Press.

Tippu Tip. 1974. *L'autobiographie de Hamed ben Mohammed el-Murjebi Tippo Tip (ca. 1840–1905).* Translated and edited by Francois Bontinck. Bruxelles: Academie royale des Science d'Outre Mer.

Tomich, Dale. 1988. "The 'Second Slavery': Bonded Labor and the Transformation of the Nineteenth-Century World Economy." In *Rethinking the Nineteenth Century: Contradictions and Movements*, edited by F. Ramirez, 103–17. Westport, CT: Greenwood.

Tomich, Dale, and Michael Zeuske. 2008. "Introduction, the Second Slavery: Mass Slavery, World-Economy, and Comparative Microhistories." *Review: A Journal of the Fernand Braudel Center* 31, no. 2: 91–100.

Trans-Atlantic Slave Voyages, Database and Estimates. http://www.slavevoyages.org/voyage/database and http://www.slavevoyages.org/assessment/estimates.

Triulzi, Alessandro. 1981. *Salt, Gold, and Legitimacy: Prelude to the History of a No-Man's Land, Bela Shangul, Wallaga, Ethiopia (1800–1898).* Naples: Istituto universitario orientale.

Vaughan, Megan. 2005. *Creating the Creole Island: Slavery in Eighteenth-Century Mauritius.* Durham, NC: Duke University Press.

Vernet, Thomas. 2011. "La première traite française à Zanzibar: Le journal de bord du vaisseau l'Espérance, 1774–1775." In *Civilisations des mondes insulaires (Madagascar, canal de Mozambique, Mascareignes, Polynésie, Guyanes)*, Mélanges en l'honneur du Professeur Claude Allibert, edited by C. Radimilahy and N. Rajaonarimanana, 477–521. Paris: Karthala.

Watts, Michael. 1983. *Silent Violence: Food, Famine, and Peasantry in Northern Nigeria.* Berkeley: University of California.

Wright, Marcia. 1993. *Strategies of Slaves and Women: Life Stories from East/Central Africa.* New York: Lilian Barber.

Yule, Henry, and A. C. Burnell. *Hobson-Jobson: A Glossary of Colloquial Anglo-Indian Words and Phrases, and of Kindred Terms, Etymological, Historical, Geographical and Discursive.* Edited by William Crooke. 2nd ed. Delhi: Munshiram Manoharlal, 1968.

Chapter 11

Dutch Capitalism and Slavery in the Longer Run

A Reorientation

Pepijn Brandon

Introduction[1]

The Netherlands seems an obvious candidate for studying the contribution of slavery to long-term capitalist development. During the seventeenth and eighteenth centuries, the Dutch Republic became a gravitational point in global capital and commodity flows, allowing it to become a dynamic center of international capitalist development (Arrighi 1994). For most of this period, the Dutch were important drivers of the expansion of transatlantic and Indian Ocean slavery. Over the period as a whole, the Netherlands was the fifth-largest participant in the transatlantic slave trade, and during a brief but significant moment in the seventeenth century it was even the leading European slave-trading nation in the Atlantic region (Postma 1990; Klooster 2016). Based on recent estimates, historians have put the Dutch involvement in the slave trade in the Indian Ocean region at par with that in the Atlantic Ocean (van Welie 2008; Mbeki and van Rossum 2017). More than just trading in slaves, the Dutch employed large numbers of slaves in commodity production in areas as far apart as the Banda Islands, Ceylon, South Africa, Brazil, and Suriname (van Zanden 1993; Nimako and Willemsen

2011; Fatah-Black and van Rossum 2014). Furthermore, especially in the Atlantic World where, after the fall of Dutch Brazil, their empire shrank to a modest size, the Dutch continued to act as the perennial interlopers, freighters, and financiers between slave-based production zones and home markets. In the eighteenth century the trade in Atlantic slave-produced commodities grew while most of the rest of the Dutch economy stagnated or declined, with the erratic expansion of slave-based coffee production in particular becoming deeply entangled with the further development of Amsterdam financial markets (van de Voort 1973; Klooster 1998; Postma and Enthoven 2003; Oostindie and Roitman 2014).

Despite such good reasons to study slavery's impact in the different phases of the development of capitalism in the Netherlands, investigations in this direction by Dutch historians in the past have always been quickly short-circuited.[2] Limiting themselves to dismissing a bowdlerized version of the Williams thesis, most historians content themselves with noting that: (1) the profits from the slave trade were low compared to those from other branches of Dutch trade; (2) there is a temporal disconnect between the period in which the Dutch made direct gains from slavery and the late emergence of *industrial* capitalism in the Netherlands; and (3) geographically, most of the time profits from the East Indies with their much more variegated modes of economic organization surpassed those from the Atlantic plantation system (Emmer and Gommans 2012, for a textbook example). Perhaps the most noticeable shortcoming of this form of reasoning is that it does not approach capitalism as a complex, evolving, global system but rather as a disjointed collection of economically independent sectors and areas of growth.[3] Establishing the importance of each becomes a simple matter of national accounting. In this methodology it becomes possible to examine the Dutch involvement in slave trade in isolation from the trade in slave-produced commodities, plantation production without the development finance, and the quest for profits from slavery as a purely economic venture, void of power relations or geopolitics. Furthermore, all the different elements of long-term capitalist development are thus reduced to the simple measuring rod of gross or net profits, without any sense of how such profits contribute to the long-term direction of development of accumulation regimes. That is not to say national accounting has no place at all in attempts to understand the long-term economic impact of slavery. However, it becomes a useful tool only when understood as shedding light on one aspect of a complex whole.

Against the one-dimensional approaches dominant in Dutch historiography, this chapter will show that in the various phases of development that characterized the

"Dutch cycle of accumulation"—rapid rise to global prominence in terms of control over trade routes and territorial expansion in the first half of the seventeenth century; economic consolidation and intensified global competition in the second half of the seventeenth century; partial decline and financialization during most of the eighteenth century; decline and readjustment of the role of Dutch capital in the world economy in the final quarter of the eighteenth and first half of the nineteenth century (Arrighi 1994; Brandon 2015)—slavery fulfilled a large variety of different functions. Apart from direct profiting from the slave trade and the trade in slave-produced commodities, among others, those included the fight over slaving zones as an instrument of geostrategy, slavery as a tool for establishing control over (segments of) global commodity chains and the laborers involved in them, and slave investments as a means of building or rebuilding transnational business networks. Each of these supported the position of Dutch capital within the world economy in different ways. Over the more than 250 years summarized here, there were large shifts in importance between these different factors as well as in the relative weight of slave-related activities within the Dutch economy as a whole. Furthermore, slavery fulfilled connected but different roles in the Indian Ocean and Atlantic parts of the Dutch global empire (Fatah-Black and van Rossum 2014). The chapter argues that the true significance of slavery for Dutch capitalist development can be judged satisfactorily only by an approach that looks at the question in its *longue durée*, that confronts both the differences and the similarities and connections between the western and eastern hemispheres, and that embraces a vision of economic processes that goes beyond mere accounting to include questions of local and global power relations.

Accidental Beginnings or Strategic Interest?

Determining how to relate to slavery and the slave trade became a practical problem for Dutch merchants and policymakers from the 1590s onward, when the newly established Dutch Republic became capable of exporting its war of independence against the Habsburg crown to the Spanish and Portuguese Empires in the Atlantic and the Indian Ocean area. At this point, potential profits from slavery did not figure largely in Dutch commercial considerations. Johannes Postma therefore has argued that the first encounters of the Dutch with the Atlantic slave trade were "more by accident than by design" (Postma 1990, 10). Most historians concur and point out that the relatively minor examples of direct involvement in both the slave trade and slavery in the Atlantic region in this period formed a by-product of privateering actions, in which the Dutch captured slaves from the Portuguese and the Spanish (de Vries 2005, 2–4).[4] However, sporadic windfalls from slaving might not be the most important factor by which to measure Dutch early interest in slavery. From the outset, merchants and statesmen acknowledged the potential strategic value of disrupting or capturing the flows of Atlantic slavery in interimperial rivalry. These military aims were not separate from economic considerations, in the same way that the two were intertwined for the newly established East and West India Companies (VOC and WIC, established in 1602 and 1621, respectively). The successful challenge to the Habsburgs in the East and partially successful challenge in the West allowed the Dutch Republic, and Amsterdam merchant houses in particular, to place themselves at the heart of early modern capitalism (Arrighi 1994; Israel 1989, chs. 3, 4). Slavery's significance for Dutch capitalism in the earliest decades of the seventeenth century should therefore not be measured in terms of profits, which were indeed small, but in terms of its contribution to commercial-military expansion.

Perhaps more than for any other period of the long Dutch involvement in global slavery, the standard view of the first half century of Dutch slaving suffers from the separation between West and East. The well-rehearsed theme of the reluctance or "innocence" with which the Dutch approached the question of slavery at the start of the seventeenth century can only be upheld by ignoring the strategic importance of slavery to the rise of the VOC in Asia in the same period (Schmidt 2001; cf. Vink 2007). In the Indian Ocean region, the VOC encountered well-established slaving practices, both indigenous and Portuguese, and the Dutch "soon accustomed themselves to the phenomenon of slavery" (Knaap 1995, 195). The number of slaves in VOC-controlled areas rose by leaps and bounds from about eight thousand in 1625 to sixty-eight thousand in 1700, and then more gradually to almost eighty thousand in 1775, to start declining after that. According to the most recent estimates by Matthias van Rossum, the size of the—largely private, not Company-operated—slave trade necessary to maintain those numbers rose from 500–850 in the first years to 4,200–7,300 in 1700, and 4,900–8,450 at the 1775 peak (van Rossum 2015a, 42). With such numbers the Dutch far outstripped their European competitors in the region (Allen 2014, 9).

The conquest of Jacatra (Batavia) in 1619 and the Banda Islands in 1621 by the aggressive VOC governor-general Jan Pieterszoon Coen formed the tipping points drawing the VOC into large-scale Indian Ocean slaving, as they did for establishing the Company as a territorial power more generally. However, it is important to note that considerations on the strategic value of slavery in colonization by VOC officials on the ground and in the Dutch Republic predated conquest. Early Dutch explorers routinely gathered information on local slave markets. To give just one example, the papers provided by the VOC directors to Pieter van der Hagen for his journey to the East Indies of December 1603 included an anonymous report on "several countries and islands . . . where trade is easy and what goods can best be acquired there." Among many other bits of valuable commercial intelligence, the report mentioned "Bourneo . . . where the Mallayans, who live on Macassar, have a large trade and bring much rice, against which they get slaves," as well as "Bouton . . . [where] the Mallayans, Moluccans and Bandanese buy many slaves, who are very cheap here," and "Lambou . . . where all the nations of diverse religions may freely buy slaves; though no men at all are sold here, most women, but cheap" (de Jonge 1865, 158–61). As early as 1614, Coen in a long letter advised the directors of the VOC of the advantages of replacing the untrustworthy "Moors" populating Ternate with Christians as well as "blacks [*swarten*] . . . , either slaves or free, all capable to do the necessary labor, so that we do not have to use our own people in this" (Colenbrander 1919, 81). In Banda, several years before the final conquest and restructuring of local nutmeg production through plantation slavery, Coen recognized the potential of using slaves to decrease the numerical superiority of the indigenous population, who were considered hostile toward the VOC, and to guarantee continuity of production under VOC control. In a letter of November 30, 1617, to the VOC official at the Coromandel Coast, Coen enthusiastically wrote: "On the *Golden Lion* and the *Neptune* we have received several sturdy blacks. Asking Your Honor to send us so many of those, as can easily be transported, young men, as well as grown boys and women, if opportunity permits, because this is highly needed for the population of Banda, since because of the lack of people there much nutmeg and mace is lost" (Colenbrander 1920, 300).

Neither was the acceptance of the slave trade merely the result of pressure from VOC officials on the ground. In May 1615 the directors in Amsterdam were the ones to exhort Coen to "buy several slaves" for the building of fortresses and other defense works needed to pacify the indigenous population of the Banda Islands, though only "in case of emergency" and provided that other sources of forced labor such as Spanish prisoners of war were not available (Colenbrander 1922, 316).

Before the turn toward full plantation slavery on the Banda Island nutmeg and mace "gardens," the VOC's involvement in slaving seems to have been more tied to colonization than to profiting per se. In many remarks like the ones cited above, VOC officials recommended slaves either as a more reliable replacement of "untrustworthy" local populations or as a cheap alternative to bringing over European laborers. The wider context was the struggle to replace the Portuguese and Spanish as a force on the ground. Considerable information gathering on slaving areas, experimentation with the use of slave labor, and a highly pragmatic attitude toward the question of slavery in general were the results, providing an easy springboard to a more systematic application of slave labor for purely economic motives.

Viewed from the East Indian side, the story of the first steps of the Dutch into the Atlantic seems one of strong parallels rather than stark contrasts. It certainly is the case that before the conquest of Dutch Brazil in the 1630s, the direct participation of the Dutch in Atlantic slavery and the slave trade was minimal (Ribeiro da Silva 2011, 251) though not nonexistent (Antunes and Ribeiro da Silva 2012). The small numbers of slaves who were traded by the Dutch were captured in privateering actions and mostly sold to non-Dutch colonies. In their African ventures, Dutch merchants initially were more interested in the trade in gold and ivory, though they used the African coastal islands as springboards to enter the trade in slave-produced sugar and brazilwood as well (Ratelband 2000; Ribeiro da Silva 2014). As in the East Indies, the Dutch were always well aware of the potential strategic importance of slavery, resulting in extensive information gathering. In the narrative of his 1600–1602 voyage to the Gold Coast, Pieter de Marees describes the Rio Forcado in the Bight of Benin: "This river is much frequented by the Portuguese and is well known, and not because of the virtue of the Country, but because of the large number of Slaves that they trade and buy there, to bring them to other places, such as St. Thomé and Brazil, to work there and refine Sugar. . . . They are on average better slaves than those of Gabom, but those that can be bought in Angola are even better" (de Marees 1912, 230–31).

Neither was there any innocence in the gathering of such information. Between the final years of the sixteenth century and the founding of the WIC, the Dutch repeatedly tried to capture São Tomé, Príncipe, São Jorge da Mina on the Gold Coast, and Luanda, both through privately outfitted and state-organized ventures. Since the Dutch had no sugar colonies of their own at this point, and had of course no chance of entering the slave trade with the Iberian colonies as more than interlopers, slavery figured mostly in those operations for purposes of disrupting the Portuguese Atlantic System. This strategic aim fitted into the global Luso-Dutch conflict, and there were tangible connections between the Atlantic and Indian Ocean theaters of war. Dutch operations along the African coast were often commissioned or led by people who were also instrumental to the earliest phase of Dutch expansion in the East Indies. Gerard Reijnst fitted out ships to establish Dutch trade on the Congo River and the Loango coast, around the same time that he also acted as director of one of the "precompanies" for Asia, and before he became governor-general for the VOC in Asia in 1613. Balthazar de Moucheron, who also played an important role in the pre-VOC trade in Asia and attempted to maintain the trade with East Africa as private trade during the negotiations to establish the company, in 1596 organized the first Dutch attempt to capture São Jorge da Mina and the island of Príncipe (Klooster 2016, 24–31). Samuel Blommaert represented the VOC as a merchant in Borneo before cofounding a company for the Angola trade in the 1610s and becoming a WIC director for Amsterdam when the Company was founded.

Despite the moral objections that at this point were still frequently aired within the Dutch Republic toward full engagement in slavery and the slave trade, many of the active investors and directors in the earliest colonial ventures showed a keen interest in slaving regions as strategic assets in the struggle against the Portuguese and as potential solutions to problems of colonization and labor supply. In the course of their operations, they gathered substantial practical knowledge about the ways in which slavery could be employed strategically in imperial ventures in the East Indies, along the West African coast, and in the wider Atlantic. Significantly, despite all propaganda on the evils of Iberian slaving practices, Dutch expansion in this field from early on explicitly aimed to take over the Spanish and Portuguese strongholds. The long-term battle for primacy in intercontinental trade at first might have had priority over short-term economic gains. However, Dutch policy in this period helped set the stage for the far more extensive and economically oriented involvement in global slavery that began in the second quarter of the seventeenth century.

From Strategic Interest to Slave-Based Accumulation

One thing that has surprised historians who accept the narrative of a "reluctant" or "accidental" first encounter with (Atlantic) slavery is the speed with which the

WIC, after its founding in 1621, turned toward an ambitious plan aiming for the conquest of the Portuguese colonies in Brazil, the main slave-trading regions on the West African coast, and the Iberian trading stations in the Caribbean. As part of the early deliberations on this "grand design," the WIC directors in early August 1623 formed a commission to investigate how the Company could disrupt or stop the Portuguese slave trade, thereby destroying the linchpin of its Atlantic commerce.[5] However, by the time the Dutch proved successful in conquering Portuguese Brazil, the aim had decisively turned from destroying the Portuguese trade to taking it over. With this intention, the Dutch repeatedly tried and eventually succeeded in replacing the Portuguese in Elmina (1637) and Luanda and São Tomé (1641) (van Groesen 2014, 9). The 1638 "Brief report on the state of the four captaincies . . . in the North of Brazil," cosigned by Johan Maurits van Nassau Siegen, explained:

> It is impossible to achieve anything in Brazil without slaves. Without them, the mills cannot crush the cane nor can the fields be tilled. The presence of slaves is essential to Brazil, and in no way can we operate without them: if any man feels offended by this, his is a useless scruple. As Brazil cannot be cultivated without blacks, and as it is essential that there should be a large number of them (simply because everyone complains about not having enough blacks), it is most important that every means possible is brought to bear to ensure the traffic along the coast of Africa. (Schwartz 2010, 245)

As the previous section makes clear, the conquest of Dutch Brazil does not signify a transition from "accidental" to "planned" participation in Atlantic slavery but one in which the predominant motive to intervene in the organization of slavery shifted from a military-strategic to a more easily recognizable economic one. Intentions and results, however, are not always neatly aligned. A rebellion of the Portuguese planters forced the Dutch colonizers to go on the defensive, and war continued to overshadow economic prospects until the Dutch were forced to return their last holdings in Brazil to the Portuguese in 1654. Between 1637 and 1645, the Dutch brought about twenty-five thousand African slaves to the colony they called New Holland to work the sugar mills (Schwartz 2014, 44). Nevertheless, the net result of two decades of warfare for the Dutch West India Company was a financial loss that crippled it so much that in 1674 it had to be dissolved and reconstituted as a slimmed-down Second WIC (den Heijer 1994). Had the Dutch managed to hold on to Brazil, it would have transformed them into the leading European power in the seventeenth-century Atlantic. The loss of the colony forced them to accept a much more modest position in the imperial pecking order.[6] However, by that time the idea that possessing slave-based plantation colonies was the key to immense profits had firmly taken root within the Dutch ruling class. Immediately after the fall of New Holland, Dutch investors started looking for "New Brazils," both through establishing new sugar colonies and through trading with and financing French and British plantations in the West Indies (Schwartz 2014; Marzagalli 2014, 105–8).[7]

A well-known tract published in 1659 by a former captain in Brazil, Ottho Keye, sums up how economic motives had taken the foreground. In this book-length pamphlet on "the true difference between cold and warm countries," Keye presented a passionate argument on why slave colonies in the equatorial zone presented an exponentially greater potential for profit than the colony New Netherland on the North American coast (Keye 1659; Davids 2010; Schwartz 2014). The greater fertility of the land, combined with the cheap and more productive labor of slaves, in his eyes could lay the basis for rapid growth. "For those Blacks or Slaves in Warm Countries can prepare twice as much land or more for cultivation of those agricultural products than hired white servants in New Netherland" (Keye 1659, 102). Frequently dismissed as mere propaganda, many historians have glossed over Keye's truly fascinating economic reflections. Those amount to an interpretation of the expansion of plantation slavery with a unique focus for the seventeenth century on capital accumulation in production as a source of national enrichment. In the final part of his tract, Keye provides a long calculation to prove that settlers "whose power is but so big that they can lay out a Capital [Dutch: *Capitael*] of 5,000 guilders for agriculture in Guajana," in four or five years could reap higher profits "than a Capital of 100,000 guilders in this country [the Netherlands]" (Keye 1659, 148). To prove this, Keye made detailed estimates of how the planter should divide his 5,000 guilders over the costs of acquisition of thirty initial slaves, their necessities, tools, and a fund to feed the planter and his family. He examined the potential return on the slaves' labor, factoring in that they would become more productive over time through the acquisition of skills and the labor they put into improving the land. He used those estimates to show how the profits from each productive cycle could be used not only for the clearing of a larger area and the acquisition of more slaves but also, over a series of years, for the building of a sugar mill. He concluded that based on such a policy, in a short time the master could employ a force of over a hundred slaves, which would accrue to him a yearly revenue on the invested capital over twice the size of the principal (Keye 1659, 155).

Of course, Keye's estimates were wildly unrealistic. What is important about them is that they show how by the mid-seventeenth century, Dutch colonizers had developed an interest in slavery far beyond the military-strategic aims that dominated their first forays into this field, or the hope for enrichment through plunder, theft, and quick trading windfalls. Keye's was an argument for the long-term potential for profit offered by plantation economies. When in the Peace of Breda that concluded the Second Anglo-Dutch War (1664–1667) the Dutch managed to trade New Netherland for Suriname on the Guyana coast, there was ample ground for celebration.[8] In the three-quarters of a century that followed, Suriname would come to harbor a slave population of almost sixty thousand, producing a continuous stream of coffee and sugar, while slave-based profits drawn from the wider Atlantic helped sustain the international position of the increasingly depressed Dutch home economy.

Dutch East Indies: Mass Slavery in a Composite Labor Empire

The introduction of commercialized mass slavery in the East Indies predated that in the West Indies. Long-term economic interests of the VOC played a key role. Its attempts to establish a monopoly in the trade in nutmeg and mace in the Asian and European market had stranded on the unwillingness to trade exclusively with the Company of the Bandanese, who were the only producers in the world of these highly coveted goods and were well aware of the disadvantages that a VOC monopoly would bring them. By wiping out the indigenous population and hiring out the harvesting grounds to white settlers who were completely dependent on the Company for the supply of slaves, the VOC obtained far greater control over the direct producers and thereby the desired monopoly. Both because of its position in the intra-Asiatic trade and because it broke the back of the Portuguese competitors, this was a turning point in the history of the Company (Prakash 1987, 193; Gaastra 1991, 45; Jacobs 2006, 13). However, slavery under VOC control on the Banda Islands did not provide a model for the organization of production throughout the VOC-controlled area in the way that Brazilian plantation production did for large parts of the Americas. Neither did it produce capitalist rationalizations of the employment of slaves like Ottho Keye's 1659 text. The reason was not that slavery remained confined to the Banda Islands, as table 11.1 shows. Neither was it that slavery in Asia was mild, household oriented, and driven by status rather than commercial interests (Allen 2014; van Rossum 2015b). Throughout Southeast Asia the Dutch employed slaves on plantations, or "gardens" as they were called by the VOC, to produce market goods. But unlike in the Atlantic where conquest and European-brought diseases marginalized indigenous labor in favor of fully European-controlled slave labor, in Asia the VOC entered from the margins into a highly developed system of production and trade governed by powerful indigenous rulers and states. Even in areas where it managed to become a large territorial ruler in its own right, most of the time Company officials deemed it more feasible and more profitable to exercise indirect control over already-existing systems of production than to supplant those with their own. The result was that throughout its vast empire, the VOC operated highly variegated zones of production and models of exploitation, based on mixed-labor systems that included wage laborers and many different forms of labor service, alongside large numbers of slaves (cf. Anievas and Kerem Nişancioğlu 2015, ch. 7).

To get a better sense of the place of slavery in these mixed-labor regimes, it helps to take a brief look at the production regimes for four key commodities: nutmeg on the Banda Islands, cloves on Ambon, cinnamon in Ceylon, and sugar in the immediate surroundings of Batavia. Bandanese nutmeg cultivation came closest to the model later generalized throughout the Dutch East Indies, with the entire economy geared toward plantation production. The earliest maps dividing the islands postconquest also show the "rationalizing" tendencies among VOC supervisors, with

Table 11.1. Slaves in Dutch Southeast Asia, ca. 1680

Region	Number of slaves	Percentage of total population
Ambon, indigenous society	7,235	12.6
Banda	3,716	55.6
Ambon City	2,870	52.3
Batavia City	14,061	49.1
Batavia, government slaves	1,273	—

Source: Knaap (1995, 197).

exact calculations for the appropriate number of slaves per "garden" in order to maximize profits. However, it is important to note that the ecological conditions and the nature of the production process of nutmeg and mace did not allow for easy rationalization through gang labor and partial mechanization introduced on West Indian sugar plantations. The transformation of production relations meant that henceforward, the VOC could set production targets, determine prices, and demand rents from the private planters (*perkeniers* or "gardeners") who actually oversaw slave production. However, as Phillip Winn has noted, "the essential method [of production] remained much the same, though intensified" (2010, 368). For the other key product in the VOC's spice trade, the production of cloves on the island of Ambon, the Company dealt with local production relations in a very different way. There, through several periods of violent subjection in the 1620s, 1650s, and 1670s, the Company nestled itself into a more or less feudal production system centered on the local nobility, the Orangkayas. The Company enforced a monopsony, set prices, favored the rise of subservient kings and nobility, demanded tribute and labor services, and regulated supply by occasionally destroying entire production areas. Both the Orangkayas and the VOC employed slaves alongside other forms of forced laborers, and the slave trade in which the Dutch became a major player facilitated this system of exploitation. But Ambon did not thereby become a slave society (Knaap 2004, chs. 6, 7).

In Ceylon, after the Dutch had managed to expel their Portuguese competitors they turned to slavery to meet their labor demands in the production of cinnamon. Widespread famine in Tanjore and Madura in 1658–1659 guaranteed a large supply of slaves from southern India, which the VOC eagerly made use of for its own government plantations. However, over the long run slave supplies proved a far less reliable source of labor than forcing the local population into obligatory labor services. This therefore became the dominant form of coerced labor employed by the Company (Arasaratnam 1985, 46). Finally, on Java the VOC increasingly supervised the production of sugar and coffee, two of the main commodities that were also produced in the West Indian plantation system (Breman 2015, 61). Sugar production itself was largely organized by Chinese farmers, who paid a rent to the Company or acted as tenant farmers for Dutch private landowners. Coercion, including slavery, was certainly a major factor in production relations but the Dutch tended to reap profits from it in an indirect way. The production of coffee was an increasingly important aspect of VOC activity in the eighteenth century, but the organization of production was for a long time left in the hands of local chiefs, on whom the VOC applied considerable external pressure to meet their prices and targets (Breman 2015). Only in the second half of the eighteenth century did the Company tighten control over production practices, at the same time establishing its own plantations, again recruiting forced labor in a variety of different forms that included slavery. The same happened for producing cinnamon on Ceylon (Jacobs 2006, 230–76).

Slavery in the VOC empire thus acted as one form of coerced labor among many. Apart from solving immediate problems of (forced) labor supply, slavery helped the VOC gain direct or indirect control over the commodity chains of key trading goods. Capital accumulation through the company and through private accounts thus relied heavily on the application of slave labor, and the Dutch were important actors in the expansion and commercialization of slavery in the Indian Ocean region.[9] However, the measure to which Dutch capital could actively shape production processes on the ground overall remained much more circumscribed by local power relations and preexisting systems of production than in the Atlantic World.

A Dynamic Sector in a Stagnating Economy

The eighteenth century saw marked change in the position of the Dutch Republic within the world economy. Depression of the main sectors of domestic manufacture and a loss of trading position to British and other competitors were indicative of the Dutch cycle of accumulation coming to an end. However, the same period saw a massive expansion of Dutch trade in colonial goods, both relative to other sectors of the Dutch economy and in absolute size. The explosion of the trade in coffee and sugar in particular, which made the Atlantic region a focal point of capital accumulation internationally, formed a lifeline for the ailing Dutch economy. Next to the continued strength of Amsterdam in international government and private finance, the outsize role of the Dutch in the trade in slave-produced goods eased the painful transition by Dutch merchant houses from the frontrunner capitalists of the late seventeenth century to a subsidiary role in international capitalism.

De Vries and Van der Woude in their authoritative overview of the early modern Dutch economy have given rough estimations for the weight of colonial trade in the total foreign trade of the Dutch Republic. According to them, between 1650 and 1770 the proportion of colonial imports grew from 11 to 44 percent, with the total value of imports remaining stable at roughly 140 million guilders. The proportion of colonial goods in Dutch exports in the same years grew from 9 to 40 percent, with the total value of exports decreasing from around 120 to 100 million guilders (de Vries and van der Woude 1995, 577). During the eighteenth century, the Atlantic slave colonies contributed most to this growth. Between 1660 and 1720, VOC imports from Asia almost doubled, from 9.2 million to 18.2 million guilders. But after that growth stagnated, with VOC imports in 1770 amounting to 20 million guilders. Reexports of Asian goods show the same pattern, growing from 7.6 million to 12.3 million guilders between 1660 and 1720 but then only slightly increasing to 13.2 million in 1770 (de Vries and van der Woude 1995, 533). While Asian trade grew only piecemeal during the eighteenth century, trade with the Dutch Atlantic colonies, coming from a much lower seventeenth-century starting point, grew exponentially (see table 11.2). Partly through Caribbean trading stations such as St. Eustatius and partly via European ports, the Dutch managed to gain a strong position in the reexport trade of Atlantic products of other European empires, especially the French (Enthoven 2003, 444).

A crucial factor in the increasing weight of the Atlantic in the Dutch economy was the steady growth of the Surinamese plantation sector for most of the eighteenth century. Suriname was a tiny colony when the Dutch took over in 1667. By 1775 Suriname's more than fifty thousand slaves produced 6,610 tons of sugar and 7,927 tons of coffee (van Stipriaan 1993, 29). Especially once the international

Table 11.2. Imports from and through the Main Dutch Atlantic Colonies (millions of guilders)

Years	Curaçao	St. Eustatius	Suriname	Total
1701–10	1.5	1.0	1.8	4.3
1711–20	1.8	1.0	1.5	4.3
1721–30	1.8	1.0	2.2	5.0
1731–40	1.7	1.0	2.7	5.4
1741–50	3.4	1.3	4.2	8.9
1751–60	1.9	3.5	4.9	10.3
1761–70	2.8	4.2	7.8	14.7
1771–80	2.8	7.0	8.8	18.5

Source: Klooster (2003, 379).

coffee boom got under way in the mid-eighteenth century, investors from Amsterdam and elsewhere pooled together under the aegis of large merchant-financiers in constructions called "negotiation funds" to provide mortgages for the establishment of new plantations, the buying of slaves, or the building of expensive equipment for improvement such as sugar mills. Financing the expansion of the plantation sector was tied to the trade, with many "negotiation funds" demanding the goods produced by the slaves to be sold in consignment (van de Voort 1973). The speculative nature of the West Indian investment boom is well-known, resulting in a serious financial crisis in 1772. However, this did not eliminate the importance of slave-related investments for the Dutch financial sector in the third quarter of the eighteenth century. Van de Voort has estimated the total size of West Indian loans at over 60 million guilders, and a contemporary memorandum using different figures asserted that West Indian loans formed 28 percent of Dutch private foreign investments through investment funds (van de Voort 1973, 101). As Van de Voort showed, these investments did not flow only into the Surinamese economy but also into the expanding neighboring Dutch colonies of Essequibo, Demerara, and Berbice that in the nineteenth century would become British Guyana, and into Danish and English Caribbean islands (see table 11.3). While some of these loans

Table 11.3. Size of Dutch Plantation Loans through Negotiation Funds, 1766–1775 (millions of guilders)

City in which the loan was floated	**Suriname**	**Essequebo-Demerary**	**Berbice**	**Danish-American Islands**	**British Islands**	**Total**
Amsterdam	24.7	5.2	1.6	13.0	2.2	46.7
Rotterdam	3.6				0.1	3.7
Middelburg		3.4				3.4
Other	1.1	2.0			0.8	3.9
Total 1766–1775	29.4	10.6	1.6	13.0	3.1	57.7
%	50.9	18.4	2.8	22.5	5.4	100.0

Source: van de Voort (1973, 103).

had to be written off or payment of interest stopped or curtailed because of the 1772 financial crisis, real and lasting blows to the investors came only with the long-term disruption of Dutch Atlantic commerce under the French occupation, and even then investors and administrators who held onto their investments into the nineteenth century saw returns turning upward again (van Stipriaan 1995).

The importance of the Atlantic colonies for the economy of the Dutch Republic was not confined to their contribution to Dutch trade, or the possibilities for productive investment that they provided to the Amsterdam capital market at a time when investment opportunities at home were receding. On a more minor scale, the boom in plantation production also provided opportunities for domestic manufacturing. Slave-related imports primarily affected the sugar-refinery sector of production, which indeed formed one of the few Dutch industries that continued to grow during the eighteenth century. Of course, such effects were not exclusive to the relationship between Amsterdam and Suriname. As the figures cited above already suggested, the Dutch became major reexporters of slave-produced goods from rival Atlantic empires, mainly France (Klooster 2003; Marzagalli 2014). Neutrality during the Seven Years' War and the American War of Independence helped the Dutch further strengthen this position. One of the main lasting results for the Dutch economy was the opening up of the Rhine trade with German hinterlands, which overwhelmingly relied on coffee and sugar in particular (Combrink 2018).

The expansion of Atlantic trade thus not only connected Dutch capital to one of the rapidly growing sections of the world economy but also made slave-related production and trade into one of the few dynamic elements of the otherwise stagnating or declining Dutch economy (van Zanden and van Riel 2004, 15). Combined with the continuing strength in East India trade, which provided its own more mixed and indirect connections between Dutch capital and mass slavery, Dutch colonial trade was fundamental for establishing the relatively high baseline under which the crisis-ridden Dutch economy of the eighteenth century did not sink. This had not only direct economic effects but geopolitical ones as well. It helped ensure that despite increasing capital flight from home-manufacture sectors outstripped by European competitors into foreign investments and state loans, the Dutch Republic could continue to function as a significant hub of international trade and finance and even establish new international links through Rotterdam and the Rhine trade or through large financial investments in the Americas.

Direct and Indirect Involvement in Slavery in the Nineteenth Century

The period of the Batavian Revolution and the French occupation forms a watershed in the study of slavery in the Dutch Empire, as it does for Dutch historiography in general. In this period territorial control over the colonial possessions in the East and West Indies was transplanted from the VOC, the WIC, and similar semiprivate bodies to the Dutch state. The first half of the nineteenth century became a period of active reform in colonial policy, aimed at restoring the Dutch role in international commerce that by now seemed inexorably lost. These attempts were highly successful in the East Indies, where the Cultivation System provided a new basis for state-led colonial exploitation through local chieftains. Slavery was gradually replaced by other forms of forced labor without this having much of an impact on colonial production, a possibility that was already built into the mixed and therefore flexible nature of the labor regimes under VOC control in the earlier period (Breman 2015).

The situation was very different in the Atlantic region. Despite the fact that Suriname continued to experience several periods of profitability, the income drawn from this colony by the Dutch home economy was increasingly dwarfed by that from the East Indies. A series of crises, beginning with the financial crisis of 1772, continuing in the imperial crisis of the 1780s–1815, and then in the crisis of adaptation caused by the abolition of the slave trade that the English forced upon the Dutch in 1814, has led historians to treat the final half century of West Indian slavery mainly as an excruciatingly slow prelude to the 1863 abolition (Oostindie 1996). This idea of the end-phase of Atlantic slavery forming no more than a "long goodbye" is problematic. It tends to gloss over the many sometimes successful attempts at modernization undertaken in Suriname itself, in collusion with some of the most prominent Dutch entrepreneurs of the nineteenth century. It also tends to play down the fact that until the late 1840s, the aim of even the more forward-looking Dutch colonial administrators was to bolster Surinamese slavery, not to abolish it (Brandon 2016). Nevertheless, it is true that after 1815 slave-related production, trade, and finance did not retain their earlier significance for the Dutch economy.

As in the previous period, the role of slavery in Dutch capitalism should not be confined to the profit drawn from bilateral trade between the Netherlands and its Atlantic colonies. Dutch capital retained many until now hardly examined links to slavery, large and small, through business connections outside the Dutch colonies. Dutch commercial and financial connections to the early American republic can serve as an example. The second half of the eighteenth century saw rapidly increasing trade between North America and Suriname. Trade with the former New England colonies became a necessary precondition for continuing Dutch plantation production when direct Dutch-Suriname trade broke down as a result of the Fourth Anglo-Dutch War (1780–1784) (Postma 1998; Fatah-Black 2015). From the standpoint of the Dutch economy, historians have usually regarded the rise of North American trade with the Atlantic colonies as pure loss. However, the connections forged between the Netherlands and the United States when North American traders started to act as intermediaries to the Dutch Caribbean were of economic significance in their own right (van Winter 1977). This can be well illustrated through the activities of the Brown family of Providence, a key North American merchant house involved in the Caribbean trade and the African slave trade (Marques 2016, 29, 34–36). For the Brown family, participation in the Suriname trade before the American War of Independence formed the springboard to increasing participation in European trade, as they profited from the disruptions in European-American trading routes caused by the wars of the late eighteenth century. The occupation of the Dutch Republic by France in 1795 and the difficulties this created for the big Amsterdam merchant houses allowed the Browns to extend their networks into Northern Europe, using Amsterdam as a hub for the trade in colonial goods that they now started to procure both from the wider West Indies and South America as well as from the East Indies. Rather than simply bypassing Dutch merchants altogether, the Browns allied themselves to the important Amsterdam merchant house Daniel Crommelin & Sons, which had long been heavily involved in Dutch Atlantic finance and trade and remained one of the most important Amsterdam houses of the nineteenth century. Thus the trade between Suriname and North America became a stepping-stone through which Amsterdam capital became integrated into the expanding global networks of US merchants (see table 11.4).

At the same time that North American merchants used the Dutch West Indies as one of their bases from which to enter European-colonial and intra-European trade routes, Dutch investors also began their financial involvement in the US plantation sector. Small in size but of great symbolic meaning were the two mortgages at the value of $1,893.21 that Thomas Jefferson contracted on May 12 and

Table 11.4. The Brown Family Shipping Network, Reconstructed through the Ports of Call in Trading Ventures, 1757–1815.

	1757–1775	**1776–1795**	**1796–1815**
West Indies and South America	63	88	61
Of which Paramaribo	27	38	7
North America	28	38	55
Northern Europe	—	22	86
Of which Amsterdam	—	4	24
Southern Europe	1	27	85
Asia	—	9	35
Of which Dutch East Indies	—	—	13
Other	2	11	38
Total number of ports of call	94	195	360
Total number of discrete voyages	81	117	178
Number of ports of call per voyage	1.16	1.67	2.02

Source: John Carter Brown Library, Brown Family Business Records, compiled from records of voyages and business correspondence.

November 21, 1796, with the Dutch financiers Van Staphorst & Hubbard, using the slaves of his Monticello plantation as collateral.[10] Throughout the first half of the nineteenth century, loans that facilitated the expansion of slavery in the US South were contracted primarily in London, Amsterdam, and Paris. These included direct plantation loans like the one that Van Staphorst & Hubbard provided to Jefferson, the sale of bank bonds to help establish the Citizens' Bank of Louisiana and other Southern banks, and state loans that went into the acquisition of slave territory (Schermerhorn 2015, 117–20). Many of these loans implicated Dutch financial houses in slavery only indirectly, as facilitators rather than conscious drivers. Among the latter, the one of most momentous impact on the evolution of slavery in the nineteenth century was never sold to Dutch investors as related to slavery at all. Out of the total sum of $12 million for the Louisiana Purchase that drew the South into the United States, $5 million was floated in Amsterdam by Hope & Co. and De Smeth & Willink, two houses that had earlier been prominent in the boom in West Indian plantation loans. Such investments overall were relatively small and did not alter the course of Dutch economic development. For most financiers on the Dutch market, they probably registered only as random elements in their investment portfolios, and their relationship to slavery might have been seen as irrelevant, as long as they delivered their yearly interest. As a result of this distance, real or perceived, the impact of Dutch capital on the second slavery has remained uncharted terrain.

Conclusions

Past attempts to discuss the role of slavery in the development of Dutch capitalism have been received with hostility by Dutch historians. The tendency to reduce the question to the technical matter of counting the net profits from the Atlantic slave trade alone, coupled with snide dismissal of the entire field of inquiry based on real and imagined inconsistencies of the Williams Thesis, have caused this potentially rich area of debate to remain barren. This chapter has suggested that in order to explore the connections between slavery and Dutch capitalism in a fruitful way, it is necessary to take into account the many different functions that slavery and the slave trade fulfilled for Dutch capital accumulation and empire building in the *longue durée*. Such a multidimensional approach breaks through the artificially created separation that Dutch historiography has maintained between Dutch slaving in the East and the West Indies, reintegrates the economics of the slave trade, finance, and slave-based production, and acknowledges the geopolitical aims that guided Dutch merchants, companies, and the state from the moment it first started to target Portuguese and Spanish slave-capturing regions. Finally, it points to the need to examine the contributions made by slave labor to the Dutch economy not simply as the net result of a series of bilateral relations between the Dutch Republic and its overseas colonies but from the widest possible geographical perspective—as elements of the changing relationship between Dutch capital and the world economy.

Notes

1. I want to thank Anthony Bogues, Tamira Combrink, Leonardo Marques, and Dale Tomich for their critical and engaging comments on an earlier draft of this chapter, and Sven Beckert for the stimulating discussions we had on this and related material on our way to Binghamton and back. Joe Miller made extensive remarks on the first draft that

have benefited me greatly. I feel deep sadness that he will no longer be there to comment on the result.

2. Piet Emmer, who was long considered the main authority on slavery in the Netherlands and could wield considerable institutional influence, played a major role in this by publicly ridiculing younger and less established scholars who dared to raise the question. See his exchange with Alex van Stipriaan in the 1990s (van Stipriaan 1995; Emmer 1996), and with Karwan Fatah-Black and Matthias van Rossum more recently (Fatah-Black and van Rossum 2015; Emmer, Eltis, and Lewis 2016).

3. Tomich (2017) makes this point about the approach to slavery within New Economic History more broadly.

4. Cf. Goslinga (1971, 342): "It may be fair, then, to conclude that, until the third decade of the seventeenth century, the Dutch were not involved in the slave trade."

5. National Archive, The Hague, Archief Oude West-Indische Compagnie, 1.05.05.01, no. 1, Minutes Heren XIX, fol. 8r-vso.

6. There is an ongoing discussion of how "imperial" the later Dutch presence in the Atlantic World was, though most now reject the more extreme position taken by Emmer and Klooster (1999). See Brandon and Fatah-Black (2015); Klooster (2016); Burnard et al. (2017).

7. Menard (2006, 49–51) challenges the old idea that Dutch finance established the plantation sector in Barbados. Nevertheless, many instances of Dutch mercantile involvement are provided by the same author in Menard and McCusker (2004, n. 315–18).

8. Incidentally, this trade-off also included the ceding to the Dutch of the English-controlled island of Pulo Run, completing the Dutch conquest of all the Banda Islands.

9. On the size of private capitals amassed under the umbrella of VOC power, see Bruijn (2011, 221–24).

10. "Deed of Mortgage of Slaves to Van Staphorst & Hubbard, 12 May 1796," Founders Online, National Archives, last modified December 6, 2016, http://founders.archives.gov/documents/Jefferson/01-29-02-0065.

References

Allen, Richard B. 2014. *European Slave Trading in the Indian Ocean, 1500–1850.* Athens: Ohio University Press.

Anievas, Alexander, and Kerem Nişancioğlu. 2015. *How the West Came to Rule: The Geopolitical Origins of Capitalism.* London: Pluto.

Antunes, Catia, and Filipa Ribeiro da Silva. 2012. "Amsterdam Merchants in the Slave Trade and African Commerce, 1580s–1670s." *Tijdschrift voor Sociale en Economische Geschiedenis* 9, no. 4: 3–31.

Arasaratnam, S. 1985. "Elements of Social and Economic Change in Dutch Maritime Ceylon (Sri Lanka) 1658–1796." *Indian Economic and Social History Review* 22, no. 1: 35–54.

Arrighi, Giovanni. 1994. *The Long Twentieth Century: Money, Power, and the Origins of Our Times*. London: Verso.

Brandon, Pepijn. 2015. *War, Capital, and the Dutch State (1588–1795)*. Leiden: Brill.

———. 2016. "'Shrewd Sirens of Humanity': The Changing Shape of Pro-Slavery Arguments in the Netherlands (1789–1814)." *Revista Almanack*, no. 14: 3–26.

Brandon, Pepijn, and Karwan Fatah-Black. 2015. "'For the Reputation and Respectability of the State': Trade, the Imperial State, Unfree Labor, and Empire in the Dutch Atlantic." In *Building the Atlantic Empires: Unfree Labor, the Imperial State, and the Rise of the Global Economy, ca. 1600–1945*, edited by John Donoghue and Evelyn Jennings, 84–108. Leiden: Brill.

Breman, Jan. 2015. *Mobilizing Labour for the Global Coffee Market: Profits from an Unfree Work Regime in Colonial Java*. Amsterdam: Amsterdam University Press.

Bruijn, Jaap R. 2011. *Commanders of Dutch East India Ships in the Eighteenth Century*. Woodbridge, UK: Boydell.

Burnard, Trevor et al. 2017. "The Empire That Never Was: The Nearly-Dutch Atlantic Empire in the Seventeenth Century." *Journal of Early American History*, 7, no. 1: 33–80.

Colenbrander, H. T. 1919. *Jan Pietersz. Coen. Bescheiden omtrent zijn bedrijf in Indië*. Vol. 1. The Hague: Martinus Nijhoff.

———. 1920. *Jan Pietersz. Coen. Bescheiden omtrent zijn bedrijf in Indië*. Vol. 2. The Hague: Martinus Nijhoff.

———. 1922. *Jan Pietersz. Coen. Bescheiden omtrent zijn bedrijf in Indië*. Vol. 4. The Hague: Martinus Nijhoff.

Combrink, Tamira. 2018. "From French Harbours to German Rivers: European Distribution of Sugar by the Dutch in the 18th Century." In *La diffusion des produits ultramarins en Europe. XVI-XVIII siècle*, edited by Marguerite Martin and Maud Villeret, 39–56. Rennes, France: Presse Universitaire de Rennes.

Davids, C. A. 2010. "Nederlanders en de natuur in de Nieuwe Wereld: Een vergelijking van visies op de natuur in Brazilië, Nieuw Nederland en de Wilde Kust in de zeventiende eeuw." *Jaarboek voor Ecologische Geschiedenis*, no. 10: 1–24.

de Jonge, J. K. J. 1865. *De opkomst van het Nederlandsch gezag in Oost-Indie (1595–1610): Verzameling van onuitgegeven stukken uit het oud-koloniaal archief.* Vol. 3. The Hague: Martinus Nijhoff.

de Marees, P. 1912. *Beschryvinghe ende historische verhael van het gout koninckrijck van Gunea: Anders de gout-custe de Mina genaemt liggende in het deel van Africa*. Edited by S. P. L'Honoré Naber. The Hague: Martinus Nijhoff.

de Vries, Jan. 2005. "The Dutch Atlantic Economies." In *The Atlantic Economy during the Seventeenth and Eighteenth Centuries: Organization, Operation, Practice, and Personnel*, edited by Peter A. Coclanis, 1–29. Columbia: University of South Carolina Press.

de Vries, Jan, and Ad van der Woude. 1995. *Nederland 1500–1815: De eerste ronde van moderne economische groei.* Amsterdam: Uitgeverij Balans.

den Heijer, Henk. 1994. *De geschiedenis van de WIC.* Zutphen, Netherlands: Walburg Pers.

Emmer, P. C. 1996. "Capitalism Mistaken? The Economic Decline of Suriname and the Plantation Loans, 1773–1850: A Rehabilitation." *Itinerario* 20, no. 1: 11–18.

Emmer, Pieter C., David Eltis, and Frank D. Lewis. 2016. "More than Profits? The Contribution of the Slave Trade to the Dutch Economy: Assessing Fatah-Black and Van Rossum." *Slavery & Abolition* 37, no. 4: 724–35.

Emmer, Pieter C., and Jos Gommans. 2012. *Rijk aan de rand van de wereld: De geschiedenis van Nederland overzee 1600–1800.* Amsterdam: Uitgeverij Bert Bakker.

Emmer, Pieter C., and Wim Klooster. 1999. "The Dutch Atlantic, 1600–1800: Expansion without Empire." *Itinerario* 23, no. 2: 48–69.

Enthoven, Victor. 2003. "An Assessment of Dutch Transatlantic Commerce, 1585–1817." In *Riches from Atlantic Commerce: Dutch Transatlantic Trade and Shipping, 1585–1817*, edited by Johannes Postma and Victor Enthoven, 385–445. Leiden: Brill.

Fatah-Black, Karwan. 2015. *White Lies and Black Markets: Evading Metropolitan Authority in Colonial Suriname, 1650–1800.* Leiden: Brill.

Fatah-Black, Karwan, and Matthias van Rossum. 2014. "Slavery in a 'Slave Free Enclave'? Historical Links between the Dutch Republic, Empire and Slavery, 1580s–1860s." *Werkstattgeschichte*, nos. 66–67: 55–73.

Fatah-Black, Karwan, and Matthias van Rossum. 2015. "Beyond Profitability: The Dutch Transatlantic Slave Trade and Its Economic Impact." *Slavery & Abolition* 36, no. 1: 63–83.

Gaastra, Femme. 1991. *De geschiedenis van de VOC.* Zutphen, Netherlands: Walburg Pers.

Goslinga, Cornelis Ch. 1971. *The Dutch in the Caribbean and on the Wild Coast 1580–1680.* Assen, Netherlands: Van Gorcum.

Israel, Jonathan. 1989. *Dutch Primacy in World Trade, 1585–1750.* Oxford, UK: Clarendon Press.

Jacobs, Els M. 2006. *Merchant in Asia: The Trade of the Dutch East India Company during the Eighteenth Century.* Leiden: CNWS.

[Keye, Ottho]. 1659. *Het waere onderscheyt tusschen koude en warme landen.* The Hague: Henricus Hondius.

Klooster, Wim. 1998. *Illicit Riches: Dutch Trade in the Caribbean, 1648–1795.* Leiden: KITLV.

———. 2003. "An Overview of Dutch Trade with the Americas, 1600–1800." In *Riches from Atlantic Commerce: Dutch Transatlantic Trade and Shipping, 1585–1817*, edited by Johannes Postma and Victor Enthoven, 365–84. Leiden: Brill.

———. 2016. *The Dutch Moment: War, Trade, and Settlement in the Seventeenth-Century Atlantic World.* Ithaca, NY: Cornell University Press.

Knaap, Gerrit J. 1995. "Slavery and the Dutch in Southeast Asia." In *Fifty Years Later: Antislavery, Capitalism and Modernity in the Dutch Orbit,* edited by Gert Oostindie, 193–206. Leiden: KITLV.

———. 2004. *Kruidnagelen en christenen: De VOC en de bevolking van Ambon 1656–1696.* Leiden: KITLV.

Marques, Leonardo. 2016. *The United States and the Transatlantic Slave Trade to the Americas, 1776–1867.* New Haven, CT: Yale University Press.

Marzagalli, Silvia. 2014. "The French Atlantic and the Dutch, Late Seventeenth–Late Eighteenth Century." In *Dutch Atlantic Connections, 1680–1800: Linking Empires, Bridging Borders,* edited by Gert Oostindie and Jessica V. Roitman, 103–118. Leiden: Brill.

Mbeki, Linda, and Matthias van Rossum. 2017. "Private Slave Trade in the Dutch Indian Ocean World: A Study into the Networks and Backgrounds of the Slavers and the Enslaved in South Asia and South Africa." *Slavery & Abolition* 38, no. 1: 95–116.

Menard, Russell R. 2006. *Sweet Negotiations: Sugar, Slavery, and Plantation Agriculture in Early Barbados.* Charlottesville: University of Virginia Press.

Menard, Russell R., and John J. McCusker. 2004. "The Sugar Industry in the Seventeenth Century: A New Perspective on the Barbadian 'Sugar Revolution.'" In *Tropical Babylons: Sugar and the Making of the Atlantic World, 1450–1680,* edited by Stuart B. Schwartz, 289–330. Chapel Hill: University of North Carolina Press.

Nimako, Kwame, and Glenn Willemsen. 2011. *The Dutch Atlantic: Slavery, Abolition and Emancipation.* London: Pluto.

Oostindie, Gert, ed. 1996. *Fifty Years Later: Antislavery, Capitalism and Modernity in the Dutch Orbit.* Pittsburgh: University of Pittsburgh Press.

Oostindie, Gert, and Jessica V. Roitman, eds. 2014. *Dutch Atlantic Connections, 1680–1800: Linking Empires, Bridging Borders.* Leiden: Brill.

Prakash, Om. 1987. "The Dutch East India Company in the Trade of the Indian Ocean." In *India and the Indian Ocean, 1500–1800,* edited by Ashin Das Gupta and M. N. Pearson, 185–200. Oxford, UK: Oxford University Press.

Postma, Johannes Menne. 1990. *The Dutch in the Atlantic Slave Trade, 1600–1815.* Cambridge: Cambridge University Press.

———. 1998. "Breaching the Mercantile Barriers of the Dutch Colonial Empire: North American Trade with Surinam during the Eighteenth Century." In *Merchant Organization and Maritime Trade in the North Atlantic, 1660–1815,* edited by Olaf Uwe Janzen, 107–31. St. John's, Newfoundland, Canada: International Maritime Economic History Association.

Postma, Johannes Menne, and Victor Enthoven, eds. 2003. *Riches from Atlantic Commerce: Dutch Transatlantic Trade and Shipping, 1585–1817.* Leiden: Brill.

Ratelband, Klaas. 2000. *Nederlanders in West-Afrika 1600–1650: Angola, Kongo en São Tomé.* Zutphen, Netherlands: Walburg Pers.

Ribeiro da Silva, Filipa. 2011. *Dutch and Portuguese in Western Africa: Empires, Merchants and the Atlantic System, 1580–1674.* Leiden: Brill.

———. 2014. "African Islands and the Formation of the Dutch Atlantic Economy: Arguin, Gorée, Cape Verde and São Tomé, 1590–1670." *International Journal of Maritime History* 26, no. 3: 549–67.

Schermerhorn, Calvin. 2015. *The Business of Slavery and the Rise of American Capitalism, 1815–1860.* New Haven, CT: Yale University Press.

Schmidt, Benjamin. 2001. *Innocence Abroad: The Dutch Imagination and the New World, 1570–1670.* Cambridge: Cambridge University Press.

Schwartz, Stuart B., ed. 2010. *Early Brazil: A Documentary Collection to 1700.* Cambridge: Cambridge University Press.

———. 2014. "Looking for a New Brazil: Crisis and Rebirth in the Atlantic World after the Fall of Pernambuco." In *The Legacy of Dutch Brazil,* edited by Michiel van Groesen, 41–58. Cambridge: Cambridge University Press

Tomich, Dale. 2017. "Slavery in Historical Capitalism: Toward a Theoretical History of the Second Slavery." In *Slavery and Historical Capitalism during the Nineteenth Century,* edited by Dale Tomich, 37–66. Lanham, MD: Lexington Books.

van de Voort, Johannes Petrus. 1973. *De Westindische plantages van 1720 tot 1795: Financiën en handel.* Eindhoven, Netherlands: De Witte.

van Groesen, Michiel. 2014. "Introduction: The Legacy of an Interlude." In *The Legacy of Dutch Brazil,* edited by Michiel van Groesen, 1–24. Cambridge: Cambridge University Press.

van Rossum, Matthias. 2015a. "'Vervloekte goudzugt': De VOC, slavenhandel en slavernij in Azië." *Tijdschrift voor Sociale en Economische Geschiedenis* 12, no. 4: 29–57.

van Rossum, Matthias. 2015b. *Kleurrijke tragiek: De geschiedenis van slavernij in Azië onder de VOC.* Hilversum, Netherlands: Verloren.

van Stipriaan, Alex. 1993. *Surinaams contrast: Roofbouw en overleven in een Caraïbische plantagekolonie 1750–1863.* Leiden: KITLV.

———. 1995. "Debunking Debts: Image and Reality of a Colonial Crisis: Suriname at the End of the 18th Century." *Itinerario* 19, no. 1: 69–84.

van Welie, Rik. 2008. "Slave Trading and Slavery in the Dutch Colonial Empire: A Global Comparison." *Nieuwe West-Indische Gids* 82, nos. 1–2: 47–96.

van Winter, Pieter J. 1977. *American Finance and Dutch Investment 1780–1805.* 2 vols. New York: Arno. First published in Dutch in 1927–1931.

van Zanden, Jan Luiten. 1993. *The Rise and Decline of Holland's Economy: Merchant Capitalism and the Labor Market.* Manchester: Manchester University Press.

van Zanden, Jan Luiten, and Arthur van Riel. 2004. *The Dutch Economy in the Nineteenth Century: The Strictures of Inheritance.* Princeton, NJ: Princeton University Press.

Vink, Markus P. M. 2007. "Freedom and Slavery: The Dutch Republic, the VOC World, and the Debate over the 'World's Oldest Trade.'" *South African Historical Journal* 59, no. 1: 19–46.

Winn, Phillip. 2010. "Slavery and Cultural Creativity in the Banda Islands." *Journal of Southeast Asian Studies* 41, no. 3: 365–89.

Chapter 12

Merchant Capital and Slave Trading in the Western Indian Ocean, 1770–1830

Richard B. Allen

Recent scholarship demonstrates that European slave trading in the Indian Ocean was not only more extensive than previously believed but also an integral component of a truly global European traffic in chattel labor. British, Dutch, French, Portuguese, and other Europeans shipped a minimum of 953,900–1,275,000 African, Indian, Malagasy, Southeast Asian, and other Asian slaves within and beyond the Indian Ocean basin between 1500 and 1850, a substantial majority of whom were exported between the late eighteenth and mid-nineteenth centuries.[1] Although these numbers pale in comparison to the estimated 11,978,700 slaves exported from West and West Central Africa to the Americas between 1500 and the mid-1860s, these Indian Ocean trades were not historically insignificant. Adding the number of slaves exported to the Mascarene Islands of Ile de France (Mauritius) and Ile de Bourbon (Réunion) between 1670 and the early 1830s to French exports from West and West Central Africa reveals that these islands consumed one-fourth of all French slave exports between 1770 and 1810 and approximately 40 percent of such exports between 1811 and 1848. The significance of this activity is underscored by estimates that Europeans carried 37–52 percent of all transoceanic slave exports away from East Africa during the eighteenth century and 58–66 percent of all such exports from 1800 to 1873. The shipment of as many as twenty-four thousand Indian slaves to the Mascarenes during the eighteenth century laid the foundations for the migration of 2.2 million mostly Indian indentured laborers throughout the postemancipation colonial plantation world as part of what is often characterized as a "new system of slavery" (Allen 2014a, 23–24).

If the general parameters of European slave trading in the Indian Ocean are now readily discernible, the economic dimensions of this traffic in chattel labor remain poorly understood. On the few occasions when historians have explored the economics of slave trading in the Mare Indicum, they have concentrated on topics such as the dynamics of supply and demand and the political economy of slavery in various locales (Clarence-Smith 1989). Basic questions about how European slaving voyages in this oceanic basin were organized and financed, their profitability, the extent to which these trades were intertwined with those in other commodities such as textiles, spices, and foodstuffs, and the ways in which European slave-trading networks overlapped or were interconnected remain largely unexplored (Allen 2017). Recent research on the Mascarene trade and Gujarati merchants in Portuguese Mozambique provides an opportunity to begin exploring the economics of European slave trading in the western Indian Ocean, and to delve more deeply into the ways in which metropolitan, colonial, and African and Asian merchants interacted to create complex, pan-regional slave-trading networks during the eighteenth and early nineteenth centuries.

The Economics of Slave Trading

Reconstructing the economic history of European slave trading in the Indian Ocean is not an easy task. Information about slave trading by the British, Dutch, and French charter companies that operated in the Mare Indicum is often sparse and widely scattered, if not problematic. While sources such as ships' logbooks can contain valuable information about how captains acquired slave cargoes in specific locales (e.g., Westra and Armstrong 2006; Hooper 2017), they rarely shed light on how these voyages were organized and financed. However, the bankruptcy of the French Compagnie des Indes in 1765, the advent of royal rule in the Mascarenes in 1767, and the subsequent opening of the islands to free trade by French subjects in 1769 and then to all foreign nationals by 1787 generated a substantial body of documentation that provides an opportunity to begin exploring the economics of European slave trading in the western Indian Ocean between 1770 and 1830. Foremost among these sources are the *déclarations d'arrivée*, statements that ship captains filed with admiralty or colonial officials upon arriving at Port Louis, and notarial acts that recorded a wide range of commercial transactions and relationships.

The decrees that opened the Mascarenes to free trade had a marked impact on the islands' economic life. The number of *négoçiants* (large merchants/traders) residing in Port Louis, the colony's capital and commercial center, rose from 25 in 1776 to 183 in 1808, while the number of ships calling at the port annually also increased dramatically, from 101 in 1773 to 347 in 1803 (Toussaint 1977, 20–21). An inventory of more than 950 slaving voyages involving the islands attests to the intensity of the Mascarene trade. More specifically, this inventory records 678 confirmed, 120 probable/possible, and 39 unsuccessful slaving voyages to or from (or both) India, Madagascar, Mozambique, and the Swahili coast between 1770 and 1809, and 115 Mascarene-based voyages to the Cape of Good Hope, the Caribbean, the Río de la Plata, and India (Allen 2014a, 68–69).

While metropolitan French merchants organized significant numbers of slaving ventures to the western Indian Ocean during the late eighteenth and early nineteenth centuries, incomplete and often problematic shipping data make it difficult to determine the number of such voyages with any certainty. The *Voyages* transatlantic slave-trade database records 109 French ventures to Southeast Africa and the Indian Ocean islands between 1770 and 1810.[2] The Mascarene inventory indicates, however, that metropolitan merchants were more deeply involved in slave trading in the western Indian Ocean than the *Voyages* database indicates. Mauritian sources reveal at least 230 confirmed/probable/possible slaving voyages between 1770 and 1806 linked explicitly to mercantile interests in France, a majority of which (123) were based in Bordeaux. Other voyages were associated with merchants in Lorient (53), Marseille (25), Nantes (14), Saint-Malo (31), and other ports including Bayonne, Brest, Dieppe, Le Havre, La Rochelle, and Saint-Brieuc (Allen 2014a, 85).

The inventory illustrates the extent of metropolitan involvement in the Mascarene trade in other ways. At least thirty-four metropolitan merchants/merchant houses participated in multiple slaving voyages involving the islands. The Bordelaise firm of Cochon, Troplong et C[ie], for example, outfitted three slavers that delivered six cargoes acquired at Mozambique and Kilwa to the Ile de France between 1783 and 1792. Another Bordelaise firm, Romberg, Bapst et C[ie], outfitted five different ships that delivered seven such cargoes, also acquired at Mozambique and Kilwa, to the island during the same period. Yet another Bordelaise house, Dominque

Cabarrus et Fils, outfitted seven ships to carry slaves to both the Mascarenes and Saint-Domingue between 1788 and 1793.[3]

Cargo manifests and other sources reveal the dynamics of some of these metropolitan ventures in greater detail. The polacre *L'Agilité* sailed from Marseille for the Mascarenes on or about September 24, 1781, with a cargo of wine, foodstuffs, clothing, and other merchandise valued at 124,013 livres 12 sols on a venture underwritten by thirteen different investors based in Cadiz (Spain), Paris, Geneva, Vevey (Switzerland), Gênes (Italy), and Marseille (Dermigny, vol. 1, 1959, 30–41). The ship arrived at the Ile de France on February 28, 1782, and remained there until September 10 when it sailed to the Ile de Bourbon to take on provisions before continuing to the Querimba Islands off the Mozambican coast where it loaded 270 slaves. The vessel returned to Port Louis on December 2 with 266 slaves on board.[4] Seven years later, *Le Scipion* departed Marseille, probably on or about August 23, 1789, for the Ile de France with a cargo of wine, liquors, soap, foodstuffs, Swedish iron, paper, and other items valued at 126,783 livres 5 sols (Dermigny, vol. 1, 1959, 328–30). The ship reached Port Louis on April 12, 1790, where it remained until May 20 when it sailed for Mongale on the East African coast, arriving there on June 5. The ship left Mongale on October 7 with 264 slaves on board, sailing first to the Seychelles where it remained for six days before proceeding to Port Louis where it arrived on November 27 with 188 slaves still alive.[5]

These ventures were facilitated by a local merchant community whose members maintained multifaceted commercial relationships that reached deep into the Atlantic World (Toussaint 1977). On May 21, 1787, for instance, Port Louis *négoçiant* René André Oury authorized Sieur Catel, an officer on the Spanish corvette *La Pepita*, to dispose of the ship's cargo, especially the slaves whom Nicholas Thomas Baudin, the ship's owner and captain, proposed to acquire and carry to Louisiana in the event of Baudin's death or failure to return to the Ile de France.[6] When the *La Petite Dorade* left the Ile de France a year later for Mozambique, where it loaded 242 slaves, it did so with a twenty-two-man crew provided by Janvier Monneron, a prominent local merchant acting on behalf of Louis Bourdon of Bordeaux.[7] On July 6, 1789, Pitot Frères et Cie, another prominent local merchant house and consignee of the 395 slaves who comprised *La Ville de Bordeaux*'s cargo, sold 386 of these slaves to Captains Jean Valeau, acting on behalf of Messrs. Letellier Frères in Bordeaux, and Jean Dufourg, acting on behalf of Messrs. Pierre Bourbon *aîné* and Jean Laroche, both Bordelaise merchants, for 428,460 livres.[8] Valeau and Dufourg had formed a partnership two days earlier to purchase the slaves and carry them to Saint-Domingue on *L'Honorine*, to be captained by Dufourg.[9] The nature and extent of these commercial ties is revealed in other ways. On October 22, 1785, Port Louis *négoçiant* Jean Mazier de Prémondière sold the 550-ton *La Garonne* to Lisbon merchants Daniel Glasche and Antonio de Govvea for 125,000 livres, a transaction in which Joseph Dasners Lion, formerly the captain of the *Notre Dame de Ste. Guitterie*, which had been outfitted by Glasche and de Govvea, acted as their agent.[10] Eighteen years later Port Louis *négoçiant* Joseph Etienne Courtois, representing the merchant house of Courtois and Borel, and Jacques Saulnier *jeune* and Antoine Serier, Port Louis *négoçiants* charged with liquidating the firm, authorized Bordelaise merchants Cabarrus and Béchade to deal with the firm's affairs in France and elsewhere in Europe.[11]

Mascarene merchants cultivated commercial relationships in the western Indian Ocean as well as the Atlantic. Portuguese Mozambique first supplied the islands with slaves in 1721 and continued to do so into the early nineteenth century. The scale of this traffic is suggested by estimates that Mozambique exported 125,306 slaves to Mauritius between 1733 and 1799 (Capela 2015, 180), and by the existence of 228 confirmed and 73 probable/possible voyages between the islands and Mozambican ports, mostly between 1770 and 1809 (Allen 2014a, 68–69). While French ships dominated this traffic, Portuguese vessels carried at least 31 slave cargoes to the islands between 1760 and 1808 (Allen 2014a: 74). The notarial record provides additional glimpses into the relationships that shaped this traffic. On November 6, 1784, Captain Manuel Justinian Dasnevez (or Dasneves) of *La Caroline* reported that the captain and supercargo of the Portuguese ship *Notre Dame de Piété et Gloire de la Mer* had offered him a one-third interest in the vessel to make three voyages from the Ile de France to Mozambique, undoubtedly to trade slaves.[12] A year and a half later, Dasnevez sold the 250-ton *Bailli de Suffren*, also called *La Stella d'Affrica*, to Port Louis *négoçiant* Jean Baptiste Pilliet for 100,000 livres pursuant to the authorization he had received from the Portuguese governor of Querimba.[13]

Mascarene involvement with regional commercial and slaving interests is revealed in other ways. Gujarati merchants based in Mozambique became involved in the Mascarene trade no later than 1780 when the Portuguese *La Ste. Antoine d'Alinas* sailed from Mozambique with a twenty-eight-man crew supplied by Assan Valy, *négoçiant maure*, and 217 slaves freighted to Pierre Antoine Monneron, a Port Louis merchant.[14] Gujarati merchants became increasingly involved in the Mozambican slave trade, often as financiers, during the late eighteenth century. The activities of Sobhachand Sowchand are a particularly noteworthy case in point. Late in 1805 or early in 1806, Sowchand purchased the *General Isidro* (or *Izidro*) from Joaquim do Rosário Monteiro, a prominent Portuguese slave trader at Mozambique. The ship had already carried three slave cargoes to the Ile de France in 1803–1804[15] and two such cargoes to the Cape of Good Hope in 1804–1805 (Machado 2014, 235). In November 1806 the ship sailed yet again for Port Louis with a cargo of Mozambican slaves only to be captured by the British (Capela 2002, 346). Sowchand subsequently purchased two slavers at Port Louis in 1806 and 1807 in partnership with Portuguese merchants (Machado 2005, 212, 223, 225).

Mascarene slave traders also maintained ties with mercantile interests in India. While the extent to which Indian merchants based in French establishments such as Chandernagore in Bengal and Pondichéry on the Coromandel Coast participated in slave trading remains difficult to ascertain, the activities of the Mahamay Kamat family, who facilitated the transshipment of Mozambican slaves from Portuguese Goa to Mauritius no later than 1777, are tantalizingly suggestive (de Souza 1989, 123–25). The instructions that Captain Alexis Joseph Bartro of *Le Chevalier d'Entrecasteaux* received from Monsieur de la Villecollet, the ship's *armateur* (outfitter), at Port Louis in April 1789 provide additional insight into the Indian slave trade to the islands. The captain was instructed to sail directly to Pondichéry where he was to call on Messrs. Coulon et Cie before proceeding to Calcutta or Chandernagore where he was to contact Mr. de Verrine, de la Villecollet's correspondent in Bengal, before procuring a cargo of 3,000 sacks of white rice, 7,450 pieces of assorted textiles, 4,000 pottery water jars, and six barrels of cigars as well as eighty male and female slaves between twelve and eighteen years of age.[16] The number of French merchants in India who may have been involved in exporting Indian slaves to the Mascarenes is suggested by an 1808 report that Pondichéry housed twenty-six merchants of "European" origin or ancestry while Yanam, another slave-exporting enclave, housed eight "European" merchants.[17]

The ability of colonial merchants to participate in the Mascarene trade stemmed from their ability to mobilize the financial resources needed to fund such ventures. Emmanuel Touche du Pujol and his associates, for example, invested more than 109,000 livres to dispatch *Le Bollé* to Mozambique in 1783.[18] Ten years later, sending *Le Bon Père* to Mozambique to trade for slaves required almost 154,000 livres.[19] The number of Mascarene merchants who invested in such voyages cannot be ascertained with any precision, but the extent of their participation is suggested by the fact that *déclarations d'arrivée* include explicit references to twenty-one local merchants or merchant houses underwriting fifty slaving voyages. Some of these individuals or houses were clearly deeply involved in this traffic. Armand Cloupet, Sieur Bouchet, and Sieurs Le Blanc et Rolland, for example, each organized at least five slaving voyages, while the firms of Le Roux K/morseven, Oury et Cie, and Janvier Monneron et Cie each organized at least four such ventures.

Partnership agreements attest that colonial merchants were able to muster the financial resources needed to mount such ventures. The assets of Pitot Frères included buildings and merchandise valued at 500,000 livres when the firm was established on August 21, 1780.[20] Other colonial merchants could mobilize even larger sums. On July 31, 1780, Port Louis's most prominent merchant, Paul de la Bauve d'Arifat, declared that he possessed cash assets (paper currency and promissory notes) worth one million livres.[21] The capital resources available to Mauritian merchants are best illustrated by d'Arifat's organization of a consortium of four firms, one of which was Pitot Frères, that contributed more than 3.8 million livres to send seven ships to China in 1782 and 1783 to trade for porcelain, silk, and tea (Keber 2002, 119–20).

Colonial merchants acquired these resources by various means, beginning with the profits from the sale of imported goods. The Abbé Raynal claimed that the Compagnie des Indes realized returns of 50 and 100 percent on merchandise imported into the Mascarenes from India and Europe, respectively (Raynal 1781, 341). The profitability of the colony's trade with Africa and India during the early 1780s was such that investors were often promised 25–35 percent returns on their investments.[22] According to reports that probably date from the early 1790s, the islands' trade with India yielded 25–30 percent profit margins, while the manipulation of bills of exchange could yield 25–33 percent returns.[23]

Information on the profitability of slaving voyages to the islands remains limited, but data on slave prices on the Malagasy and East African coasts and in the Mascarenes suggest that slaves could easily sell for twice their original purchase price, if not more. Such prices are not, however, necessarily an accurate indication of a slaving venture's profitability since they make no allowance for the expenses incurred while outfitting the ship, during the voyage, and when selling the slaves who reached the islands alive.[24] The transshipment of slaves from Mauritius to Réunion could also be remunerative. The thirty-six slaves purchased on the Ile de France in May 1787, probably by Louis Bonneau, for 32,400 livres subsequently sold on the Ile de Bourbon for 36,550 livres, a 12.8 percent return.[25]

Privateering provided another important source of the capital needed to finance slaving ventures. In September 1781 Pitot Frères reported that the prizes taken by local privateers since 1778 had sold for 12 million livres, a sum that, the firm noted, represented only one-half of their true value given the depredations that had been committed on board these ships when they were captured.[26] Individual privateers could provide investors with huge profits. On March 26, 1781, Pitot Frères informed the Comte de St. Maurice that his 2,400-livre investment in the *La Philippine* had yielded a 440 percent return.[27] Five months later the firm reported that a share in the privateer purchased originally for 1,200 livres was now worth 7,481 livres, an increase of 623 percent.[28] Privateering during the wars of the French revolutionary and Napoleonic eras was no less lucrative. According to one British source, Mascarene privateers captured shipping worth £2.5 million between 1793 and mid-1804 (Milburn 1813, 566). Auguste Toussaint estimated the value of the prizes taken by Mauritian privateers between 1793 and 1802 at 30–40 million francs, and those captured between 1803 and 1810 by local privateers and French naval frigates operating in the Indian Ocean at approximately 17.7 million and 32 million francs, respectively (1979, 273–74).

The notarial record reveals that the colony's inhabitants likewise invested in slaving ventures. During October and early November 1782, Armand Cloupet raised 68,500 livres in amounts ranging from 1,500 to 12,000 livres from sixteen individuals and merchant houses, lured by the promise of a 30 percent return on their investment, to finance *La Pintade*'s successful slaving voyage to the African coast.[29] The following year, eighteen individuals and firms invested 75,000 livres with him on similar terms to underwrite *La Sainte Anne*'s voyage to the East African coast for the same purpose.[30] Some ventures attracted even greater levels of local investment. Between April and June 1784, Pierre Bertrand and Pitot Frères et Cie raised 118,000 livres from twenty-two investors to underwrite *Le Maréchal* (or *Marquis*) *de Castries*'s voyage to Kilwa on the promise of a 4 percent return each month that the ship was away from the Ile de France.[31] Colonists continued to invest in slaving voyages during the 1790s. Between May 7, 1791, and August 26, 1793, more than twenty-five individuals and merchant houses invested 185,272 livres in seven ships sailing for Mozambique and the Swahili coast.[32]

Securing adequate supplies of the Spanish silver pesos ($), known as piastres by the French, patacas by the Portuguese, and Spanish dollars by the British and others, needed after 1750 to cover at least part of a slave's purchase price (Hooper 2017, 143–50), remained a central concern in mounting such ventures.

Surviving cargo manifests reveal that some French ships left metropolitan ports for the Mascarenes and India with large quantities of piastres on board. Such was the case when *Le Consolateur* sailed for the Ile de France, the Coromandel Coast, and Bengal on January 12, 1784, with $50,000 valued at 267,825 livres on board (Dermigny, vol. 1, 1959, 162). Three years later *L'Olimpe* left Marseille for the Ile de France carrying some $13,005 valued at 71,423 livres (Dermigny, vol. 1, 1959, 260). In February 1792 *L'Indien* loaded six chests containing $18,600 worth 167,400 livres at Bordeaux in preparation for its voyage to the Ile de France and India (Dermigny, vol. 1, 1959, 397). Other sources indicate that large quantities of piastres were readily available in the Mascarenes. In July 1795 Port Louis *négoçiant* Pierre Monneron proposed to supply the colonial government with two million pounds of grain for $66,665 to be paid for in *piastres effectives*, i.e., silver coin.[33] An inventory of the treasure taken from the *Laurel*, an English ship captured by the privateer *L'Appollon* in 1797, likewise attests to the large quantities of silver coinage circulating in the Indian Ocean during this era. The ship carried 6,063 *écus d'empire* (probably Maria Theresa thalers [MT$]),[34] 5,642 *écus turcs*,[35] 10,610 Indian rupees, and 1,879 other gold and high-value silver coins of Arab, Indian, Turkish, and Venetian origin, as well as smaller-denomination coins in such quantity that they were weighed rather than counted, and 954 pounds of silver ingots.[36]

Unfortunately, information on the quantities of piastres carried by French slavers operating from the islands remains scarce. In 1792 *Le Sauveur de l'Ile de France* left Port Louis for Kilwa to trade for slaves with $8,074 on board, $6,973 of which remained when the ship was wrecked at Soug Soug Island en route to Mozambique.[37] The following year the captain of *Le Paquebot* reported that his second mate had saved $2,000 and twenty captives when the ship's large cutter sank while returning to Kilwa from Guingera [*sic*] where he had traded for slaves.[38]

The declaration made by the captain of *Le Général Moreau* following its capture by the British on December 2, 1806, provides a unique opportunity to trace the activities of a metropolitan-based slaver in some detail. The ship, outfitted at Saint-Malo by Sieurs Deschais and Cosson, left port on January 27, 1803, with $7,810 on board and arrived at the Ile de France on May 18. After loading rice and other provisions needed to feed a slave cargo, the ship sailed on May 29 to Kilwa where it arrived on June 6. The ship departed Kilwa on August 11 with 219 slaves on board and put into the Seychelles on August 29 to "refresh" its human cargo, ten of whom were sold there before the ship departed for the Ile de Bourbon on September 27 where it arrived on October 16 with 177 slaves still alive. These slaves, together with the ten disposed of in the Seychelles, sold for $17,551. The ship then sailed on December 1 to the Cape of Good Hope where it acquired a cargo of wine, eau-de-vie, butter, iron, cordage, beer, etc. for $2,000, which sold for $10,740 following its return to Réunion on April 17, 1804. On June 23 the ship sailed again to Kilwa with $8,000 on board where it acquired 170 slaves. Those who survived the return to the Ile de Bourbon on October 19 and the ship's subsequent arrival at the Ile de France on December 1 sold for $13,950. On February 12, 1805, the ship departed for Mozambique with a cargo of piastres and mixed merchandise worth $10,751 where it purchased 110 slaves before returning to Réunion on October 6. On October 27 the vessel sailed for Foulpointe, returning to the island with a cargo of Malagasy slaves of unknown size on November 21, some of whom were subsequently carried to the Ile de France on February 6, 1806, for sale; altogether these slaves yielded $12,695. On April 24 the ship left the Ile de France on the first of what appear to have been four other voyages to Madagascar that year, the last of which ended in disaster for its owners when the vessel, valued at $7,000, with its cargo of rice, valued at $8,000, was captured by a British warship on December 2 after leaving Foulpointe.[39]

It is difficult to ascertain how much specie the Mascarene trade funneled into the regional economy between 1770 and 1810 with any precision. Calculations based on slave prices in Madagascar in 1769 ($27–$34)[40] and on the Swahili coast in 1776 (an average of $25),[41] projected slave exports to the islands,[42] and an 1820 report that 35 percent of a Malagasy slave's purchase price had to be paid in coin[43] suggest that Malagasy, Mozambican, and East African dealers may have realized $3.5–$4.7 million from the sale of slaves destined for the Mascarenes between 1770 and 1810, at least $1,241,000–$1,644,000 of which may have been paid in coin. Calculations based on reports that adult male and female slaves usually cost $30–$40 at Mozambique and Kilwa during the second half of the 1780s[44] suggest that dealers may have actually realized closer to $4.0–$5.9 million from such sales during this period, at least $1,400,000–$2,047,000 of which may have been paid in coin.

These estimates are broadly in line with Pedro Machado's estimate that French slavers paid as much as $1.5 million in coin to Portuguese and Gujarati merchants in Mozambique during the 1790s. Machado (2014, 241) notes that this silver contributed to Gujarati bankers' ability to discount the bills of exchange that were crucial to commercial activity in the region. However, these estimates may understate the Mascarene trade's regional economic impact by a substantial margin because they do not take into account the taxes, commissions, brokerage fees, and other expenses that were an integral component of any slaving voyage. Guillaume Bonne's report that it cost $31 in 1818–1819 to ship a Malagasy slave purchased for $50 to Mauritius,[45] together with information about the taxes, brokerage fees, and other expenses that *Le Succès* incurred at Zanzibar in 1820–1821 (see below), suggest that the value of the Mascarene trade's direct impact on economic life in the western Indian Ocean between 1770 and 1810 can be increased by at least 40 percent to a minimum of $4,962,000 and perhaps as much as $8,228,000.

The trade's economic impact is also suggested by comparing the amount of specie that the Mascarene trade may have injected into the regional economy with the quantity of precious metal exported from France to India during the late eighteenth century. French ships carried coined money and ingots worth some 41,455,000 livres to India between 1770 and 1790 (Dermigny, vol. 2, 1960, 123). The piastre's value fluctuated during this period; those loaded on *Le Consolateur* in 1782 and 1786 were valued at 5 livres 7 sols while those carried on *L'Indien* in 1792 were valued at 9 livres (Dermigny, vol. 1, 1959, 162, 243). Calculations based on an average exchange rate of 7 livres 7 sols to the piastre during this period suggest that the Mascarene trade may have consumed the equivalent of at least 11.0–18.2 percent of the value of the precious metal shipped from France to India during the 1770s and 1780s.

The Economics of Illegal Slave Trading

Mauritius and Réunion's capture by a British expeditionary force in 1810 inaugurated a new era in the Mascarene trade. In 1811 the islands were made subject to the 1807 Act of Parliament that prohibited British subjects from trading slaves, a ban that remained in place in Mauritius and its lesser dependencies of Rodrigues and the Seychelles following their cession to Britain in 1814. Slave trading to the Ile de Bourbon became legal again following that island's return to French control in 1814 and remained so until France formally abolished its slave trade in 1818. Despite these bans, an estimated 119,000–145,000 East African, Malagasy, and Southeast Asian slaves were exported to the islands between 1811 and the early 1830s, perhaps 52,500 of whom reached Mauritius and its dependencies before the Mauritian trade ended circa ca. 1827, while some 55,000 slaves may have been landed illegally on Réunion between 1818 and ca. 1833 (Allen 2004, 41; 2014a, 147).

Both metropolitan and colonial mercantile interests participated actively in this illicit traffic. Ten of eighty-nine ships involved in the Réunionnais trade between 1818 and the early 1830s came from Nantes, a port closely associated with illegal French slave trading during the early nineteenth century, while others hailed from Bordeaux, Honfleur, Marseille, Paimbeuf, and Saint-Malo (Gerbeau 2005, 1311–12). The extent of Réunionnais involvement in this traffic is suggested by evidence that 54 of the 94 ships known to have participated in this trade were based at the island (Daget 1996, 336) and that the island's inhabitants outfitted at least 79 of 212–216 known or probable slaving voyages to the island (Gerbeau 2005, 1312).

While the number of illegal voyages to Mauritius remains unknown, the intensity of this traffic is suggested in various ways. The Commission of Eastern Enquiry, which investigated social, economic, and political conditions in the colony between 1826 and 1828, reported that *Le Coureur*, a notorious slaver, landed 150–200 Malagasy slaves on the island during each of six voyages in 1819 and 1820.[46] The commissioners also reported that an average of 150 ships cleared Port Louis each year between 1815 and 1821 destined mostly for Madagascar and the Seychelles.[47] According to Edward Byam, the colony's chief of police from 1815 to 1823, this coasting trade provided ample opportunities for slaves to be introduced onto the island, so much so that only 39 of 100 such ships returning to Mauritius in 1822 did not include slaves in their cargo.[48] French metropolitan and Réunionnais interests were also involved in the Mauritian trade; on September 9, 1816, Governor Robert T. Farquhar informed London that French vessels were more heavily engaged in the Mauritian trade than those of any other nation.[49] The extent of French involvement remained a source of consternation five years later.[50] This concern was given substance by Charles Dorval, a well-known local slave trader, who presented evidence to the Commission of Eastern Enquiry that 23 of the 48 (possibly 51) vessels engaging in the illegal Mauritian trade ca. 1826 were based at the Ile de Bourbon.[51]

Papers recovered from the captured slaver *Le Succès* provide a rare opportunity to examine the economics of this illicit traffic in greater detail. These documents reveal that constructing and outfitting the ship in France cost 156,586.89 francs, 34,222.30 of which was spent to procure approximately 6,518 piastres.[52] The ship's captain purchased 248 slaves for $6,474 at Zanzibar between June 28 and August 30, 1820. Taxes, brokerage fees, and miscellaneous expenses at Zanzibar raised the cost of this cargo to $9,465. Disembarkation fees, food, guards, a doctor's services, "gratuities" to local authorities, and commissions cost another $5,592.55 following the vessel's arrival at the Ile de Bourbon where the 226 slaves who reached the island alive sold for $35,157, a 133 percent return on the voyage's known expenses. On December 28 the ship embarked 5,548 piastres and 4,452 *écus d'empire* in preparation for a second voyage to Zanzibar where it acquired 309 men, women, and male youths between February 10 and March 4, 1821, for $6,947. Taxes and expenses increased the cargo's total cost to $10,314. Unfortunately for its owner, the ship was captured by HMS *Menai* on March 21, 1821, near the Amirantes in the Seychelles archipelago (Allen 2014a, 152–53).

The illegal Mascarene trade's potential profitability is illustrated in other ways. Mozambican slaves who sold for $150 on Réunion in 1821 fetched $300–$400 in the Seychelles.[53] The Commission of Eastern Enquiry reported that slaves purchased for $20–$25 on the East African coast sold readily for $100–$200 in Mauritius, a price, the commissioners noted, that was "calculated to cover the expenses, and the losses, and to afford a profit adequate to the risks incurred."[54] What we know about these cargoes' demographic structure underscores their potential profitability. Males outnumbered females by a ratio of 3:1 among 2,998 "prize Negroes" landed in Mauritius between 1813 and 1827, while three-fifths of the 1,343 liberated captives whose age was recorded were the kind of "prime" hands between 15 and 24 years of age who regularly commanded high prices in European slave markets.[55]

Assessing the illegal trade's regional economic impact remains a problematic undertaking. Projections on the basis of slave prices in Madagascar in 1818 ($50)[56] and in Zanzibar in 1821 ($18–$28),[57] estimated exports to the islands after 1810, and the 1820 report that 35 percent of the purchase price of Malagasy slaves had to be paid in coin suggest that East African, Malagasy, and Mozambican traders realized $3,523,000–$5,056,000 from the sale of slaves destined for the Mascarenes between 1811 and ca. 1833, at least $1,233,000–$1,769,000 of which was paid in coin. These estimates are broadly consistent with Pedro Machado's assertion (2014, 241) that as much as $2.9 million in specie circulated in the region between 1811 and 1831, and with reports about the amount of revenue that the illegal trade generated for local governments. By most accounts the capitation tax on slaves exported from Tamatave added almost $33,000 to Merina royal coffers in 1821 (Munthe, Ravoajanahary, and Ayache 1976, 55; Campbell 1981, 208; 1987, 400), although some Mauritian officials put this figure at $40,000 a year (Scarr 1998, 132). According to Sultan Seyyid Said, the 1822 Moresby Treaty, which banned European slave exports from Omani possessions on the Swahili coast, cost him MT$40,000–MT$50,000 a year in revenue (Sheriff 1987, xix, 50). When allowance is made for the taxes, brokerage fees, etc. that also had to be paid, the illegal trade may have injected $4,932,000–$7,078,000 into the western Indian Ocean's economy between 1811 and the early 1830s.

A striking feature of the period after 1814 is the extent to which Réunion supplanted Mauritius as the Mascarene trade's financial center. The colony's former chief of police, Edward Byam, writing ca. 1824, described the "regular and well concerted scheme" by which some Mauritian inhabitants financed their involvement in the illegal trade, a "scheme" that entailed sending goods to the Ile de Bourbon where "where Metallic Money (which alone is received in Madagascar & on the neighbouring Coasts of Africa)" was to be readily had "without that immense Loss at which only it was to be procured in this Island."[58] This state of affairs was a product of the various problems that afflicted the Mauritian economy after 1810. In 1812 Governor Farquhar reported that four-fifths of the island's estate owners were in debt, only one-half of whom could be expected to repay their loans because high interest rates doubled the amount of money they owed every three years.[59] The French colonial government's failure to pay the $2 million it owed to the island's inhabitants before the island's capture in 1810 clearly contributed to this debt crisis.[60] The colony's financial condition was further compromised by significant capital flight after it was subjected to the Navigation Acts in 1815, the destruction of property worth £1.5 million ($7.5 million) by a fire in September 1816 that devastated much of Port Louis, a scarcity of specie brought about by the "drain to Madagascar and the eastern commerce," and the local hoarding of coinage.[61] These developments left the colonial government with no other option than to make loans of $100,000 in 1816 and $200,000 in 1818 to the Mauritius Bank to stave off severe credit crises.[62] Finding the specie needed to underwrite the importation of tens of thousands of slaves between 1811 and 1819 undoubtedly stretched capital liquidity in the colony still further.

There is good reason accordingly to believe that the illegal Mauritian trade began to wane after 1820 at least in part because of the unrelenting pressure it placed on the colony's capital resources and liquidity. The cholera epidemic that killed 7,000–8,700 slaves in 1819–1820 probably brought this simmering financial crisis to a head. These deaths represented an irretrievable capital loss of at least $1.2–$1.5 million, sums equal to 16–20 percent of the estimated $7.5 million colonists paid to purchase 43,700 slaves imported into the colony between 1811 and early 1819. The need to recover from this loss and stanch the flow of specie to Madagascar and East Africa also helps explain significant demographic changes in the local slave population during the early 1820s. A slave census in early 1827 described one-half of the island's slaves as Creole (i.e., locally born) compared to 27.6 percent in 1806; the census also revealed that almost 55 percent of these Creole slaves were under seventeen years of age and that 9,050 Creole slave children were six years of age or younger.[63] These figures suggest that despite their disdain for imperially inspired slave amelioration, many Mauritian colonists came to realize during the late 1810s and early 1820s that encouraging natural reproduction was the only way they could hope to maintain a viable chattel workforce into the future (Allen 2014a, 172–73).

The Mascarene Slave Trades in Perspective

While the "history of silence" that surrounded slave trading in the Indian Ocean is not nearly as deafening as it once was (Gerbeau 1979), our knowledge and understanding of forced migrant-labor systems in this oceanic world continues to be limited by a failure to situate these systems in more fully developed regional and pan-regional contexts (Allen 2017). The need for historians of slavery to shake off this "tyranny of the particular" is underscored by recent scholarship on the Dutch East India Company's multinational labor force (Lucassen 2004), the politics and ideology of the early East India Company state (Stern 2007), the geography of color lines in Madras and New York (Nightingale 2008), identity and authority in eighteenth-century British frontier areas (Wilson 2011), the geographies of colonial philanthropy (Laidlaw 2012), transoceanic humanitarian and moral reform programs (Lambert and Lester 2004), and the origins of the postemancipation indentured-labor system (Allen 2014b).

What we now know about European slave trading in the Indian Ocean demonstrates that this activity cannot be studied, much less understood, in isolation from that in the Atlantic, and vice versa. As the Mascarene case study attests, coming to terms with the economics of European slave trading requires us to explore the nature and dynamics of trade and commerce within and beyond the Indian Ocean world. The complex economic relationships that existed between French metropolitan and colonial merchants, their Portuguese and Indian counterparts in Mozambique and the Estado da Índia, and their Dutch counterparts at the Cape of Good Hope (Harries 2014a, 2014b, 2016; Thiébaut 2017) highlight the need to remember, as Om Prakash (2002) has noted, that Europeans cooperated as well as competed with one another for slave cargoes. What we now know about the dynamics of European slave trading in the western Indian Ocean during the late eighteenth and early nineteenth centuries clearly invites comparison with the ways in which the Atlantic trades were financed and organized (Morgan 2005; Haggerty 2009; Eltis, Lewis, and McIntyre 2010; da Silva 2011; Mouser 2013; Radburn 2015; Hicks 2017). The same can be said about the need to compare the illegal Mauritian and Réunionnais trades with those that flourished in the Atlantic (Harris 2016). The activities of Assan Valy, Sobhachand Sowchand, and their counterparts in Mozambique and India highlight the need to pay closer attention to the complex ways in which African, Asian, and European mercantile interests interacted in ways that shaped transoceanic slave trading within, if not beyond, the Mare Indicum (Nadri 2007; Mbeki and van Rossum 2017). The well-documented connections between the Malagasy rice, beef, and slave trades (Hooper 2017) likewise invite comparison with recent scholarship on the ways in which the production of foodstuffs in West and West Central Africa could be intertwined with the slave trade (e.g., Oliveira 2015; Dalrymple-Smith and Frankema 2017). The decade-long commercial relationship between the Mascarenes and the Río de la Plata that began in the mid-1790s (Cooney 1986; Tardieu 2010) not only illustrates the seamless quality of European slave trading between these two oceanic basins but also raises additional questions about the economics of European slave trading, including the role that silver played in shaping the commerce in chattel labor within, if not beyond, the Indian Ocean world (Bowen 2010; Parthasarathi and Riello 2014). Mauritian merchants traded African slaves, exotic tropical goods, and merchandise taken by local privateers to their counterparts on the Río de la Plata for foodstuffs and quantities of the American silver needed to sustain European slave trading in the western Indian Ocean. In so doing, their activities exemplify the complex, multifaceted economic relationships that were at the heart of European slave trading within the Mare Indicum.

Notes

1. Estimates based on a review of published scholarship. See Allen (2014a, 15–19, 22–24).

2. *Voyages: The Trans-Atlantic Slave Trade Database*, http://www.slavevoyages.org (accessed February 13, 2018).

3. Richard B. Allen, unpublished inventory of slaving voyages to or otherwise involving the Mascarenes, 1639–1816.

4. Mettas (1984, 635); Mauritius National Archives (hereafter MNA): OB 21/122, December 7, 1782.

5. Mettas (1984, 645); MNA: OB 28/532, November 27, 1790.

6. MNA: NA 27/20/4, May 21, 1787.

7. MNA: OB 50/180, May 20,1788; OB 28/75, November 1, 1788.

8. MNA: OC 4/126, [Contrat] entre Jean Pascal Dufourg et Valleau, Capitaines de Marine Marchande et Pitot frères compagnie Négoçiants de cette Isle, consignataires du V[au] La Ville de Bordeaux, July 6, 1789.

9. MNA: OC 4/126, [Société] entre J[n] Valeau cap[ne] du Navire le Comte de fumel et Jean Dufourg Cap[ne] du Navire l'honorine de Bordeaux, July 4, 1789.

10. MNA: NA 27/13/1, October 22, 1785.

11. MNA: NA 38/10A/26, 6 nivôse An XII [December 28, 1803].

12. MNA: NA 32/2/14, November 6, 1784.

13. MNA: NA 32/4A/51, May 10, 1786.

14. MNA: OC 40/237, November 18, 1780.

15. MNA: F/4/1360, 11 thermidor An XI [30 juillet 1803]; GB 26/210, 15 prairial An XII [4 juin 1804] and GB 40 40/30, 16 prairial An XII [4 juin 1804]; GB 26/300, 1 complémentaire An XII [September 18, 1804] and GB 40/56, 2 complémentaire An XII [September 19, 1804].

16. MNA: JH 10, Instructions, et conditions de Mr Bartro Capitaine du N[re] le Ch[r] Dentrecasteaux en avril 1789.

17. India Office Records, British Library, London: F/4/302/6960, pp. 51–70, 94–95.

18. MNA: OB 21/243, October 14, 1783.

19. MNA: F 23/73, January 15, 1793.

20. MNA: NA 25/3A/22, August 21, 1780.

21. MNA: OB 18/4, July 31, 1780. See also Keber (2002, 96).

22. Pitot Frères et Cie à M. de Maurville, au Port-Louis, June 27, 1781, printed in *The Commercial Gazette* [Mauritius], August 27, 1870.

23. Joseph Regenstein Library, University of Chicago: ms. f-1051, vol. 2, doc. 15, fol. 1, and vol. 2, doc. 1 (Culture Des Isles de France et de Bourbon), fol. 10, respectively.

24. For a detailed account of some of the expenses incurred during two slaving voyages to Madagascar and Mozambique in 1763 and 1764, see Jauze (2012). See also the information on *L'Aventurier*'s expenses during its 1777 voyage to Ibo/Querimba (Allen 2014a, 96).

25. MNA: JH 9, Etat Des Noirs que Jai Vendu a Bourbon.

26. Pitot Frères et Cie à MM Frin et Cie, Banquiers à Paris, September 14, 1781, printed in *The Commercial Gazette* [Mauritius], September 3, 1870.

27. Pitot Frères et Cie à M. le Comte de St. Maurice, Gouverneur de Bourbon, March 26, 1781, printed in *The Commercial Gazette* [Mauritius], August 20, 1870.

28. Pitot Frères et Cie à MM Frin et Cie, Banquiers à Paris, September 14, 1781, printed in *The Commercial Gazette* [Mauritius], September 3, 1870.

29. MNA: NB 13, fols. 45r–46v.

30. MNA: NB 13, fols. 54v–56r.

31. MNA: NB 13, fols. 65r–67v.

32. MNA: NB 33, fols. 113r–118v.

33. MNA: E/23, Comité de Sûreté Publique, Marchés passés avec divers armateur et autres personnes pour des fourniteurs de vivres et autres articles, 1795–1800.

34. The term *écu d'empire* could also refer to *rixdales* (rixdollars). See Peuchet (1798–1799, 1:196, 4:689, 5:176; and Palaiseau (1828, 169). My thanks to Claude Chevaleyre for bringing these works to my attention.

35. The type and value of these "Turkish" (undoubtedly Ottoman) coins remains unknown.

36. MNA: NA 39/8/43 & 44, 9 pluviôse An VI [January 28, 1798].

37. MNA: F 37/2, Amirauté, Procès verbale établis à bord du navire *Le Sauveur de l'Ile de France*, ci-devant le *Stanilas*, cap. Fournier, 1792.

38. MNA: F 10/540, September 6, 1793.

39. MNA: GB 14/55, July 4, 1810.

40. MNA: HB 16/9, Compte des noirs particuliers embarqués par connaissement sur la Corvette *La Normande*—Année 1769.

41. Ross (1986, 334–35).

42. Allen (2004, 41).

43. Colonial Office records (hereafter CO), National Archives of the United Kingdom, Kew, 167/49, Enclosure No. 32, Deposition of Guillaume Bonne . . . in Despatch No. 9, Major-General R. W. Darling to Earl Bathurst, February 26, 1820.

44. Dermigny (vol. 2, 1960, 109).

45. See n. 43.

46. British Parliament Sessional Papers (hereafter PP) 1829 XXV [292], Report of the Commissioners of Inquiry Upon the Slave Trade at Mauritius (hereafter Slave Trade Report), 22–23.

47. Slave Trade Report, 23.

48. CO 172/38, Three Years Administration of the Isle de France (otherwise called Mauritius) and particularly in those Parts in which the Commissary of Police (Byam) has been connected with some Reference to the whole Administration of Sir R. Farquhar since the Commencement of his Government, 259.

49. PP 1826 XXVII [295], 105, R. T. Farquhar to Captain Curran, September 9, 1816.

50. CO 167/57, Despatch No. 46, R. T. Farquhar to Earl Bathurst, June 11, 1821.

51. CO 415/10/A.298, List of French & Colonial Vessels engaged in the Slave Trade; French Vessels Engaged in the Slave Trade as stated by Mr. Dorval; List of French and Colonial Vessels engaged in the Slave Trade [1826–27].

52. Based on an exchange rate of Fr. 5.25 to the piastre (Palaiseau 1828, 169).

53. CO 167/57, Extracts from the Secret records of Governor Farquhar's private office relative to the intended formation of Depots of Slaves in the Archipelago of the Seychelles, April 8, 1821. Enclosure No. 5 in Despatch No. 46, R. T. Farquhar to Earl Bathurst, June 11, 1821.

54. Slave Trade Report, 42.

55. CO 167/43, Returns of Prize Negroes condemned by the Court of Vice Admiralty in the Colony, June 1, 1816, to January 28, 1828; CO 167/71, Detailed Statement of Blacks Seized Since the Last Return dated 31st December on board different vessels, or on Shore in the Island of Mauritius and Dependencies . . .

56. See n. 53.

57. CO 167/92, Compte courant de la deuxième traite de noirs du brick le succès a zanzibard, côte oriental D'affrique [March 7, 1821]; Commencé le present bouillard de traite à zanzibard le 9 Février 1821. Prie possetion de la maison du Gouverneur le 9 Février 1821 à raison de Commancé la traite le 10 Février.

58. CO 172/38, Three Years Administration . . . , 256–57.

59. CO 167/10, Despatch, R. T. Farquhar to Earl of Liverpool, July 28, 1812.

60. CO 167/5, Despatch, R. T. Farquhar to Earl of Liverpool, February 15, 1815.

61. CO 167/29, Despatch No. 41, R. T. Farquhar to Earl Bathurst, October 11, 1816; CO 167/50, Despatch No. 28, Maj.-Gen. Darling to Earl Bathurst, April 20, 1820.

62. CO 167/29, Despatch No. 41, R. T. Farquhar to Earl Bathurst, October 11, 1816; CO 167/39, Despatch No. 32, G. J. Hall to Earl Bathurst, June 22, 1818.

63. MNA: ID 14, Return of the slave population of Mauritius [1827]; CO 167/141, Return of Slaves Registered in Mauritius between the 16th of October 1826 and the 16th of January 1827. . . . For 1806 census figures, see Milbert (1812, 233*bis*).

References

Allen, Richard B. 2004. "The Mascarene Slave Trade and Labour Migration in the Indian Ocean during the Eighteenth and Nineteenth Centuries." In *The Structure of Slavery in Indian Ocean Africa and Asia*, edited by Gwyn Campbell, 33–50. London: Frank Cass.

———. 2014a. *European Slave Trading in the Indian Ocean, 1500–1850.* Athens: Ohio University Press.

———. 2014b. "Slaves, Convicts, Abolitionism and the Global Origins of the Post-Emancipation Indentured Labor System." *Slavery & Abolition* 35, no. 2: 328–48.

———. 2017. "Ending the History of Silence: Reconstructing European Slave Trading in the Indian Ocean." *Revista Tempo* 23, 2. doi: 10.1590/TEM-1980-542/ x2017v230206.

Bowen, H. V. 2010. "Bullion for Trade, War, and Debt-Relief: British Movements of Silver to, around, and from Asia, 1760–1833." *Modern Asian Studies* 44, no. 3: 445–75.

Campbell, Gwyn. 1981. "Madagascar and the Slave Trade, 1810–1895." *Journal of African History* 22, no. 2: 203–27.

Campbell, Gwyn. 1987. "The Adoption of Autarky in Imperial Madagascar, 1820–1835." *Journal of African History* 28, no. 3: 395–409.

Capela, José. 2002. *O tráfico de escravos nos portos de Moçambique, 1733–1904*. Porto, Portugal: Edições Afrontamento.

Capela, José. 2015. "Slave Trade Networks in Eighteenth-Century Mozambique." In *Networks and Trans-Cultural Exchange*, edited by David Richardson and Filipa Ribeiro da Silva, 165–93. Leiden: Brill.

Clarence-Smith, William Gervase, ed. 1989. *The Economics of the Indian Ocean Slave Trade in the Nineteenth Century*. London: Frank Cass.

Cooney, Jerry W. 1986. "Silver, Slaves and Food: The Río de la Plata and the Indian Ocean, 1796–1806." *Tijdschrift voor zeegeschiedenis* 5, no. 1: 34–45.

da Silva, Filipa Ribeiro. 2011. "Crossing Empires: Portuguese, Sephardic, and Dutch Business Networks in the Atlantic Slave Trade, 1580–1674." *The Americas* 68, no. 1: 7–32.

Daget, Serge. 1996. "Révolution ajournée: Bourbon et la traite illégale française, 1815–1832." In *Révolution française et océan Indien: Prémices, paroxysmes, héritages et déviances*, edited by Claude Wanquet and Benoît Jullien, 333–46. Paris: Éditions L'Harmattan.

Dalrymple-Smith, Angus, and Ewout Frankema. 2017. "Slave Ship Provisioning in the Long 18th Century: A Boost to West African Commercial Agriculture?" *European Review of Economic History* 21, no. 2: 185–235.

de Souza, Teotonio R. 1989. "French Slave-Trading in Portuguese Goa (1773–1791)." In *Essays in Goan History*, edited by Teotonio R. de Souza, 119–31. New Delhi: Concept.

Dermigny, Louis. 1959–1960. *Cargaisons indiennes: Solier et Cie, 1781–1793*. 2 vols. Paris: SEVPEN.

Eltis, David, Frank D. Lewis, and Kimberly McIntyre. 2010. "Accounting for the Traffic in Africans: Transport Costs on Slaving Voyages." *Journal of Economic History* 70, no. 4: 940–63.

Gerbeau, Hubert. 1979. "The Slave Trade in the Indian Ocean: Problems Facing the Historian and Research to Be Undertaken." In *The African Slave Trade from the Fifteenth to the Nineteenth Century*, edited by UNESCO, 184–207. Paris: UNESCO.

———. 2005. "L'esclavage et son ombre: L'île Bourbon au XIXe et XXe siècles." Thèse pour le doctorat d'État, Université de Provence (Aix-Marseille I).

Haggerty, Sheryllynne. 2009. "Risk and Risk Management in the Liverpool Slave Trade." *Business History* 51, no. 6: 817–34.

Harries, Patrick. 2014a. "Middle Passages of the Southwest Indian Ocean: A Century of Forced Immigration from Africa to the Cape of Good Hope." *Journal of African History* 55, no. 1: 173–90.

———. 2014b. "Slavery, Indenture and Migrant Labour: Maritime Immigration from Mozambique to the Cape, c. 1780–1880." *African Studies* 73, no. 3: 323–40.

———. 2016. "Mozambique Island, Cape Town and the Organization of the Slave Trade in the South-West Indian Ocean, c. 1797–1807." *Journal of Southern African Studies* 42, no. 3: 409–27.

Harris, John A. E. 2016. "Circuits of Wealth, Circuits of Sorrow: Financing the Illegal Transatlantic Slave Trade in the Age of Suppression, 1850–66." *Journal of Global History*, no. 11: 400–29.

Hicks, Mary E. 2017. "Financing the Luso-Atlantic Slave Trade, 1500–1840: Collective Investment Practices from Portugal to Brazil." *Journal of Global Slavery* 2, no. 3: 273–309.

Hooper, Jane. 2017. *Feeding Globalization: Madagascar and the Provisioning Trade, 1600–1800.* Athens: Ohio University Press.

Jauze, Albert. 2012. "Les campagnes du *Ruby* en 1763–1764—étude des colonies françaises des Mascareignes, de Madagascar et de la côte orientale de l'Afrique: Contribution à la connaissance de la traite indian-océanique au XVIIIe siècle." *Outre-mers, Revue d'histoire* 100, nos. 374–75: 119–89.

Keber, Martha L. 2002. *Seas of Gold, Seas of Cotton: Christophe Poulain DuBignon of Jekyll Island.* Athens: University of Georgia Press.

Laidlaw, Zoë. 2012. "'Justice to India—Prosperity to England—Freedom to the Slave!': Humanitarian and Moral Reform Campaigns on India, Aborigines and American Slavery." *Journal of the Royal Asiatic Society* 22, no. 2: 299–324.

Lambert, David, and Alan Lester. 2004. "Geographies of Colonial Philanthropy." *Progress in Human Geography* 28, no. 3: 320–41.

Lucassen, Jan. 2004. "A Multinational and Its Labor Force: The Dutch East India Company, 1595–1795." *International Labor and Working-Class History*, no. 66: 12–39.

Machado, Pedro. 2005. "Gujarati Indian Merchant Networks in Mozambique, 1777–c. 1830." PhD diss., School of Oriental and African Studies, University of London.

———. 2014. *Ocean of Trade: South Asian Merchants, Africa and the Indian Ocean, c. 1750–1850.* Cambridge: Cambridge University Press.

Mbeki, Linda, and Matthias van Rossum. 2017. "Private Slave Trade in the Dutch Indian Ocean World: A Study into the Networks and Backgrounds of the Slavers and the Enslaved in South Asia and South Africa." *Slavery & Abolition* 38, no. 1: 95–116.

Mettas, Jean. 1984. *Répertoire des expéditions négrières françaises au XVIIIe siècle.* Vol. 2. *Ports autres que Nantes.* Edited by Serge et Michèle Daget. Paris: Société Française d'Histoire d'Outre-Mer.

Milbert, M. J. 1812. *Voyage pittoresque à l'Ile de France, au Cap de Bonne-Espérance et à l'Ile de Ténériffe.* Vol. 2. Paris: A. Nepveu.

Milburn, William. 1813. *Oriental Commerce.* Vol. 2. London: Black, Parry.

Morgan, Kenneth. 2005. "Remittance Procedures in the Eighteenth-Century British Slave Trade." *Business History Review* 79, no. 4: 715–49.

Mouser, Bruce L. 2013. "The Trial of Samuel Samo and the Trading Syndicates of the Rio Pongo, 1797 to 1812." *International Journal of African Historical Studies* 46, no. 3: 423–41.

Munthe, Ludwig, Charles Ravoajanahary, and Simon Ayache. 1976. "Radama I and les anglais: Les négoçiations de 1817 d'après les sources malgaches ('Sorabe' inédits)." *Omaly sy anio*, nos. 3–4: 9–71.

Nadri, Ghulam Ahmad. 2007. "Commercial World of Mancherji Khurshedji and the Dutch East India Company: A Study of Mutual Relationships." *Modern Asian Studies* 41, no. 2: 315–42.

Nightingale, Carl H. 2008. "Before Race Mattered: Geographies of the Color Line in Early Colonial Madras and New York." *American Historical Review* 113, no. 1: 48–71.

Oliveira, Vanessa S. 2015. "Gender, Foodstuff Production and Trade in Late-Eighteenth Century Luanda." *African Economic History*, no. 43: 57–81.

Palaiseau, Jean-François-Gaspard. 1828. *Encyclopédie commerçiale dédiée à MM: Les Banquiers, négoçians, fabricans, agens de change, courtiers, etc.* Nisme, France: Gaude.

Parthasarathi, Prasannan, and Giorgio Riello. 2014. "The Indian Ocean in the Long Eighteenth Century." *Eighteenth-Century Studies* 48, no. 1: 1–19.

Peuchet, Jacques. 1798–1799. *Dictionnaire universel de la géographie commercante; contenant tout ce qui a raport à la situation et à l'étendue de chaque Etat commerçante.* 5 vols. Paris: Blanchon.

Prakash, Om. 2002. "Cooperation and Conflict among European Traders in the Indian Ocean in the Late Eighteenth Century." *Indian Economic and Social History Review* 39, nos. 2–3: 131–48.

Radburn, Nicholas. 2015. "Guinea Factors, Slave Sales, and the Profits of the Transatlantic Slave Trade in Late Eighteenth-Century Jamaica: The Case of John Tailyour." *William and Mary Quarterly*, 72, no. 2: 243–86.

Raynal, Guillaume-Thomas. 1781. *Histoire philosophique et politique des établissemens et du commerce des européens dans les deux indes.* Génève: Jean-Leonard Pellet.

Ross, Robert. 1986. "The Dutch on the Swahili Coast, 1776–1778: Two Slaving Journals, Part I." *International Journal of African Historical Studies* 19, no. 2: 305–60.

Scarr, Deryck. 1998. *Slaving and Slavery in the Indian Ocean.* London: Macmillan.

Sheriff, Abdul. 1987. *Slaves, Spices and Ivory in Zanzibar: Integration of an East African Commercial Empire into the World Economy, 1770–1873.* London: James Currey.

Stern, Peter J. 2007. "Politics and Ideology in the Early East India Company-State: The Case of St. Helena, 1673–1709." *Journal of Imperial and Commonwealth History* 35, no. 1: 1–23.

Tardieu, Jean-Pierre. 2010. *La traite des noirs entre l'océan Indien et Montevideo (Uruguay) fin du XVIIIe siècle et début du XIXe.* Paris: L'Harmattan.

Thiébaut, Rafaël. 2017. "An Informal Franco-Dutch Alliance: Trade and Diplomacy between the Mascarenes and the Cape, 1719–1769." *Journal of Indian Ocean World Studies,* no. 1: 128–47.

Toussaint, Auguste. 1977. *Le mirage des îles: le négoçe française aux Mascareignes au XVIII*[e] *siècle.* Aix-en-Provence, France: Edisud.

———. 1979. *Les frères Surcouf.* Paris: Flammarion.

Westra, Piet, and James C. Armstrong. 2006. *Slave Trade with Madagascar: The Journals of the Cape Slaver Leijdsman, 1715/Slawe-handel met Madagaskar: Die joernale van die Kaapse slaweskip Leijdsman, 1715.* Cape Town: Africana.

Wilson, Kathleen. 2011. "Rethinking the Colonial State: Family, Gender, and Governmentality in Eighteenth-Century British Frontiers." *American Historical Review* 116, no. 5: 1294–1322.

Chapter 13

Coerced Labor in Cameroon and Industrial Progress in Wilhelmine Germany, 1884–1914

Samuel Eleazar Wendt

Over the last fifteen years, several studies have reminded us of the fact that German lands were not landlocked and therefore were not separated from the process of European expansion (Weber 2015). Merchants, industrialists, and financiers such as the Fuggers and the Welsers from Augsburg were involved with Portuguese trade on the African coast from the late fifteenth century and with the Spanish and Portuguese slave trade and plantation economies on the Canary Islands, on Hispaniola, and in Brazil (Häberlein 2008; Denzer 2005). Linen from specific German regions like Silesia and Westphalia, Rhenish metal manufactures, brassware from Nuremberg, and glass beads from Bohemia were in demand as barter commodities on the West African coast well into the nineteenth century (Steffen and Weber 2016; Małowist 2009). There are many examples of French and British slavers from the eighteenth century most of whose cargo consisted of German-made barter products (Brahm and Rosenhaft 2016). Since the mid-seventeenth century, German entrepreneurs were also increasingly investing in large slave-trading companies such as the Dutch West India Company and the British Royal African Company. During the eighteenth century Germans owned plantations on Saint-Domingue, in Virginia, and so on (Foubert 2004; Häberlein and Schmölz-Häberlein 1995). Both the commodity flows and the flows of capital from German lands into the Atlantic Basin were poorly visible because they were being carried out under foreign flags.

Nonetheless, a fairly coherent picture of the major protagonists, their activities, and their commercial networks has been obtained. Hundreds of German merchants had settled in places like London, Amsterdam, Lisbon, Cadiz, and Bordeaux in order to secure outlets for all these Central European export goods and to channel imports of foreign colonial produce from the respective colonial empires into the Holy Roman Empire (Poettering 2013; Schulte Beerbühl 2007; Weber 2004). With the disruptions brought about by the Atlantic Revolutions, starting with the American War of Independence in 1775, places like Bordeaux and Cadiz lost their importance, hitherto regulated systems of trade (like the Carrera de Indias) were abolished, and the Atlantic slave trade was banned. At the same time, Napoleonic rule over much of Germany made the Holy Roman Empire collapse. Territorial reshuffling, reforms, the revolutions of 1830 and 1848, and the intra-German wars of the 1860s followed. Therefore, the picture of German maritime activities is even much messier and more blurred for the period from ca. 1810 to 1871, when the German Kaiserreich was established, than it was in the earlier period.

This new nation became quite zealous in its effort to equal and even challenge the long-established colonial powers, in particular Britain and France. It thus acquired its own colonies, mostly in Africa, and had them recognized internationally at the Berlin Conference in 1884–1885. Only in the last twenty years has this period of German colonial history been examined more systematically. Andreas Eckert (1998) has carried out microstudies on labor exploitation in several African colonies. Jürgen Zimmerer (2011) has examined whether the extremely violent oppression of revolts, in particular the Revolt of the Nama and Herero in Southwest Africa in 1904–1908, were precursors of National Socialist genocides. Rebekka Habermas and Alexandra Przyrembel (2013) focused on the production and circulation of knowledge in colonial contexts. Dirk van Laak (2005) and Sebastian Conrad and Jürgen Osterhammel (2004) have placed Wilhelmine Germany in a global context, challenging some of the assumptions about a German *Sonderweg*, i.e., the notion of a special path to modernity that places Germany's historical development apart from that of its European neighbors. Yet these two strands of research—the one on the Holy Roman Empire's older links with the Atlantic World and the one on Imperial Wilhelmine Germany—are still rather unconnected. The aim of this chapter is to suggest continuities and changes between Germany's early modern and modern African trade. In so doing it retraces the significant contribution of German merchants in establishing colonial rule in Cameroon, as well as the exploitation of its land and people for German industrial development. As stated by Bradley Naranch in his seminal article, "the German turn toward colonial power could not have been achieved without the willing participation of Hanseatic merchants and shippers" (2011, 129), who wanted to secure access to and directly participate in the exploitation of tropical riches like cacao, ivory, palm oil, and rubber.

Abolition and Industrialization

After the abolition of the British transatlantic slave trade (1807) and with the new emphasis on legitimate trade, European merchants sought alternative commodities that would help maintain existing commercial relations with West Africa or establish new ones. Palm oil, then rubber, and subsequently other cash crops were sought-after alternatives. Contemporaries defined legitimate commerce as trade in anything other than slaves, including nonagricultural commodities such as gold and ivory. However, over time legitimate commerce came to primarily denote trade in goods obtained from commercial agriculture. In 1839 the prominent abolitionist Thomas Fowell Buxton (1768–1845) founded the Society for the Extinction of the Slave Trade and for the Civilization of Africa. Like many of his contemporaries, he conceived of West Africa as a new America: as the potential main supplier of tropical products to Europe, with African free labor retained and employed locally. Presuming that all plants from America, Australia, India, and Europe would "flourish there in perpetual spring" (1840, 328), Buxton mistakenly estimated that all efforts and investments made in African agriculture would render more value than similar investments made in America. Missionary societies like the Basler Mission took up the idea of commercial agriculture and began to instill a European work ethos in baptized Africans, thereby enforcing a proto-Marxist system of religious conversion "in which change in the ideological sphere depended upon transformation of the economic base" (Law, Schwarz, and Stickroft 2013, 5). The idea of civilizing the peoples of sub-Saharan Africa, either through religious conversion or later by formal colonial rule, was thus linked to the idea of incorporating them into the world-economy as producers of raw materials obtained through exploitation of naturally available resources.

German trade with West Africa followed similar patterns. For decades, and even centuries before the abolition of the slave trade, merchants from the port city of Hamburg and from protoindustrial provinces established and maintained *indirect* trade relations with West Africa (under British, Dutch, French, and other flags). German-made linen textiles, spirits, household effects, weaponry, tobacco, and glass beads were the principal commodities, complemented with cowrie shells from Asia. During the first decades of the nineteenth century only a few merchants and ships from Hamburg were directly engaged in trade with this region. In the 1840s the Hamburg merchant and shipowner Adolph Jacob Hertz (1800–1866) began trading cowries for palm oil around the estuaries of the Niger and Volta Rivers. He successfully substituted shells (money cowries) from the Maldives with blue-tinged cowries from Zanzibar (gold-ring cowries), obtained at a lower price. Soon more Hanseatic merchant companies like Wm. O'Swald & Co., Spies, Galles & Co., Hansin & Co., and C. Woermann became interested in the trade and established trading posts along the West African coast. Even though their number was small compared to those from other European nations, Hanseats succeeded in securing their share of the local market and enforced their commercial interests in the region. Trade with the hinterland had been in the hands of the coastal people for centuries and they were not willing to give up their status to European merchants, who wanted to dispose of the middlemen and gain control of the whole supply chain (Eleazar Wendt 2018).

At the same time, European and leading African entrepreneurs sought to increase the overall volume of the African products in legitimate trade. Palm oil was in demand not only as an ingredient for foodstuffs but also for cosmetic products, detergents, etc. Before the advent of mineral oil, it was also widely used as a lubricant for the ever-growing number of machines and tools in European industries. Another raw material, rubber, was even more closely linked to the Industrial Revolution. Only with the rediscovery of a rubber-curing process in 1839 did it become possible to transform natural rubber into durable goods with entirely novel qualities, combining elasticity with impermeability, a hitherto unknown combination in Europe.[1] Seals for hydraulic and pneumatic machinery, and for reliable railway brakes, elastic insulation of electric cables, rubber boots, condoms, surgical gloves, and a whole array of other medical equipment were not even conceivable before the introduction of vulcanized rubber. By 1900 tires for bicycles and cars were added to the assortment—and the gas mask during the First World War. Rubber was also essential in shaping new concepts of hygiene and cleanliness. The material is both indispensable and emblematic of modernity. For nations with industrial ambition, tropical regions suitable to produce such raw materials became ever more important.

The most important trading company in Cameroon was C. Woermann, based in Hamburg. The Woermann family was originally established in Bielefeld (in Westphalia), one of the most prestigious centers in the production and trade of linen, Germany's major export item throughout the seventeenth and eighteenth centuries. The Woermanns were among the protagonists of a global dimension in early modern Germany. Like his uncle David Friedrich Weber, Carl Woermann (1813–1880) started his own business in 1837 with export of linen to Central and South America. In 1849 the company started to trade in Liberia, building on the palm oil trade. From there it expanded its business into Cameroon in the 1860s, seeking to establish a trade monopoly by buying out European competitors. Carl's youngest son, Adolph Woermann (1847–1911), who was to become the most prominent German merchant in West Africa and largest private shipowner in the world, became involved in the company in 1874. Throughout the colonial period he sought to eliminate the indigenous competition of the Duala, who traditionally dealt with the hinterland nations (Bavendamm 1987, 49–57). In the 1870s Bismarck still rejected the idea of establishing formal colonies; he favored a system regulated by the government but financed by the businessmen active in the colonies. Even though Adolph Woermann would come to benefit greatly from the Cameroon venture, he utterly rejected Bismarck's idea of financing it (Stoecker 1986, 63). Therefore, in 1883, he convinced the Hamburg Board of Trade to lobby in Berlin for his plan to dispatch warships to the unstable areas of West Africa in order to secure trade interests and to punish local communities for attacks on German citizens or on their property (Pogge von Strandmann 2009, 21–22). Adolph Woermann was a member of the Hamburg Parliament (1880–1904) and of the Reichstag (1884–1890). As such, and with the major shipping companies backing this plan, he managed to convince Chancellor Bismarck of the need to establish protectorates (colonies) in the areas where German firms had vested commercial interests (Möhle 2011a, 27).

Penetration of the Hinterland

Only two days before July 14, 1884, when the German Protectorate of Cameroon was created, representatives of C. Woermann and Jantzen & Thormählen[2] signed a treaty with the principal kings and chiefs of the Cameroon (Wouri) River Delta. This document, dated July 12, 1884, stipulated that the "Rights of Sovereignity [*sic*], the Legislation and Management of this our Country" were "entirely [assigned] to Mr. Eduard Schmidt, acting for the Firm C. Woermann and Mr. Johannes Voss, acting for Messrs. Jantzen and Thormählen both in Hamburg." The treaty also listed five limitations made by the kings, the third of which stated that "the land cultivated by us now and the places the towns are built on, shall be property of the present owners and their successors" (Ramsay 1911, 175). This provision was deliberately violated by German planters and colonial officials soon after the colonial government was put in place. The seizure of land began in the coastal areas surrounding Mount Cameroon, inhabited by the Bakweri, Bamboko, Balong, Isubu (Bimbia), and Wovea peoples. Then the territory belonging to the Victoria Division, initially founded as an English Baptist settlement in 1858, was bought out by arrangement with the Basel Mission in 1887 (Ardener 1996, 151).

To establish and secure their trading monopoly in the coastal areas and later in the hinterlands, C. Woermann and Jantzen & Thormählen sought backing from the German Foreign Office (Auswärtiges Amt) in 1885. The Duala, specifically the members of the influential Bell and Akwa families, hoped that the treaty with the German merchants would help strengthen their political and economic standing. Similar hopes were held toward the British by Ndumbe Lobe Bell (1839–1897) and Dika Mpondo Akwa (1836–1916) when they unsuccessfully petitioned Queen Victoria to annex their lands and formally establish British colonial rule over those lands in 1879. Historian Ralph A. Austen has perfectly summarized the dynamic of the power struggle, stating that "both Duala and Germans appeared confused or divided in their own objectives as well as in their respective perceptions of how the other party to the conflict was behaving" (1977, 478). On the one hand, the Reichstag took the Duala petition against the Cameroon governor Jesko von Puttkammer (1855–1917) under consideration in 1905–1906, which led to his dismissal. This success gave the Duala a sense of German benevolence toward their interests. On the other hand, the Duala faction was at odds with the commercial and political interests of the Akwa and Bell families, a cleft that deepened even more during the colonial period (Eckert 2003, 172–73). The German faction was also divided. Economic imperialists sought to expand and protect the market conditions for modern German industry and to secure raw-material supply through large-scale, monoculture plantations. In contrast, missionary societies like the Basel Mission, a number of members of the Reichstag, and even quite a few merchants favored the development of *Volkskulturen*, i.e., peasant production on small-scale units. Both perspectives relied, as will become clear, on evaluations of the nature and capacities of indigenous peoples.

By 1891, after fierce and bloody struggles with Duala traders, German military expeditions broke up the control exercised by these middlemen and established a route to Yaoundé in the hinterland. The main expedition led by Major Curt von Morgen (1858–1928) was followed by representatives of Jantzen & Thormählen and C. Woermann with their respective carriers, who bought out all ivory available on the route (Rüger 1968, 190). With the opening of the route to Yaoundé and the repression of Duala resistance in the coastal areas, C. Woermann and Jantzen & Thormählen initiated the exploitation of the fertile lands, specifically the region extending west of the Mungo River from the coast to the volcanic slopes of Mount Cameroon, through monocultures for profitable cash crops like cacao, rubber, palm oil, and coffee, all much in demand by Wilhelmine Germany's growing industry and by its consumer society (Austen and Derrick 1999, 117; Smith 1978, 123). The first large estate (approximately 140 square kilometers) in Cameroon was the Kamerun Land und Plantagen Gesellschaft Woermann, Thormählen & Co. (KLPG). The business enterprise for the Cameroon endeavor was established in Hamburg in 1885. The directorate was formed by the heads of six merchant houses (A. Woermann, C. F. W. Jantzen and J. Thormählen, E. Bohlen, E. Barth, and C. P. Dollmann, all in Hamburg, and W. Oechselhäuser from Dessau). Representatives came from twenty-six banking houses and from industrial and wholesale corporations (Rüger 1960, 162). Between 1897 and 1909 more large estates were established on the western slopes of Mount Cameroon and in the region between the Wouri estuary in the south and the Mungo River to the northeast.

In January 1897 leading industrialists and bankers founded the Westafrikanische Pflanzungsgesellschaft Victoria (WAPV), which soon held Cameroon's largest plantation.[3] Another large estate, the Westafrikanische Pflanzungsgesellschaft Bibundi (WAPB), was established in the same year; the renowned agronomist and promoter of tropical agriculture Ferdinand Wohltmann (1857–1919) was one of its founding members. In 1899 the two companies joined forces in and founded the Moliwe-Pflanzungsgesellschaft. Figure 13.1 indicates the location and extent of the plantations surrounding Mount Cameroon as well as the areas owned by missionary societies and by natives, the major roads, and, more important, the reservations in which the first inhabitants of the lands were concentrated after the plantations were established.

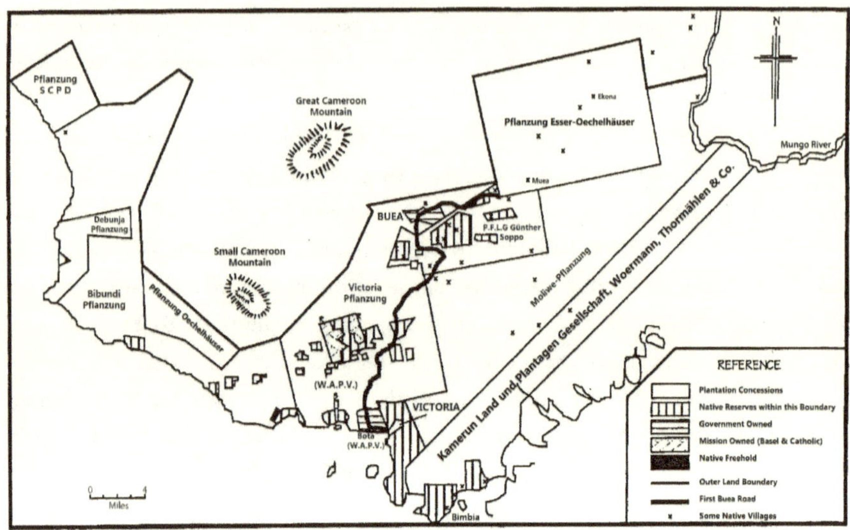

Figure 13.1. Plantations and reservations in the Victoria Division 1897–1899. Source: Ardener (1966, 153), used and printed with permission of Berghahn Books.

The Labor Regime

Initially, land acquisition followed no predefined pattern or legal procedure. Some plots were simply squatted, others acquired through treaties and purchases from local chiefs, as was the case for the WAPB. The Crown-Land Decree of 1896 (Kronlandverordnung), in contrast, promulgated all unused land *res nullius* and declared it property of the German emperor, *de facto* expropriating the land from its traditional occupants and constituting the first coherent approach to land grabbing. Land could now be bought directly from the government at an average of five marks per hectare, including all the people living on the purchased area (Ardener 1996, 152). In compliance with the policy of the colonial government, all those hitherto resident on the acquired plot were to be concentrated in reservations. This reservation arrangement showed striking similarities to the system of serfdom prevalent on East Elbian Junker estates. Even after the abolition of serfdom, previous spatial arrangements and patterns of property persisted well into the early twentieth century. In Cameroon, each dwelling (*Hütte*) was assigned one hectare of land for the sustenance of its inhabitants, who were banned from leaving the reservations. As the yield from many of the plots did not suffice, its owners were forced to engage in wage labor on the plantations to make ends meet (Rüger 1960, 187). In contrast to the East Elbian model, provisions and wages paid in Cameroon were far below the individual subsistence level, which caused very high mortality rates on the plantations. In 1913, 30.5 percent (65 of 213) of the workers employed on the Woermanns' Bimbi plantation died of dysentery and cachexia within seven months of their arrival (Möhle 2011b, 60). This was not exceptional. Estimates indicate that a 30–50 percent death rate was common on the Cameroon plantations (Eyongetah and Brain 1974, 88). Already in 1900, Deputy Governor August Köhler (1858–1902) had informed the Colonial Department in Berlin that "their diet is unsuitable, and they are ill-housed and treated in the most savage fashion. This is how matters are on average. So, you will no longer find anyone who is willing to work on the plantations" (Stoecker 1986, 75).

Because of the high mortality rate and the rising demand for labor that expanded with the growing plantation ventures, estate owners and colonial officials addressed the *Arbeiterfrage* not on the question of working conditions but rather on how to continue providing workforce to the plantation ventures. The first mention of this issue can be traced to a letter from Jantzen & Thormählen to the Prussian representative in the Hanseatic Cities, Heinrich von Kusserow (1836–1900), who forwarded it to Chancellor Bismarck on May 31, 1886. Here the merchants indicate that domestic slaves (*bakom*), common in Duala society, posed a considerable obstacle to the economic development of the colony as they inhibited the free Duala (*wonja*) from seeking employment as wage laborers on the German-held estates. To solve this problem they suggested a ransoming of slaves while giving them long-term contracts of at least ten years, and the promise of providing them with a plot of land after their time of service (von Kusserow 1886). Instead of following the merchant's suggestion, Governor Julius von Soden (1846–1921) decided to maintain the status quo for humanitarian and political reasons, as the colonial government wanted to avoid disturbing the established treaty by overruling the social order prevalent in Duala society. The governor, like many of his contemporaries, held the conviction that the steady economic transformation of the colony would bring about the disappearance of slavery and thus make any direct legislation on this matter superfluous (von Soden 1886). Thus, in the meantime, recruiting workers from other colonies was considered. This practice had already been adopted by the colonial government for the recruitment of auxiliary troops for the Polizeitruppe (police force) and Schutztruppe (protective force). Both were made up of mercenaries from other African regions (Liberia, Togo, Ghana, Sierra

Leone, Dahomey). As this very costly practice did not seem to be compatible with the profit-oriented agrobusiness, nor with the demands of building a colonial infrastructure with roads, railroads, bridges, train stations, telegraphy, brickyards, etc., the workforce had to be recruited locally. In general, recruiting workers from other colonies had become increasingly difficult for the Cameroon ventures. August Humplmayr (1864–1920), the former German consul to Monrovia, stated in a letter to the Imperial Colonial Office (Reichskolonialamt) that Liberian workers were "reluctant to go, as some private firms in Cameroon had mistreated workers and refused to pay the contracted wages in full."[4] Likewise, the British government had issued a directive forbidding the recruitment of workers in their colonies, owing to the "disorganization of the labour market and [its interference] with the agricultural development of the country" ("Labour Question" 1902, 49). A similar measure had been adopted in Cameroon in the 1880s.

In this scenario, the densely populated hinterland regions promised to hold the much-needed relief. There workers could either be enlisted through labor contractors or gathered by the Schutztruppe as reparation to be paid from unruly villages and tribes. The expeditions of 1892–1893 against the Abo, Buea, Bakoko, Jaunde, and Mabea not only promoted the forceful opening of the hinterland for the commercial interest of the Cameroon firms but also provided the workforce needed on the plantations near the coast. In 1899 Governor Puttkamer, also an advocate of the plantation system, ordered the Schutztruppe to stop freeing slaves they encountered during their expeditions *in situ*. These should rather be resettled with their families to the reservations in the coastal areas and subjected to contract labor on the plantations there (Rüger 1960, 196). Thus the colonial government became responsible for supplying and distributing workers to the plantations, which required approximately 8,200 workers in 1909 and more than twice as many in 1913 (Rathgen 1920, 72). Further, convicts were coerced into plantation labor or deployed for public works, where they were kept in chains day and night. Their treatment was the worst among all unfree workers. Still, the status of contract workers differed from that of convicts only insofar as their work was compensated with a small remuneration.

German observers often concurred in assuming that the peoples of sub-Saharan Africa were lazy, dishonest, crude, and barbarous (von Richelmann 1908). As put by August Boshart, colonial officer, mercenary in the Belgian Congo, and plantation owner: "The negro is a bloodthirsty and cruel beast of prey that can only be held at bay by the eye and whip of the tamer."[5] Other observers considered them to be like children, and as such they had to be treated and punished when mistakes were made. In an interview with the London-based financial weekly *Finanz-Chronik*, one of the longest-running German newspapers in Britain (1898–1912), Major Morgen elaborates on this notion: "It is a difficult task to motivate the negro . . . to engage in labor. There is only one solution to this problem: obligation to work. . . . This will raise him morally, allowing him to abandon his vegetating being, in which he has been living so far, and turn him into a hardworking person. . . . One cannot forget that the negro is culturally lacking, behind by hundreds of years, that he is like a child, who has to be guided and punished."[6] At first sight this view might be considered benevolent, and in line with the predominant view on child education in Wilhelmine Germany, but in Africa, punishment meant whipping.

The use of heavy whips made of rhinoceros hide was widespread throughout the German colonial realm. The disciplinary instruction issued by Governor Puttkamer in 1901 gives a fair impression of the disproportion between crimes, or rather misdemeanors, and punishment of workers: (1) continued indolence—a fine of twenty marks, (2) impertinence against the master—ten strokes with the rod, (3) absence from work without valid excuse—ten strokes, (4) contumacy against the master—five lashes and ten days of arrest in shackles, (5) neglect of duty—10 marks, (6) disobedience against the master—eight days of arrest in shackles, (7) breach of contract—thirty marks, (8) laziness—ten lashes (Rüger 1960, 218). Given the fact that plantation workers received remuneration worth about six to nine marks per month, most of which was handed out in kind during the contract period (six to eighteen months depending on the contract), monetary fines pushed workers into debt bondage. Employers could also deduct significant amounts from salaries, for example, in case a worker fell sick. Furthermore, goods sold to the workers during their employment period were heavily overpriced. It was thus possible that workers would leave the plantations without ever receiving any monetary payment.

The overall policy of the German protectorate obviously subordinated native interests to those of merchant houses and profit-oriented plantation estates. The indigenous peoples of Cameroon rebelled repeatedly against the system of oppression and coerced labor. As Catherine Coquery-Vidrovitch (1983) and most recently Sengulo Albert Msellemu (2013) have compellingly argued, protests, noncompliance, passive resistance, and even armed upheavals against European interests and colonial rule were frequent in Cameroon, as they were in other colonies throughout the continent. Plantation owners and administrators in Cameroon constantly complained about workers not complying and even contesting instructions.

Because of the primitive and harsh working conditions, workers often refused to follow instructions, went on strike, and, if the circumstances allowed, even fled the plantation (Rüger 1960, 235–41). Stressing their powerlessness, the Kamerun Land und Plantagen Gesellschaft suggested to Governor Puttkamer in 1901 that the government should hand over the right of punishment to the planters, as the "insubordination of the negroes has reached unbearable proportions" (Friederici 1901, 51). Regardless of legal formalities, plantation supervisors drove and punished the workforce by use of the cudgel and whip if they deemed the workers disrespectful, laggard, or insubordinate. The Duala, who largely opposed the imposition of German colonial rule all along, had already staged a rebellion in December 1884 (Jaeck 1960, 71–76), one year before the first German estate, the KLPG, was founded in 1885. Ten years later the people of Buea were defeated as well and the colonial expansion to Mount Cameroon was secured. This move toward the inland prompted the rebellion of the Bafut (city of Bamenda), which lasted from 1891 to 1907. In 1893 even the Dahomian members of the police force staged a rebellion over the ongoing mistreatment of their wives and themselves; all of them were executed as soon as the uprising was quelled. From 1894 to 1910 six more major uprisings erupted in Cameroon alone. Throughout the existence of German colonies in Africa, twenty-six such revolts contested colonial rule, but to no avail.

Even though missionary societies approved the notion of the superiority of German culture and thus of the civilizing mission, they actively opposed expropriation of Africans, resettling, and the imposition of forced labor. It was because of their efforts that the land assigned for the reservations was increased, as shown in figure 13.2. Also, missionaries advocated against the labor regime that was jointly established on large estates by the plantations and the colonial government during the Puttkamer era. As a result, Puttkamer's name became a synonym for exploitation, avarice, and deceit. From a Christian perspective, missionaries acknowledged the necessity of teaching the peoples of Cameroon regular daily work, that is, as a moral obligation bestowed upon mankind after the expulsion from paradise. The missionaries feared that excessive exploitation and high mortality on the plantations would negatively affect the converted Christians, as they would reject work and thus be unable to fulfill their obligations to God. Hence they rejected the plantation regime and favored small-scale farming, believing that "only if the Christians are attuned to the cultivation of their own land will they understand the value of work and learn to perceive it as a fountain of opulence, allowing for their lives to become orderly and purposeful."[7] In 1913 the Deutsche Gesellschaft für

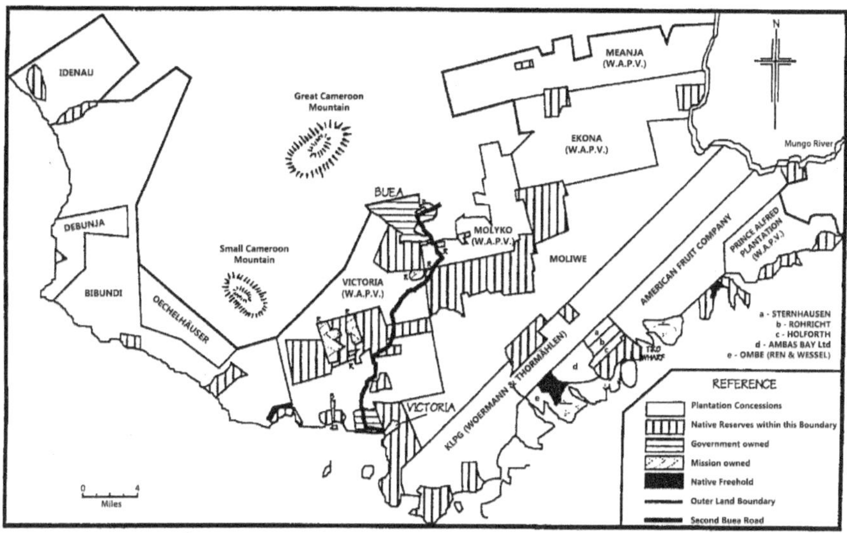

Figure 13.2. Plantations and reservations in the Victoria Division 1914. Source: Ardener (1966, 157), used and printed with permission of Berghahn Books.

Eingeborenenschutz (German Society for the Protection of Natives) was founded in Berlin. Its purpose was to counteract the damages that racist and exploitative colonial policies had wreaked throughout the colonies. Its paternalistic policy did not aim to restore precolonial conditions or to compensate the indigenous African people but to form and educate the Africans in a manner that would allow for the "master and ruled races to coexist peacefully" (Schnee 1920, 300).

Conclusion

Despite the critique of faith-based organizations like the missionary societies and of secular bodies like the Reichstag, the exploitative regime largely persisted until the end of German colonial rule in Africa in 1918. German industry benefited from it, as the example of rubber demonstrates. By 1910 rubber-processing factories, mostly established in Hamburg and Berlin, imported fourteen thousand metric tons of raw rubber per year. They employed a total of about thirty-five thousand people and produced goods worth two hundred million marks annually, 40 percent of which were destined for export. It is true that more than half of the rubber came from South America and from Dutch and British plantations in Asia, but the share from German colonies was considerable. The German rubber industry had become the third largest worldwide after the American and the British.

Even if Germany was a belated nation, and the era of German colonialism was rather brief compared to that of other European nations, its economy had been intertwined with African trade for centuries. With intimate knowledge of African markets, German merchants from Hamburg and from seemingly landlocked hinterlands found and adapted their niches long before German colonies had been established. A continuity from precolonial to colonial trade was provided by C. Woermann, whose son succeeded in luring even the otherwise very prudent Chancellor Bismarck into a policy that protected and subsidized private colonial endeavors. In 1885 A. Woermann created one of the largest plantations in Cameroon, the KLPG, and also Germany's major African shipping line, making him the principal profiteer of Wilhelmine Germany's colonial policy.

In their efforts to impose a capitalist mode of production on the people subject to colonial rule, as described by Catherine Coquery-Vidrovitch, German investment and plantation companies were as successful as their French or British counterparts. This case study shows that the German colonial empire even fits into the periodization she proposed, with a "pre-colonial latency phase" ca. 1850–1880 and with the "colonial stage proper" beginning in the 1890s (1976, 25–29).

The Kronlandverordnung promulgated in 1896 fits perfectly into this concept. As argued above, between 1885 and 1896 land acquisition was unsystematic. Local communities could, even though the power relation was unequal, appear and act as a contracting party. With the expropriation brought about by the 1896 decree, the status of local communities changed for the worse. This shift marks the intent of consolidating German colonial rule over Cameroon. The plantation system launched by German merchants, industrialists, banks, colonial officials, etc. around Mount Cameroon aimed to satisfy the needs of the metropolis. The systematic exploitation of the fertile lands by cultivating rubber, palm oil, and other crops in monoculture fundamentally changed local communities' lifestyle and social order, as indicated by the prevalent mortality rate on German plantations.

The self-proclaimed sense of mission of the Gesellschaft für Eingeborenenschutz also fits into Coquery-Vidrovitch's conceptualization. African people and their culture were considered inferior, and subjecting them to paternalistic educating missions, civil and religious, was regarded favorably. This in turn highlights the fact that German colonial rule did not follow a *Sonderweg*. Even though it was belated and not as long-lasting as the colonial ventures of, for example, Britain and France, German colonial rule still accorded with the prevailing Eurocentrism and the procedural methods implemented by other European imperial powers. Thus Germany's territories and its merchants were not secluded or landlocked; they actively engaged in and contributed to shaping the European colonial enterprise.

Notes

1. Jens Soentgen (2013) and others (Tarkanian and Holster 2011) have reminded us of the fact that functional equivalents to vulcanization had been developed by the indigenous peoples of Central and South America, where cured rubber had multiple uses in pre-Columbian times as shown by Emilie Carreón Blaine (2006).

2. The firm was established in Hamburg in 1874 by Wilhelm Jantzen (1800–1880) and Johann Thormählen (1821–1895), both former employees and representatives of C. Woermann in Liberia and Cameroon, respectively.

3. Through different intermediaries the WAPV was able to create subsidiary companies, which in turn acquired approximately sixteen thousand hectares of land: Pflanzung Günther-Soppo-GmbH (1898), Molyko-Pflanzungsgesellschaft mbH (1901), Bolifamba-Pflanzungsgesellschaft mbH (1901), Lisoka-Pflanzungs GmbH (1901), Ekona-Pflanzungs GmbH (1901), Koke-Pflanzungs GmbH (1901), and Meanja-Pflanzung GmbH (1901).

4. "Große Abgeneigtheit, nach Kamerun zu gehen, . . . weil sie . . . von einigen Privatfirmen in Kamerun schlecht behandelt wurden und nicht die richtige Bezahlung erhielten" (Humplmayr 1902, 136). My translation.

5. "Der Neger ist ein blutrünstiges, grausames Raubtier, das nur durch das Auge und die Peitsche des Bändigers in Respekt gehalten werden kann" (Schröder 1997, 30). My translation.

6. "Schwer bleibt es immerhin, den Neger . . . zur Arbeit heranzuziehen. Hier gibt es nur zwei Mittel: Arbeitspflicht. . . . Welche den Neger auch moralisch heben wird. Aus einem bislang vegetierenden Wesen wird man einen fleißigen Menschen machen. . . . Man vergesse nicht, dass der Neger um Hunderte von Jahren in der Kultur zurück ist, dass er einem Kinde gleicht, welches geleitet und erzogen werden muss" ("Die Arbeitspflicht in den Kolonien" 1901, 78). My translation.

7. "Nur dadurch, dass die Christen an die Landwirtschaft auf eigener Scholle gewöhnt werden und in ihr eine Quelle des Wohlstandes kennen lernen, wird auch ihr äußeres Leben ein geordnetes und zielbewusstes" (Steiner 1909, 50). My translation.

Sources Cited

"Die Arbeitspflicht in den Kolonien." 1901. *Die Finanz-Chronik*, December 28, 1901. Bundesarchiv: R1001/3228: 78.

Friederici, R. 1901. Letter to Gouverneur von Puttkammer regarding plantation workers. Bundesarchiv: R1001/3228: 51–53.

Humplmayr, August.1902. Letter to the Imperial Colonial Office regarding worker recruitment from Liberia. Bundesarchiv: R1001/3228: 136.

"The Labour Question in West Africa." 1902. *African Review*, September 9, 1902. Bundesarchiv: R1001/3229: 48–49.

von Kusserow, Heinrich. 1886. Letter to Chancellor Bismarck regarding the request made by Jantzen & Thormählen. Bundesarchiv: R1001/3223: 3–5.

von Soden, Julius. 1886. Letter to Chancellor Bismarck regarding the request made by Jantzen & Thormählen. Bundesarchiv: R1001/3223: 12–17.

References

Ardener, Edwin. 1996. *Kingdom on Mount Cameroon: Studies in the History of the Cameroon Coast, 1500–1970*. Providence, RI: Berghahn Books.

Austen, Ralph A. 1977. "Duala versus Germans in Cameroon: Economic Dimensions of a Political Conflict." *Revue française d'histoire d'outre-mer* 64, no. 237: 477–97.

Austen, Ralph A., and Jonathan Derrick. 1999. *Middlemen of the Cameroon Rivers: The Duala and Their Hinterland.* Cambridge: Cambridge University Press.

Bavendamm, Dirk. 1987. "Wagnis Westafrika." In *Wagnis Westafrika: 150 Jahre C. Woermann: Die Geschichte eines Hamburger Handelshauses*, edited by Dirk Bavendamm, 49–57. Hamburg: Verlag Hanseatischer Merkur.

Brahm, Felix, and Eve Rosenhaft, eds. 2016. *Slavery Hinterland: Transatlantic Slavery and Continental Europe 1680–1850.* Woodbridge, UK: Boydell.

Buxton, Thomas Fowell. 1840. *The African Slave Trade and Its Remedy.* London: John Murray.

Carreón Blaine, Emilie. 2006. *El olli en la plástica Mexica: El uso del hule en el siglo XVI.* Mexico City: Universidad Nacional Autónoma de México.

Conrad, Sebastian, and Jürgen Osterhammel, eds. 2004. *Das Kaiserreich transnational: Deutschland in der Welt 1871–1914.* Göttingen, Germany: Vandenhoeck & Ruprecht.

Coquery-Vidrovitch, Catherine. 1976. "La mise en dépendance de l'Afrique noire: Essai de périodisation, 1800–1970." *Cahiers d'Études africaines* 61/62, no. 16: 7–58.

———. 1983. "Révoltes er résistance en Afrique noire: Une tradition de résistance paysanne à la colonization." *TRAVAIL* 16, no. 1: 34–63.

Denzer, Jörg. 2005. *Die Konquista der Augsburger Welser-Gesellschaft in Südamerika (1528–1556): Historische Rekonstruktion, Historiographie und lokale Erinnerungskultur in Kolumbien und Venezuela.* Munich: C. H. Beck.

Eckert, Andreas. 1998. "Slavery in Colonial Cameroon, 1880s to 1930s." *Slavery & Abolition* 19, no. 2: 133–48.

———. 2003. "Widerstand, Kooperation und Nationalismus: Afrikanische Politik in der Kolonialzeit zwischen den 1880er und 1950er Jahren." In *Afrika: Geschichte und Gesellschaft im 19. und 20. Jahrhundert*, edited by Inge Grau, Christian Mährdel, and Walter Schicho, 169–84. Vienna: Promedia.

Eleazar Wendt, Samuel. 2018. "Hanseatic Merchants and the Procurement of Palm Oil and Rubber for Wilhelmine Germany's New Industries, 1850–1918." *European Review* 26, no. 3 (June): 430–40.

Eyongetah, Tambi, and Robert Brain. 1974. *A History of the Cameroon.* London: Longman.

Foubert, Bernard. 1990. "Les habitations Laborde à Saint-Domingue dans la seconde moité du XVIIIè siècle: Contribution à l'historie d'Haiti." PhD diss., Université de Paris IV, Sorbonne.

Häberlein, Mark. 2008. "Jakob Fugger und die Kaiserwahl Karls V. 1519." In *Die Fugger und das Reich*, edited by Johannes Burkhardt, 65–81. Augsburg, Germany: Wißner.

Häberlein, Mark, and Michaela Schmölz-Häberlein. 1995. *Die Erben der Welser: Der Karibikhandel der Augsburger Firma Obwexer im Zeitalter der Revolutionen.* Augsburg, Germany: Wißner.

Habermas, Rebekka, and Alexandra Przyrembel, eds. 2013. *Von Käfern, Märkten und Menschen: Kolonialismus und Wissen in der Moderne.* Göttingen, Germany: Vandenhoeck & Ruprecht.

Jaeck, Hans-Peter. 1960. "Die deutsche Annexion." In *Kamerun unter deutscher Kolonialherrschaft: Studien*, vol. 1., edited by Helmuth Stöcker, 29–148. Berlin: Rütten & Loening.

Law, Robin, Suzanne Schwarz, and Silke Stickroft, eds. 2013. *Commercial Agriculture, the Slave Trade and Slavery in Atlantic Africa.* Woodbridge, UK: Boydell & Brewer.

Małowist, Marian. 2009. "Portuguese Expansion in Africa and European Economy at the Turn of the 15th Century." In Malowist, *Western Europe, Eastern Europe and World Development, 13th–18th Centuries: Collection of Essays of Marian Małowist.* Edited by Jean Batou and Henryk Szlajfer. Leiden: Brill.

Möhle, Heiko. 2011a. "Aus Freihändlern werden Kolonialherren: Hamburgs Handelskammer und Fürst Bismarcks Afrikapolitik." In *Branntwein, Bibeln und Bananen: Der deutsche Kolonialismus in Afrika: Eine Spurensuche*, edited by Heiko Möhle, 25–30. Berlin: Assoziation A. Originally published 1999.

———. 2011b. "Bittere Schokolade: Die Früchte der Plantagenwirtschaft." In *Branntwein, Bibeln und Bananen: Der deutsche Kolonialismus in Afrika: Eine Spurensuche*, edited by Heiko Möhle, 55–61. Berlin: Assoziation A. Originally published 1999.

Msellemu, Sengulo Albert. 2013. "Common Motives of Africa's Anti-Colonial Resistance in 1890–1960." *Social Evolution & History* 12, no. 2: 143–55.

Naranch, Bradley N. 2011. "Between Cosmopolitanism and German Colonialism: Nineteenth-Century Hanseatic Networks in Emerging Tropical Markets." In *Cosmopolitan Networks in Commerce and Society 1660–1914*, edited by Andreas Gestrich and Margret Schulte Beerbühl, 99–132. London: German Historical Institute.

Poettering, Jorun. 2013. *Handel, Nation und Religion: Kaufleute zwischen Hamburg und Portugal im 17. Jahrhundert.* Göttingen, Germany: Vandenhoeck & Ruprecht.

Pogge von Strandmann, Hartmut. 2009. *Imperialismus vom Grünen Tisch: Deutsche Kolonialpolitik zwischen wirtschaftlicher Ausbeutung und zivilisatorischen Bemühungen.* Berlin: Ch. Links.

Ramsay, Hans G. F. 1911. "Die Festsetzung der deutschen Herrschaft in Kamerun, I. Teil." In *Jahrbuch über die deutschen Kolonien*, vol. 4, edited by Karl Schneider, 173–92. Essen, Germany: G. D. Baedeker Verlagshandlung.

Rathgen, Karl. 1920. "Arbeiter." In *Deutsches Koloniallexikon*, vol. 1, edited by Heinrich Schnee, 71–75. Leipzig: Quelle & Meyer.

Rüger, Adolf. 1960. "Die Entstehung und Lage der Arbeiterklasse unter dem deutschen Kolonialregime in Kamerun (1895–1905)." In *Kamerun unter deutscher Kolonialherrschaft: Studien*, vol. 1, edited by Helmuth Stoecker, 149–242. Berlin: Rütten & Loening.

———. 1968. "Die Duala und die Kolonialmacht 1884–1914: Eine Studie über die historischen Ursprünge des afrikanischen Antikolonialismus." In *Kamerun unter Deutscher Kolonialherrschaft: Studien*, vol. 2, edited by Helmuth Stoecker, 181–257. Berlin: Deutscher Verlag der Wissenschaften.

Schnee, Heinrich, ed. 1920. *Deutsches Koloniallexikon.* Vol. 1. Leipzig: Quelle & Meyer.

Schröder, Martin. 1997. *Prügelstrafe und Züchtigungsrecht in den deutschen Schutzgebieten Schwarzafrikas.* Münster: LIT Verlag.

Schulte Beerbühl, Margrit. 2007. *Deutsche Kaufleute in London: Welthandel und Einbürgerung 1600–1818.* Munich: Oldenbourg.

Smith, Woodruff D. 1978. *German Colonial Empire.* Chapel Hill: University of North Carolina Press.

Soentgen, Jens. 2013. "Die Bedeutung indigenen Wissens für die Geschichte des Kautschuks." *Technikgeschichte* 80, no. 4: 295–324.

Steffen, Anka, and Weber, Klaus. 2016. "Spinning and Weaving for the Slave Trade: Proto-Industry in Eighteenth-Century Silesia." In *Slavery Hinterland: Transatlantic Slavery and Continental Europe, 1680–1850*, edited by Felix Brahm and Eve Rosenhaft, 87–107. Woodbridge, UK: Boydell.

Steiner, P. 1909. *Kamerun als Kolonie und Missionsfeld.* Basel: Verlag der Basler Missionsbuchhandlung.

Stoecker, Helmuth. 1986. "The Conquest of Colonies: The Establishment and Extension of German Colonial Rule, Cameroon 1885–1906." In *German Imperialism in Africa: From the Beginning until the Second World War*, edited by Helmuth Stoecker, 62–82. London: C. Hurst.

Tarkanian, Michael J., and Dorothy Holster. 2011. "America's First Polymer Scientists: Rubber Processing, Use and Transport in Mesoamerica." *Latin American Antiquity* 22, no. 4: 469–86.

van Laak, Dirk. 2005. *Über alles in der Welt: Deutscher Imperialismus im 19. und 20. Jahrhundert.* Munich: C. H. Beck.

von Richelmann, Georg. 1908. "Art und Charakter des Negers." In *Jahrbuch über die deutschen Kolonien*, vol. 1, edited by Karl Schneider, 125–31. Essen, Germany: G. D. Baedeker Verlagshandlung.

Weber, Klaus. 2004. *Deutsche Kaufleute im Atlantikhandel 1680–1830: Unternehmen und Familien in Hamburg, Cádiz und Bordeaux.* Munich: C. H. Beck.

———. 2015. "Mitteleuropa und der transatlantische Sklavenhandel: Eine lange Geschichte." *Werkstatt Geschichte*, nos. 66/67: 7–30.

Zimmerer, Jürgen. 2011. *Von Windhuk nach Auschwitz? Beiträge zum Verhältnis von Kolonialismus und Holocaust.* Berlin: Lit Verlag.

CONTRIBUTORS

Richard B. Allen is the author of *Slaves, Freedmen, and Indentured Laborers in Colonial Mauritius* (1999), *European Slave Trading in the Indian Ocean, 1500–1850* (2014), and numerous articles, book chapters, and essays on the social and economic history of Mauritius, slavery and indentured labor in the colonial plantation world, and slavery, slave trading, and abolition in the Indian Ocean world. He is currently editing a book on slavery and bonded labor in Asia between 1250 and 1900. He also serves as editor of Ohio University Press's Indian Ocean Studies Series and research consultant to the Aapravasi Ghat UNESCO World Heritage Site.

Pepijn Brandon is assistant professor at the Vrije Universiteit, Amsterdam, and senior researcher at the International Institute of Social History. He is the author of *War, Capital, and the Dutch State* (1588–1795) and has published widely on the Dutch role in transatlantic slavery. He is a member of the editorial committee of the *International Review of Social History.*

Mariana P. Candido is associate professor of history at Emory University. Her publications include An African Slaving Port and the Atlantic World: Benguela and Its Hinterland (2013) and Fronteras de esclavización: Esclavitud, comercio e identidad en Benguela, 1780–1850 (2011), which has been translated into Portuguese as Fronteras da escravização (2018). Candido has coedited with Adam Jones, African Women in the Atlantic World: Property, Vulnerability and Mobility, 1680–1880 (2019); with Carlos Liberato, Paul Lovejoy, and Renée Soulodre-La France, Laços Atlânticos: África e africanos durante a era do comércio transatlântico de escravos (2017); and with Ana Lucia Araujo and Paul Lovejoy, Crossing Memories: Slavery and African Diaspora (2011).

Catherine Coquery-Vidrovitch is professor emerita of modern African history at the University Paris-7 and was adjunct professor at Binghamton University, SUNY, 1981–2005. In 1999 she received the African Studies Association's Distinguished Africanist Award. Four of her books have been translated into English: *Africa*

South of the Sahara: Endurance and Change (1987), *African Women: A Modern History* (1998), *The History of African Cities South of the Sahara: From the Origins to Colonization* (2006) (selected by *Choice* as one of the best books of the year), and *Africa and the Africans in the 19th Century: A Turbulent History* (2009). Recently published in French: *Les routes de l'esclavage africain du 6e au 19e siècle* (2018).

Christopher R. DeCorse is professor and chair of the Department of Anthropology in the Maxwell School of Citizenship and Public Affairs, Syracuse University. His research interests include African archaeology and history, general anthropology, and archaeology in popular culture. His work in West Africa focuses on the Atlantic period, particularly the impacts of the slave trade and the understanding of these transformations in terms of Africa's pre-Atlantic past. His principal publications include: *An Archaeology of Elmina: Africans and Europeans on the Gold Coast, 1400–1900* (2021), available at http://www.eliotwerner.com, and *West Africa during the Atlantic Slave Trade* (repr., 2016).

Samuel Eleazar Wendt is a doctoral student in history at Europa-Universität Viadrina Frankfurt (Oder, Germany). His research interests include the history of tropical botany and the extraction of colonial cash crops for industrial purposes, transnational history, and commodity-chain analysis. His most recent publications are "Hanseatic Merchants and the Procurement of Palm Oil and Rubber for Wilhelmine Germany's New Industries, 1850–1918," *European Review* 26, no. 3 (2018), and "Securing Resources for the Industries of Wilhelmine Germany: Tropical Agriculture and Phytopathology in Cameroon and Togo, 1881–1914," in *Environments of Empire: Networks and Agents of Ecological Change*, edited by Ulrike Kirchberger and Brett M. Bennett (2020).

Janet J. Ewald is associate professor emerita at Duke University. Her first book, *Soldiers, Traders, and Slaves: State Formation and Economic Transformation in the Greater Nile Valley, 1700–1885* (1990), situated the emergence and development of a Nuba Mountain kingdom in the regional context of large Sudanic kingdoms and Egyptian colonial expansion, with the consequent rapid expansion of enslavement. Her publications also include essays on historical methodology and state power, especially in Sudanic East Africa; African enslavement in the Indian Ocean; and bondsmen and freedmen as maritime and port workers, most notably in "Crossers of the Sea: Slaves, Freedmen, and Other Migrants in the Northwestern India

Ocean," *American Historical Review* 105, no. 1 (2000). She is currently writing a manuscript based on some of the themes of her chapter in this volume.

Henry B. Lovejoy is assistant professor at the University of Colorado, Boulder. He is the creator of Liberated Africans (http://www.liberatedafricans.org) and Yoruba Diaspora (http://www.yorubadiaspora.org), as well as the director of Slavery Images (http://www.slaveryimages.org). His most recent book is *Prieto: Yorùbá Kingship in Colonial Cuba during the Age of Revolutions* (2018), which was awarded the Chief Isaac Oluwole Delano Prize for best book in Yoruba studies. He is also coeditor, with Richard Anderson, of *Liberated Africans and the Abolition of the Slave Trade, 1807–1896* (2020).

Paul E. Lovejoy is Distinguished Research Professor at York University, fellow of the Royal Society of Canada, founding director of the Harriet Tubman Institute for Research on Africa and Its Diasporas, Canada Research Chair on the African Diaspora (2000–2015), and member of the UNESCO "Slave Route" Project—Resistance, Liberty, Heritage (Section du dialogue interculturel). His latest books include *Jihad and Slavery in West Africa during the Age of Revolutions (1775–1850)* (2016), *Calabar on the Cross River: Historical and Cultural Studies* (2017), *Slavery in the Global Diaspora of Africa* (2019), and *Notorious Massacre at Calabar in 1767*, with David Imbua and Randy Sparks (forthcoming in 2021). See Freedom Narratives (http://www.freedomnarratives.org), Project Baquaqua (http://www.baquaqua.org), and Gustavus Vassa, aka Olaudah Equiano (http://www.equianosworld.org).

Patrick Manning is Andrew Mellon Professor of World History, emeritus, at the University of Pittsburgh, where he was founding director of the World History Center. His research includes quantitative analysis of slavery, slave trade, and population in Africa and the African diaspora. He is author of *The African Diaspora: A History through Culture* (2009), *A History of Humanity: The Evolution of the Human System* (2020), *Methods for Human History: Studying Social, Cultural, and Biological Evolution* (2020), and recent articles with new estimates on the volume of the Atlantic slave trade.

Rafael Marquese is professor of history at the University of São Paulo and the author of *Administração & escravidão: Ideias sobre a gestão da agricultura escravista brasileira* (1999), *Feitores do corpo, missionários da mente: Senhores, letrados e o* *controle dos escravos nas Américas* (2004), and coauthor with Tâmis Parron and Márcia Berbel of *Slavery and Politics: Brazil and Cuba, 1790–1850* (2016).

Tâmis Parron is research professor at the Universidade Federal Fluminense (Niterói, Rio de Janeiro, Brazil). He coauthored *Slavery and Politics: Brazil and Cuba, 1790–1850* (2016). Currently he is writing a book on the rise and crisis of black slavery in the United States, Brazil, and the Spanish Empire within the world-historical transformations of nineteenth-century industrial capitalism.

Dale W. Tomich is professor of sociology, emeritus, and deputy director of the Fernand Braudel Center at Binghamton University. He is the author of *Slavery in the Circuit of Sugar: Martinique in the World-Economy* (rev. ed., 2016), *Through the Prism of Slavery: Labor, Capital, and World Economy* (2004), and coauthor (with Rafael Marquese, Reinaldo Funes, and Carlos Venegas) of *Reconstructing the Landscapes of Slavery: A Visual History of the Plantation in the Nineteenth-Century Atlantic World* (2021). He has also authored various articles on Atlantic history and the world-economy.

Michael Zeuske was professor of Iberian and Latin American History at the University of Cologne until his retirement in 2018. He is currently senior professor at the Bonn Center for Dependency and Slavery Studies, Universität Bonn. His most recent books include *Sklavenhändler, Negreros und Atlantikkreolen: Eine Weltgeschichte des Sklavenhandels im atlantischen Raum* (2015), *Sklaverei: Eine Menschheitsgeschichte: Von der Steinzeit bis heute* 2018) (in Spanish: *Esclavitud: Una historia de la humanidad*, http://katakrak.net/cas/editorial/libro/esclavitud-una-historia-de-la), and *Handbuch Geschichte der Sklaverei: Eine Globalgeschichte von den Anfängen bis heute*, 2 vols. (2019, 2nd ed.).

INDEX

www.ingramcontent.com/pod-product-compliance
Lightning Source LLC
LaVergne TN
LVHW090804070826
844660LV00022B/1075

* 9 7 8 1 4 3 8 4 8 4 4 4 0 *